Sa

20^{00}
13x 8/10 1/11

Dynamic Implementation of SAP R/3

The SAP® Series

Edited by Bernhard Hochlehnert, SAP AG.
Other titles in Addison-Wesley's SAP® Series include:

Greg Spence
SAP R/3 & Oracle: Backup & Recovery
(1999, ISBN: 0-201-59622-9)

Norbert Welti
Successful SAP R/3 Implementation: Practical Management of ERP Projects
(1999, ISBN: 0-201-39824-9)

Rüdiger Buck-Emden
SAP R/3: An introduction to ERP and business software technology
(2000, ISBN: 0-201-59617-2)

Erich Draeger
Project Management with SAP R/3
(2000, ISBN: 0-201-39835-4)

Stefan Huth, Robert Kolbinger and Hanns-Martin Meyer
SAP on Windows NT
(1999, ISBN: 0-201-39837-0)

Gerhard Keller
SAP R/3 Process Oriented Implementation
(1998, ISBN: 0-201-92470-6)

Mario Pèrez, Alexander Hildenbrand, Bernd Matzke and Peter Zencke
The SAP R/3 System on the Internet
(1999, ISBN: 0-201-34303-7)

Liane Will, Christiane Hienger, Frank Strassenburg and Rocco Himmer
SAP R/3 Administration
(1998, ISBN: 0-201-92469-2)

Dynamic Implementation of SAP R/3

Marcus Geiss and Roland Soltysiak

An imprint of **Pearson Education**

Harlow, England · London · New York · Reading, Massachusetts · San Francisco
Toronto · Don Mills, Ontario · Sydney · Tokyo · Singapore · Hong Kong · Seoul
Taipei · Cape Town · Madrid · Mexico City · Amsterdam · Munich · Paris · Milan

PEARSON EDUCATION LIMITED
Head Office:
Edinburgh Gate
Harlow CM20 2JE
Tel: +44 (0)1279 623623
Fax: +44 (0)1279 431059

London Office:
128 Long Acre, London WC2E 9AN
Tel: +44 (0)20 7447 2000
Fax: +44 (0)20 7240 5771
Website: www.awl.com/cseng/

First published in Great Britain in 2000

The right of Marcus Geiss and Roland Soltysiak to be identified as
Authors of this Work have been asserted by them in accordance
with the Copyright, Designs and Patents Act 1988.

ISBN 0-201-67483-1

British Library Cataloguing-in-Publication Data
A catalogue record for this book is available from the British Library

Library of Congress Cataloging-in-Publication Data
Applied for.

The programs in this book have been included for their instructional value. The publisher does not
offer any warranties or representations in respect of their fitness for a particular purpose,
nor does the publisher accept any liability for any loss or damage arising from their use.

Many of the designations used by manufacturers and sellers to distinguish their
products are claimed as trademarks. Pearson Education Limited has made every
attempt to supply trademark information about manufacturers and their products mentioned
in this book. A list of the trademark designations and their owners appears on this page.

10 9 8 7 6 5 4 3 2 1

Trademark notice
Word, Excel, PowerPoint, Project and Windows are trademarks of the Microsoft Corporation.
Visio is a trademark of the Visio Corporation. ARIS-Toolset is a trademark of IDS Prof. Scheer.
SAP R/3 is a registered trademark of AG SAP Aktiengesellschaft Systems, Applications and
Products in Data Processing, Neurottstrasse 16, D-6 9190 Walldorf, Germany. The publisher
gratefully acknowledges SAP's kind permission to use its trademark. In this publication. SAP AG
is not the publisher of this book and is not responsible for it under any aspect of press law.

Typeset by Pantek Arts, Maidstone, Kent.
Printed and bound in the United States of America.

The Publishers' policy is to use paper manufactured from sustainable forests.

Contents

Foreword

Large concerns that operate internationally have one primary goal for an SAP R/3 implementation: to implement business systems that are restricted neither to company nor to country. Nowadays, consistently and successfully implemented regional or even global concepts (for example, as part of supply chain management) represent a decisive competitive factor. This second generation of R/3 projects far exceeds the single-company solution of earlier R/3 installations, in both sophistication and complexity.

The ideas for this book arose in conjunction with a large SAP R/3 project in the Henkel group. This project focused on the European market and the creation of an integrated business system that was to be rolled out to the parts of a business division in Europe.

The demands made by such a project immediately raised the question of an appropriate methodology. Intensive discussions resulted in a plan with the goal of providing and implementing short-term subfunctionalities at a defined time, in the sense of 'time-to-market'. The first solutions and the major changes to the business processes that in any case resulted from R/3 functionality and integration should provide initial practical experience for all those involved (both in the project team and in the user areas), to be used appropriately to produce new ideas and to improve the business system continuously. Thus, the European rollout of the new business system became a 'dynamic development project', in the course of which significant changes to the system occurred.

The procedure concept presented in this book provides solution strategies that should ensure that, in particular, fixed project deadlines are met – a problem that has plagued software development and implementation for decades. Furthermore, the involvement of and cooperation between IT departments and user areas is described – one of the critical success factors of every SAP R/3 project, which is also always an organization project. Finally, I would like to mention a special aspect of this book, the statements concerning quality management. In particular, mention should be made of the documentation of the business processes and R/3 customizing as well as the statements concerning test plans and automatic test procedures, which in many projects do not attract the attention they deserve because of the deadline pressure they are under.

To summarize, I have been able to determine that DSDM strategies have been a significant factor in the current success of our project. The strength of the method lies particularly in its flexible usage and adaptation of project planning to take account of everchanging project situations.

Heinz Minx, Dipl. Commerce
IT Account Manager Chemical Business Systems, Henkel KGaA

The dynamic procedure model with which this publication is concerned was developed in 1997 by Dr Roland Soltysiak and Marcus Geiss as part of an SAP R/3 project for Henkel KGaA in Dusseldorf. The arrival of Marcus Geiss in our company in 1998 caused Mummert + Partner to analyze this procedure model in more detail.

The ongoing investigation of proven SAP implementation strategies for their improvement potential is a central task for Mummert + Partner. Speedy incorporation of the newest scientific results is essential here to permit cooperation with institutes and universities in order to subject a solution concept to a careful test both in and for practical use.

The unstoppable international internetworking of market economies and capital markets that will require both middle-sized and large companies to initiate specific action in the short-term emphasized the special importance of this strategy. SAP R/3 – the integrated application scenario for system-controlled business economics functions in business processes – provides the transparency that for many industries permits the effective economic control appropriate to the business economics requirements.

Technical consultants for specific industries must know down to the smallest detail how these industries function. Such a consultant must take time in the planning phase to understand the special needs and requirements of the individual companies in order to save long-term costs both during realization and at the start.

Consequently, Mummert + Partner incorporates the development of information processing strategies in their complete consulting principle.

The results of the accompanying book also reflect the concrete experience gained from larger SAP R/3 projects. In a surprisingly short time, the requirements of the companies involved were realized to the highest quality standards, and this in extremely dynamic markets with continuously changing determining factors. This is also the major advantage of the solution strategy presented here, which, in particular, has the capability to make continuous use of these requirements dynamics.

The results are very promising. To propel further development, Mummert + Partner can only encourage young university graduates, together with innovative companies and consultancies, to become involved in this improvement process.

Franz T. Müller, Dipl.-Economics
Director, Mummert + Partner Unternehmensberatung AG

Preface

In 1995, a consortium in Great Britain first published the Dynamic Systems Development Method (DSDM), which focused on the following principles:

A Active user involvement is imperative.
B DSDM teams must be empowered to make decisions.
C The focus is on frequent delivery of products.
D Fitness for business purpose is the essential criterion for acceptance of deliverables.
E Iterative and incremental development is necessary to converge on an accurate business solution.
F All changes during development are reversible.
G Requirements are baselined at a high level.
H Testing is integrated throughout the life cycle.

A collaborative and cooperative approach between all stakeholders is essential.

Now, more than 1,000 companies belong to this DSDM consortium, and an international roll-out of the method is being prepared. The enthusiasm for this new method was the motivation to develop a DSDM- based procedure model to realize SAP R/3 projects.

Naturally, DSDM principles also guided us in the creation of this book. We concentrated on the following goals:

- On-time delivery

- Largest possible benefits for the reader

We achieved the first goal. With regard to the second, we would like to encourage the reader to send us criticism or suggestions for improvements regarding this first edition of the book, so that we can include the improvements, remove any errors and thus meet the dynamic requirements of the reader.

E-Mail: *Marcus.Geiss@mummert.de*

E-Mail: *Roland.Soltysiak@henkel.de*

At this point, we would like to thank all those involved with the success of the book project. The Addison Wesley team played an important role here, supporting us from the first day to the last day of the book project, and were always available to answer questions. In particular, we would like to thank Mr James Kimathi whose professional support was very helpful in the creation of the case study.

I would also like to thank my employer, Mummert + Partner Unternehmensberatung AG, who were very interested and provided much support for the book project. This applies particularly to Mr Franz T. Müller and Mr Hans Werner Püttmann who provided me with sufficient time, particularly in the very stressful end-phase of the book project, and so permitted the book to be completed on time.

My special thanks go to Ginevra, my love, who, despite all the time sacrifices, always supported, encouraged and motivated me.

Cologne, October 1998
Marcus Geiss

My thanks go to all managers and colleagues at HENKEL KGaA and the ICM consultancy, from whom I learnt so much about the SAP R/3 system and the importance of human factors in projects.

My special thanks go to my dear wife, Sabine, who took care of me with so much understanding.

Duisburg, October 1998
Roland Soltysiak

Part A
SAP and DSDM

Of central importance to the DSDM-based procedure model for the realization of SAP R/3 projects presented in the following chapters is the question of how or whether the basic ideas of the Dynamic Systems Development Method (DSDM) can be adapted to the properties of an SAP R/3 project.

To answer this question, Part A of this book first presents various concepts for the realization of SAP R/3 projects. The DSDM method is then explained in more detail and finally the question of whether or why the use of DSDM is appropriate for an SAP R/3 project is answered.

However, first we briefly present the individual concepts with their advantages and disadvantages.

1 The various methods for the realization of SAP R/3 projects

So far, more than 16,000 SAP projects have been realized worldwide. Almost all of these SAP projects have one thing in common.

Either the traditional SAP procedure model or the newer ASAP (AcceleratedSAP) procedure model, which has been available for some time, was used as the basis for these projects. In addition to these two procedure models, there is also a wide range of company-specific procedure models that are at least based on the traditional SAP procedure model or extend or modify it. In general, these models have comparable characteristics and so exhibit the same advantages and disadvantages.

The principal advantage of all these procedure models is certainly the complete and precise representation of all the tasks to be mastered in an SAP project. Furthermore, it is now possible to make use of the comprehensive wealth of experience gained with the traditional SAP procedure model. ASAP also provides a wide range of examples, checklists and samples that can be used to increase the speed with which SAP R/3 systems can be implemented.

Although the models described have many advantages, they must also counter several disadvantages. In particular, these disadvantages result from the associated procedure model being based on the so-called waterfall model (refer to Section 1.1.4).

Another method, Iterative Process Prototyping (IPP) from Keller and Teufel, takes account of the frequent requirement to have an iterative procedure for SAP R/3 projects. This method uses an iterative process to master the activities from the business process analysis and description. However, even this method is normally embedded in the traditional, waterfall-based SAP procedure model.

In the following section, we describe the individual methods with their advantages and disadvantages, and also provide an overview of software development which has been concerned with comparable problems over many decades.

1.1 The traditional SAP procedure model

Before we discuss the typical problems associated with the traditional procedure model, we first provide an introductory overview of SAP R/3 projects as they are currently normally realized using the SAP procedure model. In addition to the SAP procedure model with its four phases, we briefly describe SAP customizing and some of the fundamental elements of SAP terminology.

Because there are now so many publications about the SAP R/3 system and its capabilities and advantages, the following section omits a comprehensive description of all these details and explains just briefly those terms essential for the understanding of the procedures described in the following chapters.

The SAP R/3 system provides a modularly constructed industry-independent standard software that covers and integrates all business areas of a company. This modular structure and industry independence require the appropriate settings and introductory work to be done to cater for the industry and company-specific particulars for the enterprise in question. This specific adaptation and implementation of the SAP R/3 system is called customizing.

In addition to adapting the supplied business-independent functionality, the main tasks of customizing are a fast, reliable and transparent implementation and expansion of the SAP R/3 applications, and the control and documentation of the implementation project.

A differentiation is made between two types of customizing projects. A customizing project can be either an implementation project, in which a specific function repertoire is to be used productively by a specified date, or a release project, in which all the work resulting from a system upgrade or a release change is to be performed.

The SAP procedure model forms the basic element of customizing. The aim of this SAP procedure model is to produce a structured organization of the customizing project. It offers a method frame for the SAP R/3 implementation process and also provides an operative tool that supports all the activities of every phase.

1.1.1   The structure and the phases of the traditional SAP procedure model

The SAP procedure model is based on the idea of the so-called waterfall model (Boehm, 1981, p. 35ff), which means that it consists of several phases, which follow each other in a fixed sequence, each of which must be completed before the next phase can start.

The results of each phase are presented before a steering committee at the milestone that occurs at the end of the associated phase. This steering committee's task is to check whether the results meet the targets set. Depending on the outcome, either the next phase is started, the current phase is repeated, return is made to a previous phase, or the project is cancelled. Figure 1.1 illustrates Boehm's waterfall process.

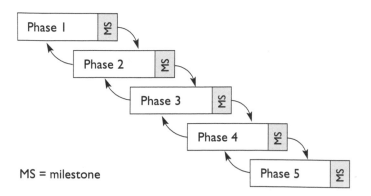

Figure 1.1   Boehm's waterfall process

However, this procedure model does not permit a new phase to be started unless the current phase has been completed. Nor is it possible to complete a phase if the expected results are not fully available.

In general, it can be said that the first phase of the waterfall model is always used to determine the requirements made of the system to be developed or implemented. Once these requirements have been defined, they remain unchanged until the end of the project. The further phases are generally concerned with topics such as design, realization, implementation and maintenance. The waterfall procedure model is normally processed just once; no iterations over the complete model are planned. The SAP procedure model, which exhibits such a structure (refer to Figure 1.2), consists of four phases.

The SAP procedure model assumes that a preliminary investigation has been performed in which the general suitability of the SAP R/3 system for the company-specific requirements has been determined. The individual phases are structured as follows:

1. Organization and conception design

2. Detailed design and system set up

3. Preparations for going live

4. Live operation

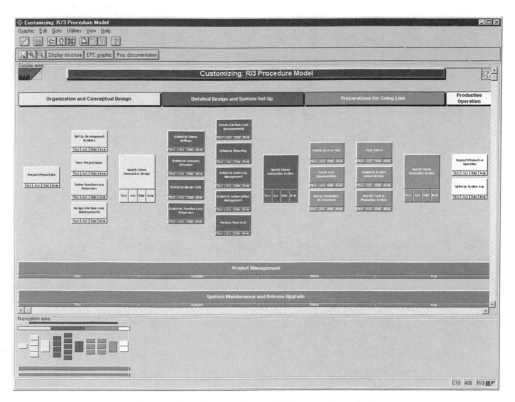

Figure 1.2   The traditional SAP procedure model

Several work packages are assigned to each phase, where each work package corresponds to an activity in the procedure model, and each work package itself consists of individual work steps. The last work package of each phase corresponds to a milestone. This milestone is used as a quality check and for the release of the results of a phase. The work packages cover the main tasks of the individual phases.

The SAP help for the procedure model provides a comprehensive description of the work packages contained in the individual phases and the steps to be performed. Figures 1.3 to 1.5 show the SAP procedure model down to the level of the phase activities for the individual phases.

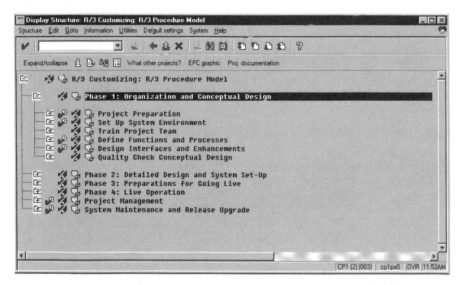

Figure 1.3   Activities of the first phase

The main tasks of the first phase (organization and conceptual design) are the organization of the project work, the training of the project team, the set-up of the test system and the test clients, and the creation of a conceptual design and the determination of requirements made on the system. The result of this phase is an approved and tested conceptual design.

The main tasks of the second phase (detailed design and realization) are the representation of the company structure, the basic data and master data, the testing of the individual business processes and the associated system settings, the realization of interfaces and system extensions, and the performance of the system test. The result of this phase is a company-specific system that has been tested and released for productive operation.

The third phase (preparation for going live) is concerned with planning for going live, the installation of the necessary hardware and software, the production of user documentation, training the users, and passing the data and the system settings to the productive system. The result of this phase is a tested and released productive system.

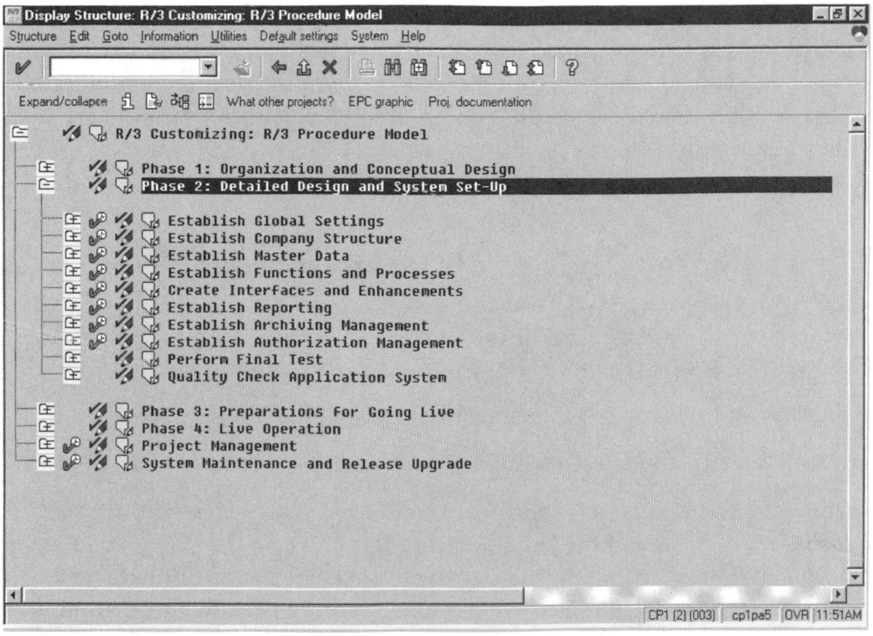

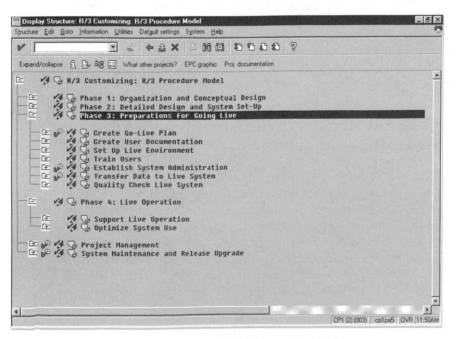

Figure 1.4   Activities of the second phase

Figure 1.5   Activities of the third and fourth phase

In the fourth phase (live operating), the users are supported in the initial productive use of the SAP R/3 system, a help desk organization is set up, system use is monitored and optimized, and any necessary modifications made to the documentation and system settings. The result of this phase is the guarantee of problem-free productive operation and further optimized use of the system.

The live operation phase ends the project.

1.1.2   Inter-phase activities of the traditional SAP procedure model

The traditional SAP procedure model has two inter-phase activities:

- Project administration and project control

- System maintenance and release change

Project administration and project control are concerned with checking the project during the processing of all phases of the procedure model as to whether the project goals have been achieved, and initiating appropriate corrective measures should there be deviations. In particular, the work packages involve detailed planning, the determination of project status, the initiation of corrective measures, and project meetings.

The inter-phase activities of system maintenance and release change are concerned with the procedures associated with the recurring corrections, improvements and extensions. The processing of the system upgrade/release change and release customizing are described as work packages for these activities.

As mentioned above, quality assurance, an additional activity considered to be an inter-phase activity in many procedure models, in the SAP procedure model is performed on completion of the individual phases.

Other inter-phase activities are not described.

1.1.3   The advantages of the traditional SAP procedure model

The major advantage of the traditional SAP procedure model is most certainly its detailed and complete description of all those activities required to perform an SAP R/3 project. Also, the very large number of projects that have now been carried out using the SAP procedure model as their basis provides an enormous wealth of experience.

In addition, SAP AG provides many integrated tools to support SAP R/3 implementation projects that are linked with the traditional SAP procedure model and so permit an integrated processing of the individual phase activities (refer, in particular, to Section 1.3 on the IPP method which discusses the use of these integrated tools).

1.1.4 Problems associated with the waterfall model and the traditional SAP procedure model

The largest problem concerned with the waterfall model and the traditional SAP procedure model lies in the enormous time difference between carrying out the requirements analysis, namely the early fixing of the requirements (first phase), and the final implementation of the system (last phase) (Gladden, 1982, p. 36; Jalote 1997, p. 20).

The user, at the time of requirements analysis, is not yet capable of predicting future needs. This problem becomes particularly apparent when it is observed that the average project duration is 6 to 12 months or, for large projects, 18 months or longer. When the increasingly faster-changing environmental conditions are taken into consideration (legal changes, new technologies/methods, even a change of currency), it becomes clear that although a system completed today may well be able to meet the requirements of the past, this makes it obsolete because the requirements are subject to continuous change over the course of time. However, the static properties associated with the traditional procedure model mean that it is not capable of satisfying the current requirements.

This problem becomes particularly apparent when the so-called 'big bang' is chosen as the implementation strategy. This requires that all business strategies are fully analyzed and described before being implemented in a single step, namely in a 'big bang'. However, because this complete business process analysis and description normally takes a very long time, such an implementation strategy should be chosen only when the requirements made on the R/3 system and the business processes themselves are very rigid, that is, not subject to any dynamic influences. If changes were made to the requirements, this would result in the implementation of an incorrect system that does not satisfy the requirements (see above).

Another important point that the SAP procedure model does not consider is the question of how teams working in parallel can be organized and managed. Because more than one team work concurrently on almost all SAP R/3 projects, this question is of particular importance.

The mastering or effective realization of the inter-phase activities is a further problem that the traditional models either ignore or disregard. An example is inadequate communication between consultants and users, and the resulting misunderstandings.

For example, as a result of these communication problems, errors often occur during system development and/or system implementation, which cause the requirements not to be satisfied and thus also fail to meet the expectations of the ordering party and the user. These errors can be subdivided into five categories (DSDM Consortium 1997, p. 13; Mumford and Welter, 1984, p. 3ff):

- The system fails to meet the actual business requirements, and either it is cancelled or expensive, adaptive maintenance tasks are preprogrammed.

- The system exhibits inadequate performance so that the user's requirements are inadequately satisfied.

- Unexpected errors (which can result either from programming errors or from misunderstandings) cause unexpected problems. These result in additional costs.

- Users reject the system. The reasons can be inadequate involvement in the development phase or lack of participation.

- Although systems are initially accepted, over the course of time they prove to be non-maintainable and so result in reduced use and consequently reduced usefulness.

Thus, to counter all these problems, the traditional waterfall model must be rejected and replaced by a model that meets the new requirements. This new model must not only satisfy the dynamic influence of the requirements described above, but must also cater for the inter-phase activities and help to speed up the project.

SAP AG reccommends the ASAP method as the solution to the problem of faster implementation.

1.2   The ASAP concept

The actual meaning of the 'asap' abbreviation is 'as soon as possible'. The adoption of this common use by SAP AG, which uses the term ASAP to mean AcceleratedSAP, is not just coincidental, but is meant to be understood as being representative of the accelerated realization of SAP projects.

ASAP was developed by SAP America in 1996, and has also been used since 1997 in Europe. The ASAP method consists of the so-called Roadmap component and various tools. The Roadmap supplies step-by-step recommendations and descriptions for all the activities to be performed. The Roadmap (refer to Figure 1.6) resulted from the traditional SAP procedure model and gives new designations to the individual phases. References are made within these phases to the work packages and the work steps of the traditional SAP procedure model.

The second component of the ASAP method consists of various tools that contain models, examples and checklists, but also pragmatic recommendations. These tools support project documentation using the usual Office programs. Furthermore, support is also provided for use of the Business Engineer, which can then be considered the basis for the R/3 configuration.

SAP AG makes the following comment with regard to the use of the ASAP method: 'ASAP resulted from the current R/3 procedure model and integrates the latest experience gained with the R/3 implementation. As such, ASAP is not a completely new methodology, but provides the collective know-how from SAP customers and partners.'

The ASAP Roadmap has the following individual components.

1.2.1 The ASAP phases

The ASAP Roadmap has five phases, one more than the traditional SAP procedure model. However, the contents of the individual phases largely correspond to those of the traditional procedure model and also exhibit the waterfall-based structure. The five phases of the ASAP method have the following names:

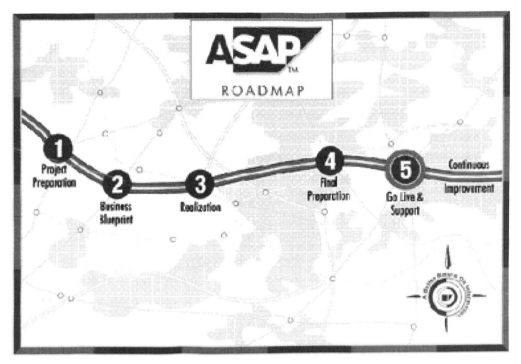

Figure 1.6   The ASAP Roadmap

Phase 1: Project preparation

This first phase is concerned with the planning and preparatory activities required for the successful realization of the R/3 project. As in the traditional SAP procedure model, the aims and the implementation strategy of the R/3 project are defined here, an estimate made of the size of the system to be implemented, and a time plan produced for the complete project.

Phase 2: Business blueprint

The second phase concentrates on documentation of the results from the requirements workshop and the business processes. The project team is also trained in the system environment and the organizational structure is defined.

Phase 3: Realization

This phase is concerned with the realization of the requirements defined in phase 2 with the aim of subsequent implementation of the R/3 system. The R/3 system must also be tested and released for productive operation. In addition, work packages such as 'develop data acceptance programs', 'define reports and forms', 'represent the authorization concept', and 'create seminar notes for the user' are prepared.

Phase 4: Preparation for production

This phase, concerned with user training and system management, provides the prerequisites for productive operation. With the completion of this phase, all defined business processes in the R/3 system can be processed in accordance with the requirements.

Phase 5: Go-live and support

The system is put into production in this phase. User support must be set up that supports not only the first days after going live but also long-term operation.

This phase ends the implementation project. Continuous optimization of the productive R/3 system then follows.

1.2.2   The ASAP tools and the accelerators

Various tools and so-called accelerators are supplied with ASAP. The ASAP tools are self-contained applications that are used to support the execution of individual work packages or individual phase activities. These tools include:

Implementation Assistant

The Implementation Assistant (refer to Figure 1.7) is an application that connects the ASAP tools, the ASAP accelerators and the ASAP Roadmap with their individual phase activities and descriptions. Thus, the Implementation Assistant represents the linkage between the work packets with provided document models and examples.

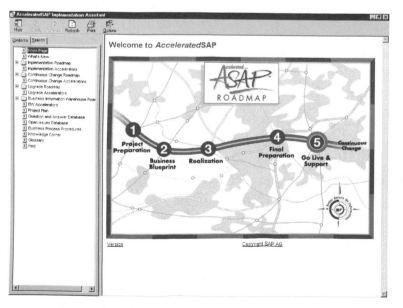

Figure 1.7   The Implementation Assistant

The Concept Check Tool

The Concept Check Tool is based on many years of experience gained in consulting and development, and provides a questionnaire that results from this experience. This questionnaire accompanies the R/3 implementation project from start to end. For this purpose, the associated phase-related questions are answered during each project phase. The Concept Check Tool generates comments on possible risks and problems from the answers, and sometimes makes suggestions indicating which methods are available for problem solution.

SAP AG designates the Concept Check Tool a dynamic tool because the answers to the individual questions determine which subsequent questions are to be answered. For example, a No answer to the question 'Do you use the MM module?' would omit all subsequent questions concerning the MM module.

The following three figures show examples of possible questions and answers for the Concept Check Tool. Figures 1.8 and 1.9 show possible dependencies between the individual questions that the Concept Check Tool takes into consideration.

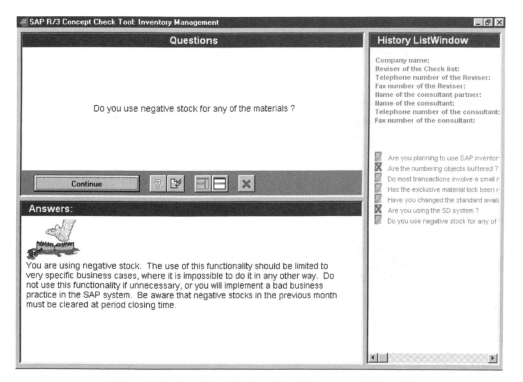

Figure 1.8   Questions for Inventory Management (Part 1)

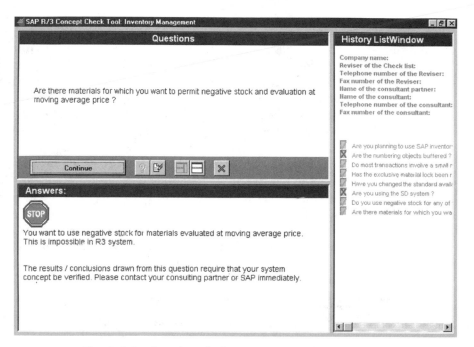

Figure 1.9   Questions for Inventory Management (Part 2)

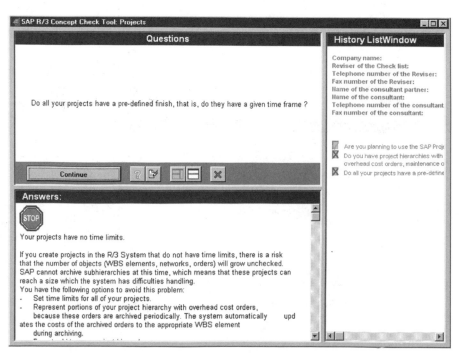

Figure 1.10   Schedule

Figure 1.10, shows an example of how references to the traditional SAP procedure model are used in the Concept Check Tool.

Question-and-Answer database

The Question-and-Answer database (Q&A database) contains all company-specific questions together with the associated answers. The business processes are taken into consideration in addition to the technical and organizational questions. This database is used as the basis for the creation of the business blueprints.

The accelerators consist of examples, models and checklists that are used to support and accelerate smaller tasks in the project. These accelerators include:

- Project plan

- Cutover Plan Template

- Knowledge Corner

For further information on the ASAP method, the reader is recommended to read *SAP R/3-Einführung mit ASAP* (SAP R/3 Implementation with ASAP) (Brand, 1999).

1.2.3   The advantages of the ASAP method

Although the ASAP method provides the same advantages as the traditional SAP procedure model, it offers more detailed job-related instructions. This means that ASAP provides an ideal support for those project employees who are working on their first SAP R/3 project or who do not yet have very comprehensive knowledge in this area. These employees are provided with very detailed instructions concerning what needs to be done in which phase, and how and when it is done.

In addition, many accelerators are supplied that not only accelerate the project but can also be used to standardize the project work.

1.2.4   The disadvantages of the ASAP method

Because the ASAP method is derived from the traditional SAP procedure model, and therefore also derived from the waterfall-based model, this method has the same disadvantages as the traditional SAP procedure model. These disadvantages are not repeated here, but rather the reader is referred to Section 1.1.4.

1.3   Iterative Process Prototyping

Keller and Teufel in their book *SAP R/3 prozessorientiert verwenden – Iteratives Prozess-Prototyping zur Bildung von Wertschöpfungsketten* (process-oriented use of SAP R/3 – iterative process prototyping to build value-added chains) describe an iterative method used to realize feasible business processes. Thus, Iterative Process Prototyping (IPP) concentrates on the 'define processes and functions' and 'form processes and functions' process activities of the traditional SAP procedure model. The following section discusses the use of IPP, critical parts of IPP and a possible embedding of IPP in the dynamic procedure model (refer to Part B).

1.3.1 The use of IPP

IPP, as part of business process modelling and in the formation of value-added chains, initially considers two levels: the business level and the system level. Keller and Teufel make use of the reference process model, the organization model and the data/object model for the business level. The business-related questions concentrate on:

- What business processes does the company require?

- Which organizational units work together? In which form?

- Which information is processed? How are the various information items related?

Prototyping, customizing and the data dictionary are available for use at the system level. This level is used to represent the requirements of the company and consideration in the SAP R/3 system.

Keller and Teufel represent the network and the possible navigation paths between the individual tools as shown in Figure 1.11.

The figure shows that it is possible to navigate from every tool of the IPP to every other tool. In practice, this navigation capability is used, for example, to jump with a transaction code from a business process of the R/3 reference model to the appropriate transaction

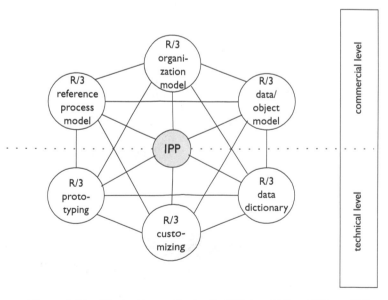

Figure 1.11   Navigation paths in the IPP (see Keller 1997, p. 198)

code in the R/3 system and so receive a prototype with default settings. In a similar manner, it is possible to jump between all the previously listed tools in the R/3 system. Thus, it is possible to discuss every business process with the user and to make the appropriate settings to meet his requirements; all changes and their effects then can be seen immediately on the screen.

1.3.2 The advantages of IPP

The iterative adaptation of the R/3 system to the user's requirements through the use of the prototype method not only provides a suitable method for correcting misunderstandings or communication problems but also provides a methodology that extends the traditional SAP procedure model and the ASAP method, and satisfies the requirement for an iterative methodology within the SAP R/3 implementation project. Thus, this iterative method corresponds to the methods actually used.

Furthermore, the use of the various integrated and SAP-specific tools is fully described and, as discussed above, prototyping reduces the communication problems.

1.3.3 The disadvantages of IPP

Although IPP's iterative method represents the reality, the business processes are processed in sequence. However, the general phenomenon of teams working in parallel remains unsolved. In addition, no explanation is provided of how the difficulties inherent in an iterative methodology can be overcome. For example, there is no indication of the necessity for version or configuration management and consequently an explanation, how this can function in an SAP R/3 implementation project.

Furthermore, the individual business processes are not discussed in the order of their importance for the business benefits, but handled or introduced successively based on their appearance in the value-added chain, and no methods are provided that could accelerate the implementation project.

The iterative method does not cover the complete process; rather it is limited to the activities that describe the business process; and makes use here of the Business Navigator, a tool that is relatively difficult to use and is seldom used in practice.

Thus, the IPP method is limited to the phase activities described above and so is also part of the traditional SAP procedure model. The IPP method therefore does not provide any solutions to the problems of waterfall-based models.

1.4 Experience from system development

When we consider the disadvantages associated with the various methodologies, it becomes apparent that these are largely based on problems that have accompanied software development for decades.

Many projects adhered to the waterfall-based method at the beginning of software development. This waterfall model in its original form described a model in which the individual phases had to be performed in a predefined sequence. The recognition that such a method does not suffice when, for example, the development has gone in the wrong direction, led to the waterfall method providing the possibility of returning to an earlier phase.

In addition, the previously mentioned fact that the waterfall model had problems with dynamic changes to the requirements resulted in the development of iterative models. Furthermore, problems with user–developer communications frequently resulted in the requirements not being met, and so the demand for a prototyping method arose.

In addition to these problems, there was criticism concerning project length and a lack of consideration of the inter-phase activities. Thus, it becomes apparent that the problems associated with software development are comparable to those associated with the implementation of a standard software package.

DSDM, a dynamic procedure model developed in 1995 as a possible solution to these problems, also corrects the typical problems that occur during SAP R/3 implementation projects, and serves as the basis for this book.

1.5   Summary

The traditional SAP procedure model has to counter many problems that largely result from the waterfall-based characteristics of the model:

- Large amount of time required

- Requirements not satisfied

- Inadequate transfer of knowhow

- Disregard of the inter-phase activities

- High cost

The ASAP method aims to speed up the implementation of SAP R/3 projects. Although this method provides various models and checklists that are suitable for supporting project management and documentation, it is still generally related to the waterfall-based model and so scarcely differs from the traditional SAP procedure model. Consequently, an SAP R/3 project realized with ASAP is confronted with the same problems.

However, countering the problems described above requires a procedure model that not only considers the individual phase activities but also describes the inter-phase activities. In particular, it is important that this procedure model exhibits fewer static properties than the traditional procedure model.

2 DSDM – The dynamic procedure model

The DSDM acronym stands for 'Dynamic Systems Development Method' and describes a dynamic procedure model for software development. This model was developed in 1995 by the DSDM Consortium and is based on the experience of various members of the consortium. Readers interested in obtaining further information on DSDM are recommended to read both the DSDM manual (DSDM, 1997) and the book *DSDM – The Method in Practice* by Jennifer Stapleton (1997)

The main application purpose of DSDM is to provide a structured and controlled procedure for software development projects. In particular, DSDM should be used to realize so-called RAD (Rapid Application Development) projects. The term RAD was first used by James Martin in his book of the same name (Martin, 1991). The main characteristics of RAD projects are the observing of a rigidly fixed time window and high development speed, with the consequence that RAD projects often have the reputation of being 'quick and dirty' or a 'licence to hack'. This negative RAD image results from the apparently unstructured and unplanned procedure adopted in RAD projects. However, the Dynamic Systems Development Method provides a procedure model that is suitable for structuring and planning RAD projects, and so counters the negative RAD image.

This chapter first introduces the DSDM idea and the principles on which DSDM is based. This is followed by a discussion of the project management and quality aspects in DSDM projects. Finally, the main benefits that result from the use of DSDM are listed.

2.1 The DSDM idea and the most important principles

DSDM is a non-trademarked procedure model that provides a skeleton that can be used to develop and maintain software systems subject to rigorous time restrictions.

DSDM is mainly used in Great Britain. The DSDM Consortium also expressed the hope that DSDM has the potential to establish itself as a standard for software development projects. Today, the DSDM Consortium describes the Dynamic Systems Development Method as being the de facto standard for Great Britain.

This statement may initially appear to be somewhat questionable because it was made by the DSDM Consortium itself. However, if you consider that the consortium has more than 1,000 members, including Oracle, IBM, Hewlett-Packard, Software AG, Cap Gemini, etc., it is quite possible to agree with this statement.

DSDM is based on the following basic assumptions:

- Although no system is perfectly developed at the first attempt,

- 80 per cent of the perfect solution can be achieved in 20 per cent of the time that would be required to achieve the perfect solution.

- End-users are not capable of predicting their long-range requirements at the time of defining their requirements (the first phase of the traditional model). In this connection, it is in any case assumed that most user requirements will become clear only when the system to be developed is actually used.

- Unlike the traditional waterfall model, DSDM assumes that the current phase does not need to be completely finished but only sufficiently complete so that the next phase can be started, in which the previous phase is then ended.

The main idea behind DSDM is an iterative prototyping that the user can incorporate very early in the development and so provide a common understanding for the system to be developed. However, prototyping, when used with DSDM, should not be understood as being the development of so-called 'throw-away prototypes' but as the development of functioning components that in the course of system development become part of the complete system.

It is important to ensure that the principles on which the model is based reflect the fundamental ideas behind the DSDM procedure.

DSDM is based on nine principles:

- Active user involvement is imperative.

- DSDM teams must be empowered to make decisions that affect system development.

- The frequent and regular delivery of products is of particular importance.

- 'Fitness for business purpose' is the main acceptance criterion, i.e., the system focuses on business benefits.

- Iterative and incremental development is necessary to converge on an accurate business solution.

- All changes made during development are reversible.

- Requirements are initially described only in general terms.

- Testing is not limited to a specific phase, but takes place during the complete life cycle.

- The collaboration and cooperation of all parties are essential.

2.2   The method

DSDM is divided into five phases (cf. the detailed explanation of the individual phases in DSDM Consortium, 1997, Chapter 4) and can be represented as shown in Figure 2.1.

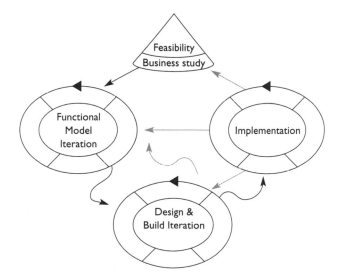

Figure 2.1   The DSDM model without inter-phase activities

The individual phases in detail:

A *Phase: The feasibility study*
One of the tests made in this phase is to determine whether DSDM can be used to realize the project. Another model is used if this is not the case.

The aim of this phase is to answer the questions: 'is the system development at all appropriate to support our company aims?', 'Is a technical realization possible, and what general form could this take?', and 'What are the expected duration and costs involved?'

The results from this phase are used in a feasibility report, which considers the area involved and the problem definitions and goals, and in a preliminary plan that represents the initial project planning.

B *Phase: The business study*
The business study involves the general definition of the main functionalities, such as the main non-functional requirements (e.g., reliability, performance). The extent to which the new system supports the business functions must be clarified.

A representative user for each user group is selected for the prototyping activities. The requirements must also be assigned a priority. The feasibility study and the business study can often be combined.

The results of this phase must provide a business area definition (users, main business processes, essential information), a list of the prioritized functions, the definition of system architecture, and a detailing of the general planning from the first phase, where this detailing then represents a general prototyping plan for the next phases.

C *Phase: Function model iteration*
This first prototyping phase focuses on determining the user's requirements or on obtaining further information on these requirements. This phase can be repeated several times and has two goals: to demonstrate the functionality and to acquire the non-functional requirements. This phase should provide the following results:

• Function model

• Implementation strategy (with detailed plan and cost/benefits analysis)

• Auditing documents of the functional prototype

• Risk analysis of future developments (optional)

D *Phase: System design and system build iteration*
It is possible to start this phase even though the previous phase has not yet been completed. The demarcation line between the third and fourth phases is not fixed and, indeed, may not be present at all.

The goal of this phase is the refining and detailing of the functional prototype and a consideration of the non-functional requirements. This phase should supply not only a tested system that meets all functional and non-functional requirements, but also a design prototype with the associated auditing documents.

E *Phase: The implementation*
The system is given to the end-users in this phase. The project success is evaluated and those components determined that still need to be completed at some later time. Depending on the result of the project audit, either a return is made to an earlier phase or the project is ended.

The tested system is embedded in the user's work environment and the future development requirements determined in this phase. The users are trained and a user's manual produced. This phase ends with a documented project audit.

Because DSDM considers maintenance normally to be a continuous development process, maintenance is equivalent to a new DSDM development iteration.

In addition to these phases, DSDM also describes a number of inter-phase activities that are essential for successful project development (DSDM Consortium, 1997). In particular, the following inter-phase activities are described:

• Project management

• Prototyping management

• Configuration management

• Risk analysis

• Testing

• Quality assurance

2.3   Navigation through the model

The representation of the DSDM procedure model shown in Figure 2.2 consists of two parts. Whereas the surface of the figure describes the DSDM life cycle, the individual slices represent the inter-phase DSDM activities.

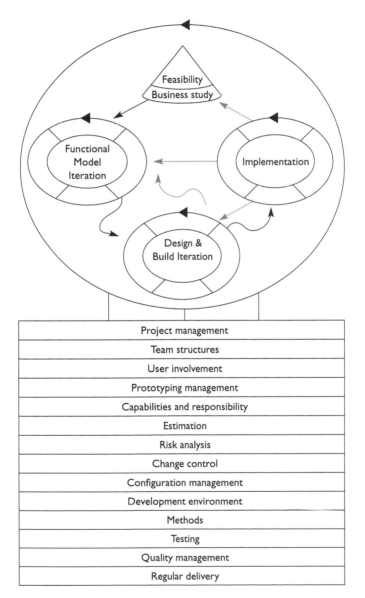

Figure 2.2   DSDM with inter-phase activities

The black arrows indicate the path through the life cycle, where, starting from the feasibility study, the transition from one phase to the next is made in an anticlockwise direction. Thus, the black arrows represent the 'planned path' through the model. In contrast, the grey arrows indicate those parts in the cycle where it is easy to return to an earlier phase. Because navigation through the individual phases can vary from project to project, the procedure model described here does not constitute a model that must be rigidly followed; rather it should be adapted for each project.

The figure also shows very comprehensively the importance of the interphase activities. These activities must not only be considered over all phases, but also form the basis of the procedure model and so are a decisive factor for project success.

2.4   DSDM and quality standards

This section investigates DSDM's conformity to common quality standards and indicates that the use of DSDM is suitable to produce quality in accordance with ISO 9000 or CMM.

DSDM and ISO 9000

The SO 9000 family is a collection of industry-independent standards for quality management, valid worldwide. To be able to judge whether DSDM meets these standards, the following statement is initially made in the DSDM manual:

> When you consider DSDM and ISO 9000, you will quickly discover a contradiction. This becomes evident when we consider two statements from ISO 9000-3 (quotations by the DSDM Consortium (1995, p. 173) 'it is not important which procedure model is used as basis for software development that conforms to the ISO standard,' and 'the functional requirements must be complete and present in an unambiguous form in order to perform software development in accordance with the ISO standard.' Thus, these statements have limited use in determining whether DSDM conforms to ISO 9000.

The discussion provided by the *British Standards Institution* (BSI), 'the Dynamic Systems Development Method & TickIT', is more useful here. The BSI describes in this discussion a detailed guide that shows how DSDM software development projects need to be realized in order that the requirements of the ISO 9000 are satisfied (BSI, 1997). These discussions come to the conclusion that DSDM satisfies the requirements of ISO 9000 (refer to Chapter 8).

DSDM and CMM

The *Capability Maturity Model* (CMM) has been in development since 1986 at the *Software Engineering Institute* (SEI) of Carnegie Mellon University. The American Defense Department which financed this development uses CMM for the selection of software suppliers.

CMM is a model that can be used to determine the maturity of software development processes and so permit specific improvements to be made (Mellis et al., 1995, p. 95). Several key process areas are defined for each maturity level. A questionnaire is used to determine whether these areas apply at the company under consideration (refer to Paulk et al. (1995) for detailed information on CMM).

Because DSDM covers all key process areas of the second maturity level in accordance with CMM, companies that use CMM are automatically at this level. The definition of the second maturity level implies that the planning, supervision and control of time, costs and quality satisfy all basic project management tasks.

2.5 The benefits of DSDM

DSDM is primarily based on the development of prototypes. Although DSDM does not apply to 'throw-away prototypes', such prototypes are realized as part of the product to be developed, in which the subsequent end-user is integrated very early in the project. This procedure provides several advantages (DSDM Consortium, 1997, p. 15), such as:

- The end-user identifies with the system.

- The cooperation of all those involved reduces possible resistance during the implementation.

- The danger of missing the end-user's requirements is reduced.

- The end-user gets a better understanding of the system. He or she knows, what, why and how something is done.

- The developed system is better suited to satisfying the requirements.

- Prototyping avoids oral misunderstandings.

- The user gets acquainted with the system during the prototyping. This reduces the training effort.

- Team and communication capabilities are trained.

These benefits apparently suffice to counteract the disadvantages of the SAP procedure model mentioned in Section 1.1.4. Thus, it appears sensible to test DSDM to see whether it can be generally used as a procedure model during the implementation of SAP R/3.

3 Test the general suitability of DSDM as a procedure model for SAP R/3 projects

The DSDM Consortium provides in the DSDM manual a guide that can be used to test software development projects for their DSDM suitability. Because this guide is based on criteria such as 'Do the requirements change over the course of time?', 'Are there clearly defined user groups?' and 'Is this a process control application or a real-time application?', and because these criteria are also relevant for standard software implementations, the guide is used in this chapter to assess the suitability of DSDM for SAP R/3 implementation projects.

In contrast to software development projects in which every single project exhibits different characteristics and so needs to be tested for its suitability, the SAP R/3 implementation project only needs to be tested once. This results from the fact that in the implementation of standard software, the main properties of the software do not change in any significant way.

Initially, this raises the question of when DSDM could be used for an SAP R/3 implementation project. A test is made of whether an SAP R/3 implementation project exhibits properties that are not compatible with DSDM. However, this would not necessarily mean that it is impossible to use DSDM, but rather that DSDM should not be used for the implementation project.

The following sections analyze DSDM-typical success factors as to whether they can be realized in an SAP R/3 implementation project.

Finally, the summary helps decide whether the development of a DSDM-based procedure model is appropriate for SAP R/3 implementation.

3.1   When DSDM can be used

The DSDM manual mentions seven criteria (DSDM Consortium, 1997, p. 37) whose existence indicates the suitability of DSDM as a procedure model ('... where DSDM should be the method of choice'):

- *The functionality is obvious because of the user interface*
  The user interface can be used to show the user the functionality of the system in the form of business processes and business functions. This means that this first point is satisfied.

- *The user groups can be clearly differentiated*
  Because every business process in the SAP R/3 system can be assigned a unique user group interface, this point is satisfied.

- *If very complex calculations are present, this complexity can be decomposed or encapsulated*
  Because it is generally possible to say that all required calculations have already been made in the SAP R/3 system or have already been implemented, this point does not need to be considered further.

- *Large systems can be subdivided into smaller functional components*
  Because the SAP R/3 system consists of many functional components in the form of individual business processes, this point is satisfied.

- *There are fixed time limits*
  Especially in the case of SAP R/3 implementation projects, there exist clearly set time limits. Reasons for this are the high consulting requirement, and thus the associated costs, and the high demand made on the users (e.g., training, support provided for business process modelling) during the implementation project, which means that they neglect their normally daily work. Consequently, this criterion is also satisfied.

- *The requirements can be prioritized*
  The individual business processes have different importance for each company and influence company success in different ways, which means that the requirements and business processes can always be prioritized. Consequently, this criterion is also satisfied.

- *The requirements do not need to be fixed early but can change over the course of time*
  Business processes are continually subject to change and so cannot be described or fixed at the start of the SAP R/3 implementation. Indeed, it is even possible to assert that an early fixing of the requirements would adversely affect the implementation project. Consequently, this criterion is also met.

Thus, the SAP R/3 implementation project exhibits all those properties that make the use of DSDM possible and those that are particularly appropriate for the use of DSDM.

The next section now tests whether the SAP R/3 implementation project possibly possesses those characteristics that are not DSDM-compatible and so would hinder the use of DSDM.

3.2   When DSDM should not be used

The DSDM manual indicates four points (DSDM Consortium, 1997, p. 39) that hinder or even stop the use of DSDM ('where special care is needed in applying DSDM'):

- *Development of real time / process control applications*
  Real time in the sense of SAP R/3 means only an 'immediate entry and updating of data' and not real time in the sense of process control. Thus, the DSDM manual does not consider this point to be critical.

- *The requirements must be fully specified before the development starts*
  It is not necessary for an SAP R/3 implementation to define all the requirements fully at the start of the project (although the SAP procedure model specifies this). Rather, it is possible to decide later whether a new business process or an additional module needs

to be implemented. Thus, the size of the system is not a constant for which there must be complete clarity at the beginning.

- *Development of security-critical applications*
  Although SAP R/3 has already been fully developed as such a system, it must be adapted to meet the individual customer requirements or be extended with customer-specific components. Because hospitals for example, are SAP customers, particular attention may need to be paid to this third point.

- *The developed components must be reusable*
  Because the individual components of the SAP R/3 system are standard software, the individual business processes and reports are also reusable. This point is also not critical.

Consequently, these criteria do not hinder the use of DSDM for an SAP R/3 implementation.

3.3 Which success factors should be observed when DSDM is used?

With the exception of the criteria for evaluation of DSDM suitability for specific projects described in the previous two sections, the success factors described in the DSDM manual cannot be discussed generally but represent company-specific properties and conditions.

Because neglect of these factors critical for success can result in failure of the DSDM project, some are listed here as examples (DSDM Consortium, 1997, p. 35ff):

- Management must understand and accept DSDM.

- The users and developers must be empowered to make decisions.

- The user must be given sufficient free time to be able to participate in the development project at any time.

- Team members must have both technical and business knowledge.

- Team members must possess strong communicative capabilities.

3.4 Test whether SAP R/3 can be implemented as a RAD tool

The DSDM manual contains a guide for the evaluation of software development systems with regard to their suitability as a RAD tool. This section aims to show that an SAP R/3 system is an ideal development system for RAD applications. The evaluation method for DSDM is also oriented to the phases of the DSDM method, i.e., it is divided into five sections, each of which corresponds to the phases of the DSDM model. Whereas the question of whether criteria are satisfied can be answered independently of the project situation in some circumstances, other criteria can only be judged in the context of the company under consideration.

Feasibility study

The decision of what is to be automated in the development work must be made during the *feasibility study* phase of the evaluation process. The highest priority here concerns the benefits, in the sense of the DSDM method, for the development.

The decision as to whether the SAP R/3 system is a suitable tool for the evaluation means deciding which activities can or should be supported by tools. The table below shows possible activities and assigns appropriate tools to each of these activities. Which of these tools are needed and the extent to which they can be used depends on each project situation. For example, if a project does not require any additional development, namely it uses only the standard functionality of the SAP R/3 system, then there is no support for new development or the use of the ABAP/4 Development Workbench. However, other activities, such as word processing, must be considered in all projects.

Action	Tool
Project management	SAP PS module
	MS Project
Configuration management	SAP DVS
	SAP CTS
Communication	SAP Office
Testing	SAP CATT
	SAP Testplan Tool
	SAP ABAP/4 Development Workbench
	AutoTester
Word processing	SAP Editor
	MS Word
Business process modelling	SAP Business-Engineer
	ARIS
	Visio
	Life-Model
Customizing	SAP IMG
Presentations	MS PowerPoint
Developments	SAP ABAP/4 Development Workbench function module library

Business study investigation

The *business study* phase should consider those risks associated with the implementation of a RAD tool.

This investigation should consider at least the following risks:

- Is the organization ready for the changes?

- Are sufficient financial resources available?

- Does the organization have a defined development process?

- Are there cultural barriers that hinder the implementation?

- Does the organization support the required technical platform?

- Can the technical support provide sufficient support for the implementation?

- Is the required infrastructure present?

The risks resulting from DSDM apply for all SAP R/3 implementations and are independent of the methods used. Consequently, because the risk questions depend on the individual company, they cannot be answered generally here.

Function model iteration

This phase investigates whether the SAP R/3 system satisfies the criteria that DSDM places on the development system. These criteria can be evaluated independently of both the project and the organization.

- *SAP R/3 supports the development process*
  All tools of the SAP R/3 system support the development process, i.e., they simplify the work of the teams. Higher costs will result for the project if the tools are not used.

- *SAP R/3 supports the modelling techniques for the project*
  The modelling techniques for the SAP R/3 project include the development of event-controlled process chains. SAP currently provides only the capability to select processes from the standard process chains and possibly omit subprocesses, but not to add new processes. Supplementary tools, such as the ARIS Toolset or Visio, must be used for such tasks. However, because the selection of the process chains within the SAP R/3 system is very long-winded, generally the major part of the required business processes is already covered. The SAP R/3 system also supports ER modelling.

- *SAP R/3 is easy to operate*
  The simple and uniform user interface provided for the developers and users meets this criterion.

- *Openness*
  The independence of the SAP R/3 system with regard to hardware, operating system, database system and presentation level meets this criterion.

- *SAP R/3 supports user involvement*
  The uniform user interface provided for the developers and the subsequent users allows the users to operate both the actual system and the development system. The users can easily operate the resulting system. The IDES training system immediately provides the users with a system that they can use to test each of the processes.

- *SAP R/3 supports iterations*
  The SAP R/3 system is supplied as the base system or as a predefined system. Because changes made in customizing take immediate effect in the system, iterations are very easy to implement. The IPP method also builds on this concept.

- *SAP R/3 supports baselines and version control*
  SAP provides the Document Management System and the Change and Transport System (CTS) for these activities.

- *SAP R/3 has a controlled repository*
  SAP supplies the Repository Information System as a tool. This system manages and checks all data elements, programs, domains, etc., for consistency. Changes are registered in the CTS.

- *SAP R/3 supports reuse*
  The CTS permits the controlled transfer and use of any objects for the SAP R/3 system on other computers. The very large number of shared objects present in all SAP R/3 systems requires that integrity is maintained. Any integrity violations are indicated. The remote function permits test runs to be started on other computers.

- *Navigation*
  The SAP R/3 Repository Information System permits arbitrary navigation to be made to the various objects. Additional navigation capabilities are provided in the test plans in the CTS.

- *SAP R/3 produces documentation*
  The R/3 system provides many standard reports. The Report Generator permits the simple creation of additional reports.

- *SAP R/3 can create the subsequent productive system from the development system (final system cut-over)*
  The subdivision of the system into development, consolidation and productive systems ensures that the productive system results from the development system.

- *Multi-user*
  The SAP R/3 system supports multiple users.

- *SAP supports standards*
  SAP supports many standards at all levels.

- *SAP supports testing*
  The SAP R/3 system supplies functions in the ABAP/4 Development Workbench, the Computer Aided Test Tool (CATT) and the Test Plan Tool to support testing.

To summarize, the SAP R/3 system satisfies all criteria of the third phase of the evaluation independent of the project and the organization.

System design and system build iteration

The phase performs a detailed investigation of the requirements made on a RAD tool. The DSDM manual specifies several criteria that should be observed. The criteria listed here, such as testing and configuration management, are not investigated in further detail because they have already been discussed elsewhere.

- *Evaluation of the suppliers (here SAP AG)*
  Criteria concerning support, references and the documentation system are listed here. SAP AG satisfies these criteria.

- *Evaluation of the server environment*
  All criteria concerning the various platforms, network capability, multi-user capability, and the hardware of the productive system are satisfied.

- *Evaluation of the user support*
  SAP AG, with the Online Service System (OSS), provides support that permits both users and consultants to send SAP AG any problems that arise with the SAP R/3 system. This system can also be used to obtain the answers; such answers are normally provided within a short time. The OSS also contains information about current errors and their correction.

  The SAP R/3 user interface also largely conforms to Windows-based user interfaces. The information is shown clearly and precisely. The hardware in use determines the response times. A wide range of seminars is provided. The IDES training system also provides tutorials to enable users to become acquainted with the R/3 system. Comprehensive online help is also provided in all areas. The quality of the online help for the associated seminars is especially good. The help is also available in printed form.

- *Evaluation of the price*
  The evaluation of the price depends on the project and the company.

- *Integration of the methods and validation of consistency*
  SAP R/3 is an integrated system that reports any inconsistencies.

Implementation

This phase evaluates the activities that need to be performed when a decision has been made to implement the R/3 system.

- *User training*
  SAP AG offers a wide range of seminars that cover all areas of the SAP R/3 system. The number of seminars required, and thus the associated costs, depends on the project and the organization.

- *Roll-out strategy*
  The roll-out strategy for the implementation of the SAP R/3 system as a RAD tool can, for example, be based on the 'from project to project' principle or have company-wide use as goal. The answer to this question is company dependent.

- *Support*
  A technical support team must be formed to support productive operation. The size and cost depend on each project and the company involved.

- *Work-arounds*
  The decision must be made as to how the new activities associated with the implementation of SAP R/3 can be combined with the old systems and development methods.

- *Monitoring of use*
  Once the system has been implemented, monitoring must be done to determine the extent to which it is being used, which errors have occurred, and whether the expected benefits have been achieved. These activities are project and company dependent.

To summarize, depending on the project and the company, SAP R/3 satisfies all criteria for project phases 3 and 4. Irrespective of the implementation of SAP R/3, each company must clarify phases 1, 2 and 5. Thus, the SAP R/3 system can be implemented in a company on the basis described and so satisfies all criteria placed on a RAD tool.

3.5 Summary

An SAP R/3 implementation project satisfies all the requirements that the DSDM manual places on the successful use of DSDM and does not contain any of the properties that would give cause in special attention in the planned use of DSDM.

In addition, the use of DSDM for an SAP R/3 implementation project also requires that the project to be realized can be divided into several parts and so permit the realization of the principal DSDM ideas for iterative and incremental development and implementation. Comprehensive practical experience shows that SAP R/3 projects satisfy these properties and so are particularly appropriate for the use of DSDM.

Thus, the use of a DSDM-based procedure model for an SAP R/3 project would appear to promise a very successful implementation.

Part B
The DSDM-based procedure model for SAP R/3 implementation

This part of the book now uses DSDM for an SAP R/3 implementation project and develops the DSDM-based procedure model which can be used as a basis for the realization of SAP R/3 projects. Our interest in the following chapters initially concerns the individual phase activities, whereas the later chapters describe the inter-phase and phase-independent activities.

At this point, we must again emphasize that the DSDM-based procedure model should not be understood as being a model that questions the usefulness of the traditional SAP procedure model, the ASAP concept or IPP, but rather aims at combining the advantages of the individual methods and rectifying the disadvantages of these concepts.

Thus, for example, there is no change to the method used for the realization of the individual work packets of the traditional procedure model or the ASAP concept, but rather the method with which they are embedded in the overall relationship of the DSDM-based procedure model and thus with regard to their use as part of an iterative and incremental strategy. This is also the reason why the contents of the individual work packets are not described in detail; this has already been done very comprehensively in the online help of the SAP R/3 systems and in the ASAP concept. Rather, the activities discussed in the following chapters are placed at a higher level, namely at the phase activity level.

This means that the contents of the individual phase activities do not change. The reader is requested to consult the associated documentation for the individual activities that has been mentioned previously. Because Keller and Teufel have already provided a detailed description of the IPP concept in their book *SAP R/3 prozessorientiert einführen* (a SAP R/3 process-oriented implementation), a detailed description of the operation of the IPP concept is also not part of this book.

Rather, the contents of the following chapters serve to describe those properties of a dynamic procedure model that fundamentally differ from the waterfall-based concepts. The focus lies on the questions used to determine the appearance of the new procedure model in order that the SAP R/3 system can be implemented iteratively and so also extended stepwise.

Furthermore, the following chapters also present those activities used to ensure that the individual iterations and the teams working in parallel in the individual iterations can be managed and their work results combined without losing sight of the real goal. Consequently, these activities have both an inter-phase and a phase-independent nature.

However, the reader is not only urged to refer to the detailed documentation for the individual work packets, but also encouraged to make extensive use of the accelerators provided with ASAP when they can be shown to be advantageous in speeding up the SAP R/3 project.

The following chapter shows the DSDM-based procedure model graphically and provides a general description of the possible model processes. The individual phase activities are then described and finally a summary provided for the DSDM-based procedure model with special identification of the DSDM characteristics of each activity.

The term 'DSDM iteration' often arises in conjunction with the DSDM descriptions. A DSDM iteration designates a cycle *within* the DSDM-based procedure model. In contrast, a 'DSDM pass' designates the processing of all phases of the DSDM-based procedure model. Thus, a DSDM pass is equivalent to a subproject within the complete SAP R/3 implementation project.

Although the inter-phase activities of the procedure model are described only in the next chapter, the description of the phase activities has already frequently made reference to these inter-phase activities, so that the study of this book can also take the form of a very dynamic process. These inter-phase activities represent the foundation on which the individual phases build and which are essential for a successful realization of the SAP R/3 implementation project. This means that the detailed phase descriptions must frequently refer to these inter-phase activities.

In particular, although the detailed phase descriptions contain the representation of the individual phase activities in the DSDM-based procedure model, it also indicates possible problem situations that can occur during the course of SAP R/3 implementation. Furthermore, an indication should be made as to which of the individual phase activities must be performed successively and which can be performed in parallel.

4 The DSDM-based procedure model

4.1 The DSDM-based procedure model

The DSDM-based procedure model for the realization of SAP R/3 projects differs significantly from the well-known waterfall-based method. A successive procedure with individual, completed substeps is no longer described, but rather an iterative method whose individual phases cannot or need not be separated. For this reason, the representation of the DSDM-based procedure model should orient itself as closely as possible to the DSDM procedure model for software development and so take account of the fundamental DSDM ideas and the DSDM philosophy.

The motive for the development of a new procedure model for R/3 implementation was the requirement to have a more modern concept that did not only describe at the individual phase activities but also handled the task and problem situations that always need to be mastered in SAP R/3 projects. These points of criticism can be generally summarized as follows:

- The dynamics of the requirements are not considered.
- The product comes into productive operation too late.
- Prototyping and the iterative methodology are neglected.
- No discussion is provided on how teams can work together in parallel.
- No discussion is provided on how it should be tested.
- The inter-phase activities are neglected.
- The transfer of know-how is not supported.

The dynamics of the requirements are not considered

The problem that the dynamics of the requirements are not considered results largely from the fact that the traditional SAP procedure model and ASAP are waterfall-based concepts. Waterfall-based here means that the individual phases of the implementation project are executed successively in a strictly predefined sequence. The first phase normally serves to analyze the requirements, which are only realized towards the end of the project. If we also take into consideration that implementation projects can take as long as one year, or even longer depending on the size of the project, it becomes apparent that

requirements determined some time previously, because of the dynamics of the requirements (changes to business processes, changes to laws, new methods, currency
conversion, etc.), do not have much in common with the current requirements. Thus, it
is possible that even though a system has been implemented to meet the written requirements, it is not capable of taking account of the current requirements. This problem
situation becomes particularly apparent when you select the so-called 'big bang' concept, in which all business processes are described down to the smallest detail (in
negative examples, this activity alone can take a year or longer!), before the actual implementation project is started. Thus, we need to take account of this problem situation in
the DSDM-based procedure model. That is, in contrast to the waterfall-based concept,
we need to select a dynamic concept that takes account of changing requirements even
during the project.

The product comes into productive operation too late

This criticism has two causes: the projects themselves take a long time, and the projects
are normally planned so that all business processes are implemented within a project.
This procedure is also the only one envisaged in the traditional SAP procedure model and
ASAP, which do not assume that several passes are made through the model. However,
from the DSDM viewpoint, not all business processes should be implemented in the first
project, but only the most important (measured according to their importance to the business benefits). This means that the first pass through the model aims at implementing an
approximately 80 per cent solution, before the special functions are implemented later in a
second pass. Thus, these special functions are functions that are used either very little or
not at all, or are relatively unimportant to the business benefits. Consequently, the DSDM-
based procedure model should help the SAP R/3 system to become productive faster and
so contribute sooner to the success of the enterprise.

Prototyping and the iterative procedure are neglected

Prototyping and the iterative procedure are two typical characteristics that occur in every
SAP R/3 project and are also normally desired. However, even here when we use the procedure in accordance with the traditional SAP procedure model or ASAP, we have the
problem that although these methods are used by everyone, they are not taken into consideration in the traditional models. This is a particularly critical weakness, because
prototyping and the associated user involvement are particularly controversial in the literature and unconsidered 'impetuous' prototyping is very susceptible to errors.

   Thus, the goal of the DSDM-based procedure model must be to establish a prototyping
management that ensures that prototyping is performed in a planned and controllable
manner. The same applies to the iterative procedure, which is also essential in all projects,
because it cannot be assumed that all business processes will be implemented directly at
the first attempt in accordance with the requirements. Thus, the procedure model must
also permit iterations to be performed in a controlled manner.

No discussion is provided on how teams can work together in parallel

Typical for SAP R/3 projects is that normally several teams are involved in parallel in the project work. This initially causes the difficulty that normally several teams, for example, must work with the same customizing settings, although this problem can be handled relatively easily. More difficult, however, is the task of combining the results of the individual teams and checking whether everything that functioned independently in each individual team also runs as expected together, i.e., integrated. Also, neither the traditional SAP procedure model nor ASAP handles the problem of teams working in parallel. Thus, the goal for the DSDM-based procedure model must be to describe how the results of the various teams can be combined and how the test effort caused by any modifications of these results can be reduced to a minimum.

No discussion is provided on how testing should be done

Although both in the traditional procedure model and in ASAP detailed descriptions are provided of what is to be tested and which tool is to be used to support the documentation of these tests, no discussion is provided regarding the tool support to be used for the actual testing. This has the consequence that naturally no discussion can be provided on how this tool is to be used and which capabilities it provides. Furthermore, no discussion is provided on how the tests can be organized. Thus, it is particularly important for the new procedure model to show how the CATT and the test plan tool can be used within the implementation project.

The inter-phase activities are neglected

A further disadvantage frequently criticized regarding the SAP procedure model is the neglect or the absence of inter-phase activities. Whereas the traditional SAP procedure model describes just project administration and project control, and system maintenance and release changes, the Roadmap, the ASAP procedure model, completely omits the description of such activities. However, in particular, project management, prototyping management, quality management, test management and configuration management also play an important role in SAP projects, so that a description of these inter-phase activities would be desirable. Thus, the DSDM-based procedure model should also consider these topics, but this book obviously concentrates on test management in this context.

The transfer of know-how is not supported

SAP projects are usually very large and very complex projects that also take a lot of time (see above). It also requires enormous SAP know-how, which is normally not available to a sufficient degree in the implementing enterprise, so it is necessary to make use of external consultants. However, suitable concepts that show how the consultants' knowledge can be passed to the internal employees during the project work are often missing. Usually the transfer of know-how takes the form that at the end the consultancy has detailed knowledge of how the implementing enterprise works and how the individual business processes function. However, the implementing enterprise has learnt too little about SAP to enable it to perform subsequent projects independently or even make isolated, small changes or modifications. Consequently, it becomes dependent on the contracted consultancy from which it can only break out with great difficulty, because every contracted consultancy would have to start by learning everything about the enterprise, which is very time-intensive (and thus cost-intensive). Thus, even during the course of the project care should be taken that the internal employees become capable of solving problems themselves. Therefore, it is necessary to find means by which the transfer of know-how can be supported, and, in particular, the transfer of know-how from the consultancy to the implementing enterprise.

4.2   The graphical representation of the DSDM-based procedure model

Thus, the graphical representation aims at illustrating the dynamic DSDM ideas, focuses on the iterative and incremental procedure, shows the importance of the inter-phase activities, and makes a clear differentiation from the familiar representation form of the waterfall model.

Figure 4.1 shows the DSDM-based procedure model for the realization of SAP R/3 projects.

Of particular importance to this concept is the fact that the DSDM-based procedure model obviously does not rediscover the typical SAP phase activities, such as 'create system landscape' or 'perform global settings', but makes use of the complete and very

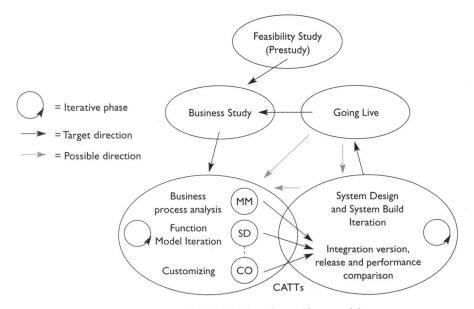

Figure 4.1   The DSDM-based procedure model

detailed activity descriptions from the traditional SAP procedure model or from ASAP. Even the use of ASAP tools and the ASAP accelerator, such as checklists or document templates, is expressly supported whenever it appears appropriate. With regard to the procedure itself, everything beyond the activity descriptions should be performed starting from the DSDM basis. Thus, the most effective project realization is possible when the project is organized using the DSDM-based procedure model 'powered by' ASAP.

The first phase of the model is the feasibility study in which a check is made on whether and the extent to which the considered project can be realized in an appropriate manner. When you leave this phase following the 'target' arrow, it becomes apparent that the first phase is performed just once and there can be no subsequent return back to this phase.

The business study always follows the feasibility study. The business study represents the true start of the DSDM cycle. This phase performs the organizational and planning activities for the next DSDM pass or for the next iteration.

The function model iteration that follows as the next phase contains primarily the business process analysis and customizing activities. As the name implies, this phase is an iterative phase. In every iteration of this phase, the business processes are analyzed, described and finally adapted to meet the special requirements.

A specific number of all the business processes to be implemented are considered each time. The basis system is implemented in the first DSDM pass. The extensions, changes or a release change are normally performed in the following passes. The number of business processes considered is the same as later found in customizing and for which a version, release, integration or performance comparison is performed in the system design and system build iteration phase. The cycles within the representation of this phase represent the individual teams that process the various modules to be implemented in parallel.

As already implied, the system design and system build iteration, which also describes an iterative phase, follows the function model iteration phase. The main activities are version, release, integration or performance comparison. During the system design and system build iteration phase, for example, a test is made as to whether the customizing settings made for a version or release change have undesirable effects on the system or whether the customizing settings cause integration or performance problems. Therefore, in this phase the results of the individual teams are combined and subjected to an integration test.

If errors occur during the integration test, changes must be made in the customizing, which in turn can affect the business processes. If the business processes are inadvertently changed in this activity, either the customizing settings must be reworked or the business processes adapted to meet the capabilities of the implementing company. This also means that it may be necessary to jump repeatedly between function model iteration (third phase) and system design and system build iteration (fourth phase). Consequently, the transition between these phases can also be considered to be an iteration.

The Computer Aided Test Tool (refer to Chapter 7) and a functioning configuration management (refer to Chapter 6) are the two most important tools for these phases. These ensure that the customizing settings of the business processes operating in parallel can be combined or integrated. If necessary, the Computer Aided Test Tool can be used to revoke the changes. It is also possible to test whether the changed individual business processes still continue to function as required. If this is not the case, the configuration management can be used to restore the last known correct state.

A pass through the DSDM-based model closes with the 'implementation/productive operation' phase from which a new jump is made to the business study and a new pass started through the DSDM-based procedure model.

However, if errors occur during implementation or productive operation, a return is made to a previous phase as appropriate for the type of error. For example, if a business is incorrectly represented, the function model iteration phase must be reprocessed, but, if the performance is inadequate, the system design and the system build iteration is repeated.

Thus, the DSDM-based procedure model for SAP R/3 implementation describes an iterative model that extends the SAP R/3 system stepwise with every DSDM pass. This idea is shown graphically by representing the individual phases as a loop and the 'target' arrows as a continuously repeating path through the model.

Suitable inter-phase activities that permit operation in the DSDM sense are required in order that the described procedure can be performed successfully. As already indicated above, these inter-phase activities describe the foundation on which the procedure model is based. The inter-phase activities of the DSDM-based procedure model are:

- Project management

- Prototyping management

- Configuration management

- Timeboxing

- Testing

- Quality management

- Risk analysis

The following sections describe the individual phases of the DSDM-based procedure model and the most important phase activities. Furthermore, differences from and features in common with the SAP procedure model are shown, new DSDM-specific activities implemented, and references made to the DSDM features and possible problem situations.

4.3   First phase: Feasibility study (prestudy)

An investigation at the start of this first phase determines whether the SAP R/3 system is generally suitable to support the company-specific requirements. Although the SAP procedure model does not explicitly take account of this investigation, it is assumed that an appropriate prestudy has already been done before the start of the first phase of the implementation project.

Although the DSDM-based procedure model theoretically starts earlier, this is a purely formal difference, because, as discussed earlier, the prestudy is also essential for appropriate use of the SAP procedure model. However, it should be indicated at this point that it may not be appropriate (even though such a procedure sometimes occurs in practice) to make an initial decision to implement the SAP R/3 system and only afterwards check what the R/3 system actually offers.

Once you have decided on an SAP R/3 strategy, the first decision to be made is whether the use of DSDM is appropriate for the project under consideration. However, because the general suitability of DSDM for SAP R/3 implementation has already been determined in Part A of this work, this decision normally does not need to be made. However, any procedure model can still be used for application developments pending within the SAP R/3 implementation. It only remains to test whether factors critical for success still need to be taken into account (refer to Chapter 3). If it transpires that the company cannot meet the specified factors, another procedure model should be chosen. A reason why the DSDM-based procedure model would not be suitable as the basis for an R/3 implementation project, would be the necessity to realize a 100 per cent solution in the first step, i.e., the need to realize all business processes in the first implementation step.

The SAP procedure model also assumes that the range of business functions and business areas to be supported has already been defined. However, this item is very important in the DSDM-based procedure model, because it corresponds to module selection. Thus, it must be decided which SAP R/3 modules are to be used and to what extent.

An implementation strategy, which must be defined in the next step, provides information on the time sequence in which the SAP applications are to be implemented, the sequence of implementation with regard to geographic business divisions, and the sequence on which implementation is to be made in the various company divisions. General planning must also be done as to how long the total implementation project (namely, all planned DSDM passes) is to take.

A further phase activity is concerned with the definition of the company goals that are to be realized with the SAP R/3 system. These goal definitions must be documented in order to permit a subsequent planned–actual comparison.

The first phase closes with the creation of a feasibility report which must substantiate why the use of SAP R/3 is appropriate (see above), and which describes the modules to be used, which goals are to be fulfilled using SAP R/3 and the form of the general time planning and timeboxes.

A final comment on this first phase of the DSDM-based procedure model: it occurs only once, namely at the start of the complete implementation project. The individual passes through the DSDM model each begin with the second phase.

4.4   Second phase: Business study

In contrast to traditional procedure models, three DSDM-specific activities are performed in the business study:

1. The business processes to be represented are generally identified.

2. The business processes are given a priority and a general time plan is produced.

3. An agreement workshop is conducted.

Note for activity 1: The most important term in this activity designation is the term 'general'. In contrast to the traditional procedure, the individual business processes at this time, namely at the start of the actual implementation project, have not yet been analyzed and described in detail, but just generally noted, i.e., the business processes to be implemented are identified generally. This general business process identification is equivalent to the determination of the business process headings, which serves two purposes: to estimate the required time and to provide a basis for the prioritization of the business process in the following section. Finally, the responsible persons or teams are assigned to the individual business processes.

Note for activity 2: Prioritization represents a very important element for project realization when the DSDM-based procedure model is used. It ensures that the individual teams do not perform the business processes according to their personal tastes or just 'somehow', but in a sequence oriented to the importance of the individual business processes to the business benefits. The prioritization is performed in workshops attended by the responsible team and an internal employee, who, in the ideal case, has an overview of the business processes to be handled in the workshop. In the workshop itself, the business processes (i.e., the headings) are presented to those involved and a sequence in agreed using a prioritization rule. The inter-phase activities in a later section describe how this prioritization works. The resulting prioritized business process list is binding and determines the sequence for subsequent processing. The list can be changed only when changed requirements arise during the course of the project or if there is a need to change the priority list as part of the reconciliation workshop.

A change of requirement within a project can have three possible causes:

• Network requirements arise.

• Known requirements have changed.

• The importance of existing requirements has changed.

If one of these situations arises, a new assignment must be made in agreement both within the team and with those external to the team.

The priority list also determines the time planning of the subsequent project, because the DSDM-based procedure model aims at implementing an approximately 80 per cent solution in the first DSDM pass. Thus, the time planning is performed on the basis of the most important 80 per cent of the business processes to be implemented.

Note for activity 3: The reconciliation workshop is a very important activity that must be performed very early, immediately after it is known which business processes are to be implemented. This reconciliation workshop should resolve all the questions concerned with inter-team work. For example, typical questions in this connection are:

• Can the time planning of the individual teams be agreed?

• Which customizing settings are made by several teams?

• Do all teams agree with the prioritization settings within the other teams?

• Are the responsibilities for the individual business processes accepted by all teams?

Of particular importance in this activity is the experience of the consultants, who are capable of providing both suitable estimates for time planning and also information about where the various teams must access shared customizing settings. Knowledge of these facts can be very useful in the subsequent course of the project and can avoid unpleasant surprises.

In addition to these DSDM-specific activities, the start of the second phase is also concerned with the organization of the project work, which must contain the items described below.

Determine the current situation

The goal of the analysis of the current situation is to obtain an overview of the organizational structure, the business areas and the existing application systems of the company. This analysis then can be used as the basis for all planning of subsequent activities.

Determine the consulting requirement

Which and how many external consultants are needed for the next planned pass through the DSDM-based procedure model must be determined. The aim is for internal employees to become increasingly independent with every DSDM pass, so that in the course of time they will be able to realize additional DSDM passes themselves. This means, in the ideal situation, that with every new project the consulting requirement will become less than that required previously. The use of the DSDM-based procedure model also has the advantage that, if necessary, the consulting company can be replaced after completion of each DSDM pass. This motivates the consultants to optimize the quality of their work (which should actually be obvious), with the aim of being given the order for the follow-up projects. Thus, the commissioned consultancy should also be given detailed information on the DSDM philosophy and be obliged to use it, and so achieve the best possible use and performance. The consultancy, for example, must be prepared to support the concepts of know-how transfer described below.

Specify the teams

The project leader, the person responsible for the business process and a representative user for every user group must be determined for prototyping activities. A single person can perform the last two roles. At this point it should be emphasized again that the teams should be given the greatest possible freedom to make decisions with regard to DSDM, and the steering committee should be requested to provide advice only in exceptional situations. Team training must be organized on the basis of the modules to be implemented, and the number of teams determined depending on the business processes to be performed per module. The team should consist of at least two members (one internal employee and a consultant), but not more than four. The team members must be aware of their roles both in the team and with regard to the DSDM principles, namely their role in the project management and thus the associated decision-making authority. It must be ensured that the selected team members conduct their DSDM roles conscientiously and possess good communicative capabilities.

The following excursion discusses the so-called 'Contextual Inquiry' method. This describes how communication within the team should take place as part of the business process analysis.

Excursion: Contextual Inquiry

The following discussion is largely based on discussions from Beyer and Holtzblatt who provide a detailed description of the Contextual Inquiry method in their book *Contextual Design*. Interested readers are recommended to consult this work for detailed information. Our special thanks go to Mr Markus Nimtz from Andersen Consulting who made us aware of the possibilities and advantages of the Contextual Inquiry. We describe this in the next section as part of an SAP R/3 implementation using the DSDM-based procedure model.

The *Contextual Inquiry* or *Contextual Interview* describes a form of customer questioning or observation that serves to analyze customer requirements; in the present case, the analysis of business processes. This method focuses on the assumption that the customer can describe his work and thus also his requirements much better when he is in the usual environment appropriate for his work. This contradicts the classical interview methods in which the user and the consultant withdraw to a conference room and discuss there in very abstract form the work of the user. It is just as difficult in this method for the user to describe his work in abstract terms outside his usual work environment as it is for the consultant to translate this abstract descriptive form. This leads inevitably to misunderstandings.

Thus, the Contextual Inquiry concentrates on understanding the customer better. Consequently, it describes a customer-oriented concept that aims at understanding the customer's daily business. Beyer and Holtzblatt also summarize the central statement of the Contextual Inquiry as follows: 'Go there where the customer works, observe him while he is working, and speak to him about his work. Do that and you cannot avoid getting a better understanding of your customer' (Beyer and Holtzblatt, 1998, p. 41).

Several important conclusions for SAP R/3 implementation projects using the DSDM-based procedure model can be drawn from this procedure. For example, it is very important that the external consultant and the internal employees work in the same room when they are working on the project. Not only do the team members get to know each other better and so also understand each other better, but it is also possible for the customer to make use of the consultant's expert knowledge at any time without the need to make a trip to the consultant's project office for every question. Consequently, when the DSDM-based procedure model is used, it expressly discourages using closed rooms and consultancy project offices isolated from the users; rather, shared workplaces are preferred. This removes both barriers and fear of contact, which results in improved communication.

However, even for the actual requirements analysis using Contextual Inquiry, there are several important principles and behaviour rules that must be observed. The most important behaviour rule is the so-called master–trainee model which focuses on role assignment during requirements analysis. This assumes that the user is the master and the consultant is the trainee. As in reality, the master in this model must explain his work to the trainee in order that the trainee understands and can later perform it alone. This avoids the consultant, who is actually the expert, thinking he knows everything better. Furthermore, it removes the customer's shyness in dealing with the consultant and the customer's requirements take precedence rather than the requirements that the consultant incorrectly thinks he knows better, unless these also happen to be the customer's requirements. However, the master–trainee model does not represent a rigid behaviour rule, but rather forms only a basis for communication that may be modified according to the requirements of the persons involved. For example, if the customer considers that it is not appropriate for him to impart his knowledge, namely to teach, he can just perform his normal work and answer any questions to correct the trainee's mis-understandings. This model is also supported by the assumption that the consultant, in contrast to the usual trainee, is better able to become acquainted with and understand the new circumstances.

Another significant aspect essential for Contextual Inquiry is the understanding and the observance of the four principles on which the Contextual Inquiry is based:

- Context

- Partnership

- Interpretation

- Focus

The *context* principle is the principle on which the whole method is built. It says that the consultant must go to where the customer works, namely the context of his work. This provides a common understanding of the work tasks and the customer's requirements (see above).

The *partnership* principle illustrates the difference from classical interview techniques, in which complete responsibility is placed in the hands of the consultant and he is expected to ask the right questions. The partnership principle ensures that the consultant asks only questions to help him understand what the customer is trying to tell him. Consequently, either partner can lead the conversation without fear that the consultant takes the interview in a direction he wants but is possibly wrong. The consultant can emphasize the partnership principle by trying to minimize any gap in physical appear-ance. For example, a worker on a conveyor belt may feel uncomfortable if the questioner appears in a pin-stripe suit.

The *interpretation* principle says that it does not suffice that the consultant believes that he has understood the customer's requirements. Rather, he is required to maintain his interpretation of the facts and then let the customer approve the correctness of his under-standing of the facts or the business process, i.e., confirm his interpretation and so provide a common basis.

The *focus* principle ensures that at any one time a single business process rather than several is discussed. The consultant is responsible for keeping the conversation on track without assuming too much control. This ensures that the necessary information is recorded completely and also that no unnecessary information is recorded.

This excursion should be closed with the comment that the Contextual Inquiry method goes hand-in-hand with the DSDM principles and that the teams already in the team building phase activity have become acquainted with the Contextual Inquiry method. Even when the method is not adopted one-to-one, an understanding of the method and thus the various roles that a team member can assume during the course of the project greatly supports communication and ensures that both parties know, for example, who is the master regarding business process analysis and customizing. This avoids the customer believing that the consultant, in his role of consultant, must know everything, even including how the customer's business processes function. Furthermore, the master–trainee model supports, for example, the transfer of know-how in customizing; on the one hand, it forces the consultant to teach, and on the other hand, it encourages the customer to ask.

Determine the training requirements

This work step should determine the extent to which those involved with the SAP R/3 implementation need to be trained, i.e., it must be determined who must be trained, when, and in what. If only SAP R/3 training requirements are to be determined in the SAP procedure model, DSDM-specific training must also be performed when the DSDM-based model is used.

The largest part of the training required takes place in the first pass through the DSDM-based model. For every further iteration, it is only necessary to determine who has been added to the project team, who needs to refresh their SAP R/3 or DSDM knowledge, and situations where possible uncertainties or weaknesses have arisen during previous iterations. The major advantage of this procedure is the model's inherent capability to use what has been learnt not just once, but repeatedly with every iteration. The achieved learning effect can not only compensate for the additional training effort required, but can also result in a reduction of the total training required.

After finishing these activities largely concerned with organization and planning, we continue with the following activity:

DSDM training

To use DSDM successfully, it is not enough just to train the individual team members in DSDM. It is just as important that the management also attend the seminars, so that they understand the DSDM philosophy and DSDM principles. This will also arouse their awareness of why it is essential to pass a suitable level of decision-making responsibility to the teams, and to provide the users with enough time for active involvement in the implementation process. In addition, because a DSDM implementation can cause extensive changes in a company, DSDM training gains special importance. The DSDM manual even mentions changes to the company culture (DSDM Consortium, 1997, Section 10.1).

In addition to the DSDM principles and philosophy, the DSDM training must also cover prototyping basics and configuration management systems. The training should pay particular attention to communication capabilities and teamwork.

SAP R/3 training

SAP R/3 training serves to introduce the commercial contents and the capabilities of the R/3 system, and should also provide an overview of the R/3 functionality. However, because the business process analysis, customizing and CATT capabilities represent a significant part of the phase activities required for SAP R/3 implementation with the DSDM-based procedure model, these should also be part of the training.

General business process description

The individual business processes represented in the SAP R/3 system are briefly discussed at this point. Particular attention should be paid to ensuring that the business processes are only described in general terms and not in detail. It suffices just to find headings for the individual business processes. A general concept must have been produced at the end of this phase activity.

Some methods of collecting the business processes are the Contextual Inquiry method described above, traditional interview methods or group-work techniques, in which representatives of the individual user departments participate. Even here, experience or methods from software development can be useful for the R/3 implementation project. For example, the so-called *Voice of the Customer Analysis (VOCA)* can be used in addition to the methods mentioned. VoCA describes an integrated method to determine customer requirements; in the case shown, the determination of the relevant business processes through to their priority assignment. Moreover, as shown below, this priority assignment, in particular, plays an important role in the further processing of the DSDM-based procedure model (for information on VoCA consult Mazur (1992), p. 1ff and Mazur and Zultner, 1996, p. 105ff).

The reference and industry models which already contain a large number of business processes provide help in finding the relevant business processes.

The non-functional requirements made on the SAP R/3 system also must be determined in this phase. These non-functional requirements, which, for example, affect performance or security, are only generally described in this phase; they are refined in phase 3, and finally checked in the fourth phase.

The general entries for the business process rules serve an important purpose that is essential for SAP R/3 implementation using the DSDM-based procedure model. The goal must be (in the DSDM sense) first to implement those business processes with which the greatest business benefits can be achieved. The question of what are the most important business processes can only be answered by evaluating the business processes with regard to their importance to the business benefits. The assigning of priorities itself is performed later. The MoSCoW rules used as a method for assigning priorities can be taken from the inter-phase activities. A list of the business processes to be implemented must exist at the end of this activity. These business processes must be put into sequence in accordance with their importance to the business benefits. Thus, a list with priorities must exist for each module. The following guideline is suggested to determine the overlapping timebox for phases 3 and 4 (see below): Estimate the time for each module required to implement all business processes that in accordance with the MoSCoW rules fall into the 'must' and 'should' groups, and the largest part of the business processes from the 'could' group. The module that takes the longest time according to these estimates determines the timebox. The least important business processes from the 'could' group and all business processes from the 'would' group are implemented only in the next DSDM pass.

The reader may consider that the consequences of the prioritization just described cause more problems than at first appears. This results from the stepwise extending procedure always needing to provide new interfaces to the existing systems.

The expected effort needed for interface programming must now be taken into consideration in assigning priorities to the individual business processes. We do not recommend ordering the business processes individually, but rather, if possible, forming groups of related processes and evaluating these as a unit, when it can be expected that either no or significantly fewer interfaces will need to be provided.

However, the problem of additional interfaces has not proved to be particularly critical in practice, because even in the first DSDM pass dealing with 70–80 per cent of the business processes, a very large part of the SAP R/3 system has already been implemented, and the remaining 20–30 per cent of the business processes are the least important and, normally, do not make intensive use of interfaces. Thus, moving these business processes often has no significant effect on the problem situation described (also refer to the appropriation sections in the case study).

Determine and update the timeboxes

Because the determination of suitable timeboxes is both an important and a difficult task for the success of the SAP R/3 implementation project, the individual timeboxes obviously should not be unique and so do not need to be determined for every pass through the DSDM-based procedure model, but instead modified on demand using the experience gained, and varied and modified depending on the extent of the business processes to be processed. This can mean, for example, that the timeboxes become increasingly shorter with increasing experience, or more time may be needed when the length of the timeboxes is not sufficient to satisfy a minimum of the requirements.

Two different timeboxes must be determined. The first must be defined so that it represents the total planned length of the third phase. Additional short timeboxes that each have new goals (which requirements should be satisfied in the timebox?) are set within this timebox. These short timeboxes ensure that the project work remains controllable and that the teams, because of the short time horizons, are better motivated and work in a more goal-oriented fashion. There is a 'small' milestone or an audit of the achieved results at the end of every timebox.

At this point in the project, i.e., in phase 2, however, only the global timebox for the third phase has been determined.

In addition to the activities described above, the SAP-typical and necessary activities of the traditional procedure model or from ASAP are also performed. Some of these are described as examples:

Create the system landscape

In parallel to the general business process description or to the above-mentioned (VoCA) workshop, it is possible to start the creation of the system landscape to the extent required for each planned pass through the DSDM-based procedure model. This step must set up the required clients for the development/test system and the user master records for the project members, etc. A functioning system environment, which is an essential prerequisite for the following activities, must also be provided. In this case also, the system environment is provided only to the extent it is required and then extended step by step for each additional DSDM pass.

Because, in order to ensure sensible continuation of the project, the system landscape must satisfy the restrictions just described, no timebox is suggested for this phase activity. It does not make sense to try to accomplish as much as possible within a specified time and then neglect to provide a solid minimum basis.

However, the DSDM assumption that 80 per cent of the work can be done in 20 per cent of the time and that the activities do not need to be fully completed in this phase also applies for the following three phase activities.

Determine the interfaces and the system extensions

The systems to be connected to the SAP R/3 system and the data to be accepted must be defined.

Perform global settings

The settings for countries, currencies and measurement units are determined in this work packet.

Represent the company structure, the basic data and the master data

Represent the company components connected hierarchically or as a network, and the basic data and the master data that serve as the basis for the realization of the individual business processes.

4.5   Third phase: Function model iteration

Together with the fourth phase, the third phase forms the heart of the DSDM-based procedure model. The principal tasks of this phase are detailed business process analysis, business process description, customizing and setting the associated CATT, where the processing of the individual business processes is performed in accordance with the priority list determined in phase 2. In contrast to traditional procedure models, the analysis and customizing of the individual business processes are performed immediately after each other and are only considered to be closed when the associated test run has been recorded and the required test data determined. This extension is very important, because recording the test case ensures that a large amount of duplicated work is avoided in the following sections. Not only is the project accelerated but it is also very simple to obtain assurance that the business processes still function as required despite the changes made to the system.

However, the timebox planning done at the start of the third phase determines how many business processes from the priority list the individual teams are to process in the next timebox. A timebox normally represents a time window of 10 workdays, namely two calendar weeks. A small milestone occurs at the end of each timebox within the teams. A check is made here on whether the set goals have been attained or whether the task planning for the timebox was realistic.

The third phase is itself an iterative phase. This means that, on the one hand, the 'Determine the next timebox within the third phase' activity must be repeated, and, on the other hand, that the activities within these timeboxes must also be performed iteratively.

Determine the next timebox within the third phase

How long the next 'short' timebox should take within the global timebox of the third phase must be determined. We suggest a length between two and maximum four weeks. Which requirements are to be satisfied within this timebox must also be planned.

Business process analysis, customizing

Thus, the parallel processing of the individual business processes takes place within this timebox. We recommend that prototyping is always used as a tool here. Iterative Process Prototyping (IPP) from Keller and Teufel (1997) and DSDM prototyping management provide two methods to perform this prototyping.

IPP uses the various integrated SAP-specific tools to set the business processes in workshops in accordance with the user requirements. The various tools used here are:

- R/3 customizing,

- R/3 prototyping,

- the R/3 data dictionary,

- the R/3 reference process model,

- the R/3 data/object model, and

- the R/3 organization model.

Thus, apparently, IPP does not suggest the use of CATT. However, the creation of the CATTs is unavoidable when the project is to be performed on the basis of the DSDM-based procedure model. Consequently, even when IPP is used for any business process, the recording of the associated CATT must be added. However, this does not contradict the concept of IPP making use of SAP-specific tools.

In particular, the use of the CATT or another automatic test tool is of great importance, because these test tools can be used at the end of each timebox to ensure the coordination of teams working in parallel. Thus, the results of the teams working in parallel are repeatedly consolidated approximately every two weeks (10 workdays) in a 'small' integration test.

Iterative (DSDM) prototyping is the second possibility for using prototyping. Although this does not demand the use of SAP-specific tools, it provides comparable questioning for the individual prototypes as is the case in IPP. Furthermore, this iterative (DSDM) prototyping is embedded in a prototype management system that should ensure that the prototyping does not become non-oriented and never-ending, but proceeds in a controllable manner. Section 4.3.3 provides a short description of how this prototyping management functions.

If iterative (DSDM) prototyping is used, R/3 prototypes of the individual business processes are produced in the individual teams. In every iteration, the questions posed in Figure 4.7 should be applied to every prototype. Typical questions are:

- Is the screen layout uncluttered?

- Are all required input fields present?

- Is the input logic intuitive?

- Are the required default values set?

- Are the response times OK?

- Can the expressed change requests be realized?

If the prototype is finally accepted as a functioning part of the system, the associated CATT must be recorded. As part of the transfer of know-how, in the ideal case, care is taken that an internal team member (under the supervision of the consultant) makes all customizing settings. This ensures that internal employees become capable of performing small tasks themselves initially and later can independently customize the settings for change requests. The same applies to the CATT activities. The internal employees should be prepared for the situation that external consultants will not be present in the enterprise for ever.

However, in the DSDM-based procedure model the CATT is used for more than just the actual test tasks. For example, the CATT can also be used to transfer old data, to read in master data, or to create training notes or other application documentation. Chapter 7 describes how these activities are performed.

The milestone within the teams that occurs at the end of every timebox clarifies how any outstanding requirements of this timebox could be satisfied and the form of the next timebox.

Irrespective of whether the tools of the Keller/Teufel concept are used, it is of particular importance for these activities that they take in the form of iterative prototyping. The case study in Part C of this book provides an example of how this iterative prototyping can appear in practice and which special questions should be considered.

The involvement of the users (refer to Chapter 5), the observance of the DSDM principles (refer to Section 2.1) and the observance of the rules for prototyping management (refer to Section 5.2) also take on special importance.

The effects of customizing settings are presented to the user in the form of a prototype demonstration and each is tested immediately after settings have been made; the CATT (refer to Chapter 7) plays an important role here. The business processes, together with their associated customizing settings and the tests, must be documented.

Depending on whether the achieved result is satisfactory, another iteration can be performed, the next business process addressed or a return made back to the start of the phase. This return can, for example, be to the last status that is known to function. This action also emphasizes the importance of configuration management (refer to Chapter 6).

We must expressly emphasize once again here that it is the user who decides whether the achieved result meets the requirements (refer to Section 5.2).

The following steps can be started in parallel to the timebox activities just described:

Update the user documentation

The user documentation must contain descriptions of the company-specific functions and business processes. This documentation provides the basis for training and for the day-to-day work with the system, and is oriented to the business processes that run in the timebox. Because of the frequently changing business requirements, ensuring that the documents are up to date is particularly important here. The continuous updating and stepwise expansion of the user documentation inherent in the DSDM-based procedure model means that this requirement is easily met.

User training

The goal of the training is to enable the user to work with the R/3 system using all the provided facilities. The training is also performed in a continuous manner, i.e., the user's knowledge is extended stepwise. The seminars are oriented to the previously created user documentation.

Extend the report system

A check must be made to see who requires which information and the extent to which the SAP R/3 system can already be used in the current DSDM pass to support these information requirements. If the standard reports are not adequate, the report system must be extended and, if necessary, external data accessed. The report system must be organized and structured in accordance with these requirements. The extended report system must be tested at the end of this step.

Represent the archive administration

An investigation must be performed to determine which data must be archived for how long and in which form, and the procedure to be adopted in the case of a system failure. The result of this investigation flows into an archiving concept, which must then be realized and tested.

Update interfaces and system extensions

Data transfer programs must be created and tested. The same applies for system extensions and interfaces to the areas affected by the business processes and business process groups to be realized. However, it is also possible that interfaces become superfluous, such as when new areas in the current DSDM pass can be included in the SAP R/3 system.

As mentioned previously, there is a smooth transition to the fourth phase. This means that the activities described do not need to be fully completed. Rather, they only need to be sufficiently advanced so that the next phase can be started. Those activities that have not yet been completed are then continued and completed in the fourth phase.

4.6   Fourth phase: The system design and system build iteration

The content of this phase can have various forms. With regard to performance compari-son, the prototypes (the designation 'prototype' should not be misinterpreted here, as they already represent much more than an initial representation) are refined to satisfy the non-functional requirements.

Once the prototypes satisfy the non-functional requirements, it must be ensured that the customizing settings of the prototypes match the customizing settings of the SAP system that is already productive (this step is obviously omitted in the first DSDM pass). This is designated as integration matching in the DSDM-based procedure model. Every change to the customizing settings must be documented and tested. To check whether the business processes have been set in accordance with the functional and non-functional requirements, the refined prototypes must be demonstrated to the user at the end of the timebox.

The tests are performed by replicating the customizing settings of the business processes in the productive system. The CATT is the most important tool used to perform these tests (refer to Chapter 7).

If at this point the SAP R/3 system does not function in accordance with the require-ments, changes are made to the customizing settings. A functioning configuration management ensures that it is possible to return to some known state at any time.

If it is not possible to make a change to the customizing settings to create a functioning state, it may be necessary to return to the start of the third phase where the individual business processes can be reconsidered, and, if possible, modified. The effects of the new customizing settings and the tests must also be documented.

If no functioning system with regard to the requirements exists at the end of the fourth phase, a return must be made either to the start of this phase or, as just described, to the third phase. Another possibility to end this phase in a sensible way is to return to some known state where the functional requirements were satisfied. The satisfying of the non-functional customizing settings in this case is moved to the next DSDM pass.

Another form of the activities of this phase can be a release or version change. In this case, the customizing settings of a functioning system are passed to the new version or release and then tested using CATT. If the system no longer satisfies the requirements, the procedure described above is adopted and a return made to the customizing settings or even back to the third phase.

The additional phase activities that can also be performed in parallel to the described activities of the fourth phase follow:

Represent the authorization administration

Authorizations and profiles must be created and tested to ensure that every user can access only those functions for which he has rights.

Refining the non-functional requirements

The non-functional requirements defined in phase 2 are refined here using, for example, the knowledge gained in the VoCA workshop. The non-functional requirements refined here serve as the basis for the matching to be performed in phase 4. This matching tests, for example, performance or security.

Prepare for productive operation

The largest part of this phase activity is performed in the first pass using the DSDM-based procedure model. The required hardware and software must be acquired, the user master records created and the data transfer to the productive system planned.

The transition to the fifth phase can be made when these activities have been completed.

4.7   Fifth phase: Implementation/productive operation

Two groups of activities must be performed in the fifth phase. Firstly, those activities that are used for the implementation of the extended customizing settings of the current DSDM pass in the existing productive system. Secondly, those activities that accompany productive operation.

Transfer the customizing settings to the productive system

The extended SAP R/3 system realized at the end of the fourth phase timebox is accepted as the new productive system. Obviously, it is assumed that the requirements of the system described in phase 4 were satisfied.

Organize the system administration

The organization of the system administration also develops with every pass through the DSDM-based procedure model. Thus, the stepwise extension of the SAP R/3 system also results in a stepwise increase in administrative tasks. It is necessary to define and assign responsibilities for task areas. The system administrators must also be prepared and trained for their extended responsibilities with every DSDM pass.

Support productive operation

Support of productive operation means that the user is supervised in the use of the SAP R/3 system, and, in particular, in the use of the extended functionality of the system. The help desk that provides this supervision may need to be extended or further trained after every DSDM pass.

Monitor system use and, if necessary, initiate measures to optimize system use

After every DSDM pass, it takes a certain amount of time before the use of the extended system becomes established. Monitoring is required to see whether the productive system has developed as expected. If necessary, corrective measures must be initiated. For example, if the business processes change, it is possible to return to the third phase of the DSDM-based procedure model, but if non-functional requirements change or these are not satisfied as expected, it is better to return to the fourth phase.

Completion of the subproject

To complete a subproject of the DSDM-based procedure model normally means to initiate the next DSDM pass. The project must be critically analyzed once again, and a closing report must be produced. An important advantage to be realized with DSDM is the continuous improvement of the individual subprojects and the associated continuous learning. To realize these advantages, it is important to close the subproject conscientiously and to make the results generally available.

Changed or new requirements and the next DSDM pass are derived from the productive operation. This pass can either represent a new subproject or, depending on the situation, mean a return to a previous phase. If, for example, there are functional problems, a return must be made to the third phase. If, however, there are non-functional problems, a return must be made to the fourth phase.

An (approximate) 80 per cent solution (basis system) should normally exist at the end of the first DSDM pass. This basis system is then extended in the second pass (second subproject). Some possible reasons for this extension are:

- new requirements,

- changed requirements, or

- error correction.

The reason for a further pass through the DSDM-based procedure model could be, for example, a release change or continuous optimization.

4.8 Summary

The significant characteristics of the DSDM-based procedure model for SAP R/3 implementation are the iterative procedure, the prototyping activities, and the use of timeboxes (TB).

Compared with the traditional SAP procedure model, the configuration management and the CATT represent new and important methods that are essential for successful use of the DSDM-based procedure model.

The same applies for the method of stepwise expansion and the repeated implementation concept of the DSDM-based procedure model, which is just as characteristic as the circular representation and the associated navigation through the individual phases.

The individual phase activities with their DSDM features are briefly summarized in the following figures. Figure 4.2 shows the meaning of the contents of the individual figures. Figure 4.3 shows the connection and the transitions between the individual phases.

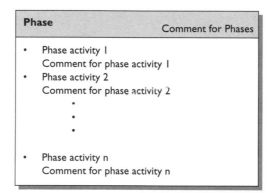

Figure 4.2   Contents of the phase description

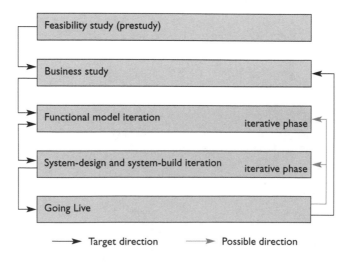

Figure 4.3   Summarized representation of the phases of the DSDM-based procedure model

The black and grey arrows, rather than the arrangement of the phases, have special significance here; the phases in fact are more reminiscent of a waterfall-based model. However, this representation form was chosen in order to group the phases of the DSDM-based procedure model. Figure 4.1 provides the actual representation of the DSDM-based procedure model and also illustrates the fundamental iterative idea.

Figures 4.4 to 4.7 briefly summarize the activities that are performed within the individual phases.

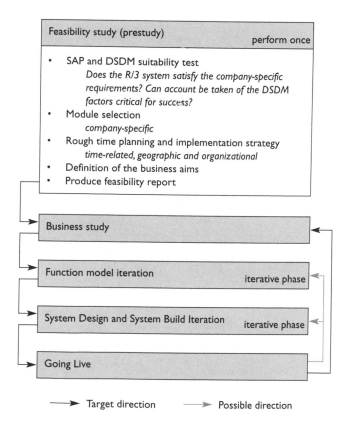

Figure 4.4   Summary (Part 1)

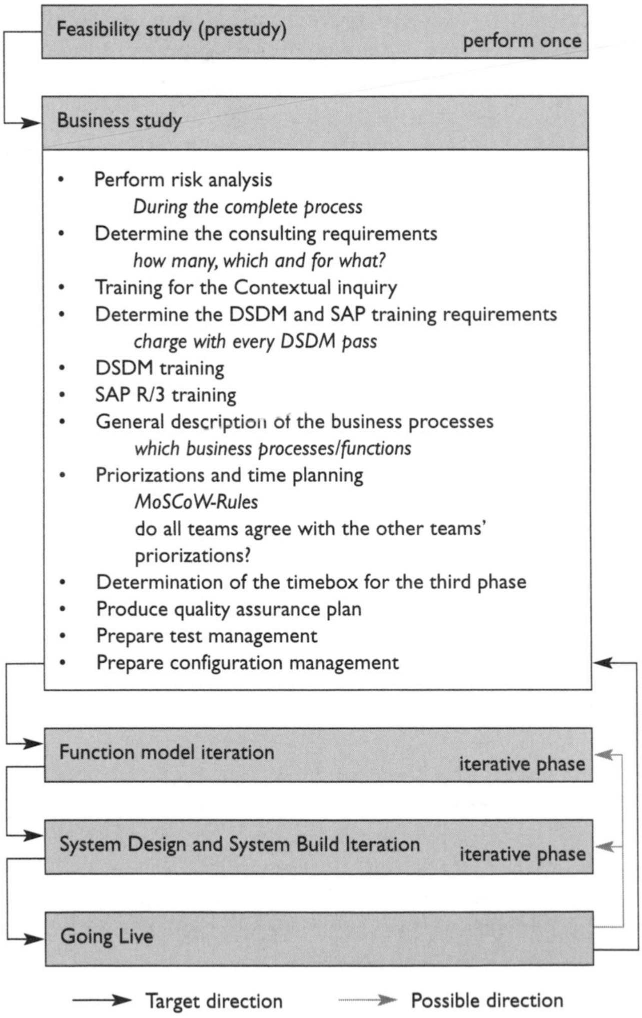

Figure 4.5   Summary (Part 2)

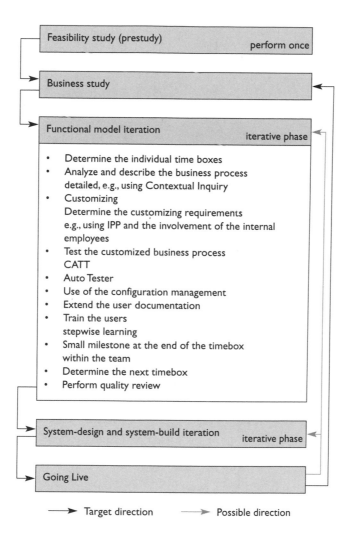

Figure 4.6 Summary (Part 3)

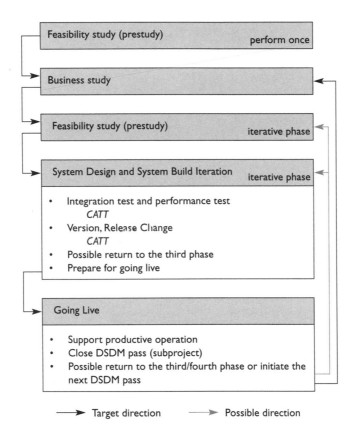

Figure 4.7   *Summary (Part 4)*

5 Project management

Project management has different aims in DSDM-based projects in that it is concerned with fast project progress and with maintaining good relationships within the teams and with the customers. Because project progress is documented in prototyping management, this also attains importance. Timeboxing and prioritizing guarantee that a deliverable product (prototype, study) is available on time.

SAP provides the PS module (Project System) for dynamic implementation. The IMG implementation guide with its implementation projects helps with the documentation of the prioritized activities.

Although the SAP R/3 system supports project management for traditional implementations with the graphical procedure model, this cannot be used for DSDM-based implementations.

Another important project management task is to perform a risk analysis that is continuously extended throughout the running project.

5.1 The project manager in DSDM

Compared with the SAP procedure model, project management with DSDM places completely new demands on the project manager, on the project team and on the communications capabilities of all those involved.

Whereas the project manager's task in traditional projects was to ensure that the requirements and goals defined at the start of the project were met, the DSDM project manager is confronted with requirements and goals that change continually. This results from the peculiarity of this method, in which the requirements and goals are never finally fixed (which takes account of the dynamics of the reality), but when required can be continually adapted to meet the changed requirements of the users and the changed environmental conditions.

If, for example, in traditional projects the requirements fixed at the beginning were not met, responsibility can be placed on the developers. If, however, the requirements were met but the system still proved to have limited usefulness, responsibility can be placed on the users who were not capable of defining their requirements sufficiently precisely in the early phases of the project to provide the company with a useful system.

Thus, the project manager was principally concerned with keeping within the specified time limits and given budget, and controlling the developers.

In contrast, DSDM projects are based more on close cooperation between developers and users. Consequently, the DSDM project proceeds with a high degree of developer–user consensus and, thanks to the continuous updating of the requirements, also produces a useful system for the company.

For the project manager in particular, this has the consequence of permitting effective cooperation between developers and users. Thus, it is not sufficient just to organize when this cooperation is to take place, but to prepare those involved for the prototyping activities and to provide support for them. The project manager must also take account of new requirements, which concerns not only communications and team management, but also prototyping management and the DSDM philosophy.

The project manager has the following tasks in the project (DSDM Consortium, 1997, p. 124ff):

- *Demand fast progress*
  When there are problems with completion in a waterfall-based project, the end date is normally moved. In contrast, the project manager in DSDM projects must ensure that the demands of the timebox are changed. This is the only way of ensuring that the customer obtains a useful product when the timebox has expired.

- *Obtain general agreement for the priority list of demands and for the detailed contents of the timeboxes*
  Once the priority list has been created, it is possible that the customers, after some time, recognize that another development sequence would be better for their business. The project manager in DSDM-based projects must cater for the customers' objections without delay and attempt to change the direction of the development to provide benefits for the customers. However, the project manager must ensure that the customers understand the consequences of such a change.

- *Manage customer relationships*
  The users are fully integrated in the teams. However, this may cause problems in the relationships between users and developers. These can be caused, for example, by the developers spending all of their time on the project, whereas the users also have to take care of their day-to-day business. The project manager must ensure that the teams do not split into 'we' and 'them' factions.

- *Promote team culture and motivation*
  A DSDM project makes more demands on those involved than a traditional project. On the one hand, the project manager must promote the motivation of the employees, but on the other hand, ensure that the project members have sufficient time to recuperate. The project manager should adopt more the role of a promoter rather than being an authoritarian.

- *Communicate project progress*
  The teams communicate very intensively within the group. The project manager has the task of informing all those involved who are not working in the teams of the project progress. This is of particular importance for fast development. If this is not done, it is quite possible, for example, that within a short time the senior management will no longer know the current state of the project.

- *Ensure that learning from errors and planning continue*
  A group meeting with the users after every timebox evaluates the delivered product. The project manager must create a speaking culture for the project in which errors can

be discussed openly. 'Learn, don't blame' is the DSDM principle. However, at the end of these meetings, the project manager must take account of critical points and make positive use of these in the project.

5.2 Prototyping management

Iterative prototyping is one of the most important activities in the DSDM-based procedure model.

Prototyping generally means that the contracting party is provided with a prototype that contains the most important functions of the system to be developed. This permits him to define, and possibly correct, his ideas (Balzert, 1992, p. 62).

Prototyping in the SAP R/3 implementation means that it is possible for the user to view or perform the specific business process within an executable system (Keller and Teufel, 1997, p. 206).

A prototype in the DSDM-based procedure model serves two purposes:

- It represents a component of the system to be developed, i.e., it will not be discarded but rather iteratively developed so that it can be used as part of the new system.

- It represents a technology used to develop and refine the functional and technical requirements.

The DSDM Consortium not only considers prototyping to be the creation of a first image but assumes that the iterative prototyping concept can be used to develop operational subsystems: 'Prototyping is not a waste of time' (Stapleton, 1997, p. 65).

Some of the advantages hoped to be obtained through the use of prototyping are (Frese et al., 1994; Hesse et al., 1992, p. 67):

- more appropriate requirements through the involvement of non-DP specialists;

- avoidance of design errors through the earliest possible test use;

- increased user acceptance;

- early user training.

However, the most important prerequisite for successful prototyping is adequate support by management, who, ideally, should feel committed to DSDM and know how essential intensive (and thus time-consuming) user involvement is. If this is not the case, the management will need to be convinced and the advantages of prototyping emphasized.

A prototype can be developed either horizontally or vertically. Horizontal means that initially all functions are covered, but not differentiated in all details. By contrast, vertical means the complete understanding, differentiation and processing of an area before starting the next area.

Because DSDM requires that functions are processed in the order of their importance to business benefits, the prototypes in SAP R/3 implementation projects are developed in a vertical direction. Thus, the individual business processes must be completely described, understood and 'customized' before the team starts the next business process.

The prototyping management concentrates on the concept of iterative prototyping. The fundamental tasks of configuration management, timeboxing and the close involvement of the end-users are essential for successful iteration management.

In accordance with the iterative prototyping concept, as a rule-of-thumb, every prototype should pass through the following development (DSDM Consortium, 1997, p. 79, Figure 5.1):

- *Initial (business process) prototype*
  To ensure that the activities to be performed within the timebox have been chosen correctly, this prototype should be created fast.

- *Refined (business process) prototype*
  This prototype represents an improvement of the initial prototype. It provides as much additional functionality as possible in the available time.

- *Consolidated (business process) prototype*
  This prototype was developed with the aim of rounding off the product and transforming it into a complete, consistent and deliverable product.

Each of these prototypes starts with goals and ends with quality checks.

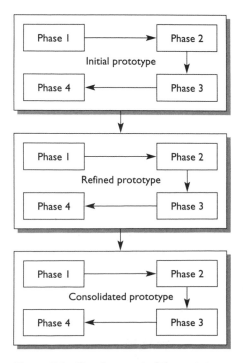

Figure 5.1   Development of the prototypes

Each prototype iteration itself consists of four phases (DSDM Consortium, 1997, p. 77, Figure 5.1):

Phase 1: Determination of the prototype

First, it must be decided which team is going to be concerned with which business processes or business process groups. Each team must then decide which of the business processes are essential for a prototype and which are supplementary. This differentiation has another importance within a prototype and so specifies a procedure for the development of the individual prototypes.

The acceptance criteria placed on a prototype have already been specified in this phase. This definition is done before the first development step has taken place and so ensures that the development takes the right direction.

Phase 2: Coordination and agreement

How much time is to be spent on each prototype must be defined. The most important aspect of this step is that it does not permit any deviation from the goal unless significant problems occur.

It is important that the end-user understands that his priorities decide whether or not a component of the system is considered to be essential.

Phase 3: Development of the prototype

The prototype is developed in conjunction with the user. It is quite possible to construct prototypes on paper, which, particularly in the early phases, can be useful and cost-effective because this quickly produces a common understanding for the problem situation to be processed. However, the decision on how the prototype is to developed must be agreed together.

Phase 4: Audit of the prototype

The aim of the audit is to check whether the set goals/tasks have been met and which tasks can be moved to later project phases. An investigation is also made as to which tasks (from the project) can be outsourced and whether the previous base functions are accepted (DSDM Consortium, 1997, p. 78).

Furthermore, it should be ensured that the development proceeds in the correct direction and that the later end-users can identify with the work.

Prototyping, being one of the significant DSDM ideas, demands excellent configuration management (refer to Chapter 6) as an essential prerequisite for implementing a successful project.

5.3   Timeboxing and setting priorities

Timeboxing means specifying a fixed end date when a specific goal must be satisfied. Thus, even here the focus is on the goal and not the activity.

Whereas the developers and users must initially decide together which goals are to be attained, i.e., which business processes within a timebox are to be described and 'customized', the developer alone must estimate how long it will take until the goal is reached. If it becomes apparent that the activities planned for a timebox cannot be met, the user must specify which missing functions and business processes should be moved to a later timebox. This means that deadlines, once they have been set, cannot be exceeded, but rather the requirements must be changed or moved. Although the result of this procedure is increased pressure on all those involved, the project management becomes more controllable.

Thus, timeboxing represents an important task in DSDM projects that prevents the DSDM teams from losing sight of their goals or even wasting time on unimportant functions or business processes.

However, timeboxing can itself also bring risks. This is exactly the case when timeboxes are repeatedly planned incorrectly, which can result either in time being wasted or in the planned tasks being unable to be adequately met in an excessively short timebox. Consequently, timeboxing is also dependent on the experience of the planning project manager and his level of knowledge of the capabilities of his employees. Thus, it can be assumed that the risks associated with timeboxing will reduce with increasing experience.

5.4   The MoSCoW rules

The so-called MoSCoW rules provide an important method for assigning priorities to the requirements (DSDM Consortium, 1997, p. 50):

Whereas the two o's have no meaning, the other letters have the following meaning:

- *Must have requirements*
  Requirements that must be realized in the future system.

- *Should have requirements*
  Requirements for which there is a possible solution by the next delivery. The system can be used even though these requirements have not been realized.

- *Could have requirements*
  Requirements that can be omitted without problem.

- *Want to have but will not have this time round requirements*
  Requirements that can be moved to a later time without problem.

5.5   Risk analysis

Risk analysis begins with the project start. In accordance with the DSDM method, it is only generally considered at the beginning and further refined during the project lifetime. The DSDM Consortium mentions the following risks (DSDM Consortium, 1997, p. 139):

The users are not sufficiently involved in the project

A success factor for the DSDM method lies in the involvement of the later users in the complete project. If the project team does not adequately cater for their requirements, an SAP R/3 system can result that the users do not accept and so make only inadequate use of it later. The developers must take account of those business benefits that only the users can judge. Consultants can also try to use in the new project the same customizing settings that brought large benefits in other companies. If the users cannot counter this, because they are not sufficiently involved, it is possible that they get a system that does not support their business or concentrates on the wrong aspects.

Users that can judge an SAP R/3 system with regard to the business benefits are normally the same employees that are urgently required for the day-to-day business. For this reason, there is the danger that executives will not want to make their employees available for such a project or at least impede their involvement.

These risks can be reduced by holding DSDM seminars for the teams and by the project manager convincing the superiors ('You get exactly that system that you need'; 'The project is not taking too long').

The time needed for decisions endangers the project schedule

Every project is slowed down waiting for decisions. This problem has particular significance for DSDM-based projects, in which the dynamism associated with the teams must not be hindered. This danger is prevalent when senior management does not have sufficient faith in the teams and would rather make all important decisions themselves. A typical example of a delay is the discussion about the works concept of SAP, which can take a very long time in a large company before a decision is reached. It is better, in accordance with the method, to decide quickly on a solution, while still taking into consideration how it would be possible to revert to a different solution. If the strategy is not consistent in a company, but rather different people follow different goals, the delay in reaching decisions can also be used as a means of moving in a different direction. The project manager should observe these styles of play and mention them.

Team members concentrate more on activities than on products

If the timeboxes are selected to be too long, the teams can achieve a life of their own that no longer concerns the product but more the activities. There are so many interesting things to discover or refine in the SAP R/3 system, that it is quite possible that the teams attempt to perfect one part while completely forgetting some other part. A shortening of the timebox with emphasis on a deliverable product reduces this risk. In addition, those employees who wish to achieve a result in a specified time should dominate in the team. Two months is too long for a timebox.

Delivered products do not bring any business benefits

One reason for the delivered system failing to achieve business benefits is caused by the project being too technically-driven and not sufficiently company-driven. This risk can be kept within limits when the teams report less about their activities and more about what has been achieved. Regular reviews in which the business benefits are evaluated can also help to reduce the risk. This is the only way of ensuring that the project maintains the right direction.

Iterative and incremental development is not controlled

If the teams do not fully understand the principles of iterative and incremental development, there is the danger that the resulting SAP R/3 system is not usable. This system is being continually changed and the development creeps forward without delivering a product. Short timeboxes can reduce the risk of retaining the waterfall method and misunderstanding the iterative and incremental principle so that only a single iteration with just one deliverable product results from the project.

It is difficult or even impossible to return to a previous development level

If the capabilities that SAP provides for configuration management are either not used or insufficiently used, there is the danger that it is difficult or even impossible to return to a previous development level. Good training in the use of the SAP tools can reduce this risk. Regular audits and reviews must ensure the use of these methods. Otherwise there is the danger that the teams will slowly neglect these important activities as they concentrate on producing products.

The general requirements have not been frozen

Long project delays can result when it takes too long for the general requirements to be agreed. The teams tend to discuss the requirements in too much detail before the requirements have been frozen. The modularization of the requirements combined with the assignment of individual modules to the timeboxes is a good way of reducing this risk. All requirements that do not belong in the current timebox are then considered to be frozen. Shortening the timeboxes is also a good method here.

Testing is not considered to be an integral part of the life cycle

The fast development in DSDM projects can mean that the teams regard testing to be an unnecessary bureaucratic task, with the consequence that it is then reduced. However, if a system that changes dynamically is not tested regularly, there is the danger that too many errors can bring the system into a non-repairable state. This is why the DSDM method places so much value on testing. To reduce this risk, someone with responsibility for the tests should be named in the team who ensures that all tests are performed and documented.

Not all these involved working cooperatively together

Different groups work together in a DSDM project. This can cause problems, with the result that the principle of cooperation no longer applies. If such a situation occurs, measures must be adopted to ensure that the focus concentrates not on guilt but on getting back to the product. A wrong approach would be to set increased contractual agreements, such as what a consultant has to achieve. It is better to hold regular reviews and to increase the sense of trust. Once trust has been destroyed, the DSDM method can cause more damage than advantages. For this reason, special attention should be paid to the choice of project members and the development of the project culture.

DSDM is not fully usable

If a business system has been described in full detail, it does not make much sense to use DSDM as the method. The SAP procedure model is more likely to produce the required goal. For this reason, it is important that the DSDM usability filter provided by the DSDM Consortium is carefully tested during the feasibility phase (DSDM Consortium, 1997, p. 239).

The team does not understand the DSDM method

A renunciation of training in DSDM can give the impression that a user can work 'part-time' in the teams while continuing to perform normal work as previously. Training in the method means that it has been appreciated that the team's work makes full use of the employee's available time. The manager must ensure that the employee is fully available for this limited time period.

The organization of the users changes dramatically as the result of implementing the system

If the discovery is made during the development process that the implementation of the SAP R/3 system will bring major changes in the business processes, this can change the way the teams work. Employees who see themselves threatened by possible changes will no longer continue working with their previous creativity in the project. Consequently, a distinct differentiation should be made between projects that dramatically change the business processes and those that are to support the existing business processes.

The original project goal can probably not be achieved

In a project in which it is only recognized late that the project goal cannot be attained, the project manager should agree to a reduction of the requirements with the user department. It is not sensible to add additional members to the project team at some late date, because experience has shown that this causes an even greater delay.

The developers do not have sufficient knowledge of the SAP R/3 system

It is absolutely essential that the developers know the SAP R/3 system very well and also master the individual tools. They should not start learning during the project work. If there are knowledge deficits, the project manager must ensure that specialists are available for specific topics. Given the current limited availability of SAP R/3 specialists, the project manager must request them early.

5.6   The graphical SAP procedure model

The graphical SAP procedure model contains a preconfigured and integrated project management system, whose the structure cannot be changed (refer to Figure 5.2).

This project management system has the advantage in providing graphical navigation capabilities using sensitive fields with direct connection to the associated work packages (refer to Figure 5.3).

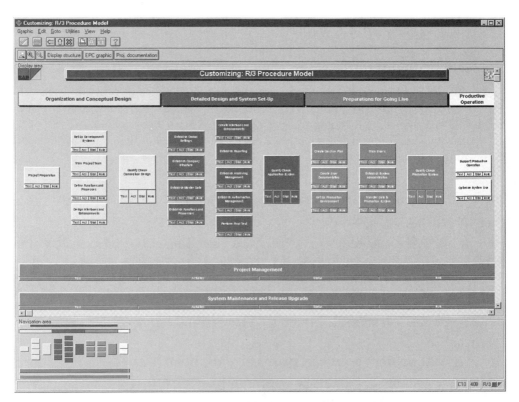

Figure 5.2   The graphical SAP procedure model

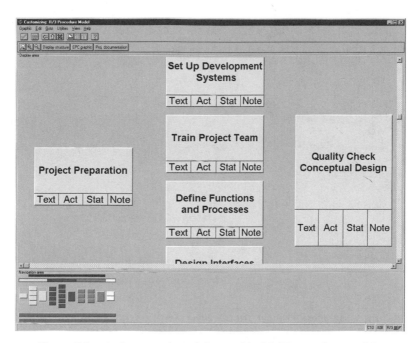

Figure 5.3   A close-up view of the graphical SAP procedure model

- This permits immediate branching from the graphical procedure model into the online documentation in order to read the associated instructions and recommendations for the work package (refer to Figure 5.4).

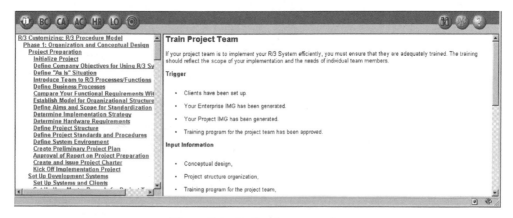

Figure 5.4   Online documentation

- Executable activities, such as access to the customizing transactions assigned to this work package and to other tools that can be used in customizing, can also be called directly (refer to Figure 5.5).

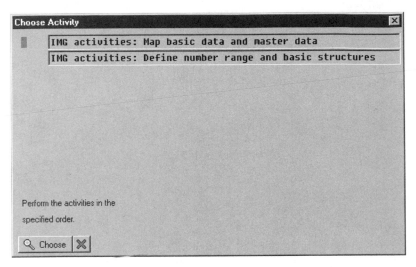

Figure 5.5   Customizing transaction

• The updating of the status information for the work package can also be directly called from the graphical model (refer to Figure 5.6).

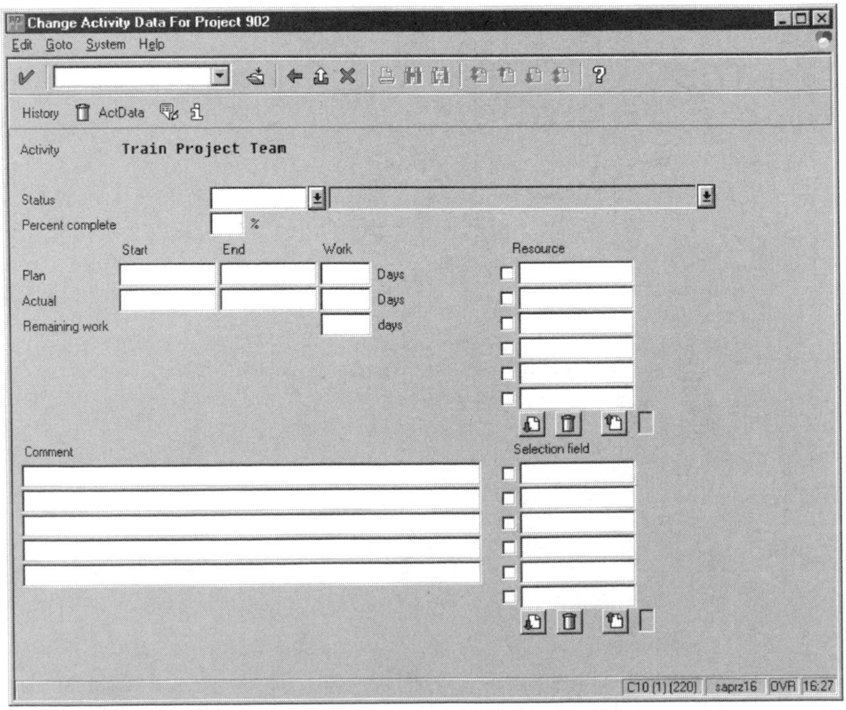

Figure 5.6   Status input

- Branching can also be made into the project documentation. This is sensible when information is to be directly documented for the work package (refer to Figure 5.7).

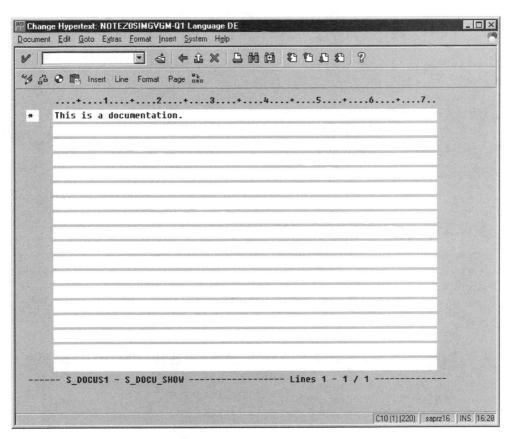

Figure 5.7   Project documentation

The graphical SAP procedure model uses project administration/controlling as an inter-phase work package that continually monitors the project to determine whether the project goals are being attained. Corrective measures must be adopted if there are any deviations.

The following specific activities should be performed:

- Perform detailed planning of the project activities.

- Determine the status of the project.

- Initiate corrective measures.

- Conduct project meetings.

When a project is developed using the SAP procedure model, this representation provides a simple means of monitoring the project. Because of their defined structure, this tool cannot be used to manage DSDM-operated projects.

5.7   The SAP Project System

The requirements list with assigned priorities is the most important project control tool for DSDM-based projects. The SAP R/3 system provides the Project System (PS) module if an additional project management tool with graphical display capabilities is to be used for controlling (Dräger, 1998).

The PS module provides the following functionalities:

- *Create and maintain a project structure plan*
  The project structure plan contains a hierarchical division of the project into subprojects, which in turn are divided into work packages. The time aspect plays a subordinate role here.

- *Create and maintain a network plan*
  The network plan contains a time-related description of the individual activities together with the dependencies between the individual activities. The network plan is displayed graphically; its structure is based on the phases and iterations of the DSDM-based procedure model. The integration of the complete R/3 system object links to documents or customizing settings can be assigned to the individual activities (refer to Figure 5.8).

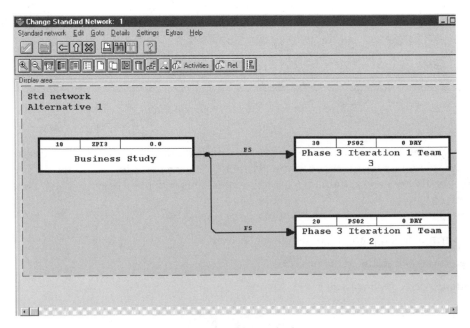

Figure 5.8   Network plan

- *Plan costs*
  The planned costs for the individual project structure plan elements are acquired. The degree of detail can be selected as required. Because change forms are written once the project has been released, any changes made to the plan can be traced.

Other functions of the project system are date planning, budget assignment, resource planning, acquisition of the actual values and project analysis.

5.8   The SAP Implementation Guide

The Implementation Guide (IMG) provides the most important aid for structured system setting. The IMG is organized hierarchically into application components, and organized into the processing sequence of the work steps within these components.
  Various functions can be initiated for each node of the IMG hierarchy:

- Invoke the customizing transaction.

- Invoke the SAP documentation.

- Invoke the project documentation (save project-specific and project-independent documents).

- Invoke project management (status, dates, degree of processing and resources).

The IMG is not a rigid system like the procedure model, rather you can include your own processing steps, such as tests.
  The information system forms an important function. This provides the capability to select standardized or freely selectable reports.
  The IMG also supports the iterative and incremental method:
  SAP provides an implementation guide, the so-called 'Reference IMG', with all system settings for the base system. This SAP Reference IMG can now be used to generate a 'Company IMG' for the associated company in which the required functions and countries can be sought. The company IMG then forms the frame for all future projects with their iterations and increments (refer to Figure 5.9).
  The company IMG is then used to develop a 'Project IMG' for the associated project. The project IMG is a further limitation of the company IMG and contains only the maximum work steps that are to be achieved in the project.
  Views can also be created for every project IMG, for example to display the priorities of the individual teams using the MoSCoW rules (refer to Section 5.4).
  The models that SAP provides are another advantage of the IMG. These models provide Word templates for many activities. For example, they can be used for customizing settings or to document function extensions (refer to Figure 5.10).
  Although the implementation guide is structured into components, a process orientation would have been more appropriate for the method.

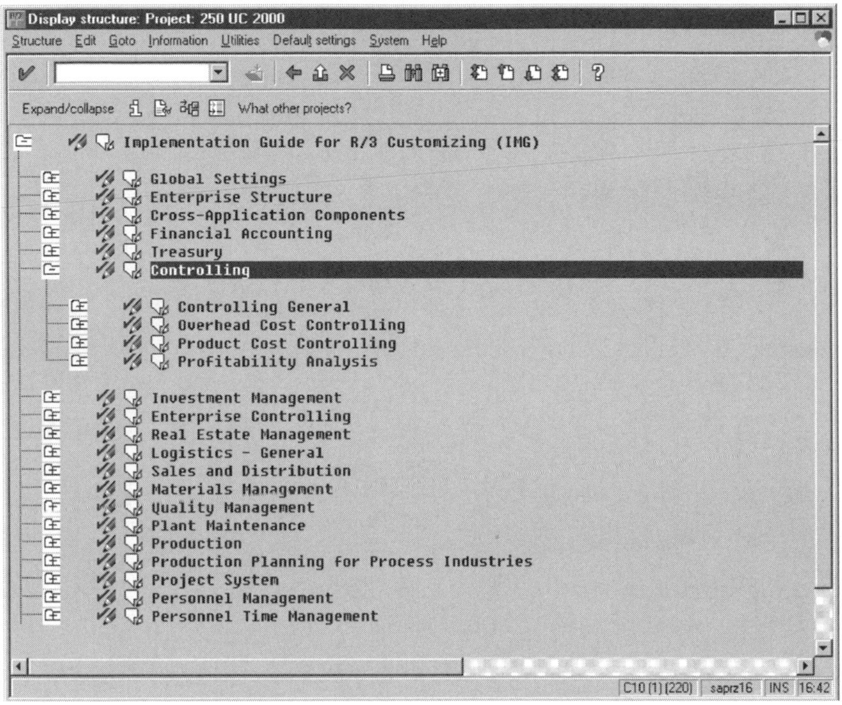

Figure 5.9 IMG project structure tree

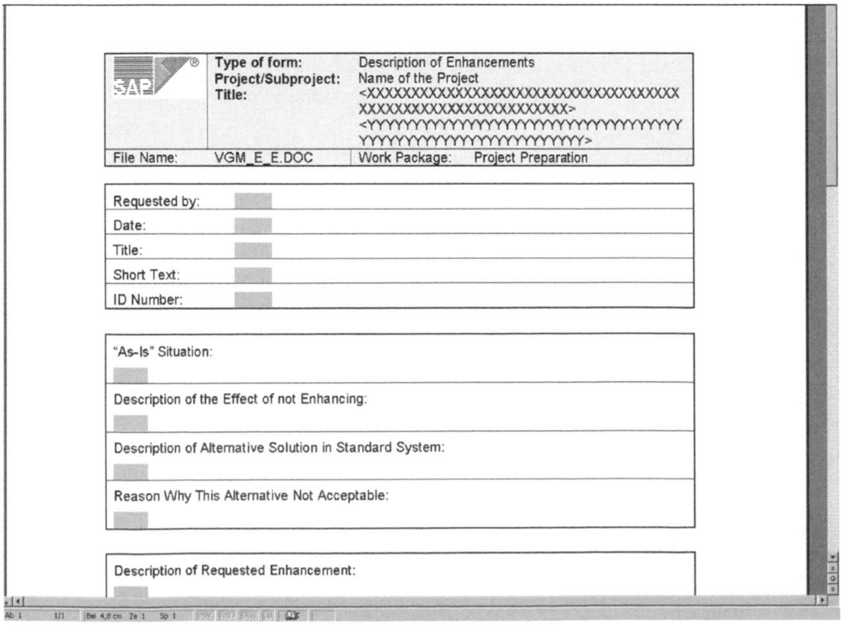

SAP	**Type of form:**	Description of Enhancements
	Project/Subproject:	Name of the Project
	Title:	<XXXXXXXXXXXXXXXXXXXXXXXXXXXXXXXXXXXXXXXXXXXXXXXXXXXXXXXXXXXXXX> <YYYYYYYYYYYYYYYYYYYYYYYYYYYYYYYYYYYYYYYYYYYYYYYYYYYYYYYYYYYYYYYY>
File Name: VGM_E_E.DOC		Work Package: Project Preparation

Requested by:	
Date:	
Title:	
Short Text:	
ID Number:	

"As-Is" Situation:

Description of the Effect of not Enhancing:

Description of Alternative Solution in Standard System:

Reason Why This Alternative Not Acceptable:

Description of Requested Enhancement:

Figure 5.10 Example of the Word template

5.9 Summary

The project management changes in DSDM-based projects. The project manager has been assigned different tasks to ensure that the project completes on time and with the best possible business benefits. The project manager makes use of the following methods: prototypes, timeboxes, the prioritization of the requirements, and risk analysis. The SAP R/3 system supports project management with the project system and the implementation guide. The graphical procedure model is available for traditional projects.

6 Configuration management

The DSDM-based procedure model pays special attention to configuration management, because during a fast development it is very easy for the teams to start working in the wrong direction and then want to continue from some previous development version. Configuration management (CM) guarantees that no old versions are lost and the development remains under control despite the dynamics.

6.1 Introduction

Configurations are managed and change scenarios organized in configuration management. Disregarding these important tasks can cause large problems, even for smaller projects (Balzert, 1998, p. 234).

For example, an SAP R/3 system consists of a number of software elements such as:

- Business process documentation
- Customizing settings
- CATT test procedures
- Training notes
- Project plans
- ABAP/4 extension programs
- Interface specifications
- Interface programs to non-SAP systems

Furthermore these elements are not isolated within the project, but rather there are many dependencies between them:

- The customizing settings must reflect the business processes.
- The test procedures with their test data must be able to run the business processes, for example in the SAP R/3 system.
- The training notes must correspond to the version of the SAP R/3 system.

  Every change to a software element can cause a change to other software elements.

- A version change in the SAP R/3 system can have effects on the ABAP/4 programs. the test procedures and the training notes.

- A change in the business process description can have effects on the customizing settings.

- A change in the interface specification has an effect on the associated interface programs.

A careless use of these elements carries the danger of a large project risk. To reduce this, configuration management ensures that which versions of these elements are valid is always known (refer to Figure 6.1).

The goal is achieved by creating a *configuration identification document* – also known as a 'configuration hierarchy' or 'element structure plan', which describes the elements that form a so-called 'configuration'. A configuration is a bill-of-materials for those software elements with their corresponding version numbers, which at a specific time match each other (refer to Figure 6.2).

A further task of configuration management is *change management*. When a single software element is changed, then, as a consequence, a new configuration must also be created and simultaneously tested to determine whether the individual elements are still compatible with each other. If this is not the case, there is the danger, for example, that a changed business process description with an incompatible customizing setting is valid in a system. To avoid this danger, version management should initially be implemented for ail important software elements. This version management assigns a version number to every element of a change. This version number, together with the name of the element, must be used in the configuration hierarchy. This can avoid a new business process description being used with an old customizing setting. Version management must obviously also be used in the configuration hierarchy. When versions are created, reference configurations (or also base configurations (baselines)) that exist at specific times represent a released state of the software development.

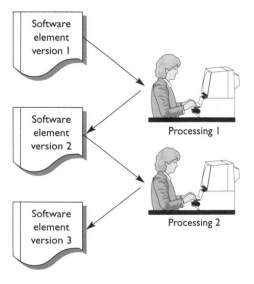

Figure 6.1   Versions

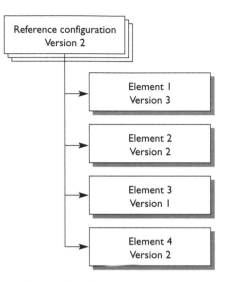

Figure 6.2   Element structure plan

The simultaneous processing of software elements by different project members brings another source of danger. An important task of configuration management is to avoid mutual overwriting. The implementation of status and reservation management inhibits the simultaneous processing of documents by two project members (refer to Figure 6.3).

Configuration management guarantees the following requirements (Wallmüller, 1990, p. 122):

• Identification of all relevant documents of the SAP project

• Documentation that describes which changes have been made on which elements

• Documentation that describes when and by whom changes have been made

• Ensure the reconstruction of old versions of all associated elements

• Documentation that describes which documents have validity and when

• Hinder inadvertent deletion of or changes to documents (safe function)

6.2   The DSDM view

Whereas in traditional SAP R/3 implementation projects the requirements made on the system were decided in the early project phases and from then onwards regarded as being stable, dynamics in the form of frequent changes, parallel processing and further development of a single object are DSDM-inherent characteristics that demand good configuration management (DSDM, 1997, p. 151).

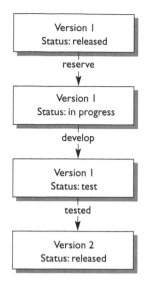

Figure 6.3   Status management for software elements

For SAP R/3 implementation projects using the DSDM-based procedure model this means, in particular, that the configuration management must be capable of managing and documenting changes made to the customizing settings, which may be made simultaneously by several teams for several business processes. This should ensure that it is possible at any time to return to a known system state. This, for example, is particularly important when the development has taken a wrong turn or when the end of a timebox has been reached, even though the current system status is not yet stable and stabilizing would require much additional time. This makes it possible at the end of a timebox to return easily to the last known and stable state.

In particular, because of the very dynamic changes in DSDM projects, the method attaches much importance to careful configuration management.

The importance of a functioning configuration management system can be derived from the nine DSDM principles and summarized as follows:

- The teams must be empowered to make decisions and without any extensive bureaucracy.

- Configuration management methods and tools must not hinder the teams.

- Changes are unavoidable in an iterative process.

- All changes are reversible.

- Every prototype is reproducible, including all development information, test scripts and expected results.

In an iterative process with many changes, it is important for the team members to know that their changes are under control and a previous version can be restored without difficulty.

For these reasons, every team member must be familiar with the configuration strategy. Thus, we do not recommend a central configuration management, rather it should be an integral part of the daily project work. When the responsibility for creating the base configurations is transferred to the teams, they are made too infrequently. For this reason, a 'CM champion', normally the technical coordinator, must be responsible for administration, for resolving conflicts and for ensuring that the strategy is adhered to. If the technical coordinator does not belong to the team, a team member should take over the role of CM champion (refer to Figure 6.4).

The configuration strategy should be defined before ending the business study phase, and the employees then trained appropriately. It is most important to define how often a reference configuration (baseline) is to be created. DSDM mentions the following possibilities:

- Produce a base configuration before presenting each prototype.

- Produce a daily base configuration. This demonstrates flexibility and the speed of development.

- As absolute minimum, produce a base configuration at the end of a timebox, but however, only when the timeboxes do not last longer than three weeks.

Another aspect of the configuration management strategy is the granularity of the configuration elements, i.e., is it sufficient just to make a system copy of the SAP R/3 system without having to know what has changed from one configuration to the next, or should all change steps up to the change of individual customizing settings be tracked. The DSDM Consortium recommends choosing as fine a granularity as possible.

Traditionally, configuration management is first performed near the end of a project, and then usually only for documentation purposes. DSDM recommends that every element should be subject to configuration control.

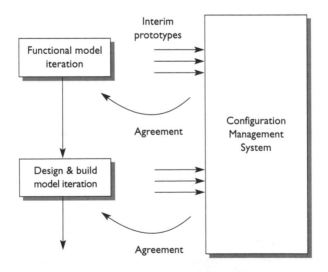

Figure 6.4   DSDM picture of the configuration

DSDM requires that the dependencies between individual elements, such as business process descriptions with their associated customizing settings and test procedures, are subject to configuration control.

In particular, for teams working in parallel, it is necessary to be able to reserve individual elements to inhibit mutual overwriting. Because inadequate configuration management provides a very high project risk, being able to analyze the changes performed is very important.

6.3   The SAP support

The various tools of the SAP R/3 system are an ideal means of meeting the DSDM requirement for reliable configuration management:

- *Change and Transport Organizer (CTO)*

- *SAPoffice*

- *Document Management system (DMS)*

6.3.1   The Change and Transport Organizer

SAP developed the *Change and Transport Organizer* to register and document all changes made to objects in the registry and in customizing. Such objects are, for example, ABAP/4 programs, screen backgrounds, documentation modules and test modules. The CTO consists of three parts:

- The *Customizing Organizer* for the registration and documentation of customizing changes.

- The *Workbench Organizer* for the registration and documentation of changes in the repository.

- The *Transport Organizer* for the controlled transfer of repository and customizing changes between the various systems.

In a DSDM-based SAP R/3 project, so-called *change requests* on which the individual teams work are created for every timebox. A change request has a tree structure in which all changed development objects and customizing settings are acquired automatically. The change requests can be defined in more detail through the tasks of the individual teams or team members.

Because the SAP R/3 system automatically records every change made to an object, the operation of the CTO is very simple for the teams. The CTO also provides a simple *navigation aid* that displays in a tree structure all change requests together with the associated tasks and changed objects (refer to Figure 6.5).

Requests and tasks are supplemented in overviews and selection lists with short descriptions or employee names.

As soon as a development object has been recorded in a change request, the developers can be sure that no further uncontrolled changes can be made to this object. It is disabled for other developers and can only be displayed (refer to Figures 6.6 and 6.7).

Every object has its original in just one system. As standard, corrections and developments can only be made to the original in its original system.

If a user attempts to change a repository object, the Workbench Organizer is invoked automatically and permits changes to be made to the system only when the user has specified a change request. This ensures that all changes made to the ABAP/4 Development Workbench and to customizing are registered.

The CTO ensures a *versioning* of all development objects and so permits both comparisons and access to earlier versions. This permits the documentation or the restoration of released versions before and after a change request or even after a development project.

The developer must produce for every *change request* a document that contains the project goals, the status and any special features. All changed development objects are also automatically logged in the object list for the request. This logging, together with the documentation and the versioning, guarantees a complete record of changes.

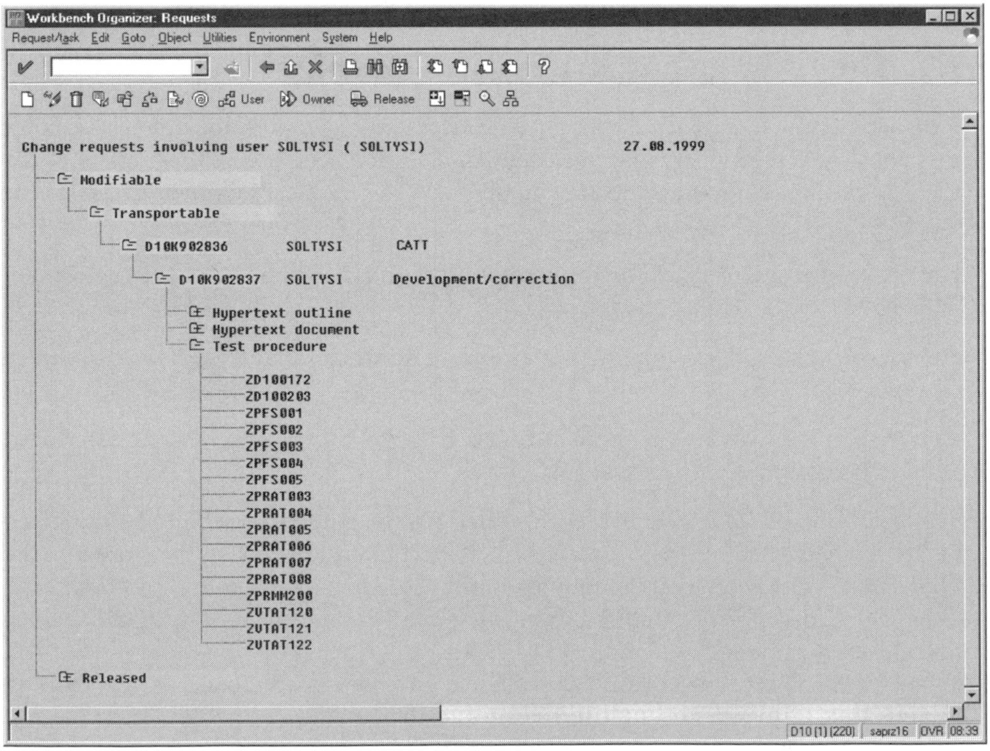

Figure 6.5   CTO tree structure

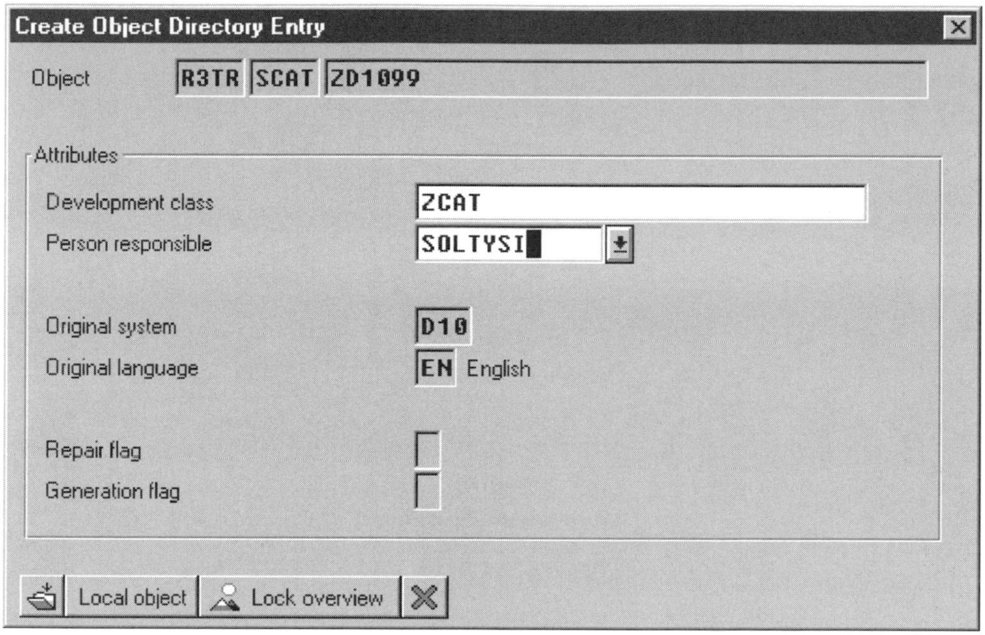

Figure 6.6   Registration

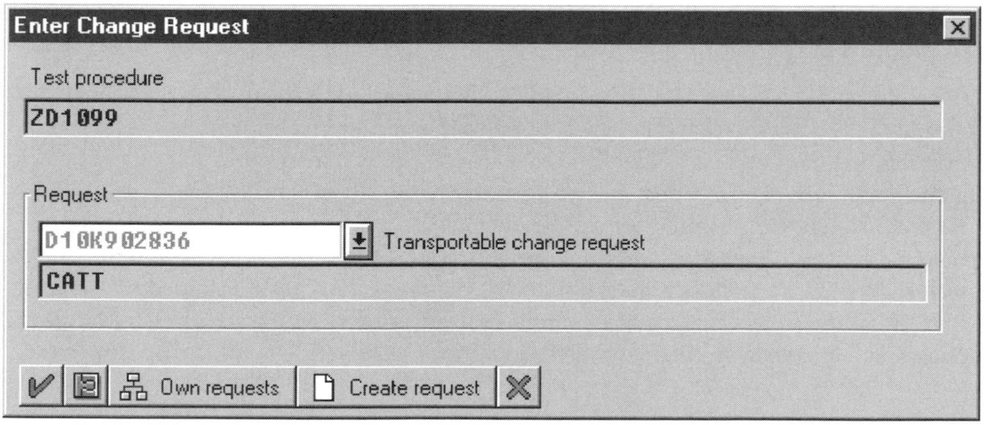

Figure 6.7   Change request

The transport system, which is closely connected to the Workbench Organizer, performs the transport of development objects and customizing settings to other systems. Transport is performed using change requests, i.e., the number of objects to be transported is obtained automatically after a release. Every larger SAP R/3 project should contain several SAP R/3 systems (also refer to Figure 6.8):

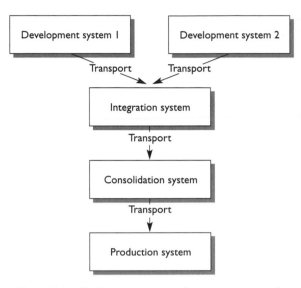

Figure 6.8   Various systems in the transport complex

- One or more development systems

- An integration system to combine the development systems

- A consolidation system for test under production conditions

- A production system

A transport log is automatically created for the transport of every change request. If, for example, a productive system behaves incorrectly after an import from the test system. It is possible to determine immediately which objects were transported, who was the ordering party and why the transport was performed.

The consistency of a transport can be checked in advance using a simulation of the transport to the destination system. The assignment of the transport type and the destination system is performed automatically, and does not need to be maintained by the user.

An information system for the search, display, processing and analysis of change requests is available to supplement the Workbench Organizer and the transport system.

6.3.2 SAPoffice

SAP provides the SAPoffice in the R/3 system as a mail and storage system. The mail functionality can be used for communication and permits the sending and receiving of mail, even within an SAP R/3 system. However, the storage system is more important for configuration management. The storage system organizes the personal and the general storage with hierarchical folder structures, a correction concept, and the storage of important documents. These documents can also be PC documents (e.g., Word documents) with different appendices (refer to Figure 6.9).

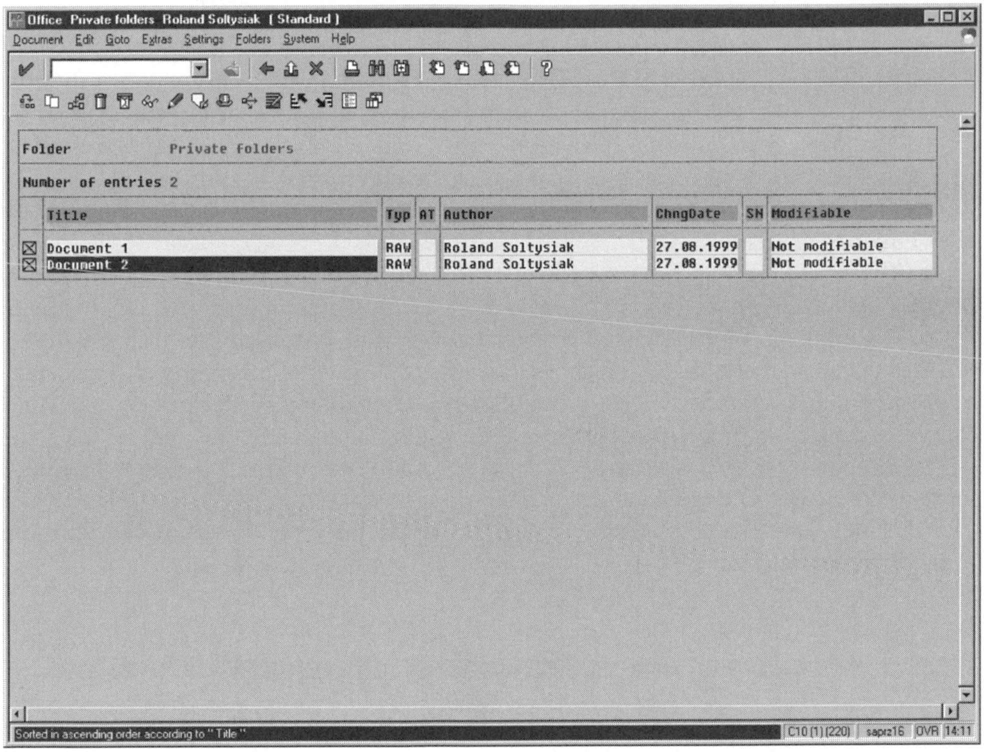

Figure 6.9   Schematic representation of the folder structure

6.3.3   The Document Management System

The *Document Management System (DMS)* is a general system for the management of all types of documents. Every document has a document information record that can specify all of its important attributes. A document key identifies every document information record. Basic attributes used for document management are also stored in the document information record. Typical attributes are:

- Document type (business process description, training notes, training schedule, etc.)

- Subdocument (in many cases, such as for training notes, it may be necessary to divide a comprehensive document into smaller documents. A list of the subdocuments is specified here.)

- Version (automatic or manual)

- Description

- Status

- Storage location

- Administration data

The *status management* ensures that it is possible to display whether a document has been released or whether it is currently being processed (refer to Figure 6.10).

The *change service* provides the capability to make a common reservation for different documents that have related content and so protect them against inadvertent change, and to identify those documents that have been frozen under a change number. For example, the change number can be used to reconstruct the correlation of old documents using their change number; this permits reversion to every old version and thus satisfies one of the essential demands of DSDM.

The *document bill-of-materials* used for structuring the documents in DMS permit a directory structure of the documents. In contrast to a file structure, several document bills-of-material can be built using different categories. For example, it is possible to sequence bills-of-material based on project aspects, i.e., ordered according to phase, team and iteration, and document bills-of-material for some overall criterion, e.g., arranged according to business process descriptions and training notes.

DMS supports the *version management* of a document, i.e., various versions of a document can be created. Old versions are retained.

Furthermore. the *SAP classification system* can be used to specify additional attributes for the documents.

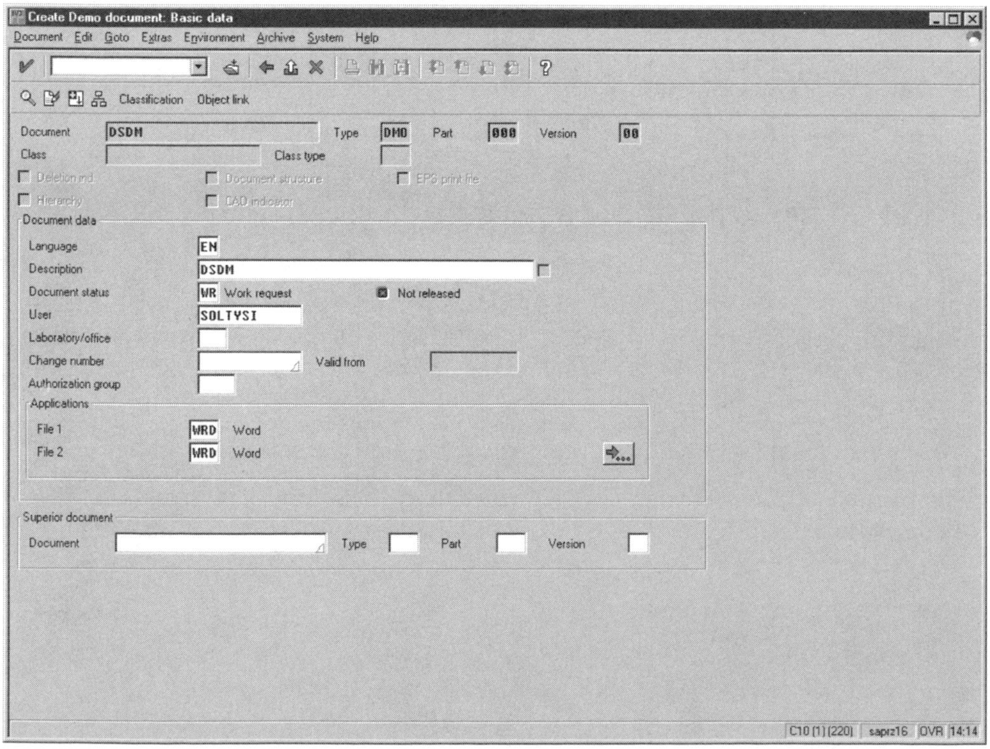

Figure 6.10   Status management

The *storage* of the documents can be done either in the SAP database or organized on an external server that the DMS manages.

6.4   Summary

Configuration management is an important feature in DSDM-based projects. Good configuration management can avoid many errors in project work: mutual overwriting of software elements, incompatible configurations and the irreversibility of each development level. This is achieved in configuration management through the introduction of versions, reference configurations and change services. SAP R/3 provides powerful tools to support configuration management: the Change and Transport Organizer (CTO), SAPoffice and the Document Management System (DMS).

7 Testing

Testing is a very important activity in DSDM-based projects that minimizes the risk of errors reducing the business benefits. The SAP R/3 tools *Computer Aided Test Tool* (CATT) and the *test plan tool*, and the supplementary product *AutoTester*, are ideal for satisfying the DSDM requirements. This provides a test method for SAP R/3 projects that to a high degree automates almost all tests and consequently reduces the test effort.

7.1 The DSDM view

DSDM does not consider testing to be a self-contained phase but rather an activity integrated in the complete software life cycle. For prototyping this means that every prototype developed by the developers and users must also be subsequently tested, with the result 'fit for purpose'.

Testing in accordance with DSDM is based on the following six principles: (DSDM Consortium, 1997, p. 159):

- Test cases are generated to find errors and not to show which components of the system function correctly already.

- Testing is done in all phases.

- If possible, the developer should not test his own work. Indeed, because the user should also be closely involved in the development, but does not himself do development work, it is a good opportunity for the user to perform the testing.

- The test must be designed so that it can be repeated.

- The aim of the testing is to ensure that the requirements have been satisfied. However, this does not mean that the testing is done to prove the absence of errors, rather only that all the requirements have been implemented and that no unnecessary functions are present.

- Testing never finds all the errors. Because testing is subject to restrictions (time, human resources), it should initially concentrate on the most important business benefits to be achieved.

7.2   CATT and the test plan tool

Prototype testing and the tool support provided in the form of the Computer Aided Test Tool (CATT) are of particular importance.

The business process prototypes must be tested in accordance with the test principles mentioned above to determine whether the requirements have been understood correctly. A test case can be considered successful when it supplies the expected information.

CATT can be used to group repeatable business or administrative activities for test purposes, and so create just once test procedures that are automated and repeatable. The CATT procedures are used to check the following settings and activities:

- Settings for the customizing tables

- Responses to changes in the customizing tables

- System messages

- Transactions

- Value determination and database updating.

A log is produced automatically for every test activity. This log is produced in a short form when there are no errors, otherwise it contains detailed information.

Thus, one of the most important functions of CATT for the DSDM-based procedure model is the documented validation of the new customizing settings and their effects on every incremental extension to the business processes. Once the test procedures have been created they are also used for new versions or releases to detect any possible negative effect of the changes (phase 4 of the DSDM-based model).

With the exception of CATT, the DSDM-based procedure model does not demand any special test techniques. We recommend the usual combination of static and dynamic methods.

7.2.1   Test procedures and test modules

A *test procedure* in CATT simulates a sequence of transactions, which, together with selected test data, normally represents a complete business process chain.

Each test procedure itself consists of individual reusable *test modules*, each of which initially contains an executable transaction, which also contains test data (refer to Figure 7.1).

A test module can also be a *manual test case*, i.e., it contains a verbal description of a test activity.

Finally, a test module can provide an interface to an *external test tool*, i.e., the test module transfers import parameters to an external test tool and receives back export parameters.

Because the individual test procedures only make references to the associated test modules, a change to a test module acts immediately on all those test procedures that reference it.

This provides a very flexible and modular system in which test procedures are formed from a set of test modules.

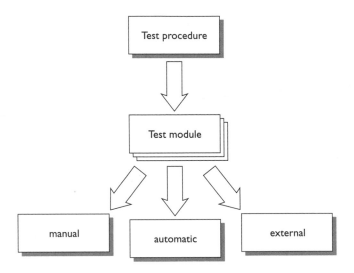

Figure 7.1   CATT terms

7.2.2 Recording functionality

Special attention should be given to the *recording functionality* in CATT with regard to the simple creation of test cases in the DSDM teams.

Transactions and customizing settings that have been accepted by one of the teams can be recorded in test modules with sample data and run later. It suffices here to activate the *recording functionality* with the specification of the transaction name. CATT then records, transparent to the user, all activities. The advantage of this method is that this activity can also be taken over by users who are later integrated in the teams without requiring extensive training. As required by DSDM the action of creating the test modules is automatically integrated in the daily work procedure of the teams (refer to Figure 7.2).

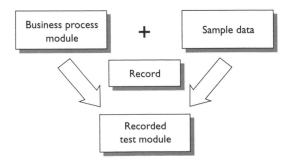

Figure 7.2   Recording of test modules

7.2.3   Expert mode and parameters

Once the test modules have been recorded, SAP experts in *expert mode* can replace the existing fixed values for the test by parameters.

Parameters describe the import and export interface for test modules. Values for import parameters can be passed at the invocation of a test module or test procedure and are available locally within the test procedure or test module. Export parameters can be used for the assignment of messages or parts of messages.

For example, the internal inquiry number returned in a test module for the creation of an inquiry can be transferred using an export parameter to the import parameter of a test module used for the creation of a quotation as the response to an inquiry.

If the fixed values in a test have been replaced by parameters, internal or external variants of the test procedures can be created, which can then be run with different values (for example, from an Excel table). Thus, the creation of a single test procedure with only a single test module produces many test variants (refer to Figure 7.3).

For example, a user records the transaction for a customer order with a customer, a material and the quantity. The SAP expert replaces these fixed values with parameters and combines these parameters as an external variant of an Excel table that contains all combinations of customers and materials. CATT then creates test runs for all combinations, and the team can be sure that this transaction can be used with all possible combinations of data (refer to Figure 7.4).

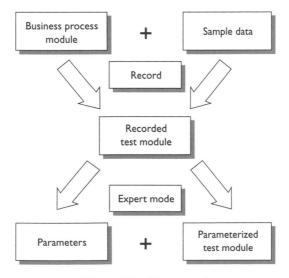

Figure 7.3   Expert mode

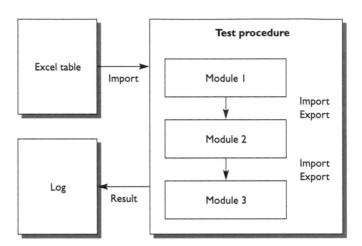

Figure 7.4   Structure of a test procedure

7.2.4 Supplementary functions

In addition to the recording functionality, the expert mode and the variants, many other functions can be used in the test procedures and test modules. These are normally required for test validation. Error messages can also be created and validated in a controlled manner without causing the test procedure to fail. Furthermore, any function modules can be used (refer to Table 7.1).

Table 7.1   Supplementary functions for CATT

TCD	Test transactions
REF	Reference test module
FUN	Include function module
TXT	Enter comment
SETTAB	Initialize table
RESTAB	Reset table
SETVAR	Assign value to variables and parameters
IF ... ENDIF	Condition
DO n ... (EXIT) ... ENDDO	Loop
EXIT	Conditional exit
CHEERR	Test error message
CHETAB	Test table contents
CHEVAR	Test variable contents

7.2.5   Start test procedures

All test procedures and test modules can be started either individually or in larger groups (mass start). There is also the capability to run one, all or none of the variants.

Furthermore, the processing mode satisfies the team's requirement for flexible processing. There are three modes here:

In *foreground execution* mode, the test procedure is performed completely in the dialog. You can change or correct field inputs here. ENTER continues the dialog with the next picture.

In *background execution*, the transactions run without any dialog.

In *display only errors* mode, the transactions run without dialog until the first error occurs or the transaction is cancelled. A switch is then made into dialog mode. Incorrect inputs can be changed. ENTER continues the transaction until the next error occurs.

7.2.6   The log

A log is created for all test procedures. The log is organized hierarchically in accordance with the test modules and test procedures that are used. All inputs and messages are listed in the log. It is possible to navigate in this structure.

Starting with SAP R/3 Version 4.0, the log can be used to retest all parts of the test procedures using the same data. There is also the possibility choosing between a short and a long log. The download functionality from CATT can be used to load the logs to the workstation. There, a difference viewer, such as provided with MS Word, can be used to test the logs for differences.

7.2.7   Attributes and the Repository Information System

Many attributes can be stored for every test procedure and every test module. The following attributes, many of which are set automatically, can be changed:

- *Header data*
  Name of the test procedure/test module, status, type, original language, short, text, keywords for the search function

- *General data*
  Application/sub-application/component or inter-application, development class, priority

- *Administration data*
  Author, changed by, person with responsibility, updated for release, valid until release

- *Dependencies*
  Front-end, platform, language, country, context, usability (application test, individual test, platform test)

- *Flags*
  Test module, external TCD data, cancel flag, inactive, external variants, released

A search can be made in the Repository Information System of the SAP R/3 system for all attributes and references. This ensures that the teams retain an overview and that fast selection is possible, even when there are very many test procedures.

7.2.8 Test plan tool

To complement the structuring of test procedures, SAP developed the Test Workbench in the R/3 system. The uppermost structure element is the *test catalog* which contains all test procedures in a tree structure. In addition to this structuring functionality, the individual test procedures can be linked with the test catalog elements. There should be only one test catalog in the project (refer to Figure 7.5).

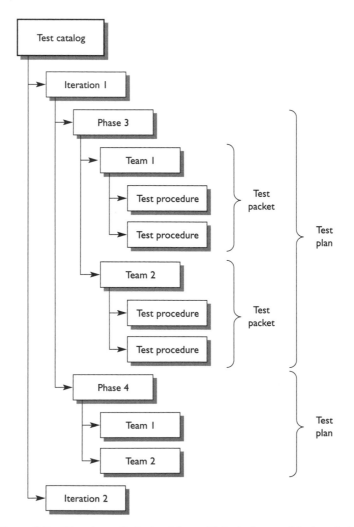

Figure 7.5   Structure of a test catalog with test plans and test packets

The *test plans* generated from the test catalog contain the test procedures for the individual iterations.

These test plans can also be used to generate *test packets* that contain the test activities of the individual teams and describe the concrete test tasks.

7.2.9   Assign status

The status of the individual test procedures can be used in the test packet to construct an administration. The individual status indicators can be assigned either automatically or manually. This makes it possible to recognize immediately which test procedures have not yet been handled. Table 7.2 shows the situations, status indicators and activities defined by SAP.

Table 7.2   Assign status

Situation	Status	Activities
You have not yet processed a test untested case.	untested	–
You wish to indicate that the work on a test case has been temporarily interrupted.	being processed	–
You have processed a test case and have not found any faults.	OK	–
You have mentioned faults that have only a limited effect on the use of the software (e.g., ergonomic weaknesses, inadequate user prompting).	OK with restrictions	Save explanation as processing note or record a problem message
You have complained about program errors or severe errors.	incorrect/retest	Record a problem message, note problem number as *recorded problem number*, update the *retest necessary* block.
You have determined during the testing of corrections that the original error has been corrected and no follow-up error is present.	retest OK	–

7.2.10   Criticism of CATT

The CATT tool also exhibits some weaknesses:

- Although values can be read from the status line, it is not possible to read any information from the individual masks.

- The contents of the individual reports cannot be processed in CATT.

- CATT cannot be used to analyze any selection lists.

- CATT supports only testing in the SAP system, but not the testing of external interfaces or supplementary programs.

In order to automate the testing in these areas, additional test tools, such as *Autotester Client/Server*, must be used (refer to Section 7.3.1).

7.3   CATT and DSDM

CATT is an ideal tool for testing SAP R/3 systems using the DSDM concept. As shown, the use of CATT makes the testing an integral part of the individual iterations. As soon as the team has represented a business process in the R/3 system, the users (and not the SAP experts) at the same time record the individual test procedures, which the SAP experts then combine as test procedures and structure in the test catalog. This provides the users and the SAP experts with a great deal of transparency on what has already been achieved.

CATT test procedures can also be run for subsequent iterations. This avoids previously accepted business processes being no longer executable after changes have been made to the customizing settings. The structure of test catalog, test plan and test packet is clearly documented as to what was tested, by which team, and in which phase.

The capability to make customizing settings using CATT procedures means that it is easy to reset old settings.

In phase 4, the test packets from the individual teams can be combined to form an integration test, which is used to ensure that the isolated processes in the SAP R/3 system also operate correctly outside the team limits. This results after several iterations in a modification of the setting for the SAP processes.

An additional advantage of CATT is that the tests developed there can also be used for training, manuals and help functions. Because the test is oriented to the business processes, it describes all business processes using examples from the user's viewpoint and returns all procedures as examples. In a training course, such procedures can initially be run in foreground and later repeated manually with other data. The existing CATT procedures can also be used to validate the assignment of master data and the initialization of the training system. The individual test descriptions can also be used for process-oriented help functions. Thus, CATT simply and easily satisfies the requirement for consistency in the documentation, the help and the training materials in every phase.

7.4   The AutoTester Client/Server

The AutoTester Client/Server product is an ideal addition to CATT and the test plan tool from SAP. In contrast to CATT, which operates at the transaction level, AutoTester operates at the presentation layer (refer to Figure 7.6).

Figure 7.6   AutoTester introductory screen

AutoTester also has a recording function that can be used in background to record all commands made to the R/3 system and then replay them later. This also takes account of actions that are not part of the CATT functionality:

- Read data fields.

- Read reports line by line.

- Search in selection lists.

- Check the authorization concept.

AutoTester provides its own script language which can be used to make changes to the recorded test procedures (refer to Figure 7.7).

AutoTester can also solve another test problem: the automation of those test procedures that are to be executed from the SAP R/3 system, such as for interfaces to old systems or with DP support for business processes, which operate both with SAP R/3 and also other products (e.g., scheduler, laboratory management systems). Because many errors arise in the interfaces as the result of a release change, it is very sensible to use this tool in this situation.

AutoTester logs all actions and the associated response times in the individual systems, and provides flexible functions for reporting (refer to Figure 7.8).

Similar to the test plan tool from SAP, the *AutoAdviser* provides the capability to store the test cases hierarchically and so structure test scenarios. The 'AutoController with Server Performance under Load Conditions', a new product from AutoTester, permits the simulation of hundreds of SAP R/3 users on a single machine. Because the response times of a new SAP R/3 release can be compared with those of an old release, this simulation is suitable for performance tests.

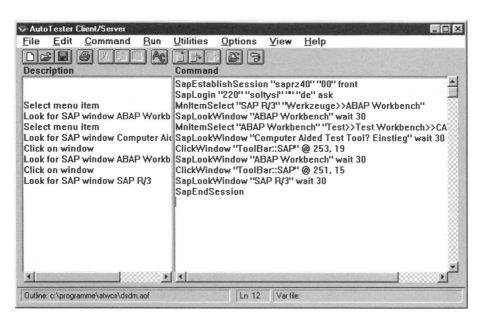

Figure 7.7   AutoTester sample script

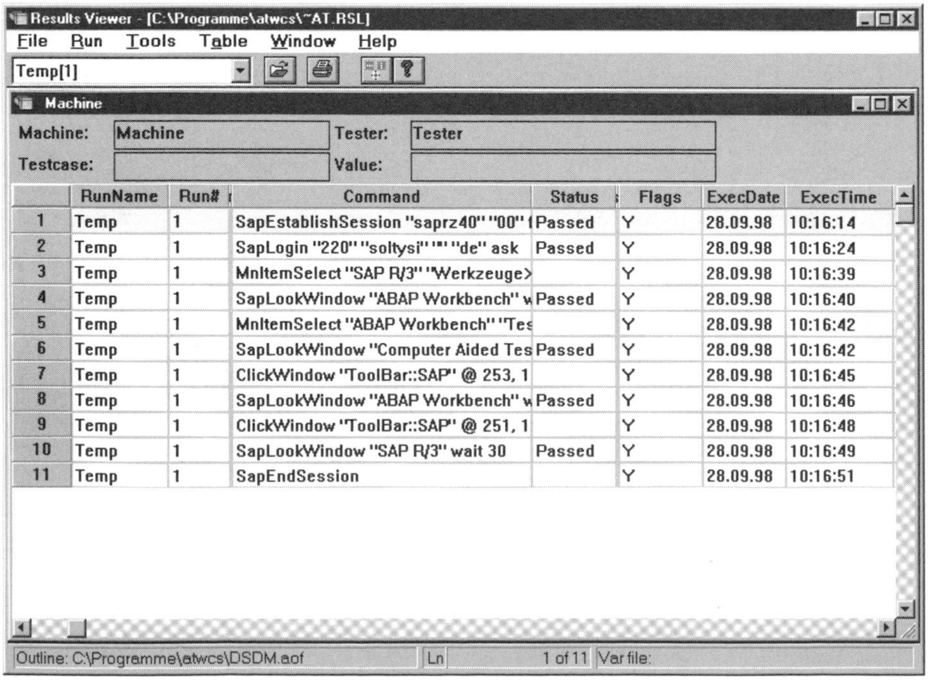

Figure 7.8   AutoTester log

7.5   Test methodology with CATT

Software development provides a wide range of methods for testing. The most important of these are (Balzert, 1998, p. 391):

- *Whitebox test of the modules*
  Select the test procedures using the program processing; this is appropriate when additional developments have been made (ABAP/4 Debugger).

- *Blackbox test of the modules*
  Test a software module (function module, screen); select the test data using the input and output parameters (ABAP/4 Tester).

- *Integration test*
  Test whether the business processes over module boundaries can be realized with SAP R/3 (CATT).

- *System test*
  Test whether the future SAP R/3 system runs without problems in the destination environment (CATT in the consolidation system).

- *Acceptance test*
  Test whether the users are satisfied with the user interface.

- *Performance test*
  Test whether the SAP R/3 system has respectable response times for both normal and heavy loading, (AutoController).

- *Regression test*
  Test whether after a release change the same functionality is available as previously (CATT).

Although the integration and regression tests are the most important test types in a DSDM-based SAP R/3 implementation, they can also be used to test whether the configured SAP R/3 system actually represents the described business processes. This requires an investigation as to whether the graphical business process descriptions can be converted into test procedures under CATT. This is the only means of ensuring that the SAP R/3 system supports every possible processing for a business process. This is an ideal method to synchronize the various viewpoints of the users and developers (refer to Figure 7.9).

This section describes a method that can be used to support this synchronization. It describes the individual work steps required to achieve this goal.

Check the prerequisites

Several prerequisites for testing must be satisfied in order to be able to make an appropriate implementation. All the business processes to be tested

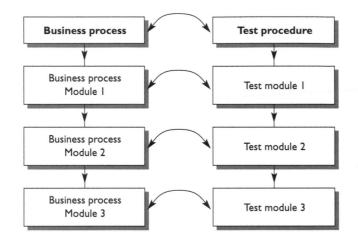

Figure 7.9   Synchronization of the business processes and the SAP system

- must be accepted by the DSDM team;
- must already be present in graphical form (e.g., as an event-controlled process chain or scenario);
- must have already been set in the SAP R/3 system.

Furthermore, a team member, preferably a user, should be capable of demonstrating on the SAP R/3 system the processing of business processes using selected sample data (refer to Figure 7.10).

Select concrete test paths

Every business process can normally be performed in many different ways. This work step determines typical paths through the business process as test paths. The test paths can be chosen either systematically or – when there is the danger that the number of combinations explodes – assigned a priority according to their importance for business support. As minimum, all individual functions of the business processes should occur as a test step on one test path (refer to Figure 7.11).

For example, the 'Acquire customer order' process consists of the following line sequence:

- Record customer inquiry.
- Record customer quotation with reference to the customer inquiry.
- Record customer order with reference to the customer quotation.

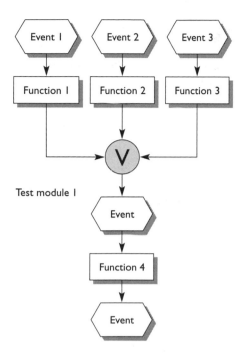

Figure 7.10   Representation of a business process

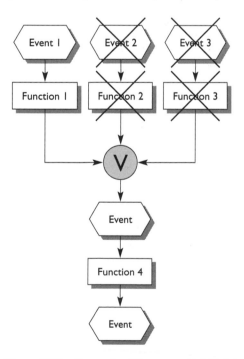

Figure 7.11   Example of the sequential division

Specify test data

The information to be entered in the individual masks must first be specified before it is possible to present the representation of a business process in the SAP R/3 system. It suffices to define one test data record per test path. The input values shown in Table 7.3 should be used for the sample process.

Table 7.3   Record the test data for the Customer Order process

Test step	Input	Value	Output
Record customer inquiry	Contracting party	101	
	Material	222	
	Quantity	100	
	Date	Current date	Inquiry number
Record customer quotation	Inquiry number	Last test step	Quotation number
Record customer order	Quotation number	Last test step	

Identify the transaction name

Every test path should be so refined that the individual test steps can be realized with a single SAP R/3 transaction. The transaction names can be determined using the status query in every mask (refer to Figure 7.12).

The names of the transactions are noted for the individual test steps. If a test step can be performed only with several transactions, the test path must be refined until every test step can be performed by a single transaction. Table 7.4 shows the transactions identified for the 'Record customer order' example.

Table 7.4   List of the transactions

Step	Transaction
Record customer inquiry	VA11
Record customer quotation with reference to inquiry	VA21
Record customer order with reference to quotation	VA01

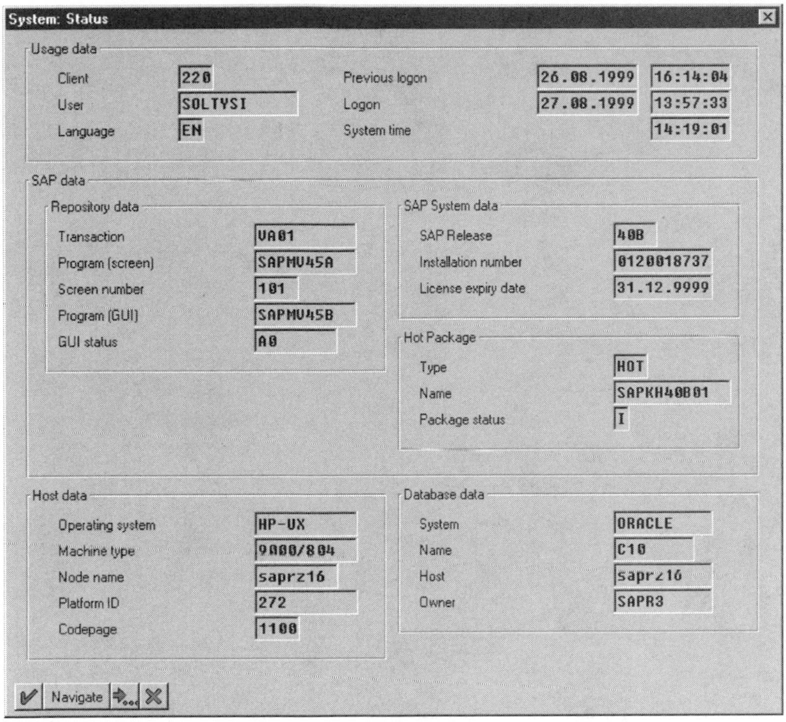

Figure 7.12 Transaction names using status query

Create test modules

A test module with CATT recording functionality for each test step is specified in this work step. The required transaction names and the test data have already been determined. The user should make the necessary entries (refer to Figure 7.13).

After this step, three CATT test modules exist for the example (refer to Table 7.5).

Table 7.5 Test modules for the example

Step	Transaction
Record customer inquiry	CREATE_INQUIRY
Record customer quotation with reference to inquiry	CREATE_QUOTATION
Record customer, order with reference to quotation	CREATE_ORDER

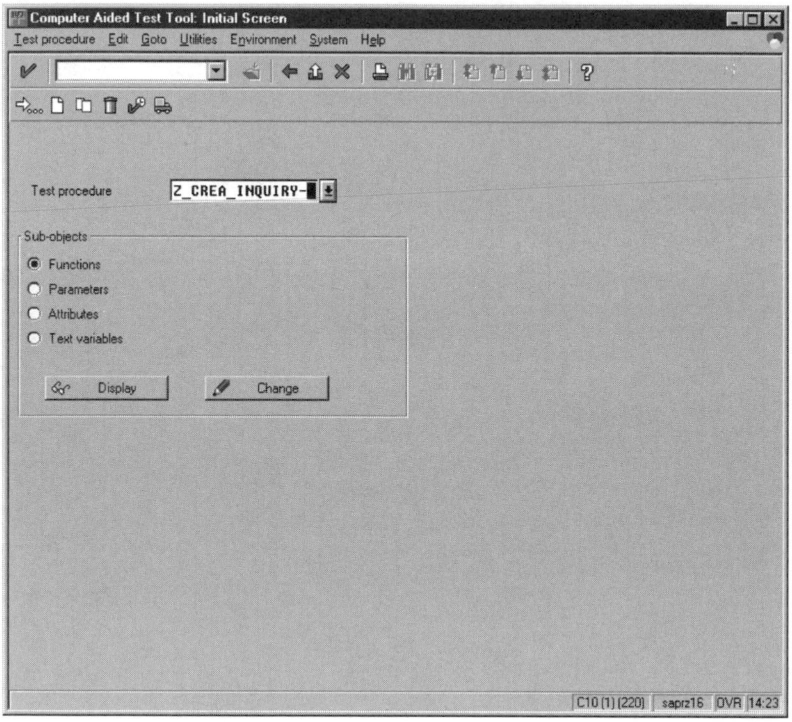

Figure 7.13   Enter a test module

Incorporate tests

Tests are added to every created test module. For example, they can query whether the transaction displays the expected message (refer to Figure 7.14).

Convert fixed values into parameters

In the CATT expert mode, the entered fixed values, such as those for the material number, can be converted into variable import parameters. This provides the prerequisite that this test module can be used for a range of input combinations. Furthermore, those output values to be used in subsequent test modules can be declared as export parameters (refer to Figures 7.15 and 7.16).

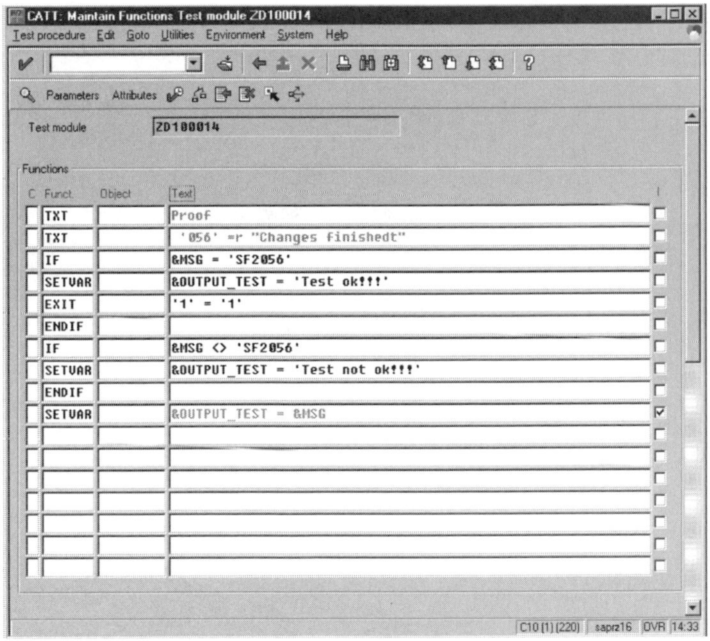

Figure 7.14   Tests in a CATT test module

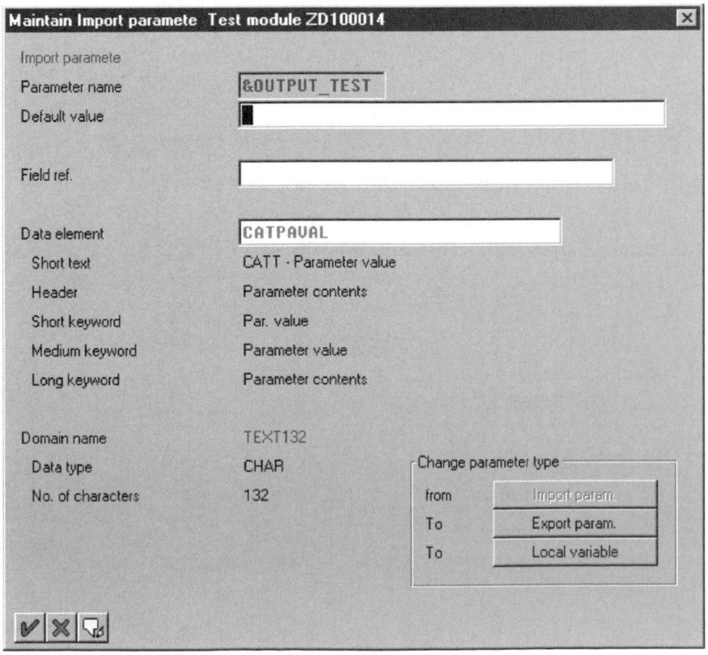

Figure 7.15   Import parameter declaration

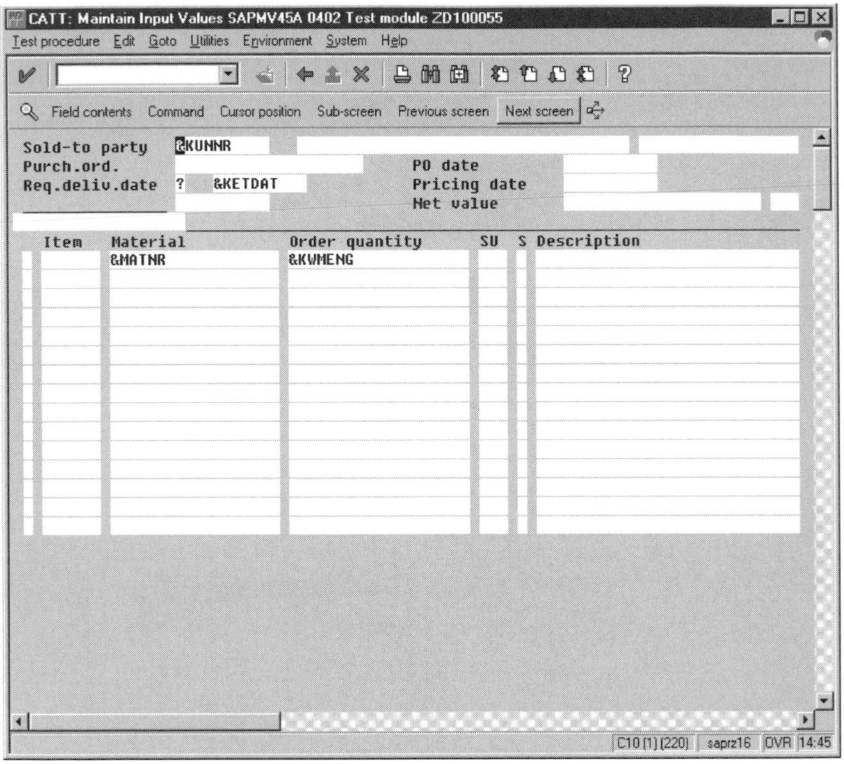

Figure 7.16   Parameterization in the expert mode

Create test procedures

For each test path a test procedure is formed from the associated test modules. The individual test modules are only referenced here. A test procedure CREATE_CUST_ORDER is created with the test modules (refer to Table 7.6, Figure 7.17) in the described example.

Table 7.6   CREATE_CUST_ORDER test procedure

CREATE_CUST_ORDER
CREATE_INQUIRY
CREATE_QUOTATION
CREATE_ORDER

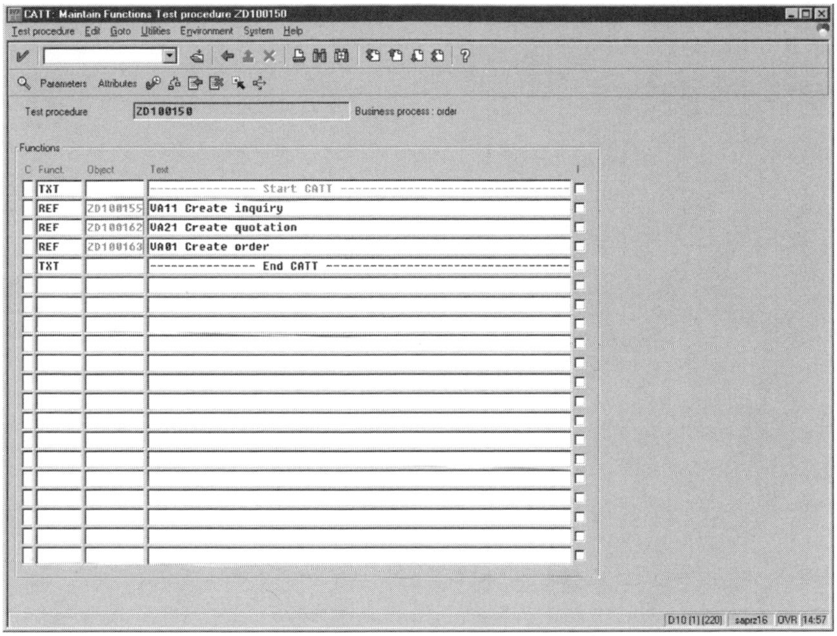

Figure 7.17   *CREATE_CUST_ORDER test procedure*

Link test modules

When the results of one test module are to serve as input for the next test module (inquiry number, quotation number), the corresponding parameters in the test procedure must be linked to each other (refer to Figures 7.18 and 7.19).

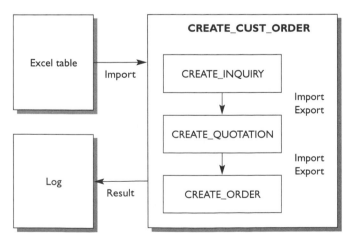

Figure 7.18   *Parameter passing scheme*

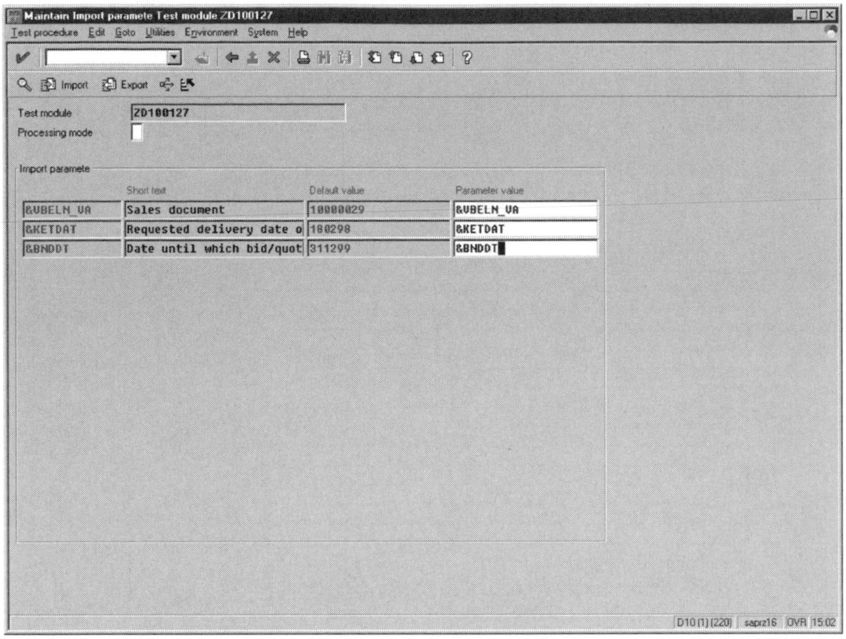

Figure 7.19   Linking test modules in the test procedure

Start test procedure

The now-completed test procedure can be started in various modes. The test procedure should initially run in foreground and then in background (refer to Figure 7.20).

Evaluate log

After every test pass, CATT automatically provides a log that documents all actions that occurred during the testing. This log should be carefully analyzed to determine whether all parameters have been passed without problem (refer to Figure 7.21).

Create variants

The completed test procedures have only a single test data record. This does not suffice for a comprehensive test. The creation of variants permits a large number of additional test data record sets to be stored as a table linked with the test procedure. In this step, for example, a single order can be generated for all contracting parties and all materials (refer to Figure 7.22).

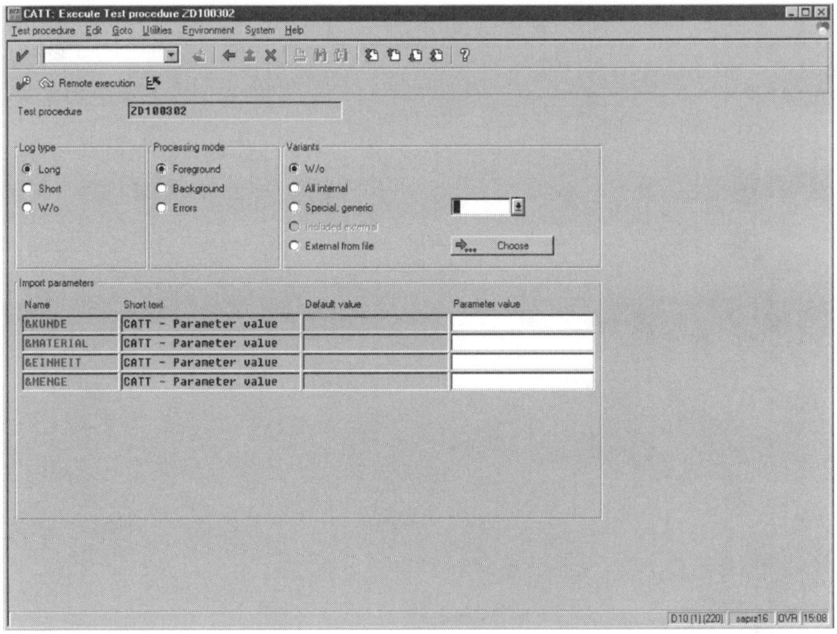

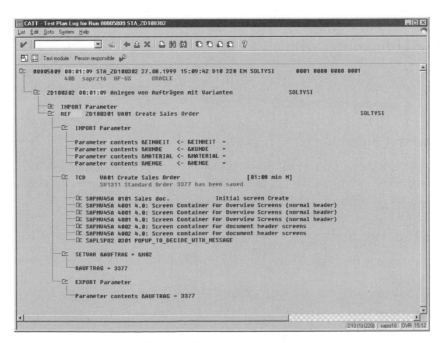

Figure 7.20   Start a test procedure

Figure 7.21   Log of a test pass

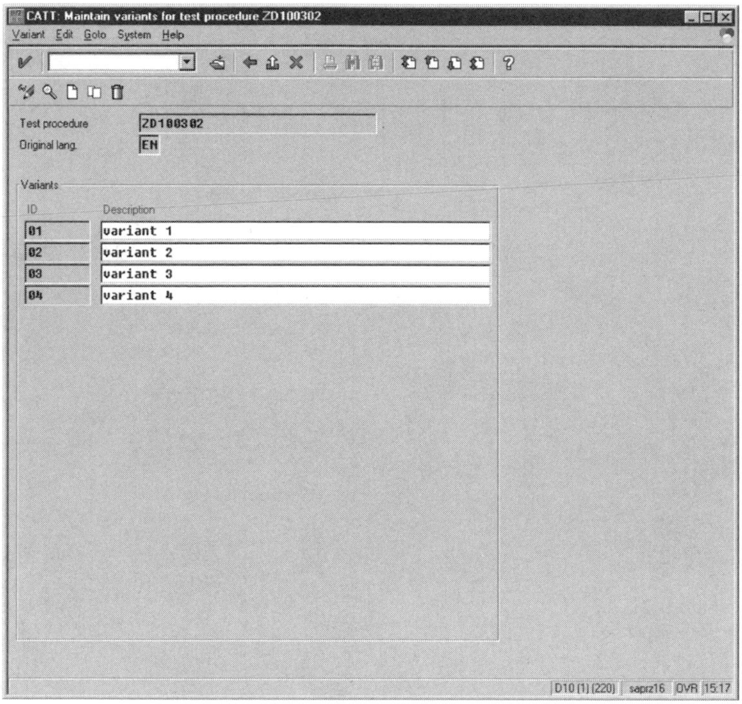

Figure 7.22   Variants

Start test procedures with all variants

This step should be performed only when the test procedure also runs without error in background mode. When the 'all variants' setting is used, the test procedure runs automatically in a loop over all variants.

Use the test plan tool

You should use the test plan tool provided with the SAP R/3 system even for a small number of test procedures. This tool can be used to structure all test procedures and manage the status flags. You should observe the following sequence here:

Create the test catalog

The test catalog is the central directory for all test procedures. Each project has just a single test catalog.

Structure the test catalog

Ideally the test catalog is structured according to teams, iterations, phases and business processes (refer to Figure 7.23).

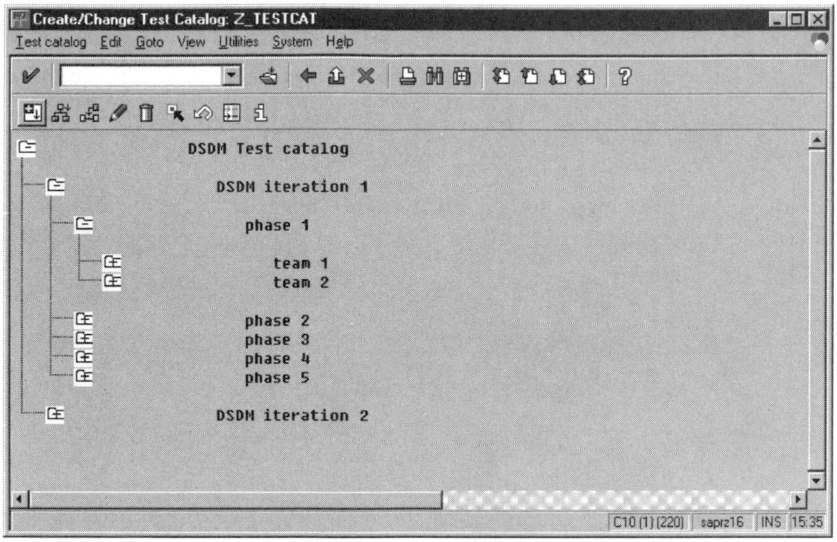

Figure 7.23   Test catalog structure

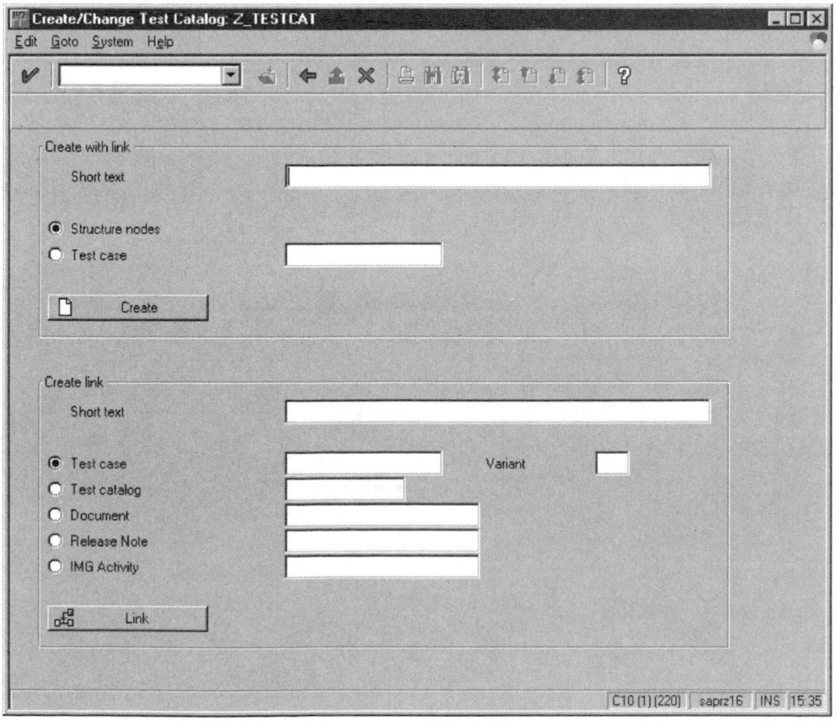

Figure 7.24   Link the CATT procedures with the test catalog

Link test procedures with the test catalog

The test procedures can be linked with the pages of the test catalog (refer to Figure 7.24).

Create test plan

A subtree from the test catalog can be generated as a test plan. This test plan, for example, can group all test procedures that belong to a certain release level of the SAP R/3 system (refer to Figure 7.25).

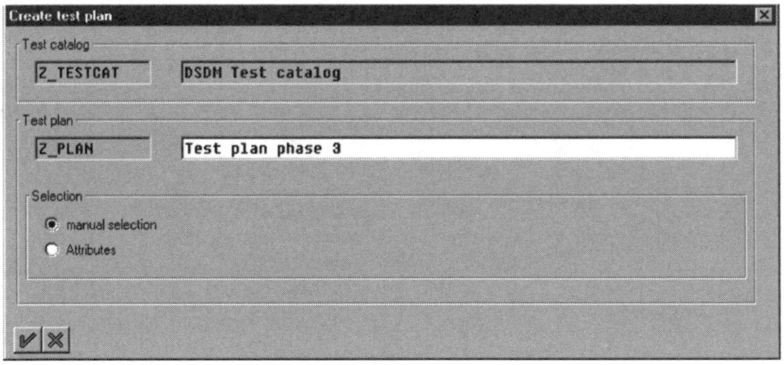

Figure 7.25   Test plan

Create a test packet

A test packet, which can be created for a test plan, specifies the test tasks to be performed (refer to Figure 7.26).

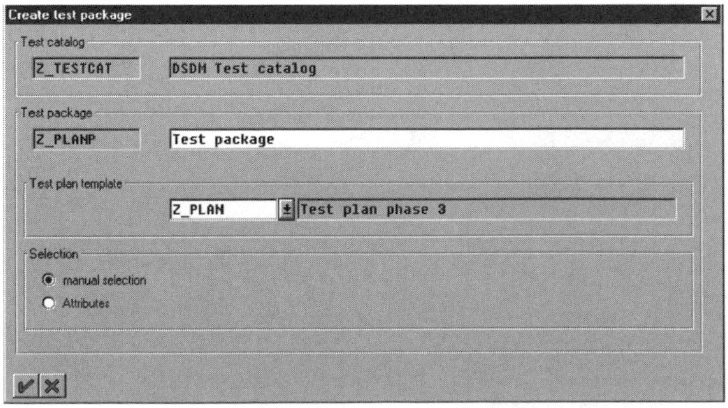

Figure 7.26   Test packet

Assign test packets

Because a test packet describes the specific concrete test tasks to be performed, someone responsible for the test must be assigned to every test packet (refer to Figure 7.27).

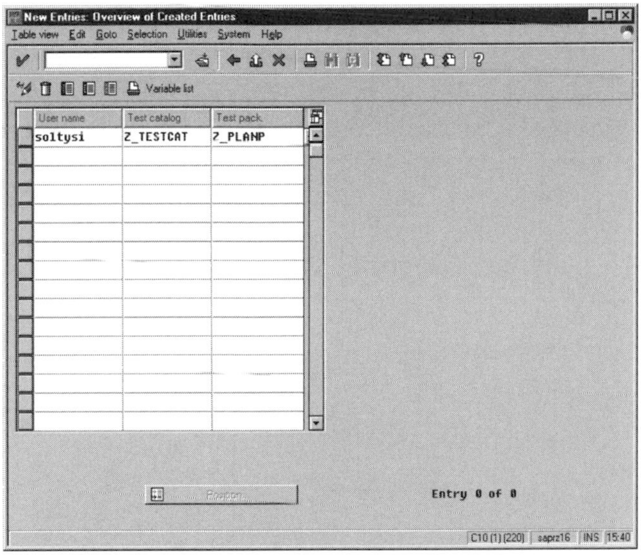

Figure 7.27   Assignment of the person responsible for the test

Execute test packets and assign a status

All test packets can now be executed automatically. A test status is assigned automatically or manually to every test run (refer to Figure 7.28).

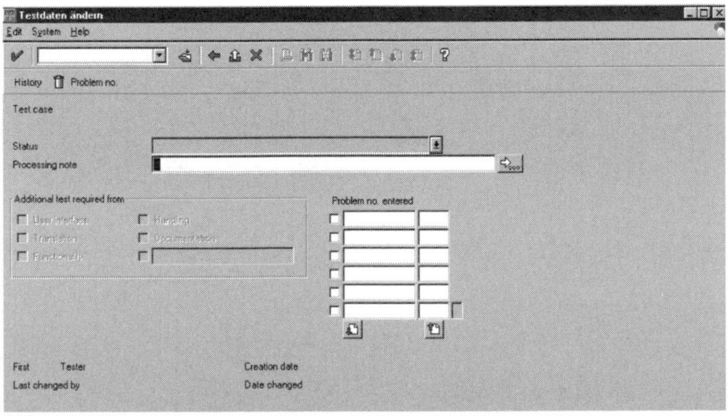

Figure 7.28   Assign test status

Archive logs

All test logs, which, for example, must be retained as proof of ISO 9000 conformance, can be archived so that they cause no further loading on the SAP R/3 system.

7.6 Summary

Testing is an important project activity that SAP supports through the provision of the Computer Aided Test Tool (CATT) and the test plan tool. CATT provides a recording functionality that even permits subsequent users of the SAP R/3 system to create test modules. All test procedures can be structured with the test plan tool. There is a method that checks whether the configured SAP R/3 system does actually cover the described business processes.

8 Quality assurance

Because of the dynamic development in DSDM-based SAP R/3 implementations, particular attention must be paid to quality management in such projects. If a company is certified in accordance with a standard such as ISO 9001, it must be proved that the SAP R/3 implementation also meets this standard. The DSDM method tries to burden the teams with as little bureaucratic activity as possible and provides help for successful quality audits.

The quality assurance plan is the most important instrument for effective quality assurance of the project. It describes all measures that affect quality assurance.

8.1 ISO 9000-3 and DSDM

ISO 9000-3 is the most important European standard for quality assurance in software development. It describes quality management for the development, supply and maintenance of software. ISO 9000-3 is divided into three main parts (Balzert, 1998, p. 327):

- *Frames*
  These indicate that the upper management of the contracting party and the supplier are responsible for quality, and describe which reviews are to be performed.

- *Life-cycle activities*
  These describe those aspects of quality assurance that require particular attention in the individual phases of the software project. These include specification of the requirements, the planning of the development, the planning of the individual phases, the testing and software acceptance.

- *Phase-independent activities*
  This section describes those aspects that can be important in every phase of the project. These include configuration management, the routeing of the documents, regulations, tools, acquisition and training.

The *British Standards Institution (BSI)*, together with the DSDM Consortium, has issued the 'The Dynamic Systems Development Method & TickIT' guide that describes how DSDM software development projects should be realized in order to satisfy the requirements of ISO 9000-3 (TickIT, 1997).

This guide contains a short introduction to DSDM, a guide for customers, suppliers and the auditor. In accordance with the organization of the Standard, a discussion of the individual requirements is also provided.

8.2   The Capability Maturity Model (CMM) and DSDM

The *Capability Maturity Model* (*CMM*) is the most important standard in the USA for quality assurance in software development. The CMM is a model that can be used to determine the maturity of software development processes and so permit specific improvements to be made (Mellis, et al., 1996, p. 95). Several *key process areas* are defined for every maturity level. A questionnaire should be used to determine whether these key process areas are appropriate in the company under consideration (Balzert, 1998, p. 361) (refer to Figure 8.1).

There are five maturity levels in CMM:

- *Level 1: Initial process*
  The development process is done ad hoc and chaotically, and no prediction can be made for the resulting costs, the required time or the achieved quality. The success of the projects depends less on the company organization and more on the capabilities of the individual employees. A company that wishes to attain the second maturity level must improve or even implement planning, progress monitoring, change management and quality assurance.

- *Level 2: Repeatable process*
  Whereas fundamental management processes such as management of projects, configurations, tests and quality have been established, there are problems with completing on time and with the quality produced. However, those projects that have already been realized successfully can be repeated with similar success. A company that wishes to attain the third level of maturity must develop process standards and introduce a methodology.

- *Level 3: Defined process*
  The development process is a qualitative process with reliable cost estimates and deadlines. Although the quality has been improved, it still cannot be predicted. There exist

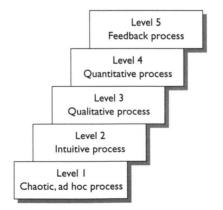

Figure 8.1   CMM display

documented project standards and the development process is independent of the individual team members. A company that wishes to attain the fourth level of maturity must measure and analyze its processes, and implement a quantitative quality assurance programme.

- *Level 4: Controlled process*
  The software development process can be controlled. The quality can be predicted and is subject to detailed measurements.

- *Level 5: Optimized process*
  The software development process can be controlled and is being continually improved. The improvements are achieved through a feedback of the quality measurement results from the process and the testing, and through innovative ideas and technologies.

So-called *key process areas* provide a more detailed description of each of these levels. Because DSDM covers all key process areas of the second level of maturity in accordance with CMM, companies that use DSDM are automatically at this level. The definition of the second level of maturity implies that through the planning, supervision and control of the time requirements, the costs and the quality, all basic project management tasks are satisfied.

8.3   Quality assurance in the traditional SAP procedure model

The SAP procedure model does not envisage the use of quality assurance measures after the first three phases.

- After the first phase (organization and conceptual design), the planned concept, the project structure and processing organization, adherence to the project standards, the system landscape, the interface and system extension descriptions and the project planning are checked against the associated specifications. A check log is then produced and the release of the next phase initiated.

- The application system, the project structure organization and project processing organization, the project standards, the implementation of the design concept, the realization of interfaces and system extensions, the report system, archive management, the correction concept, the system test and the project planning are tested at the end of the second phase (detailed planning and system set-up).
  Once again a check log is produced and the release of the next phase initiated.

- The productive system, the user documentation, the productive environment, the user training performed, the organization of the system administration, data acceptance and the project planning are tested for their quality at the end of the third phase (preparation for going live). Once again a check log is produced and the release of the next phase initiated.

- No further quality test is made after the fourth phase (live operation). Although the SAP procedure model provides a detailed guide for every test, no reference to the international standards is made.

8.4   DSDM and SAP

In contrast, in the DSDM-based procedure model, because of the fluid phase transitions and the non-uniquely prescribed way through the model, there are no longer any clearly defined milestones. This then raises the question: when and how should quality assurance activities be performed in DSDM projects?

The DSDM-based procedure model no longer has a few large milestones, but many small milestones. These milestones must occur at the end of every timebox and at the end of the complete DSDM iteration. In addition, it may be necessary to perform milestone sessions on demand. This can take place at the end of each prototyping iteration in a small group, i.e., within the teams, or in a larger group, i.e., together with the affected user groups in the form of demonstrations of the prototypes.

8.5   The quality assurance plan

The DSDM procedure model contains few details for a *quality assurance plan* (QAP), but instead refers to the existing standards (e.g., IEEE Standard 730–1989). Also, with regard to a possible request to supply proof that the project has been realized using an appropriate standard, e.g., ISO 9000-3, it is important to produce a quality assurance plan for the project. The quality assurance plan describes all quality assurance measures that were used in the project. The size of the QAP should be kept sufficiently short so that it can also serve as an aid for the teams. It should contain only that information that the teams require for their day-to-day work. It should also be accepted by all team members. The following section shows an example of a QAP that has proved itself in practice. This QAP is based on the requirements specified in the IEEE standard.

The IEEE 730-1989 Standard makes a suggestion as to how the QAP should be structured. This suggestion must be adapted to cater for the changed situation regarding the procedure model and the implementation of SAP R/3. This QAP should be changed during the project if it causes too much bureaucracy or if the QAP does not provide any business benefits. Someone with responsibility should be appointed for all the following topics.

8.5.1   The title page

The title page should contain at least the name of the project, the type of the document ('quality assurance plan' in this case), the name of the person responsible for the QAP, the version number, and the status of the QAP.

8.5.2 History

The QAP is not a document that is defined at the start of a project and then never changed. Rather, the plan should be continually adapted to meet the needs of the teams. This requires maintaining a table with the change history of the plan that contains at least the following information: version, status, reason for making the change, name of the person who made the change, date.

8.5.3 Referenced documents

This section lists all documents referenced in the plan. These can be general standards or internal guidelines.

These references could include the following documents:

- *ISO 9000, Part 3* – Guide for the development, supply and maintenance of software
- *IEEE 730-1989* – IEEE Standard for Software Quality Assurance Plans
- *IEEE 828-1990* – IEEE Standard for Software Configuration Management Plans
- QM manual for the enterprise based on ISO 9001, if present
- DSDM Version 3 methods manual
- The Dynamic Systems Development Method & TickIT (guidance to assist software developers using DSDM to meet the requirements of ISO 9001)

8.5.4 Implementation

This section provides a short overview of the goals and the content of the QAP. The following questions have proved themselves:

- What effect does the project have on the quality management manual?
- What quality demands does the quality management manual have on the project?
- How is the quality management organized?
- What are the quality goals of the project?
- Which procedure model is used?
- Which reviews are performed, and how are they structured?
- Which tests are performed, and how are they structured?
- Which documents are produced during the project lifetime, and where are they stored?
- Which tools, methods and models are used to process the documents?
- How are problems reported and processed?
- What training is required to perform quality management?

- What are the risks of the project?

- What means are used to ensure that all those involved are informed adequately and on time?

- How are the data backups organized?

8.5.5 Terms

The wide range of terms creates a large problem during the day-to-day work in the teams. The SAP R/3 terminology is normally different from that used in the company. SAP has tried to counter this problem by issuing a comprehensive glossary. However, normally a reference between the SAP R/3 terms and the current terminology in the company does not exist. Although DSDM avoids the problem through close cooperation between users and developers, it should still be made clear at the start of the project whether a terminology list or reference list is to be maintained. The teams should be responsible for the decision, and they should also maintain the entries.

8.5.6 QA management for the project

This section describes how quality assurance is organized. In accordance with DSDM, the project manager has overall responsibility for quality. There should also be two quality assurance representatives for the project: one from the information system department and one from the user's division who represents the interests of the general quality management.

8.5.7 Reference to the QM manual in the company

If a quality management (QM) manual exists in the enterprise, this section describes how the quality assurance plan relates to this manual, and in particular, how the changed business processes can be integrated in the QM manual.

8.5.8 Quality goals and measurement

The most important quality goal in DSDM projects is to provide the maximum possible support for the business system. This includes the observance of cost restrictions and deadlines, and providing a high level of maintainability.

The goals can be measured through informal questioning of the teams.

8.5.9 Procedure model

This section should document that the project is to be realized using the DSDM procedure model. The fundamentals should at least be listed and references to the relationship between DSDM and the international standards emphasized.

8.5.10 Reviews

This section describes at which parts of the project (e.g., after every timebox and after every iteration) a quality check should be made. It also describes which tests take place in these reviews (tests, documentation, configuration, etc.).

Various questions are posed in the DSDM manual. Some of these follow here (DSDM Consortium 1997, p. 149):

- Have the goals been achieved?

- Are the users sufficiently involved?

- Are the users authorized to make decisions?

- Have the results from the prototyping been used?

- Have the priorities been taken into consideration?

- Have the timeboxes been met?

8.5.11 Tests

This section not only describes how the individual tests are performed within these timeboxes using CATT, but also the appearance of the individual tests and thus the associated test recordings.

8.5.12 Configuration management

This section describes how configuration management (CM) is organized and how SAP R/3 tools should be used. These tools can be the Change and Transport Organizer (CTO), the Document Management System (DMS), SAPoffice or others. It describes where the individual software elements are stored and how it is possible to ensure that every project member has access to the required information.

8.5.13 Quality questions concerning the products

Every software project produces a number of products. This also applies to SAP R/3 projects. and especially those SAP R/3 projects that have been implemented with the DSDM-based procedure model. These products consist not only of such things as project plans, customizing settings, business process descriptions, test plans and documentation, but also the trained end-users. The DSDM manual specifies which products must be produced in which phase. who is responsible for their acceptance, with which goal they are to be produced, and which quality criteria are to be tested in a review to determine whether they have been satisfied. Although the individual products are assigned to specific phases of the DSDM model, they can be extended or improved during the project in other phases (DSDM Consortium, 1997, p. 81).

Feasibility study

The feasibility report describes many aspects of the project at a very high level: project goals, affected business processes, required interfaces, restrictions, hardware requirements, and expected changes to the business processes as the result of the SAP R/3 implementation.

- Does the problem definition conform to the goals of senior management from the user department?
- Is the project goal sufficiently clear so that it can be further refined during the project?
- Are the business and technical goals achievable?
- Can DSDM be used?
- Has management agreed what belongs to the project, and what not?
- Have all associated external systems been identified?

Feasibility prototype

The feasibility prototype should provide a first impression of the SAP R/3 system and, through its 'look and feel', support the feasibility report. The IDES training system from SAP is useful for this purpose in an SAP R/3 project. SAP also provides many presentations that can be used to provide a first impression of the software.

- Does the prototype provide benefits for the feasibility study?
- Does the prototype support the decision-making process with regard to the use of DSDM?

Project outline plan

The outline plan describes the organizational aspects of the project. These include: costs, resources, time frame, acceptance criteria, ensuring that management allows the development teams to make their own decisions, configuration management, test management, risks, project standards, external factors that can affect the project. An investigation is also made whether DSDM can be used as method.

- Are the cost and manpower estimates realistic?
- Are the time estimates consistent with regard to the business benefits?
- Have the business benefits of the supplied products been described?
- Can the user department management provide the necessary users?
- Can the IS management provide sufficient developers?
- Are configuration management, change management, and testing organized in accordance with the DSDM principles?
- Can all required computers and rooms be made available?

- Have the acceptance criteria for the product been described – also for the changed requirements?

- Have all expected standards and regulations been described, or has sufficient time been planned in the project for their development or acquisition?

Definition of the business area

The definition of the business area identifies those business fields that the SAP system is to support. This can be done using the reference model. Furthermore, the outline plan is refined with regard to the benefits, risks, costs, changes in the business processes and interfaces. The user groups that will later work with the R/3 system are also specified.

- Have the business context, the business processes and the business goals been defined and agreed?

- Have all requirements been assigned a priority?

- Have the priorities been agreed with the users?

- Have general acceptance criteria for the delivered system been agreed?

- Have the business areas been clearly documented?

- Have the risks been taken into consideration in the time frame?

- Have all classes of end-users been identified for the new system?

- Is it still clear that the new system must increase the business benefits?

- Has a person been appointed to be responsible for every business process?

- Have all important business events been identified?

Prioritized requirements list

The prioritized requirements list describes and assigns priorities to the expected functions of the SAP R/3 system. It is part of the definition of the business area.

- Have all identified requirements been assigned a priority?

- Have all the priorities been discussed with the users?

- Does the user department management accept that those requirements with a lower rating may need to be realized later?

Definition of the system architecture

The definition of the system architecture describes the technical structure of the SAP R/3 system. Because this system allows many technical possibilities, it should be decided here which hardware, operating system database system, front-end system and network are to be used.

- Is the system architecture appropriate for the requirements?

- Have the risks for the selected architecture been considered; in particular, can all components be delivered and are they compatible?

- Is the migration from the development platform to the target platform easy to realize? If not, have all possible problems been identified?

- Can the architecture be changed without difficulty after the project has started?

Prototype outline plan

The prototype outline plan refines the outline plan for the functional phases, and the design and build iteration phases. Planning is made to determine which types of prototypes are expected in which phase and which priorities they should have. Those persons who are to work on the individual iterations are also assigned here. In addition, the type of configuration management and the test methods to be used are also specified.

- Do the time periods agree with the planned business goals in the feasibility study and in the business area definition?

- Does the sequence of activities within the prototyping plan correspond to the list of prioritized requirements?

- Has the plan taken account of the risk areas for time estimation?

- Can all the user classes involved identify themselves with the prototyping plan?

- Does the required user involvement take account of the work they reed to do for existing activities?

- Will the user involvement be possible when the project needs them?

- Is the configuration management suitable for the business area definition?

- Is the configuration management method adequate for the systems used?

- Does the extent, depth and degree of formality of the testing meet the requirements?

Functional model

The functional model describes all those functions and data requests in the project that are important for the company. It should also be possible to derive the non-functional requirements.

- Does the functional model meet the user's requirements as developed in discussions and prototypes?

- Does it meet the goals of the business area definition?

- Do all parts of the functional model satisfy a test of consistency?

- Does the model have a minimum-usable subset?

- Does the functional model cater for all essential aspects of integrity and security?

- Is the consistency of all static models (data model) satisfied with regard to the functional prototypes and vice versa?

- Does the model provide confidence that the correct degree of performance, capacity and maintainability is achieved?

- Is all necessary documentation available and at an appropriate standard?

Functional prototypes

The functional prototypes demonstrate the feasibility of the functional requirements. The users can see whether they can use the set system to perform their day-to-day work. This provides agreement as to the direction in which the project should continue.

- Are all documents available in the development environment?

- Have all important interfaces been clarified?

- Is it probable that some interfaces can also be realized later?

- Are all important business process requirements apparent in the prototypes: if not, is supplementary support documentation available?

- Are all important data apparent in the prototypes; if not, is supplementary support documentation available?

- Have all non-functional requirements been clearly mentioned in the functional prototypes?

Non-functional requirements list

This document describes the non-functional requirements list in more detail for the design and build phase.

- Are all non-functional requirements quantified in sufficient detail?

- If non-functional requirements have already been addressed by the functional prototypes, has this been documented?

- Have all areas of the feasibility study been considered?

- Is the group of non-functional requirements consistent in itself and does not contradict the functional requirements?

- Do all non-functional requirements provide benefits for the company?

- Are all non-functional requirements realistic and realizable?

Review histories for the functional model

The feedback from users concerning the functions of the prototypes is recorded in the review histories. This supports the subsequent planning, because any following projects can make use of this information.

- Were all functional prototypes discussed in the review?

- Have all user comments been noted to the user's satisfaction?

- Has the user department management agreed to all those areas for which the user wishes further development?

- Have all unsolved problems been described for management or for technical coordination?

- Has all information been noted for those prototypes that do not meet the expectations?

- Have all areas that are to be frozen been described?

Implementation strategy

The implementation strategy refines the project plan for the subsequent phases and so provides the management with the means to judge the accumulated and future costs.

- Do the design and build time-frames still meet the business recruitments?

- Are the cost and manpower estimates (for both users and developers) adequate to fulfil the plan?

- Have the procedures to hand-over for maintenance and to the support personnel been clearly formulated?

- Have the procedures for data acceptance or system acceptance been adequately described?

Risk analysis

The risk analysis report produced during the whole project helps the management evaluate the project for the future.

- Have all factors that endanger the success of the project been described?

- Have all risks been described in sufficient detail to enable a decision to be made?

Design prototype

The design prototype is used to demonstrate that the non-functional requirements can also be fulfilled.

- Can the prototype describe the requirements?

- Have all design risks been clearly identified?

- Does the design represent all user requirements?

- Does the design conform to all development standards and regulations?

Review histories for the design prototype

The review histories record the feedback from the users concerning the design prototypes. This information provides support for the subsequent planning and is available for any follow-up projects.

- Does the review document refer to all design prototypes?

- Have all comments from users and developers been recorded to their satisfaction?

Tested system

The tested system is ready to be accepted for production. It meets all functional and non-functional requirements, and can be accepted into the end-user's system environment.

- Does the tested system satisfy all the user's acceptance criteria?

- Can the developers guarantee that the system is robust enough for operative use?

- Was the system tested sufficiently so that it can be used?

- Is it evident that all expected requirements have been tested and, where necessary, presented to the users?

- Have all security-relevant and reliability aspects been validated?

- Have all functions required for the implementation phase been tested (data acceptance. conversion)?

- Can all components of the tested system be executed stepwise in accordance with the functional model?

- Have all components that were rejected in the design review been removed from the system?

- Is the system documentation consistent with the software?

Test histories

The test histories show that the development took place analogously to the test plan.

- Have all tests been documented sufficiently?

- Has the test specification been subjected to a review?

- Has it been recorded that all tests took place and that the users were involved in the tests?

- Have all problems that arose during the testing been noted and corrected?

- Have adequate regression tests been performed?

- Have the tests been described in sufficient detail so that they can be repeated in the future?

User documentation

The user documentation describes how the end-users can use the supplied system.

- Is the user documentation accessible for all users, and is it available in an appropriate format (as file, in paper form, as help file)?
- Does it contain a clearly understandable step-by-step guide for the supplied system?
- Does it explain how the system works in conjunction with other systems (manually or otherwise)?
- Does it cover all functionalities supplied with the system?
- If different classes of user are present, is an explanation provided as to who should read which sections?
- Is it easy to 'jump' through the user's guide for business-process oriented tasks?
- Is it written in language that is understandable to the users?
- Does it provide, when necessary, step-by-step instructions for manual tasks associated with the system?
- Does it contain instructions on what needs to be done should errors occur (e.g., who can be asked, standard problem solutions)?
- Does it contain a tutorial? Is it easy to read? Have the users tried it out?

Trained user population

All users are able to operate the system.

- Do the trained users have adequate knowledge and capabilities to work with the system?
- Have all the users involved received training?
- Are the seminar notes available for future users?
- Is the user documentation readily available for all users?
- Is there a training strategy for future users?
- Is there a training strategy for users should there be system extensions?

Supplied system

The supplied system is the actual end product.

- Have all changes made to the tested system been accepted, implemented and retested?
- Does the system operate as expected in the target environment?
- Can it be operated at the planned service level?

- Are there unexpected problems in the target environment that still need to be solved?

- Have all data been accepted and conversions completed successfully?

- Have all configuration modules been archived securely?

- Have the correct versions of every configuration been recorded?

- Have all outstanding problems been documented?

Project review document

The project review document judges the success of the project, and describes decisions about any future work and results that can be used on other projects.

- Have all areas not considered in this project been documented?

- Has management been supplied with sufficient information so that they can decide whether further development is to be made in the future?

- Have the lessons that were learnt during the project been documented?

Customizing description

The customizing description is produced in the implementation guide (IMG). All customizing settings must be documented.

- Have all the performed customizing settings been documented?

- Is the documentation easily understandable?

- Has a reference been made to the business processes?

Administration guide

The administration guide describes all procedures required to administer the system. These include, for example, the organization of user administration, a description of valid systems and clients, and data backup.

- Has it been described how to set up new users?

- Has it been described who can change user rights?

- Has it been described which systems and clients can be used for which tasks?

- Are there administrative tasks that have not been documented?

Seminar notes

The seminar notes are produced to satisfy two requirements: to provide a reference for previously trained users, and to give new users a source material that they can use to become acquainted with the system. The seminar notes also include a seminar plan that provides details of who is to be trained, when, where, about what and by whom.

- Are seminar notes provided for every business process?

- Are the seminar notes up to date (SAP R/3 version, changes to business processes)?

- Is the form of the seminar notes appropriate?

- Are the seminar notes available?

8.5.14 Tools and guidelines

This section describes which tools and guidelines are to be used for the project. These can be internal programming guidelines or other standards.

The programs used as tools are listed with their version number and the tasks for which they are appropriate.

8.5.15 Problem reporting

This section describes which procedures have been defined for problem reporting. When a user or developer is confronted with a problem, he is provided with a detailed description of how to solve the problem.

8.6   Summary

Quality management plays a major role in DSDM-based projects. Despite the very dynamic character of this method, it is still possible to produce certifiable procedures in accordance with international standards when a carefully defined quality assurance plan is used. However, the quality assurance should be as non-bureaucratic as possible, and, in particular, serve the business benefits.

9 Communication in the project

In a DSDM-based project, all persons involved in the project work more closely together than in traditional projects. This means that the structure of communication in such projects has become a major success factor. This fact should be taken into consideration in project planning so that the correct selection of the project members and their roles in the project team favours successful project progress. The DSDM model describes various roles, for which it is essential that suitable employees are assigned.

A further possibility of improving communication is to hold workshops. They serve to speed up communication and to develop new ideas.

The size and the form of the project teams also play an important role in communication.

Particular attention should be paid to ensuring that a project culture grows in which the teams can work productively together. The methods of topic-centred interaction provide information here.

9.1 Roles in the project

Great care must be taken in the selection of project members. It is essential that various roles for the project have been assigned. However, one person can also be assigned to several roles. DSDM demands the assignment of the following roles (DSDM Consortium, 1997, p. 107):

The executive sponsor

The executive sponsor is the true ordering party for the SAP R/3 system. He should belong to top management and demand fast project progress, reduce unnecessary bureaucracy and make decisions quickly. He ensures that the users involved are indeed released from their normal work and that sufficient financial resources are made available.

The ambassador

The ambassador must be accepted by all users – not just the management – so that he can also enforce decisions that cause changes in the procedure or the assignment of priorities. If the decision processes take too long, this can be caused by too many ambassadors belonging to the team. Their number should be reduced in this case.

The visionary

The visionary has a view of the business that is more global (helicopter perspective). He is involved with the feasibility study and the business study, and should also be included in the development process to avoid the work drifting away from the business needs. Often a single person combines the tasks of the ambassador and the visionary.

The consulting users

Consulting users are not active during the complete project, but only during evaluation and for the testing of important prototypes. The consulting users pass their experience on to all users. Because of their detailed knowledge of the business, they can very quickly judge the business suitability of the prototypes developed by the teams.

The project manager

The project manager who undertakes the supervisory role for the teams can come either from the commercial or the information processing side. However, it is important that he has sufficient knowledge of both areas and can appreciate the user's viewpoint. Obviously, he must provide the usual qualities of a project manager, such as communication ability. The project manager cooperates closely with the lead consultant from the external business consultancy and should ideally have an established SAP R/3 knowledge gained in many implementation projects. This close cooperation in project management should result in a knowledge transfer, which in the course of time should permit the project manager to perform all significant project tasks independently.

The technical coordinator

The technical coordinator is responsible for ensuring that the SAP R/3 system and the complete technical environment are available to all those involved with the project. He must also promote the use of SAP tools, such as CATT or CTO. He must have detailed knowledge of the basis system and the inter-component functions of the SAP R/3 system. It is quite possible that he also has responsibility for configuration management and quality management.

The team leaders

The team leaders must have good communicative capabilities so that they can provide good guidance for the team and also justify the results to the project manager. They have good knowledge of both the business processes and the SAP R/3 system. They motivate the team and ensure a productive working atmosphere. The team leaders report to the project manager.

The SAP experts

The SAP experts should have many years of experience with SAP projects. Although they are experts in the customizing of many modules, even less-experienced employees can also be involved in this role in the project. However, to ensure that project progress is not slowed, it is important that novices are not used exclusively.

The workshop moderator/organizer

The workshop moderator/organizer does not belong to the project team. He is responsible for the context but not for the content of the individual workshops. His area of responsibility involves obtaining agreement on the goals, performing the planning, presenting the results and ensuring that all preliminary work has been done. He also has the task of investigating whether the set goals have been achieved.

The transcript writer

The transcript writer attends the team sessions and documents all important items. These items should be presented to the team for them to agree on the written formulation. Important items are: decisions, outstanding questions, business process descriptions. The transcript writer should have an easily understandable writing style, and possess both business and technical knowledge.

The specialists

Specialists work periodically in the teams to speed up the development process through their knowledge. Specialists can be, for example, business consultants, business modellers, technical consultants, specialists for user interfaces, or planners for the capacity and performance of the SAP R/3 system.

9.2 Team structures

The individual teams in SAP R/3 implementation projects using the DSDM-based procedure model consist of developers, users and a team leader. Further specialists can also be brought into the project, such as internal or external consultants, a quality manager or a configuration manager (DSDM Consortium, 1997, p. 99).

We suggest two to four members, but certainly not more than six persons, as the team size, half of whom should be employees from the user department (namely the users). The team is complemented with SAP R/3 specialists who provide special capabilities in business process modelling and customizing. Although the SAP R/3 specialists in the first DSDM phases will probably be external consultants, attention should be paid to ensuring that internal employees adopt their roles over the course of time, so that finally there will be no need for consultants.

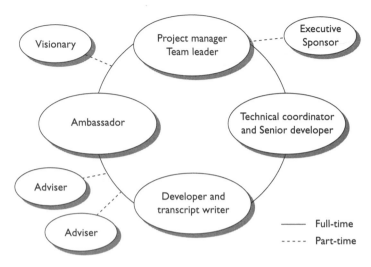

Figure 9.1   Example of a project structure for small projects

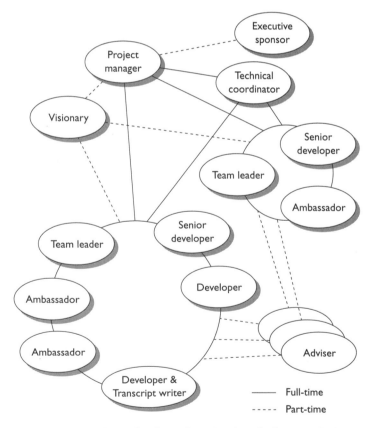

Figure 9.2   Example of a project structure for large projects

If possible, the team members should work full-time in the project. For limited periods of time, employees with other roles can be brought into the team. Figure 9.1 shows a typical project structure for small SAP projects. The technical coordinator and the SAP expert are a single person in this example. This is also the case for the project manager and the team leader.

Because the size of the teams is restricted, larger projects can only be realized with several teams. Naturally, different people occupy the various roles in the project. Figure 9.2 shows the project structure for a larger project.

9.3   Workshops

The traditional SAP procedure model or the ASAP approach places much value on holding appropriate workshops. An example is the guide for performing a workshop for the kick-off meeting of the implementation project.

From the SAP viewpoint, the goal of such workshops is to bring all the members involved together, to emphasize common goals, to motivate, to illustrate the procedure used, to explain the determining factors, to explain the cooperation, responsibility and competencies, and to answer the questions from those who did not participate in the project preparation process.

The workshop preparation should first consider the topics of the workshop. These include: the aims of the kick-off, project goals, project determining factors, implementation strategy, R/3 procedure model, project plan and implementation tools, project scope, introduction to SAP AG, short introduction to the R/3 system, project organization, project standards, project success factors, presentation of the next steps, and questions and discussion.

The following groups of people should be invited: the steering committee, the management board, the project team, the works council and the consulting company.

The following documents should be distributed: copies of the presentation documents, the project charter and the report resulting from the project preparation.

A supporting workshop in the DSDM sense is a technique that is used with the following aims (DSDM Consortium, 1997, p. 189):

- To make decisions

- To develop ideas

- To exchange knowledge

- To solve business problems

Workshops have the following advantages over individual conversations:

- Increase the speed of the decision-making process

- Identification with the decisions

- Improve the productivity

- Broaden the consensus

- Improve the quality of the decisions

- Understanding of the problems in the project

The workshops listed in Table 9.1 can be held in the individual project phases.

Table 9.1   DSDM phases and workshop types

DSDM phase	Workshop contents
Feasibility study	General requirements made on the SAP R/3 system Business benefits resulting from the SAP R/3 implementation Technical decisions
Business study	General requirements made on the SAP R/3 system Business benefits resulting from the SAP R/3 implementation General business process modelling Assigning priorities to the requirements
Function model iteration	Refining the business process descriptions
System-design and system-build iteration	Planning of the integration tests
Implementation/productive operation	Satisfaction analysis Acquisition of new, changed or improved business processes

The DSDM principle also applies to conducting a workshop: 'achieve the greatest possible benefits in a limited time'. To achieve this goal, every workshop is divided into five time-limited phases that under no circumstances may be exceeded (refer to Table 9.2).

Table 9.2   Workshop phases and activities

Phase	Activity
Definition	Clear and understandable description of the results expected from the workshop
Preparation	Description of the topics and problems
Execution	Study the ideas and solutions of the problems
Logging	Description of the problems/topics and suggested solutions
Review	Presentation of the results and the agreement

It is also sensible that the participants attend a workshop appropriate to their possible roles. DSDM suggests the roles shown in Table 9.3.

Table 9.3   Roles in the workshop

Role	Description
Workshop sponsor	Top manager who presents an introduction at the start and receives a summary at the end
Workshop owner	The workshop owner is often the project manager. He is responsible for the results and cooperates closely with the moderator
Workshop moderator	The moderator guides the group through the workshop and ensures that the participants do not lose sight of the goal while working on the topic
Participant	Participants should be selected on condition that they can contribute to providing the solution for a problem. Pure observers should not participate in the workshops
Transcript writers	The transcript writers document all the results of the workshop. These include technical topics and discussion points. They should be able to prepare the information so that it can be used later for reference
Prototyper	If prototypes are also created in a workshop, it is essential that technical specialists are present.

9.4 Topic-centred interaction

The DSDM model does not say anything about the methods to be used in a team to achieve optimum results. However, even the best procedure model does not provide any benefits when those involved in a project do not cooperate. The management should take this association very seriously, because non-observance can endanger the whole project. Ruth C. Cohn with her so-called 'topic-centred Interaction' (TCI) provides a strategy that aims to achieve real, and thus productive, work. It forms the foundation for productive work in the teams (Cohn, 1977, p. 120).

The starting point of this method is the awareness that a team must not be regarded as being just a machine that can be used at any time to produce results. Rather, a team must be led so that it is capable of developing productive results. Many interruptions can hinder this and so block the teamwork.

Every consideration of the interaction in a team should take account of three factors:

- The individual

- The team

- The topic

These three factors are embedded in the environment in which the group acts. This environment consists, for example, of the time, the location and the company situation (refer to Figure 9.3).

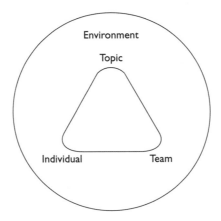

Figure 9.3   Factors of a group interaction

The team leader must analyze the following environment before a team meets for the first time:

- Who has an interest in achieving successful teamwork (organization, persons)?

- Who wants to hinder results?

- What roles can the individual team members play?

- What working times are to be chosen?

- What is the most suitable location?

- Has the team leader earned the necessary trust?

- Do the team members meet willingly?

The personality of the team leader is naturally just as important as the use of this method, because no method can replace the ability to empathize, to show tolerance and to have a positive attitude towards people.

The team leader has the goal to keep a balance between the three factors: the individual, the team and the topic. If the team becomes too interested in one person, the team leader must return to the team or to the topic. If the team becomes too interested in itself, there is the danger of an unproductive genial gathering taking place. If the team becomes too interested in just the topic, there is the danger of an academic discussion developing.

The *topic-centred interaction* from Ruth Cohn is based on two postulates and nine auxiliary rules that should be agreed as being the rules governing the team. The described postulates are obviously the team's daily work. However, it should not be considered just in absolute terms. The more productively a team works together, the more responsive it can be to any interruptions made to its activity.

Postulate 1: Be your own chairman

This postulate means that the team members should practise being aware of themselves and others. All team members in the meetings should try to remain aware of their requirements and goals. These include bodily sensitivities, thought, some inspiration, changing feelings, prevailing moods, appreciation of group behaviour, intuitions, judgements and evaluations. All members should offer something that they can do well and so can be an authority in at least one area for every other member. All facts and statements should be respected, and so increase the room for decisions.

Postulate 2: Interruptions have priority

Interruptions have de facto priority, and indeed, have so, irrespective of whether, for example, the team leader calls to order. Interruptions make themselves apparent in the form of aggression, fear or blockades. Antipathies between different team members can petrify individuals and so undermine the group. The teamwork takes the wrong direction or turns in a circle. The work results are then no longer based on real considerations but are subject to the dictates of the interruptions, i.e., they are senseless and often destructive.

- **Auxiliary rule 1:** Make your statements recognizable as such by making use of 'I'; do not hide behind 'we' or 'one'.

  Generalized idioms such as 'but we all have the opinion', 'no sensible person believes that ...', 'as everyone knows ...' are almost always personal pretences. The speaker hides behind a majority decision that has not been critically tested and does not accept responsibility for his words. If you believe your statements, you do not need any fictive, quantitative support. The use of the I-form produces responsible statements, avoids projections and hides neither your own creativity nor your own errors. 'We' should only be used when it actually represents the group opinion. 'One' should only be used for statements about all persons or a specific larger group.

- **Auxiliary rule 2:** When you ask a question, say why you are asking and what your question means for you. Speak for yourself and avoid the interview.

  A true question serves to obtain the information needed to better understand something. Such information questions become clearer and more understandable when the reason for the information is provided. Questions not aimed at obtaining information are not genuine and can support avoidance and power games. Such spurious questions produce spurious counter-questions and spurious replies. The interview then replaces the dialogue. When, however, the team members make statements rather than asking questions, this promotes further cooperation, because true communication is just as infectious as defence.

- **Auxiliary rule 3:** Be authentic and selective in your communication; be aware what you think and feel, and take care what you say and do.

  When a team member says something only because it is demanded of him, this is not independent, and is done without consideration of the situation. The chance to make use of the experience and the knowledge of all members is then no longer possible. The basis for the decision-making process is then only the opinion of the managers or the unreflected team opinion.

If everything is said unfiltered, there is the danger of reducing trustworthiness and understandability. Once trust has been established within the group, the filtering between experience and assertion becomes unnecessary. The cooperation of the members becomes more productive, and fewer filters are required. However, this process needs time, because neither the pressure to conform nor excessive speed can achieve trust within the work group.

- **Auxiliary rule 4:** Refrain from making interpretations from others as long as possible. Give your own personal reactions instead.

  Interpretations are often a sign of self-inflicted actions, which, at best, do not cause any damage. If they are not correct or are made at an inappropriate time, they invoke a defensive response and slow the productive process. Otherwise they can only cement what the interpreting person already knows. However, it turns a non-interpretative, direct personal response into a spontaneous and positive response.

- **Auxiliary rule 5:** Use generalizations sparingly.

  Because generalizations made during the meetings have the characteristic of interrupting the productive process, they should only be uttered when one subtopic has been finished and a transition is about to be made to another.

- **Auxiliary rule 6:** If you say anything about the behaviour or the character of one of the other participants, also say what it means to you (i.e., how you see him).

  Direct assertions about the behaviour or the character of a participant without adding your own motivation are often diversionary manoeuvres or attacks. The addition of your own motivation shows that this is your own opinion and not a general assertion. Only in this way can true dialogues be supported.

- **Auxiliary rule 7:** Side conversations have priority. They interrupt and are normally important. They would not take place if they were not important (perhaps would you like to tell to us what you have been discussing together?).

  If a side conversation takes place, this is an indication that a team member has something important to say. However, he hesitates to present this directly to the team or he is stifled by faster speakers. Possibly, he is no longer part of the team and is attempting to take part in the team activities again. Even if it is initially found disturbing, this attempt should be evaluated positively and the request answered by making the content of the conversation available to the complete team, otherwise possibly important aspects of the work would be lost. However, such a request should not being a blackmailing nature.

- **Auxiliary rule 8:** Request only one person to speak at any one time.

  This rule is important because nobody can concentrate on two partners at the same time. If necessary, work can continue in smaller groups. However, the results of this work should be made available to the complete team.

- **Auxiliary rule 9:** If more than one of you wish to speak at the same time, use keywords amongst yourselves to agree what you intend to speak about.

All contributions that the team members wish to provide should be briefly discussed. This avoids explosive requirements and the team itself can decide the sequence of the envisaged conversation points. Such a procedure also arouses recognition within the team members of the range of opinion that can prevail a specific aspects. This avoids unproductive contributions that are aimed only at rivalry. If this rule is not enforced, the role behaviour of individuals is often enhanced: a timid member participates even less and the dominant member increases his dominance and does not let any other member express himself. Thus, important aspects that could be presented in the group remain unheard.

9.5 Summary

Many factors influence communication in a DSDM-based project. Initially, attention should be paid to ensuring that all important roles have been assigned to the appropriate project members. Workshops can speed up the finding of solutions for problems and make the information available more quickly. The *topic-centred interaction* method supports productive behavior in the team.

10 Special features and advantages of the DSDM-based procedure model

Before the advantages resulting from the use of the DSDM-based procedure model are mentioned at the end of this last chapter of the theoretical part, we provide here again a short summary of how the DSDM-based procedure model differs from the known strategies for the realization of SAP R/3 projects:

- Iterative procedure

- Implementation of a basis system

- Stepwise extension of the basis system

- Prototyping

- Assignment of priorities

- Timeboxing

- Intensive user involvement

- Shifting of the decision-making process

- Support of the test activities using CATT

- Simplified release change by taking over the CATTs

- Description of the inter-phase activities

- Description of the phase-independent activities

It can generally be said that SAP R/3 implementation projects currently being developed using the standard SAP procedure model take between 12 and 18 months, or – depending on the size of the project – even longer. Furthermore, the lack of know-how in the company requires a very large consultancy requirement with the correspondingly high expenditure on consultants.

The use of the traditional SAP procedure model is countered by the problems described in Chapter 1, some of which can be directly taken from Figure 10.1.

In the traditional SAP procedure model, for example, the demands made on the SAP R/3 system can be acquired and also fixed very early (in the first phase, at the very left of the time axis), so that the implementation of a system comes at the end of the time axis, which, because of the dynamics of the requirements described in Chapter 1, no longer necessarily has very much to do with the current demands made on the system. Thus, a company that implements R/3 is not only confronted with an implementation cost but

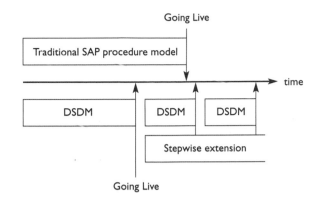

Figure 10.1   Time axis: DSDM vs. SAP

also with the follow-up costs of an implementation that no longer conforms to the initial requirements. Although the problems described can be overcome in large companies, this general state of affairs is not satisfactory.

All this has the consequence that most middle-sized companies currently forgo the use of SAP R/3. However, particularly in the current situation in which SAP AG has started an 'attack on the middle-sized companies', it is a challenge to demonstrate that it is also possible to implement an SAP R/3 system without enormous costs and the disadvantages described in Chapter 1.

The use of the DSDM-based procedure model for SAP R/3 implementation is suitable for eliminating the described disadvantages and also brings many advantages with it. Some of these advantages can also be taken directly from Figure 10.1.

- *The requirements are satisfied*
  The enormous time difference between collecting the requirements and the productive use of the system (in traditional implementation projects up to one year, or even longer) vanishes, i.e., the business processes can be implemented as they actually are. Thus, the dynamics of the requirements are taken into account.

- *Changing requirements can be taken into consideration*
  When those business processes important for business benefits change, this change not only becomes apparent but also can be taken into consideration, because these requirements are always analyzed or updated. Whereas the requirements in the traditional model were considered to be constant quantities, because they are initially described only in general terms and fixed only at the moment of realization in the DSDM-based procedure model, changes can now be taken into consideration even up to the last moment just before implementation.

- *Although the training effort reduces, the training becomes more effective*
  Because the close involvement of users has a large learning effect even during implementation, the subsequent training effort can be reduced. Furthermore, the users now learn stepwise and no longer need to learn everything at once. This advantage is based on the assumption that continuous learning coupled with use (namely additional

learning) is easier than mastering large amounts of material without having made pre-vious use of parts of it (see, for example, Chapter 4, 'Effizientes Lernen' (Efficient Learning), in Nagel (1990)).

- *The close involvement of users reduces resistance to the new system*
  Even although in the literature the active involvement of users is subject to controver-sial discussion (also refer to the discussions on user involvement as part of prototyping in Section 5.2), this involvement, can help users to identify themselves with the new system and also serve to reduce their fears, resistance and prejudices.

- *The SAP R/3 system serves to speed the company's success*
  As shown in Figure 10.1, the SAP R/3 system is no longer implemented in just one step, but rather extended stepwise. Thus, the SAP R/3 system can be used productively earlier and so serves to speed the company's success.

- *The know-how remains in the company*
  Because the DSDM-based procedure model is used for many small implementation projects, it may be desirable for the implementing company to train its own employees to become SAP R/3 specialists who can then assume increasing responsibility from project to project. This means that the SAP R/3 know-how remains in the company.

- *The consulting companies become controllable*
  Whereas consulting companies in traditional projects were automatically sure of get-ting the complete order and left the company only after the complete implementation had finished, consulting companies must now operate on the customer's behalf to receive the order for the next subproject. Thus, the stepwise implementation of the SAP R/3 system has the result that it is now possible to judge the success of the consulting company after each subproject.

- *The company retains its independence*
  The company implementing SAP R/3 is no longer dependent on the consulting com-pany. The use of the DSDM-based procedure model opens the possibility of changing the consulting company after each subproject or at least making the consulting com-pany aware of this possibility.

- *The maintenance activities reduce*
  Because the probability that the requirements made on the SAP R/3 system are not met is lower, the maintenance activities and the maintenance effort are less.

- *The costs sink*
  The reduction of the consulting and maintenance effort, and the training costs, together with the increased degree of meeting the requirements, has an overall effect of reducing the costs.

However, the use of the DSDM-based procedure model can also bring the following disadvantages:

- *The user neglects his day-to-day business*
  Because close user involvement is naturally very time-intensive, the users can probably no longer dedicate themselves so intensively to their usual day-to-day business as would be the case if the DSDM-based procedure model was not being used.

- *The additional interface programming causes additional effort*
  Because new modifications to the interfaces are needed in every subproject, the continuous changes to the overall system can increase the effort involved in interface programming. However, practical experience has shown that this problem situation does not play a significant role, because the implemented basis system normally covers at least 70 to 80 per cent of the complete system and the modifications to the other interfaces (the ones less important to company benefits) are not particularly significant.

However, if we assume that criteria such as the degree of meeting the requirements, know-how transfer and cost play the most important role for most companies, we can summarize: the use of the DSDM-based procedure model developed and presented in this book for an SAP R/3 implementation can prove to be very appropriate for many companies.

Consequently, the DSDM-based procedure model may well have the potential to establish itself as an alternative procedure model for SAP R/3 implementation projects.

Part C
Case study

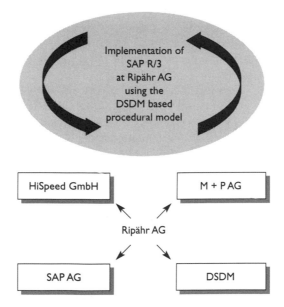

C.1 Structure of the case study

The case study presented in the following chapters refers largely to a project actually realized in practice. However, the names of the companies involved and the individual business processes have been radically changed or reduced to the extent required to understand the peculiarities of a DSDM-based implementation project without the reader becoming bored with company-specific detailed knowledge. Rather, the case study concentrates on the special features of the DSDM-based procedure model and not the special business economics relationships.

In addition to these extracts from the practical project, some parts of the case study also refer to the business processes of the model company from Keller and Teufel's book *SAP R/3 prozessorientiert anwenden* (process-oriented use of SAP R/3) and show that it is quite possible, even desirable, to use the concept of IPP within the DSDM-based procedure model in such a manner that IPP is performed within the individual teams and in accordance with the priority list for the associated modules and business processes. In addition, this book is also recommended to those readers who, in the course of the

DSDM-based case study shown in the following chapters, develop an interest in obtaining a more detailed business process knowledge, the possibilities for the use of the integrated SAP-specific tools, or the general business economics terms and relationships. The detailed representation and the numerous examples permit us to concentrate fully on the DSDM features in this book.

The case study is divided into three chapters. The first, and most detailed, chapter (Chapter 11) describes the first pass through the DSDM-based procedure model and so presents the implementation of the basis system. All the phase activities and inter-phase activities described in the theory are represented in the first pass. Moreover, the reader can always refer to this first part of the case study when the descriptions in one of the following DSDM passes are not detailed enough. The purpose of the second and third part of the case study is to explain the peculiarities of the individual subprojects and not to represent all the activities again.

The second part of the case study (Chapter 12) is concerned with the possible form of a second pass through the DSDM-based procedure model. The first part assumes that the implementation of the basis system has already been completed successfully and the business processes that now needed to be implemented are low on the priority list or have left the timebox. In addition to this extension to the basis system, this chapter also discusses the handling of the requirements, the improvement of the productive system, and the correction of any faults in the productive system.

The third and last part of the case study (Chapter 13) finally describes how to proceed, when, in accordance with the DSDM-based procedure model, a release change is to be performed. In particular, this chapter explains how the business processes from the previous DSDM passes, which are still present as test cases stored in CATT, can be used to perform a regression test and so ensure that the SAP R/3 system still functions in accordance with the company-specific requirements.

Thus, as previously discussed, the case study concentrates on showing the special features of a DSDM-based procedure. At suitable places, in particular in the first and most detailed part of the case study, a short description is provided of those SAP work packets that originated in the traditional SAP procedure model but need to be performed, and also reference is made to the relevant places in the ASAP concept.

Value is also placed on a complete study being made of the theoretical part of this book, even though this is not essential to understand the case study. Rather, it aims at permitting the reader to better understand the case study and thus the DSDM features. The theory is only used as reference to supply background information or when the theoretical basis is needed for knowledge obtained practically.

Depending on his previous knowledge or interests, it is up to reader to decide whether he starts with the theoretical or the practical part.

C.2 Current situation

The case study considered here concentrates on Ripähr AG (abbreviated to RAG in the following chapters). The business activities of RAG include both the production of spare parts for vehicles and the assembly of so-called 'sets'. Although these sets also include

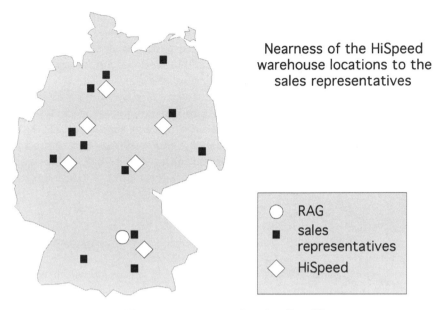

Figure C.2   *Current situation (Part II)*

spare parts, these do not come from the company's production, but are purchased from third parties and later assembled to form these sets.

Although RAG currently supplies only Germany, intensive discussions are being held about a possible expansion to Switzerland and Austria. As the map in Figure C.1 shows, RAG has only a single location, in southern Germany. Both the production and the warehouse are at this location. The total of 12 sales managers are spread throughout Germany. Each of these sales managers has his own storage area (normally the size of a garage) that stores both sets and s-parts. The parts and sets stored at the sales manager's location mainly serve as samples. RAG generally differentiates between sets (see above), s-parts (small) and l-parts (large).

The sales manager assigned to each customer forwards the orders to the head office and, in cooperation, the two coordinate the deliveries to the customer. However, in certain emergency situations, the sales manager can accept the delivery of sets and s-parts and supply them directly from his warehouse.

From the technical viewpoint, RAG currently has a very heterogeneous system landscape that is characterized by the high level of in-house development.

As a goal for the future, RAG mentions the implementation of a standard software and the realization of the associated advantages. The standard software should cover the complete business economics area of RAG, namely the areas of purchasing, production and logistics, marketing, and financial services. Long-term, the area of human resources should also be included.

As part of the implementation of a standard software package, RAG intends to commission an external service provider to supervise the delivery and warehousing tasks, and so reduce the company's stock levels and minimize delivery times. In addition to the warehousing costs, the number of warehouses and the distance to the customers were important decision criteria for the selection of the transport company shipper. HiSpeed Corp., which has six warehouse locations near the customers, is currently favoured (refer to Figure C.2) and, according to its own information, can provide unlimited warehouse space.

RAG commissioned the Mummert + Partner Consultancy (abbreviated to 'M+P') to provide support for the selection of the standard software. The two companies had already worked together successfully on a wide range of problem situations for many years. It was also planned to commission M+P to realize the actual implementation project.

A team of M+P and RAG employees was selected and commissioned to produce a criterion catalogue that was to contain all important requirements that RAG placed on the standard software and later was to be used as the basis for making the decision.

11 The first DSDM pass

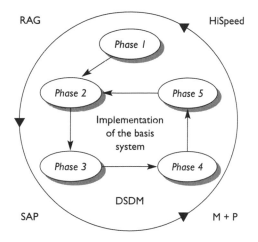

Figure 11.1   Implementation of the basis system

11.1 Phase 1: Feasibility study

Because the DSDM-based procedure model requires, as part of a prestudy, an investigation as to whether the SAP R/3 system and the DSDM-based procedure model are indeed appropriate to satisfy the company-specific requirements, it starts earlier than the traditional SAP procedure model. Consequently, it normally also uses external business consultants earlier and so permits more precise planning in which the commissioned consultancy can make use of its own experience.

11.1.1 Test the suitability of SAP and DSDM

The preliminary investigation of possible standard software products had the result that the SAP R/3 system appeared to be the most suitable product with which to satisfy the requirements of RAG detailed in the criteria catalogue. The results of the preliminary investigation were presented to the steering committee, which agreed with the decision to use the SAP R/3 system and thus gave the start signal for the implementation project. At the same time, M+P was named as the consultancy and given the task of supervising the implementation.

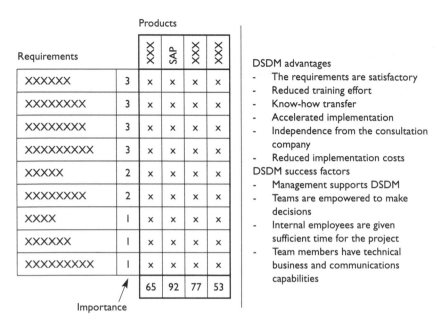

Figure 11.2   SAP and DSDM suitability test

The M+P company, which already has many years of experience in the area of SAP migrations and SAP R/3 implementation projects, planned to use the DSDM-based procedure model as the basis for the new project and so ensure a customer-oriented, fast and economical implementation.

Because the use of the DSDM-based procedure model required not only the approval of the steering committee, but also its support, M+P initiated a workshop that presented the advantages of the DSDM-based procedure model. It was also determined whether RAG considered itself both capable of and willing to conform to the DSDM principles (refer to Figure 11.2). This, however, would mean passing the decision-making process to individual teams and require intensive user involvement.

The decision was made at the end of the workshop to use the DSDM-based procedure model as the basis for the implementation project.

11.1.2 Determine modules and internal employees

RAG determined the modules MM, SD, PP, FI and CO as being the modules to be implemented in the first DSDM pass. It was now necessary to determine the number of suitable employees to accompany and organize the project.

Of particular importance in determining the number of possible employees was not only their knowledge in the user area and previous knowledge of SAP R/3, but also consideration of the large amount of time that the employees involved with the project would need to provide. This time effort must be taken into consideration for the planning of the day-to-day business, and so avoid this work not being performed adequately and the employees being taken off the running project.

Available resources/required resources

Module	available resources	required resources	requirement
MM	1	2	1
SD	3	1	0
PP	2	2	0
FI	3	2	0
CO	1	1	0

Although the QS and HR modules appear to be suitable, they were initially postponed for an indeterminate time.

Figure 11.3   Employees and modules

Furthermore, a general estimate was made of the number of person-days that would be missing from the individual user areas. M+P was also involved with this estimate, and, because of their large project experience, could significantly improve the estimate. Because it was essential for the subsequent course of the project to ensure the uniform progress of the teams operating in parallel, the efforts concentrated on balancing the time involved with the individual modules.

This estimate should also be used as the basis for the determination of the consulting requirement needed in the following phase. Thus, the goal of this phase was only to determine how many internal employees were available or should be used. Figure 11.3 shows the number of employees estimated to be needed for the individual modules and how many suitable employees could be assigned to these modules. Although there was no lack of qualified employees for the MM module, the inclusion of an additional employee in the project team would have had significant effects on the ability to perform the day-to-day business.

11.1.3   Time planning and implementation strategy

Figure 11.4 shows the estimates for the first general time planning over all planned DSDM passes for the SAP R/3 implementation project. The timeboxes were already included in this time planning, which are valid over phase boundaries for both the third and fourth phases of the DSDM passes. However, the time planning shown was not final but merely an initial estimate for the size of the project. The time planning in total, and in particular for the timeboxes, was corrected with the creation of the general concept and fixed only with its acceptance. The timeboxes starting at this time represented a fixed quantity and could no longer be changed. All those involved had to be aware both of this inviolability of the timeboxes and also the concept behind the timeboxes. In this connection, a reference was made to the subsequent DSDM training in which all project members were informed about the basic ideas and principles.

With regard to the implementation strategy, here this is an activity that could be processed independently of the DSDM-based procedure model. For this reason, a refer-

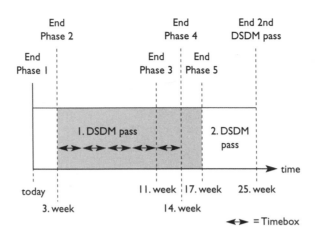

Figure 11.4   Time planning

ence should be made at this point to the traditional SAP procedure model and the corresponding documentation in the ASAP concept. ASAP in this context provides, for example, a detailed description that discusses, in particular, the activities 'test the implementation suggestion', 'confirm the implementation method' and 'test the rollout strategy of the company'.

11.1.4 Company goals, feasibility report

The results of the first phase were contained in the feasibility report. In particular, the feasibility report contained the following points:

- Why was the decision made in favour of the SAP R/3 system?

- What is the general time planning for the first DSDM pass?

- How long should the complete implementation project take?

- Who are involved in the project?

The goals to be achieved with the SAP R/3 implementation were again formulated here. Particular value was attached to the goals being formulated in such a manner that they could be measured and so could be used for the subsequent planned–actual comparison.

This activity ended the first phase of the first DSDM pass. Thus, the general decision was made to implement the SAP R/3 system on the basis of the DSDM-based procedure model. Because the higher-level decisions had already been made and all subsequent DSDM passes were then built on an existing SAP R/3 'base' system, this phase no longer needed to be performed for any of the following DSDM passes. Thus, the decision for each additional subproject was made at the end of the previous project and no longer needed to be made in the comprehensive manner described here.

11.2 Phase 2: Business study

11.2.1 Perform risk analysis continuously

The project manager started the investigation of risks to the project right at the beginning of the project. He initially used the checklist from the DSDM Consortium.

This meant that risk analysis began at the project start. In accordance with the DSDM method, initially it was performed only generally but was further refined during the course of the project. Additional risks were added later.

The users are not sufficiently involved in the project

Project manager: 'This risk is very high, because it is to be expected that the users will not be given sufficient time to work on the project'. To reduce this risk, the project manager spoke again with his superiors and attempted to convince them that the involvement of the users is very important. Experience has shown that this risk remains high throughout the complete project.

The time required to make decisions endangers the project plan

Project manager: 'Because senior management supports the DSDM-based strategy, this risk can be ignored.'

Team members concentrate more on activities than on products

Project manager: 'There is the danger that a new tool such as the AutoTester attracts too much of the team's interest.'

The delivered products do not provide any business benefits

Project manager: 'The expected business benefits must be discussed again with the senior management.'

Iterative and incremental development is not controlled

Project manager: 'If we really take our timeboxes and configuration management seriously, this risk is very low.'

It is difficult or impossible to return to an old development level

Project manager: 'Because the Change and Transport Organizer, the Document Management System and SAPoffice provide excellent configuration management, we do not have any of these problems.'

The general requirements have not been frozen

Project manager: 'This has already been done.'

Testing is not an integral part of the life cycle

Project manager: 'CATT, the test plan tool and AutoTester provide us with excellent support.'

Not all those involved work cooperatively together

Project manager: 'This will become a problem. Some consultants have already worked on similar projects for other customers. There is the danger that our users will not accept their suggestions and then there will be a division of the group into the "we" and "they" factions.'

DSDM cannot be used fully

Project manager: 'This risk does not apply at the moment.'

The teams do not understand the DSDM method

Project manager: 'We do not know whether the teams, despite the extensive training, have really understood the reason behind the method.'

The organization of the users has changed dramatically through the implementation of the system

Project manager: 'Top management has guaranteed that no dramatic organizational changes will take place during the project lifetime.'

The original project goal can probably no longer be attained

Project manager: 'This cannot be judged at the moment.'

The developers do not know the SAP system sufficiently well

Project manager: 'This is why we have consultants to support our developers.'

The project manager recognized that currently no larger risks are known in the project. He repeated this analysis at the end of the next timebox.

11.2.2 Determine the consulting requirement

The graphs shown in Figures 11.5 and 11.6 were presented to the RAG project management at the start of the SAP R/3 implementation project to emphasize the advantages of the DSDM-based procedure and so make clear to the management the effect of intensive

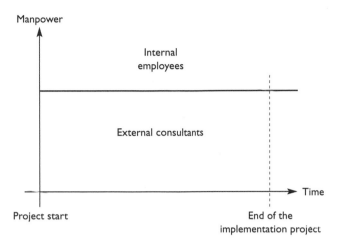

Figure 11.5   *Development of the consulting requirement for an SAP R/3 implementation on the basis of the traditional SAP procedure model*

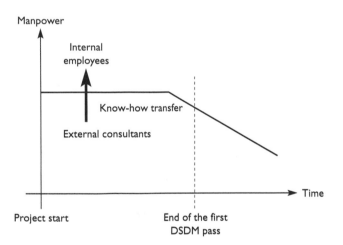

Figure 11.6   *Development of the consulting requirement for an SAP R/3 implementation on the basis of the DSDM-based procedure model*

user involvement. It became clear here that the amount of consulting effort remains constantly high over the complete period of the implementation project (where this period is larger than that required for the implementation of the basis system using the DSDM-based procedure model) and also no reduction can be expected for subsequent projects. Thus, Figure 11.5 illustrates how high the consulting effort will be in the total effort for the consulting project.

The same applies for Figure 11.6, which shows how the consulting effort develops in a DSDM-based implementation project. This shows that the required consulting effort reduces during the base project implementation. This is caused by the internal employees that have been chosen as having module responsibility (see above) being ready to take over tasks near the end of the first DSDM pass. They then only needed supervision or support from the consultants. This transfer to the lower-cost internal employees resulted from the transfer know-how inherent in the DSDM method. Figure 11.6 also graphically illustrates this transfer.

This transfer know-how also represented one of the significant criteria against which the external consultancy was measured with regard to the granting of follow-up projects. In this connection, a criterion catalogue was presented to M+P that contained the most important points for RAG and should give M+P the capability and the motivation to pay special attention to these points. In addition to the transfer of know-how, this catalogue also contained items such as work effort and speed for business process analysis and for the customizing settings made.

Just these points were realized later in the accompanying practical example. The consulting company was very concerned with supporting the transfer of know-how, and tried to prove this, for example, by not making any customizing entries themselves, but rather explaining every time to the internal employee responsible for the module, what, why and how it functioned, so that he would be able to perform all necessary activities himself.

The project was also realized at high speed, which resulted not only from the special motivation, but also from the timeboxes being set to the very short time of two weeks. This forced all those involved to work and cooperate in a goal-oriented and effective manner.

11.2.3 Specify the teams and the project organization

The traditional project organization shown in Figure 11.7, being independent of the DSDM-based procedure model, describes a typical organization that can apply for every project. A differentiation is made between three levels. At the highest level is the steering committee, followed by the project management and finally the individual teams. The

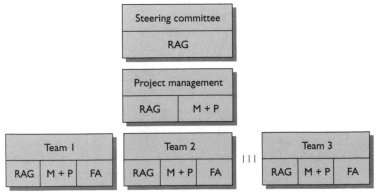

FA = employee from the user department

Figure 11.7   Traditional project organization

individual teams consist of the person responsible for the module, who possesses not only know-how in the module he has been assigned but also comprehensive knowledge of the associated user department, an M+P employee who possesses the appropriate component knowledge, and one or more employees from the user department, who have detailed knowledge about the business processes to be implemented.

However, the DSDM-based procedure model demands a team structure oriented more to the individual roles to be adopted within the team. For this reason, the DSDM Consortium recommends the team structures shown in Figures 11.8 and 11.9.

Thus, characteristic of the project organization in the DSDM-based procedure model was less the hierarchical structure of the individual bodies, but rather role distribution and decision-making competencies. These competencies were largely delegated to the individual teams. This had the consequence that, for example, a 'large' milestone in the form of a presentation was no longer announced in front of the steering committee as being attained, but rather announced as a small milestone to the teams. The teams at the end of a timebox reported just to the project manager.

Furthermore, of particular importance to the project organization was adherence to the DSDM philosophy, and thus terms such as user involvement and transfer of know-how.

New tasks were assigned to both the project management (refer to Chapter 5) and the individual teams, which were then given new roles with new tasks and responsibilities. Furthermore, the overcoming of communication problems in DSDM-based projects and within a DSDM-typical project organization had gained additional importance. Consequently, the decision was made in the accompanying project to hold additional communication training for all team members and project managers.

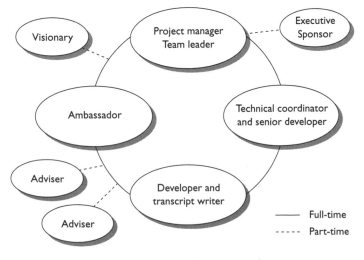

Figure 11.8   Team structure 1

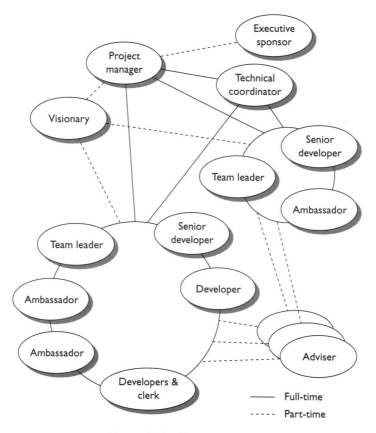

Figure 11.9   Team structure 2

11.2.4 Training for the contextual inquiry

As mentioned previously, all team members and project managers attended the Contextual Inquiry seminar. However, this did not apply to the CO team, which had decided to use the IPP concept to analyze and set the associated business processes. This meant that a workshop should be held that was to take place not in the work context of the user departments but in a neutral conference room.

For all other team members, this meant that not only the internal employees responsible for modules, but also the consultants and the employees from the user departments with whom it could be expected that they would most often come into contact had to be taken into consideration. Consequently, it was essential that all those involved were informed about their respective roles in the various project situations.

Figure 11.10 shows the specific content that was provided in the training. Once the participants had been made aware of why communication problems or misunderstandings can arise, the principles of the Contextual Inquiry and their special meaning for the current project were presented.

```
┌─────────────────────────────────────────────────────────────┐
│  Contextual Inquiry                                           │
├─────────────────────────────────────────────────────────────┤
│   1.  Overview                                                │
│   2.  Communication                                           │
│        2.1. What does communication mean                      │
│        2.2. Behaviour patterns                                │
│        2.3. What misunderstandings arise                      │
│        2.4. Other communication problems                      │
│   3.  Contextual Inquiry                                      │
│        3.1. Overview and goals                                │
│        3.3. The master–apprentice model                       │
│        3.2. Context                                           │
│        3.3 Partnership                                        │
│        3.4. Interpretation                                    │
│        3.5. Focus                                             │
│   4.  Exercise                                                │
│   5.  What have we learnt?                                    │
├─────────────────────────────────────────────────────────────┤
│  Training material for the contextual Inquiry   Master+Partner│
└─────────────────────────────────────────────────────────────┘
```

Figure 11.10   Content of the training for the Contextual Inquiry

Initially the master–trainee model was used to show the specific roles that the various persons involved with the project would assume during the course of the project. For example, it was emphasized that the employees from the user departments and the internal employees responsible for modules would assume the role of the master as part of the business process analysis, while the external consultants had to accept that they were the trainees. In contrast, during the realization of the customizing settings, the consultant would adopt the role of the master while the employee responsible for the module adopted the role of the trainee; however, this does not mean that the consultant makes the customizing settings himself, but, rather, as part of the transfer of know-how required by DSDM, explains to the trainee what is to be done and just supervises these actions.

Another important point was that the business process analysis did not take place as part of a workshop in some neutral conference room, but in the context of the associated business processes to be performed.

Furthermore, it was shown that the partnership principle should ensure that all those involved understood that they are working together towards the same goal. Thus, no time was allowed to be wasted in constantly providing an alibi for oneself and so prove one's own innocence should the project not proceed optimally. All those involved must be made aware that the fulfilment of the requirements of a timebox is judged as the success or failure of everyone. The shortness of the timebox, which does not allow any time for non-goal-oriented communication or recriminations, supports this principle. The shortness of every timebox should also ensure that misunderstandings can be uncovered quickly and thus permit fast help. Consequently, those problems that affect partnership cooperation do not become apparent only near the end of the project but can be corrected directly. Thus, the partnership principle and the timeboxes avoid a 'large crash' occurring at the end of the project.

The principles of interpretation and focus were responsible for providing a common understanding rather than business processes being handled concurrently. This exclusive handling of individual business processes also adhered to the concept of the DSDM-based procedure model, which requires that the business processes are handled individually, namely according to their importance to business benefits.

Together with improvement of the understanding of communication and the cause of misunderstandings, the goal of the training to provide a common view and goal-oriented working was also achieved.

11.2.5 Determination of the training requirements

When the DSDM-based procedure model is used, it does not suffice just to determine the training requirements for the SAP area; all the parties involved must also have the necessary DSDM knowledge.

11.2.6 General business process description

The requirements made on the SAP R/3 system, i.e., the requirements made on the business processes, were initially generally described in this phase activity. This general business process description should be used only to provide an overview of the size of the project and to prepare a basis for the subsequent priority assignments.

Consequently, differentiation into general and detailed business process description was particularly important because one aim of DSDM is to perform the detailed analysis and the true realization as close together as possible. This avoids the requirements changing during the time between the analysis and the realization, as is typically the case for the waterfall-based model. This problem assumes particular importance when the so-called 'big bang' is chosen as the implementation strategy. In this case, the requirements

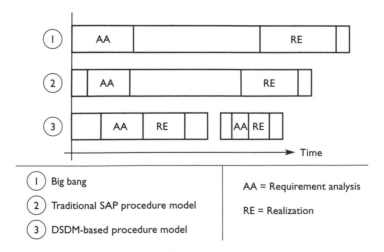

Figure 11.11   Time axis with requirements

are initially analyzed and described down to the smallest detail prior to the actual project start, before being realized at the end of the project, i.e., after a very long time. Figure 11.11 also illustrates this problem situation in which the effects of the time differences between requirements analysis and realization for the three different strategies are compared.

The figure shows, in particular, that the large time difference between requirements analysis and realization in models 1 and 2 does not take account of the dynamics of the requirements. This means that the realized requirements may not necessarily have anything to do with reality. This results either in the implementation of the wrong requirements or in a lengthened realization time because the requirements must be analyzed and described a second time.

Because the analysis and the realization are combined in the DSDM-based procedure model, the figure also shows that this problem does not arise in this case. Indeed, because the figure implies that the DSDM-based procedure model is realized successively in these two blocks, it is not quite accurate. However, DSDM goes even further: every requirement is analyzed and realized separately before starting the next requirement. This achieves the shortest possible time between the analysis and the realization.

The requirements in the case study shown were also initially determined only in general terms, before they were first prioritized in another step and finally individually analyzed in detail and realized quasi-concurrently.

However, before these steps are further described in detail, the question must first be answered as to which business processes need to be considered. Because the methodology and the DSDM specifics do not change for the various modules, this consideration was ignored for all business processes in the case study. For this reason, the following section considers only those business processes that primarily lie within the task area of the MM and CO teams.

Because the methods adopted by these two teams differ so much, these teams should be considered in more detail. Whereas the MM team used a DSDM-specific method, the CO team adopted the IPP concept which was very suitable for embedding in the DSDM-based procedure model.

The following section also discusses the special characteristics of the SD team, which are not primarily linked with the analysis and setting of the business processes, but rather result from this team being concerned with the problems associated with electronic connection to external warehouses.

11.2.7   MM general business processes

To determine the business processes that lie in the area of the MM module, the consultants and the MM representative first produced a list that contained both the user department employees and a general overview of the business processes as seen by the MM representative. The two MM teams used this list to assign the employees to be questioned. The MM teams then went to the user departments to conduct interviews in the form of a Contextual Inquiry. One consultant, a module representative and the associated employees took part in each of these interviews.

The Contextual Inquiry produced the following business process headings that were relevant to the MM area:

- Process the material master data

- Process the supplier master data

- Order request

- Order

- Goods arrival

- Subcontracting

- Stocktaking

- Invoice receipt

- Invoice validation

- Restocking

- Rebooking

- Inventory comparison

- Returns from the sales representatives

- Returns from customers

- Return old goods

- Stock destruction

Once the interviews had been completed, this list was presented again to all those involved so that it could be checked for completeness.

11.2.8 CO general business process description

The CO team chose a different method to determine the general requirements. The internal module representative invited all the employees responsible for the user departments and the relevant consultants to a workshop.

This workshop comprised of two parts. Initially the individual employees were asked to describe the day-to-day tasks that they had to perform. The module representative and the external consultant now tried to formulate the general requirements from these descriptions. Those involved had the possibility of making additions or asking questions at any time. In the second part of the workshop, the person responsible from the user department was presented with a list containing the referenced business processes. His task was to ensure that business processes had not been forgotten and that no additional business processes were required. The following listing of relevant business processes was provided at the end of the workshop:

- Cost/revenue element processing

- Cost centre processing

- Cost centre analysis

- Activity type processing

- Standard cost estimate with quantity structure

- Determination of deviation

- Profit planning

- Billing transfer and evaluation

- Profit centre report

- Profit analysis

This list was also given to all those involved for them to check for completeness.

11.2.9   EDI connection to external warehouses in the SD area

The business processes (e.g., order processing, delivery to customer, delivery to travelling salespersons, invoicing interface) in this case, i.e., for the case study, play only a subordinate role with regard to the SD area. Consequently, because we wish to show how EDI interfaces to an external warehousing are handled in a DSDM-based SAP R/3 implementation, the SD area is also included in the case study.

The main problem in the case shown was that the creation of the EDI interfaces would take the largest amount of time. This meant that not all EDI interfaces could be realized within the time frame of the SAP R/3 implementation. This was caused not only by the particular difficulty with this problem situation, but also the large number of interfaces. Thus, overcoming this problem represented one of the most critical factors in the complete project and caused much anxiety at RAG.

However, M+P could counter this anxiety by showing that M+P not only has special know-how in the area of migration, the handling of customs' formalities, euro conversion and HR, but also provide excellent capabilities with regard to EDI connection to external warehouses or external service providers.

DSDM activities should also be prioritized here. The question was asked as to which interface is the most important to the business benefits when the frequency of its use is also taken into account. However, the following phases of the case study should not describe the interface code, but just provide an overview of the tasks to be mastered.

The connection to HiSpeed Corp. can be described as follows:

- Bookings are always specified from RAG. Confirmations are made by HiSpeed.

- The inventory is maintained on the SAP R/3 system for RAG. HiSpeed does not maintain its own inventory but receives goods movements electronically and confirms these.

- HiSpeed should use the designations of materials, debtors, deliveries, etc. from RAG.

- Although, primarily, the transfer of transaction data is concerned, the exchange of master data (at the very minimum, the material) should also be realized.

- HiSpeed must permit RAG to track in electronic form the shipping of all deliveries and returned orders.

- SAP organizational elements are used to separate the data to be sent, i.e., works and storage location.

- HiSpeed employees have no access to the SAP R/3 system.

11.2.10 Prioritizing rule and time planning

The goal of the use of the MoSCoW rules was to prioritize the business processes. This prioritization had two purposes: firstly, to give a sequence in which the business processes should be processed, and, secondly, to provide a basic planning of the timeboxes.

The critical question used to determine the importance of the individual business processes is: 'How important is the business process to the business benefits?'. The specific prioritizing was done with the associated team initially deciding for each business process the group to which it belonged. The sequence within the individual groups was determined by assuming in the first pass than the first business process was the most important and then asking whether the next business process was more or less important than the first. This produced a list starting at the most important business process and ordered in decreasing importance.

This grouping was included in the planning to the extent that the estimate of the processing time required for the first three groups was included in the planning of the timebox for phase 3 (refer to Figure 11.12).

If a business process changes or a new one is added during the processing of the individual business processes, this business process is added immediately to the prioritized list and processed in accordance with its assigned importance. The length of the timebox is not subsequently changed in this situation.

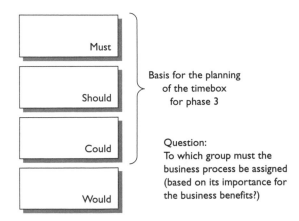

Figure 11.12   The MoSCoW rules

11.2.11 MM: Priority list and time planning

The priority list shown in Figure 11.13 represents the business processes of the MM team sorted according to their importance to the business benefits. This priority list is the result of a workshop in which the persons in charge agreed with the arrangement into a group and the sorting within this group. Thus, this prioritizing also generally defines the appearance of the basis system to be implemented in the first DSDM pass.

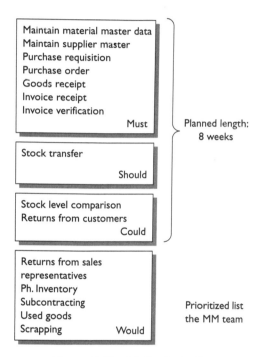

Figure 11.13   MM priority list

11.2.12 CO: Priority list and time planning

The same applies for the priority list of the CO team as for the priority list of the MM team. Agreement on the importance of the individual business processes with regard to the business benefits was also attained here in a workshop.

Figure 11.14 shows how this priority list appeared in detail.

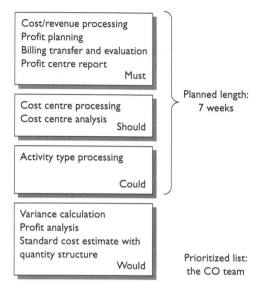

Figure 11.14   CO priority list

11.2.13 SD: Priority list and time planning

As already discussed above, the case study for the SD area should concentrate on the EDI interfaces and not the business processes. Because of the limited time available for the creation of the EDI interfaces, the following procedure was chosen. The interfaces should be realized successively according to their importance. In parallel, plans were created for the interfaces that probably will not be realized within the first DSDM pass. These should provide a temporary data exchange by sending faxes. The 'worst case' for the creation of EDI interfaces was considered during the planning of the data exchange using paper, i.e., fax plans were also created for interfaces even though it was more probable that the electronic variant would already have been realized.

Single, short timeboxes that extended over several DSDM passes rather than a global timebox were defined for the third phase of the EDI task.

11.2.14 General concept

The general concept must contain all business processes to be represented for all modules. In the case study, every business process was described with one or two sentences, and the person in charge named both for RAG and for M+P. However, the most important features of a general concept within a DSDM-based implementation project show themselves in the weighting of the individual processes and the definition of the specification of an acceptance procedure for them. The position in the prioritized list and the estimated time were defined for each business process. Thus, this prioritized list also provided an initial estimate of when the individual business processes were to be processed, and so provided the basis for the planning of the first timebox within the third phase.

The acceptance procedure for the general concept is that the internal persons in charge together with the external consultants are responsible for the general process description and planning, and they accept the associated item into the general concept only when they consider that it has been described and prioritized in accordance with the requirements. Thus, the team members themselves must accept each individual item in the general concept. The overall general concept is then considered to have been accepted when all signatures for all business processes have been provided. In the case study, the general concept was also presented to the steering committee, even though this presentation was only for information purposes. Responsibility for decision making had already been passed to the teams when the general concept was produced and so account taken of one of the most important DSDM principles.

11.2.15 Determination of the timebox for phase 3

Figure 11.15 illustrates the form of time planning over the individual modules when the MoSCoW rules are used. As the figure shows, the resource-usage planning in the project presented was very successful because the largest planned time difference between the modules was just two weeks.

To ensure that all Must, Should and Would requirements can be satisfied in accordance with the planning in the third phase, this timebox would need to be nine weeks long in order to take account of the bottleneck with the PP module. However, after consulting the PP team, and to avoid giving the teams the impression that they had sufficient time in any case, the global timebox for the third phase was set to eight weeks. It was also planned to subdivide this eight-week timebox into four additional timeboxes each of two weeks. However, the final decision for these short timeboxes was made only at the start of the third phase of the first DSDM pass.

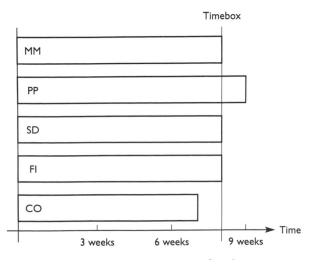

Figure 11.15   Timebox time planning

Consequently, the form of the basis system to be implemented was already relatively clear at this time. It was also explained again to the teams how they should react if the timebox is too short should new requirements become apparent during the timebox, and in which sequence the individual requirements are to be processed.

11.2.16 Setup the system landscape, make general settings

The 'Setup system landscape' and 'Perform global settings' phase activities are traditional SAP activities that are performed fully independent of DSDM. For this reason, the reader should also refer to the documentation in the SAP online help and the ASAP documentation, which both describe what is to be done for these activities. Although these are mandatory activities that must be embedded in the DSDM-based procedure model, they do not require any special handling.

It is possible, for example, to select the model structure procedure in customizing and then click there on 'Setup system landscape' to perform the relevant activities (refer to Figure 11.16).

With regard to the 'Perform global settings' phase activity, the SAP online help indicates that the contents to be represented apply to countries, dimensions, currents, measurement units and the calendar, and these details must be provided from the conceptual design.

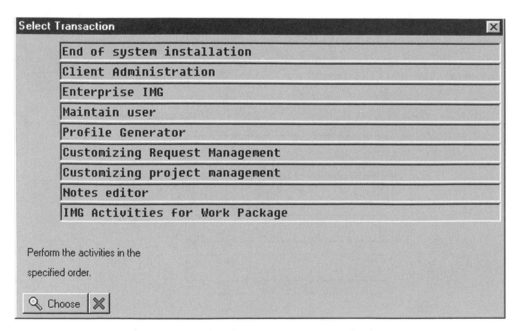

Figure 11.16   Setup the customizing system landscape

11.2.17 Define interfaces and system extensions

The same applies for the phase activities in Section 11.2.16 as for the 'Define interfaces and system extensions' phase activity. This activity is also a mandatory activity in SAP R/3 implementation projects. However, the fact that the interfaces in the DSDM-based procedure model can change or reduce in every DSDM pass makes them a special activity.

The SAP online help describes this phase activity as follows: 'With the implementation of the R/3 system you normally replace existing systems and connect external systems with the R/3 system using interfaces. If necessary, you develop your own functions to close any functional gaps.' This replacement of the existing systems is done stepwise in the DSDM-based procedure model.

The SAP help provides detailed instructions within the following work packets on how this phase activity must be performed:

- Create a detailed description for the interfaces.

- Create a detailed description for the system extension.

- Produce a concept for data migration.

11.2.18 Represent company structure, base data and master data

This phase activity also does not exhibit any special DSDM features, and so it can be performed as usual. The customizing settings, as shown in Figure 11.17 for example, are performed fully.

As an example, at this point we would like to refer you to ASAP, which supports all DSDM-independent phase activities and describes three work packets for the 'Represent company structure' phase activity:

- *Recommend the company structure and agree to it*
  Because of the many integration characteristics of the SAP R/3 system, it is necessary that the final company structure within the system is agreed with all business areas, and they understand and accept this suggested structure. For this purpose, ASAP also provides a standardized release form that supports the documentation of the attained results.

- *Determine the company structure*
  The release form mentioned above goes into this work packet and serves as the basis to conduct a workshop used to finalize the determination of the company structure. ASAP also describes how this workshop should be held.

- *Hold company structure workshop*
  At the end of this workshop there will be the definitive specification of the company structure within the system. ASAP provides details for such a workshop and suggests comprehensive presentations that support the determination of the company structure.

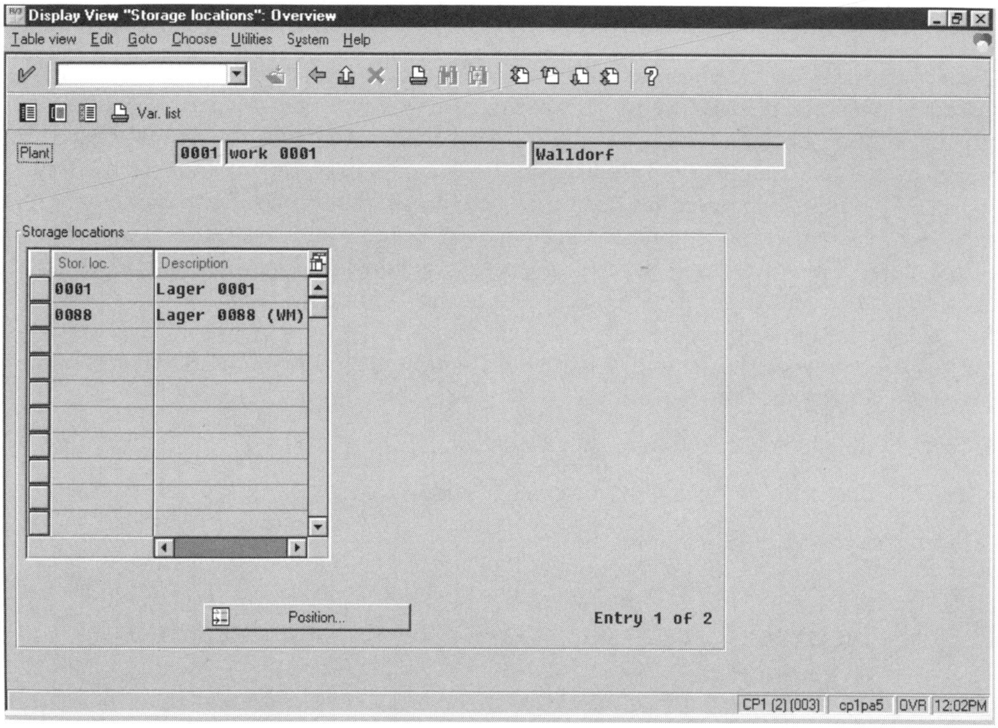

Figure 11.17   Customizing the company structure

11.2.19 Produce quality assurance plan

The technical coordinator received the order to produce a quality assurance plan. This plan should be kept as short as possible and the teams given practical notes to help them with their day-to-day work in determining which activities need to be performed for quality assurance.

The plan should be discussed with the teams and also accepted by them (refer to Figure 11.18). Although the quality assurance plan does not need to conform to the strict international standards such as ISO 9000-3 or CMM, it should support the business benefits without requiring unnecessary bureaucracy. The technical coordinator uses the IEEE standard 730-1989 and the TickIT recommendations from the DSDM Consortium as the basis for creating the quality assurance plan.

The expansion of the quality assurance plan then had the following structure (see Figure 11.18)

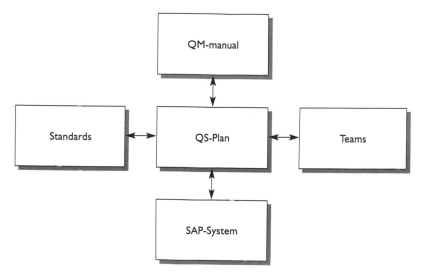

Figure 11.18   Quality assurance

The cover page

The cover page contained the heading 'Project <name> – Quality Assurance Plan', the current version number, the date of the last change, and the name, the department and the telephone number of the technical coordinator. This made clear who is the contact partner should any questions arise regarding quality assurance.

Project <name> *Quality Assurance Plan*	
Author	<name of the technical coordinator>
Telephone	<telephone number>
Department	<department>
Last change	<date of the last change>
Status	in progress
Version	2.0

History

The technical coordinator noted in this section which versions he has assigned previously, which version numbers have been assigned, what was the reason for the new version and who was responsible for it.

Table 11.1   History of the quality assurance plan

Version	Status	Person in charge	Date	Reason
Version 0.0	created	<name>	8.7.1997	Created in the DMS
Version 1.0	review	<name>	31.7.1997	Completed without agreement
Version 1.1	review	<name>	8.8.1997	Changes after response from the teams
Version 1.3	reviewed	<name>	21.8.1997	Agreed
Version 2.0	in progress	<name>	11.11.1997	Correction after the integration test

Referenced documents

The quality assurance plan made reference to the following literature:

- ISO 9000, Part 3, Development Guide, Delivery and Maintenance of Software
- IEEE 730-1989, IEEE Standard for Software Quality Assurance Plans
- IEEE 828-1990, IEEE Standard for Software Configuration Management Plans
- QM manual for RAG
- Methods Manual DSDM Version 3
- The Dynamic Systems Development Method & TickIT (guidance to assist software developers using DSDM to meet the requirements of ISO9001)
- RAG programming standards

Implementation

The technical coordinator here used the quality questions from Chapter 8.

Terms

The QM representative indicated here that there was inconsistency in the terminology concerned with the QM representative of the company:

- Whereas the international standards for software development use the term 'Quality Assurance Plan', the ISO 9001 standard refers to quality *management*.

It was then documented that a glossary is to be maintained for the project to avoid the SAP terms clashing with the company's terms:

- A glossary in the <name> database is created for the <name> project.

- All terms relevant to the company and the project are documented in this database.

- The QM representative assumes responsibility for the terminology database.

QS management for the project

The project manager has responsibility for quality management of the project.

This responsibility for the software and for the company as a whole is delegated to the technical coordinator and the quality manager of the company, respectively.

A QM representative is also named in each team.

Reference to the company's QM manual

Because the <name> project has an effect on RAG's quality management manual (QMM), the business process documentation is structured according to the QMM, namely following ISO 9001. The structuring of the business process documentation, the seminar notes and the user manual correspond to the QMM structure.

The company's QM representative is responsible for reference to the QM manual of the company.

Quality goals

The project has the following quality goals:

- Observance of deadlines

- Observance of the costs

- Meeting the requirements

- Simple maintenance for a release change

The quality measurement is made using an actual–planned comparison for items 1–3 and for the time required for a release change.

Procedure model

The nine principles of DSDM are noted here, and a reference is made to the DSDM manual.

Reviews

A review is a formally planned and structured analysis and evaluation process in which the project results are presented to a team of experts who commented on or approved them.

Every timebox ends with a review. All quality criteria listed in this manual are checked at every review. The reviews can be held within the teams. A log is maintained of the results of the reviews. The QM representatives are responsible for the reviews.

Tests

- All important business processes in an SAP R/3 system must be tested.

- If a test can be performed with CATT, it must actually be performed with CATT.

- If a test cannot be performed with CATT but with the AutoTester, it must be performed with the AutoTester.

- If a test cannot be performed with either CATT or the AutoTester, it must be performed and documented manually.

- All tests are structured with the test plan tool in a test catalog and specific instances made in test plans and test packets.

- The test logs are archived.

Configuration management

The Change and Transport Organizer is used for configuration management.

Those objects that cannot be controlled with the CTO are managed with the Document Management System.

The technical coordinator is responsible for configuration management.

Quality questions for the products

All the products produced with the quality questions from Chapter 8 are listed here.

Tools

The tools listed in Table 11.2 are used.

Table 11.2   Tools and tasks

Tool	Task
SAP R/3 4.0B	Development system
MS-Word (Format 97)	Word processing
MS PowerPoint (Format 97)	Presentations
Visio Version 5	Diagrams
AutoTester Version 3.2	Tests for non-CATT procedures

Problem reporting system

The problem reporting system is handled using a company-internal help service. Chapter 8 contains further details.

The technical coordinator presented this quality assurance plan to the teams. Because the technical coordinator told the teams that the DSDM method permits changes in the quality assurance plan after each review, they agreed immediately to the quality assurance plan. Acceptance was also encouraged because only those quality requirements were recorded that the teams knew at this point in time. The fear that an excessive bureaucracy would occur was not expressed.

11.2.20 Prepare the test management

Once it had been agreed in the quality assurance plan to use the SAP R/3 tools CATT, test plan tool and AutoTester to automate as many tests as possible, the technical coordinator had to make preparations for the use of these tools.

He first created a test catalog in the test plan tool. He called this Z_TESTCAT and described it as being the 'test catalog for the project'. He created a tree structure in the test catalog that is classified into phases, iterations and teams.

The teams could now link CATT test procedures with the individual structures.

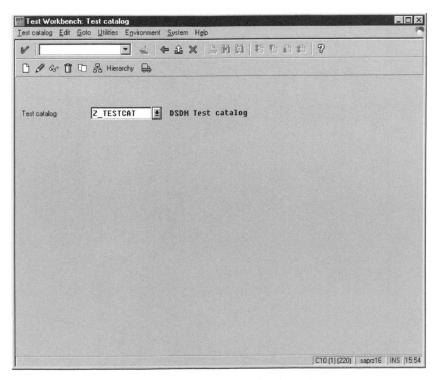

Figure 11.19   Test catalog for the project

11.2.21 Prepare configuration management

Three SAP R/3 systems were set up for configuration management: a development system, a consolidation system, and a productive system.

A project IMG was generated that covered all important tasks of the project. The Change and Transport Organizer was set so that it supported these transport paths.

The Document Management System (DMS) controlled supplementary programs for the external systems. The use of DMS also permitted the realization of version management for all external program modules.

The project documents and the customizing settings were documented in SAPoffice and in the project IMG, respectively.

Change requests were created for the individual tasks of the teams. The Change and Transport Organizer automatically registered and documented all changes in these change requests.

A base configuration should be created after every timebox.

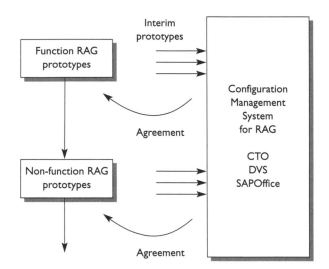

Figure 11.20   Configuration management

The technical coordinator then presented the configuration management plan to the teams.

11.3 Phase 3: Function model iteration

11.3.1 Determination of the individual timeboxes for the third phase

Four timeboxes, each taking two weeks, were planned for the third phase. However, it was not sufficient just to define the end dates for the individual timeboxes. Rather, it was much more important to plan what was to take place within these timeboxes. These exact time details for the requirements to be satisfied had the main task of improving project control, in which a 'small' milestone or a review of what the individual teams had achieved was performed at the end of every timebox within the teams.

The following requirements were defined as the task for the MM teams in the first timebox:

- Process the material master

- Process the supplier master

- Order request

- Order

- Goods arrival

The CO team planned for their first timebox their following business processes as the requirements to be achieved:

- Cost/revenue element processing

- Profit planning

- Billing transfer and evaluation

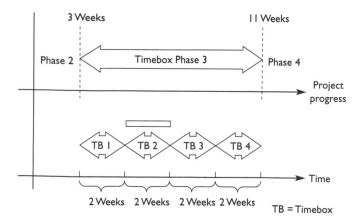

Figure 11.21   Timebox planning within the third phase

All teams were required to go on to process the next request from the associated priority list once all planned business processes had been completed (even before the end of the timebox).

The following section uses a business process to show how the MM team and the CO team process a business process or, in other words, how a business process runs through the various phases of prototyping management (MM team) or of IPP (CO team).

11.3.2 MM: business process description

The MM team, together with module representatives, questioned the persons in charge from the user departments about the individual business processes in their work context, namely in a Contextual Interview.

They took the most important business process from the priority list and processed this completely. This work involved expanding the associated entry for the general concept and creating a Visio graph that showed what the consultant and the module representative had understood about the requirements. Figure 11.22 shows an example of such a Visio graph for the MM business process 'Process material master'.

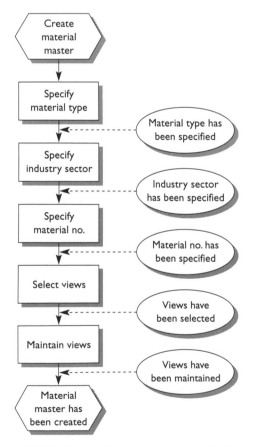

Figure 11.22   Process business process material master

Because the R/3 reference process model was considered to be very difficult to handle and also cluttered, the MM team decided to create Visio graphs. These graphs should also avoid the business process analysis taking a wrong path should the internal module representatives consider that their own business processes could be pressed into predefined templates by the reference model and so miss the actual requirements.

The initial prototype was now derived from this graphical and verbal business process description.

11.3.3 MM: Management of iterative prototyping

This initial prototype was presented to the persons in charge from the user department. On the one hand, the team wanted to gain more exact information about the requirements made on the system and to determine any modifications required, and, on the other, to be able to demonstrate to subsequent users how the SAP R/3 system functioned with regard to their individual tasks.

Every prototype normally passes through the phases of iterative prototyping management shown in Figure 11.23.

The phases shown for iterative prototyping management do not represent a fixed specification for prototyping that must be performed under all circumstances. Rather, they provide a framework to ensure that the prototype iterations are not continued endlessly.

If, for example, the user has already accepted a prototype in its original form, additional demonstrations do not need to be held, but rather the status of the prototype is set immediately to 'consolidated'.

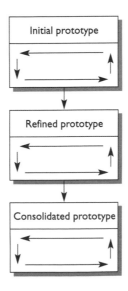

Figure 11.23   Phases of the iterative prototyping management

The individual forms of a prototype have the following purposes:

- *Initial (business process) prototype*
  This permits fast creation or acceptance of the standard settings to ensure that the correct requirements are processed.

- *Refined (business process) prototype*
  This contains changes to the original prototype and serves as a basis for the determination of the consolidated prototype.

- *Consolidated (business process) prototype*
  The consolidated prototype represents the business process in the form that it will later be passed to the productive system.

Figure 11.24 shows the form of the individual iterations within the prototyping management phases.

Thus, Figure 11.24 describes how a prototype can develop within a phase of iterative prototyping. Normally four levels are passed through here:

- Demonstration

- Comparison

- Change requests

- Customizing

The following section lists typical questions that were asked more than once or needed to be considered during the case study.

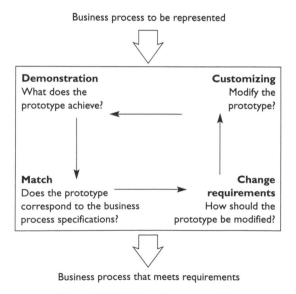

Figure 11.24   Iterative prototyping

Before the prototype was demonstrated for the first time, it was first necessary to clarify to whom the prototype should be presented, i.e., whether the prototype should only be presented to the persons in charge from the user department or whether other representative users from the user groups should be included. This can be very useful because a large number of end-users normally also have a wide range of wishes. The question should also be considered whether all relevant screens and input fields are shown. In conjunction with this, reference should be made to all change capabilities, which include not only the input fields and their positions, but also the screen sequence. The question was also asked whether the input logic is appropriate, whether the screen is well laid out, and whether the response times are acceptable.

The comparison focuses on the questions of whether the prototype matches the requirements for the business process, whether all mandatory input fields are present, whether superfluous input fields are present, and whether the default values and the mandatory fields have been set correctly.

When requests for changes are made, it must be taken into consideration who makes the change request, whether the change request can be made, whether a modification needs to be made to the business processes or whether it would not be better to change that of the prototype, and how it is possible to ensure that changes do not respond to two conflicting wishes that exclude each other and so result in a never-ending loop.

With regard to the customizing settings, those involved must realize that the customers' requirements are paramount and not the consultants' ideas. They must also question whether the requirements have been set in accordance with their importance and whether the customizing entries have an effect on other customizing settings.

Problems can arise even during the iterative prototyping, the cause of which has been discussed many times in the theoretical part of this book. These questions are, for example: Is the same 'language' spoken? Are the tasks and roles clearly defined? Are there any fears of making contact? Does the consultant claim to know the business processes better than the customer? Or does the customer expect that the consultant already knows the business processes in all companies (he is, after all, a consultant)? Are the DSDM principles taken into consideration? Are the internal employees given sufficient time to do the prototyping?

These change requests were added to the prototypes using customizing.

11.3.4 MM: Customizing

Because in the project under discussion great importance was placed on the transfer of know-how, RAG and M+P considered it to be very important that the internal employees themselves made the customizing settings and so the transfer of know-how was supported effectively. Even during the course of the first DSDM pass, the internal employee responsible for the module could himself solve customizing tasks and correct any errors that arose during the testing.

Figure 11.26 shows the refined prototype that then resulted from the modified customizing settings.

This was also presented to the users and further modified when necessary. The next step should bring the prototype to the 'consolidated' status.

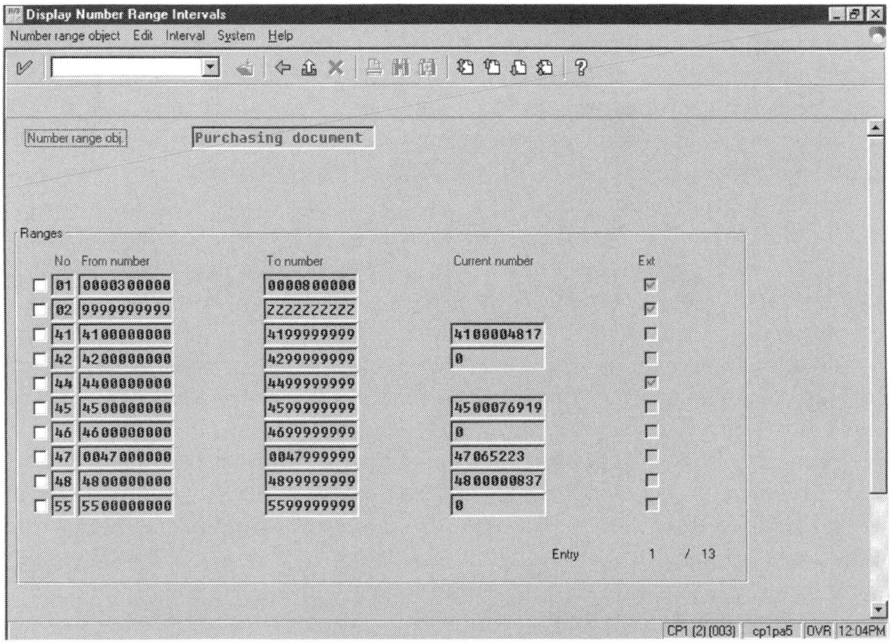

Figure 11.25   Customizing

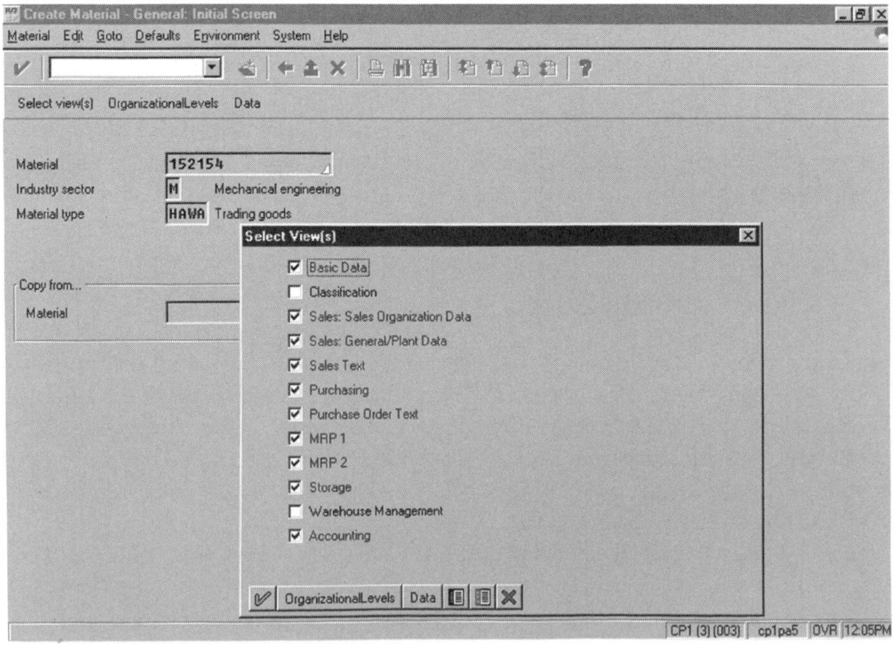

Figure 11.26   Refined 'Process material master' prototype

At the end of iterative prototyping management, those involved passed the business process to the detailed concept.

11.3.5 MM: CATT

As soon as a business process has attained 'consolidated prototype' status in iterative prototyping management, the CATT records a test procedure for it, which is then passed to the organization of the test plan tool (refer to Figure 11.27). The recording of every single business process makes it very easy and quick to check whether changes to the customizing settings (even with regard to other business processes) have any undesirable effects on the business processes that have already been consolidated.

The test plan tool, in agreement with RAG, was organized in a modular form that made it possible to test either individual processes (lowest level) or individual modules (middle level), or to perform a test over all modules (highest level). In the case study, the individual test procedures were also parameterized using comprehensive Excel tables, in which the rows represented test cases for the individual test procedures.

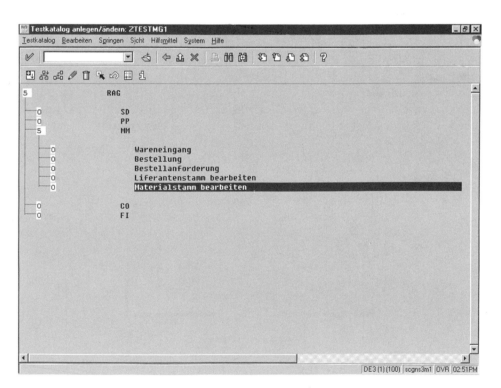

Figure 11.27   MM test plan

11.3.6 Perform tests

Once the teams had graphically described the first business processes and the users could execute these processes in the SAP system using sample data, the SAP specialists gave the users a brief introduction to the use of CATT. The users learnt how they could use CATT to record transactions with the sample data.

The users decided to record, using the appropriate sample data, the 'Process customer order' process chain which consists of the 'Create customer inquiry', 'Create quotation', 'Create customer order' process chains. For this purpose, they noted the associated transaction names and recorded this under the control of CATT.

The SAP specialists in expert mode then processed these recorded CATT test modules. They named variable import and export parameters for the inquiry number, the quotation number, the customer name, the material, the order quantity and the delivery date. They then created an Excel table with all combinations of customer names and materials each for two quantities.

They created a test procedure from the three created test modules that executed in succession, and then ran the Excel table with the 3000 combinations as external variants of the test procedure. Errors occurred for 30 combinations. These could be traced back to the master data having been updated incorrectly. The complete test procedure with all its variants was rerun once these incorrect settings had been corrected. All 3000 test variants ran without problem in this test. The team could now be sure that there were no further incorrect master data for this business process.

This test procedure was now linked with the test catalog. This linking permitted all additional test runs to be represented clearly as a tree structure. Another advantage was that both the manual test cases and those test cases that had been processed with the

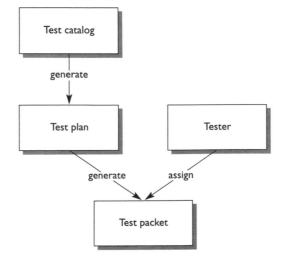

Figure 11.28   Generation path of the test packet

AutoTester were also stored in this test catalog, and so all test cases could be invoked in a clear manner.

For an integration or regression test, the test catalog was now used to generate a test plan with those test cases that were to be processed. Various test packets sorted into teams are then generated from this test plan.

These test packets are then used to perform the tests and to manage the states of the individual test cases. The SAP R/3 system uses a 'traffic light' to support status management. This shows at a glance which tests are OK (green), incorrect (red) or still untested (yellow). In order to estimate the testing effort still required for the remaining cases, the teams also used the statistical functions that the test plan tool offers.

After making use of this impressive tool for some time as an exercise, the teams recognized that testing a system is not a necessary evil that is often performed only inadequately, but that testing can indeed be a demanding and interesting task. The number of test cases recorded with CATT increased steadily and the old test cases could be rerun for every new iteration.

11.3.7   CO: Business process description

As already discussed above, the CO team decided to use the IPP method for business process description and creation. This method uses SAP-specific, integrated tools. Thus, the business process shown in Figure 11.26 returns to the Business Navigator, which, for example, permits a direct branch from individual nodes of the business processes into the corresponding transaction of the SAP R/3 system.

The following section shows how the IPP method operates in detail.

11.3.8   CO: The IPP workshop

The business processes from the reference process model are normally used as the starting point for the method (refer to sample business process above). To analyze the business processes, all relevant processes are printed and distributed to the participants in a workshop. An IPP workshop should have the following content (Keller and Teufel, 1997, p. 246:

- 6–8 customer employees and a moderator with industry and R/3 knowledge

- Relevant R/3 reference models in printed form for the selection of the required functionality using text markers

- R/3 system access and visualization capability using an LCD display to present the business solution in the R/3 system

- 2–3 partition boards for the flexible arrangement of process modules, etc., using card to create a value-added chain for the customer

- Optional, a spreadsheet program for the structured acquisition of the requirements with open points during the workshop

- Optional, depending on the associated investigation spectrum, additional technical consultants with special knowledge in the area to be handled

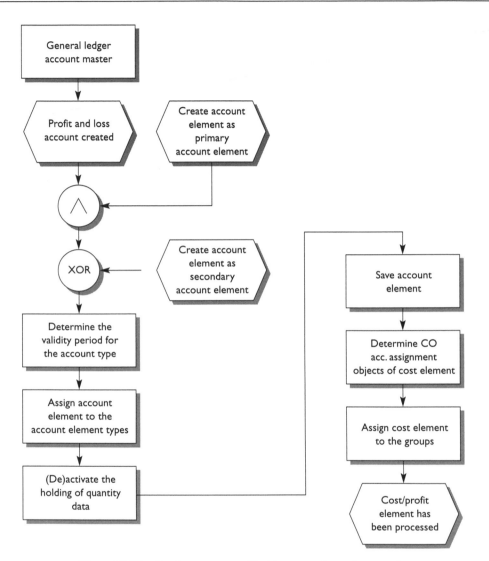

Figure 11.29   Business process: Cost/revenue element processing
(from/Keller and Teufel, 1997, p. 322ff)

In this workshop, those involved discuss and develop the business process to be represented.

A typical question that is asked during the workshops is whether it is possible to regard the business process as being a prototype in the system. The major advantage of the IPP that provides for the use of the integrated tools becomes apparent here. If, for example, you click on the 'Assign cost elements' element in the 'Cost/revenue element processing' business process from Figure 11.29, you reach the corresponding transaction in the SAP R/3 system as shown in Figure 11.30.

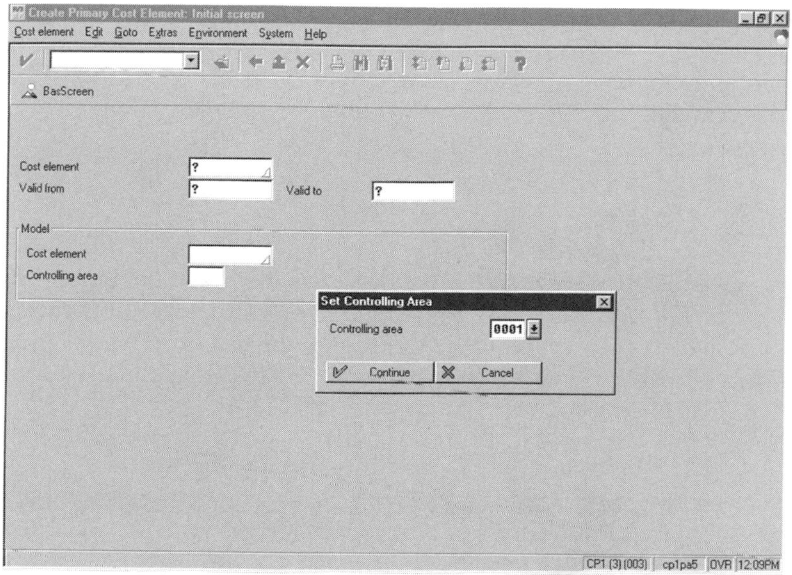

Figure 11.30   IPP prototype

The same applies to the so-called 'iterative jumps' that can also be made from the business process into the customizing. Figure 11.31 shows the customizing screen that you reach when you click on the 'Determine the cost elements CO for the consolidation objects (FI)' element in the business process.

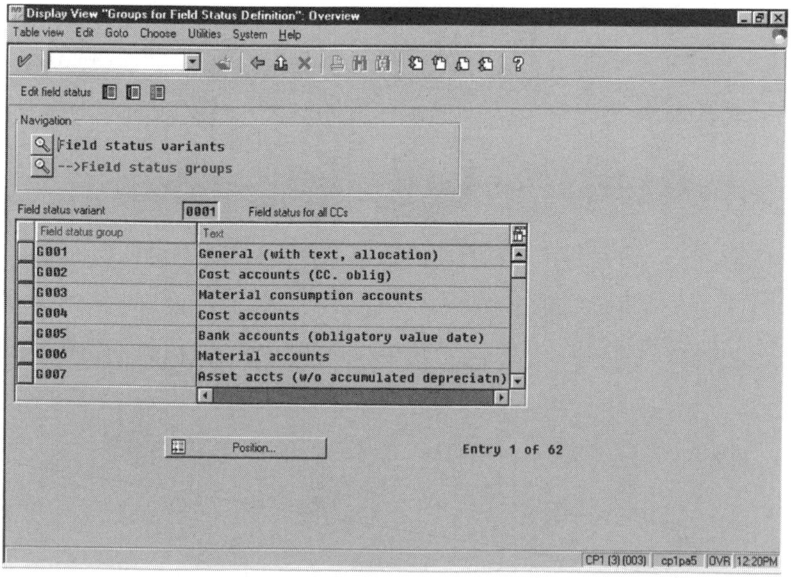

Figure 11.31   IPP jump into customizing

The described method is used to jump within the associated business processes using the IPP method until the business process has been set in accordance with the requirements. In addition to the jumps into customizing or into the transactions, a branch can also be made into the data dictionary, the data/object model, the reference process model or the organization model.

11.3.9 CO: CATT

As soon as agreement has been reached in the workshop about the form of the business process in the SAP R/3 system or as soon as this has been set, the Computer Aided Test Tool is used to record a test procedure and pass it to the test plan. Figure 11.32 illustrates how the 'Process cost/revenue element' business process considered as our example is received in the test plan.

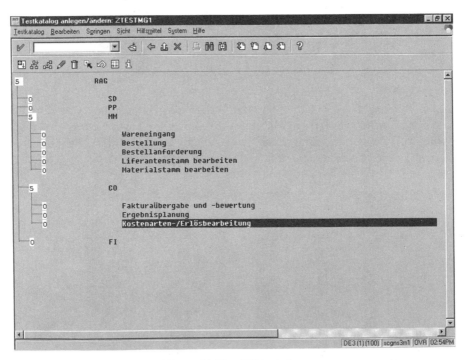

Figure 11.32   CO test plan

11.3.10 Use of configuration management

The property of reversibility of the previous development is a basic requirement of DSDM-based procedure models. It means that every step in customizing, in business process description, and also in the development of supplementary programs can be reversed, and the team can then restart at an old state. This increases the development speed, because the teams can be sure that an old, functioning state is reachable at any time. Configuration management provides the most important support here.

A requirement for the team was to produce an interface to an old system. This meant a large programming effort outside the usual ABAP/4 environment. Because the Change and Transport Organizer only references SAP R/3-specific objects, it could not be used in configuration management. For this reason the DMS document management system from SAP was chosen for configuration management of the externally written programs to this interface.

The team had created a functioning interface after the first timebox. The programs that belong to this interface were archived in the DMS document management system at the end of the timebox and assigned the version number 1. A bill-of-materials was created for all the software elements that belong to this interface and stored as a reference configuration (baseline). To ensure that this reference configuration could not get lost, it was assigned a validity date in the DMS.

The team wanted to further refine this interface in the second timebox and undertook great effort to change many modules. These changed modules were regularly archived in the DMS and a version number was assigned for each new version. A new reference configuration was to be created only at the end of the timebox when the extended interface was finished.

Technical difficulties in the development became apparent shortly before the end of the second timebox. The team realized that the goal could no longer be reached in the timebox. The careful configuration management made it immediately clear which modules belonged to the valid reference configuration. However, because the modules developed in the second iteration could be used in a further DSDM pass, the previous work was not done in vain.

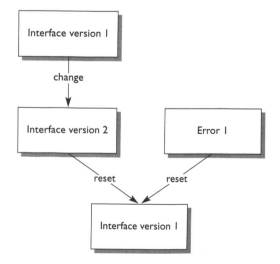

Figure 11.33   Schematic representation

11.3.11 Testing with AutoTester

Even though CATT is a very flexible test tool, the team became aware that not all test tasks can be performed with CATT. Although CATT can read and process all messages from the status line, it cannot read the result fields in the masks. However, because it was important for the team to test whether the correct prices are automatically displayed in the screens when a quotation was created, it quickly became apparent that this test cannot be automated with CATT. For this reason, it was decided to use AutoTester for those tasks that cannot be performed with CATT.

Similar to CATT, AutoTester has a recording function for test cases, the so-called AutoCommand. This made it very easy for the users to become acquainted with this new tool. Indeed, because they could also call the individual transactions easily using the menu without needing to determine the transaction number first, they found the operation of AutoTester to be even simpler than with CATT.

Because all activities in the SAP R/3 system can be programmed with special commands, the reworking of such test scripts did not provide any difficulties for an experienced software developer.

Table 11.3 shows some examples.

The software developer can use the *SapVerifyFieldValue* command to write test scripts, and to automatically test whether the correct prices are displayed in the screens when the quotation is produced.

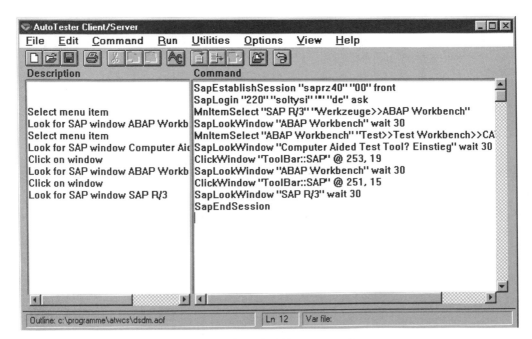

Figure 11.34   AutoTester example

Table 11.3   AutoTester commands

Command	Meaning
SapLogin	Log in to an SAP R/3 system
SapEndSession	Log off from an SAP R/3 system
SapRetrieveFieldValue	Read the value of a field
SapVerifyFieldValue	Check the contents of a field
SapListItemCount	Determine the number of elements in a selection list
SapListItemExists	Check whether an element is present in the list
SapListItemSelect	Read an element from the list
SapPossibleEntriesSelect	Select matchcode
SapFindInstance	Find a value in a table

11.3.12 SD: Requirements for the interfaces

Figure 11.35 shows the processes that are to be realized in cooperation between RAG and HiSpeed. Two problems must first be solved here:

The interface to be designed assumes a flexible data extraction mechanism that can be used to obtain the business data from the application data. The following requirements should be satisfied:

- The software should be able to send data to the service provider at regular, but arbitrary, intervals.

- If transmission problems occur, it should be possible to repeat the data shipping.

- Data flow tracking should be an integral component of the software.

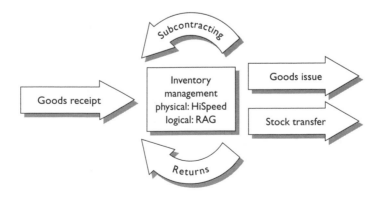

Figure 11.35   Business processes and inventory management

- Any errors that occur should be forwarded immediately to the assigned staff members.

- Corrected business transactions should be further processed automatically.

The coupling system between HiSpeed and the RAG should satisfy the following requirements:

- It must ensure secure data transfer.

- The data transfer should run completely disconnected from the software.

- The archiving of the send or receive data should take place at the server level.

Because IDocs (*Intermediate Documents*) can avoid all problems that could occur for a conventional software solution, its use was favoured to provide a software solution to the above-mentioned requirements. The IDoc technology is an integral part of the SAP R/3 applications and provides you with the capability to incorporate your own extensions which are retained even over release changes.

The standardization of this format made it possible to convert these documents without difficulty into common transaction data formats such as EDIFACT. This made the realization of communication between an SAP system and an external system relatively simple.

ALE (*Application Link Enabling*) also supports the IDoc system. ALE can be used to solve the following tasks:

- Partner finding is set in the customizing and is thus flexible.

- The definition is made as to which partner can exchange which information.

- Data can be filtered, if, for example, certain information is to be suppressed.

No detailed description of the technical realization is provided here.

11.3.13 Extend the user documentation

The user documentation in the example considered was created or extended when a business process was sufficiently advanced that the prototype had attained 'consolidated' status. The task of creating this documentation was given to an employee from the user department. Care was taken that this user department employee was also involved with the development and acceptance of the prototypes, and so was already acquainted with the operation of the corresponding applications in the SAP R/3 system, i.e., with the processing of the business processes. This documentation was also used as the basis for training the users.

11.3.14 Training the users

In the ideal situation, the same person who was already responsible for creating the user documentation for the associated business process would also be given the task of training the users. The same concept used for the creation of the user documentation also applied to the individual seminars. Rather than holding just a single seminar in which all the functionalities of the SAP R/3 system were handled in a single step, many small seminars were held that were dedicated to the complete processing of a business process and its documentation.

Thus, the DSDM-based concept with its methodology of extending stepwise required at the same time the principles of further learning in steps. This concept is based on the assumption that the complete learning, understanding and processing of small subtasks is easier for the trainees than the mastering of the complete task in a single step. Thus, the users get to know and master the SAP R/3 system piece by piece. Indeed, the concept of this further learning in the DSDM-based procedure model continues over several DSDM passes. The user also gets to know which business processes are the most important for the business benefits, because these are handled in a prioritized and periodized sequence.

11.3.15 Milestone at the end of a timebox

The milestone at the end of the timebox is performed within the teams. The first question to be answered was to determine everything that had been achieved in the previous time-box. The result was that the MM team and the CO team had not been able to complete the 'goods arrival' business process and the 'billing transfer and evaluation' process, respectively. However, the creation of the interface in the SD team had progressed faster than planned. The project management indicated that it was very satisfied with the result of the first timebox.

The following questions were also asked in the milestone meeting:

- How successful was the timebox planning?

- Were the users given sufficient time to become actively involved with the project work?

- Were the teams empowered to make decisions?

- Was the cooperation between internal and external team members successful?

- Were the roles adopted?

- Are there new requirements?

- Have the requirements changed?

In particular, with regard to the question of new or changed requirements, it must be clarified how they are to be assigned in the priority list to form the basis for determining the next timebox for the third phase.

11.3.16 Determine the next timebox

With regard to determining the next timebox within the third phase, the individual teams suggested distributing the remaining six weeks of the function model iteration over just two rather than three timeboxes. However, because the central consideration was to reduce pressure on the limited time assignment, the project manager decided to retain the original planning, with three timeboxes each of two weeks. He made this decision because the concept of timeboxes is aimed precisely at giving the team members no time to leave non-completed tasks to the last moment. The project manager was also supported by the fact that all requirements, except the least important, planned for the first timebox had been fulfilled, which also represents the ideal case for timebox planning.

If, however, all planned requirements have been processed completely, this is a sign that too few requirements had been planned, although it would be possible to argue that this does not play any role in this case, because the next requirement from the priority list will be processed if there is any excess time. However, experience has shown that if the teams are not fully loaded, they will organize their work effort so that they complete the required work at precisely the deadline.

However, if many planned requirements were not fulfilled, either the timeboxes were overloaded or the team members were given too little time to working on the project.

Thus, the original timebox planning was retained and the activities of the next timebox again given a time interval of two weeks. The following activities were specified to be performed by the MM team:

- Goods arrival

- Invoice receipt and checking

- Restocking

  The CO team was to process the following business processes in the next timebox:

- Billing transfer and evaluation

- Profit centre report

- Cost centre processing

The timebox planning was performed in the same manner for the rest of the third phase. Section 11.3.22 shows which business processes were introduced at the end of the function model iteration.

11.3.17 Extend the report system

Except for the fact that it does not need to be completely represented, but only extended stepwise, the creation of the report system is not a typical DSDM phase activity. For this reason, no reference is made here to the SAP help nor to ASAP. SAP describes the following work steps for this item:

- Determine the information requirement.

- Check whether the information requirement is covered.

- Work through the suggested solutions for the outstanding requirements.

- Realize reports.

- Define the organization of the report system.

- Test the report system.

11.3.18 Represent the archive administration

The figure for archive administration is independent of DSDM and described in detail by SAP. The following individual items must be performed:

• Create the concept for archive administration.

• Perform the system settings.

• Test the archiving activities.

11.3.19 Update the interfaces and system extensions

Because the system is not implemented from one day to the next in one 'large' project, but extended stepwise, the system extensions and interfaces must be tested and adapted in each DSDM pass.

11.3.20 Perform the quality review

A quality review was performed at the end of the timebox. For this purpose, the quality assurance plan in the team with the individual quality assurance measures was considered with regard to their observance in the timebox. Questions were prepared for configuration management, for observance of the test specification, and also quality questions prepared for the currently available products. The review can be conducted either internally in the team or by an external moderator, such as the technical coordinator or the project manager. Because reviews, in contrast to the traditional methodology, take place very frequently, such a review should not take too long. The result of the quality review is a list of quality faults and measures for their correction. Particular attention in the quality review is dedicated to communication. Intensive discussions about the communication problems in the team sessions took place in this session. The team members had the impression that they did not produce optimum results in the discussion. Countless, ever-recurring, arguments interrupted the constructive running of the creative group process and disturbed the close cooperation between users and developers. The team leader, who had little previous experience in team leadership, was helpless. The moderator noticed these remarks and attempted, in discourse with the team members, to agree measures. At first it transpired that all team members suffered under this situation and worked to achieve improvement for the benefit of the real project work.

The moderator showed in a short extract the principles of the *topic-centred interaction method* from Ruth Cohn. He explained that the cooperation in a team depends on three factors: the individual team member, the team and the subject. These factors are embedded in an environment that consists of space, time and the company situation. To ensure effective work on the team topic, it is necessary to consider not only the subject, but also the other factors.

It transpired that the project room had several faults that the team leader had not noticed when he selected it. The room was easily accessible by the team members' superiors. This had the consequence that the team was very often interrupted in its work. The frequently ringing telephone added to this effect because it frequently attracted the attention of individual team members and kept them from their intensive work.

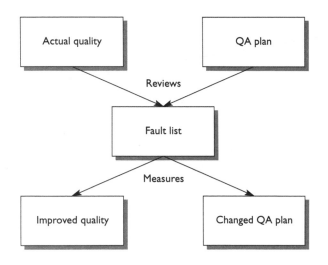

Figure 11.36   Quality review

It was decided that the team be given a new, more isolated project room and that during team meetings the telephone was switched to the number of another employee who did not belong to the team.

However, because there was a real communication problem in the team, these measures by themselves did not suffice. For this reason, the moderator offered to take part in the next team meeting and to observe the behaviour of the group in observing the rules of the topic-centred interaction method, and at the end of the team meeting to give the participants feedback about their behaviour in the team and so improve the work situation.

11.3.21 Topic-centred interaction

In the last review it was decided to use Ruth Cohn's topic-centred interaction in the team. The moderator of the quality review, at the start of the meeting, once again presented the postulates and the associated auxiliary rules, and wrote these on a flipchart:

Postulate 1: Be your own chairperson.

Postulate 2: Interruptions have priority.

Auxiliary rule 1: Represent yourself when you speak; use 'I' and not 'we' or 'one'.

Auxiliary rule 2: When you ask a question, say why you ask and what your question means for you. Speak for yourself and avoid the interview.

Auxiliary rule 3: Be authentic and selective in your communication; be aware what you think and feel, and choose what you say and do.

Auxiliary rule 4:   Refrain as long as possible from making interpretations of others. Instead of this, tell you personal reactions.

Auxiliary rule 5:   Avoid making too many generalizations.

Auxiliary rule 6:   If you say anything about the behaviour or the characteristic of another participant, also say what it means to you (i.e., how you see him).

Auxiliary rule 7:   Conversations on the side have priority. They disturb and are normally important. They would not take place if they were not important (perhaps you would like to tell us what you are discussing amongst yourselves?).

Auxiliary rule 8:   Only one person at the same time please.

Auxiliary rule 9:   If more than one person wants to speak at the same time, use keywords to indicate what you intend to speak about.

The moderator then adopted the role of silent observer and noted situations in which auxiliary rules were violated.

When he analyzed his notes, he noticed that the participants often spoke in the We-form, even though not all shared this opinion. He also noted that the developers very often attempted to interpret the users' statements, which violated Rule 4. Generalizations were regularly used in the discussion, which were not allowed.

It became apparent in the subsequent presentation that the participants had not been previously aware of this behaviour. Thus, the team meetings concentrated on showing individual team members that they saw things too globally. This meant that the group action focused more on the individual members than on the subject. Better observation of the rules resulted in improved concentration on the subject. But when the team consciously attempted to work on the subject at hand, they adopted a working methodology that concentrated too much on the topic. The result was work that was too academic and that had lost sight of the actual goal, to achieve a contribution to the business benefits. The team leader, who in the meantime had become sensitized to such problems, recognized that the team members, fearing to send the wrong signals to the other participants, treated each other too distantly. He brought the team back by steering the conversation in the meetings to the team and its members. It became clear to the team leader and the team during the course of the project that neither involvement with the subject, nor individual team members, nor the team as a whole could be allowed to be the centre of attention. Rather, it was the task of the team leader to achieve a balance here, which from the company's viewpoint provides the optimum benefit. After several weeks of use and supervision of the topic-centred interaction method, the team stopped using it consciously. They had won trust in each other, and each member had become an authority for the others in at least one area.

11.3.22 End of the global timebox for phase 3

Figure 11.37 shows which requirements were satisfied in the MM and CO modules, i.e., it shows the form of the basis system with the basic functionality. With regard to the SD, PP and FI modules, the planned requirements were also satisfied in these areas. The EDI interfaces that had been assigned to the SD area could also be satisfied in accordance with the planning and so already replace some fax concepts.

As described above, the function tests had already been performed. The result of this function test was that each business process functioned alone in accordance with the requirements, i.e., independent of the other business processes. The integration test now planned in the next step should ensure that the business processes also functioned together, i.e., integrated.

MM	PP	SD	CO	FI
- Returns from customers - Inventory - Stock transfer - Invoice verification - Invoice receipt - Goods receipt - PO - PR - Vendor master - Material master	XXX	XXX	- Variance calculation - Cost centre analysis - Cost centre processing - Profit centre report - Billing transfer and evaluation - Revenue planning - Cost element/ revenue element processing	XXX
The SAP R/3 basis system of the RAG				

Figure 11.37   Set business processes

11.4 Phase 4: System design and system build iteration

11.4.1 Integration test

Now that all teams had worked intensively and independently of each other, an integration test was carried out to see whether the settings and results still matched. For this purpose, larger inter-team CATT procedures were formed from the existing CATT procedures. These new test procedures concentrated on the interfaces between the teams. In this way, the integration capability of the independently developed SAP R/3 subsystems could be tested and the subsystems changed when necessary (refer to Figure 11.38).

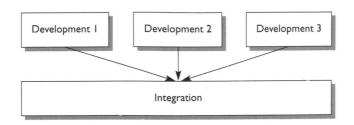

Figure 11.38   Integration of the systems

11.4.2 Define the authorization concept

An authorization concept for all subsequent users was created in this work packet. This defined which functions, in which system organization unit, from which position could be executed, and which functions were not available to every user (refer to Figure 11.39).

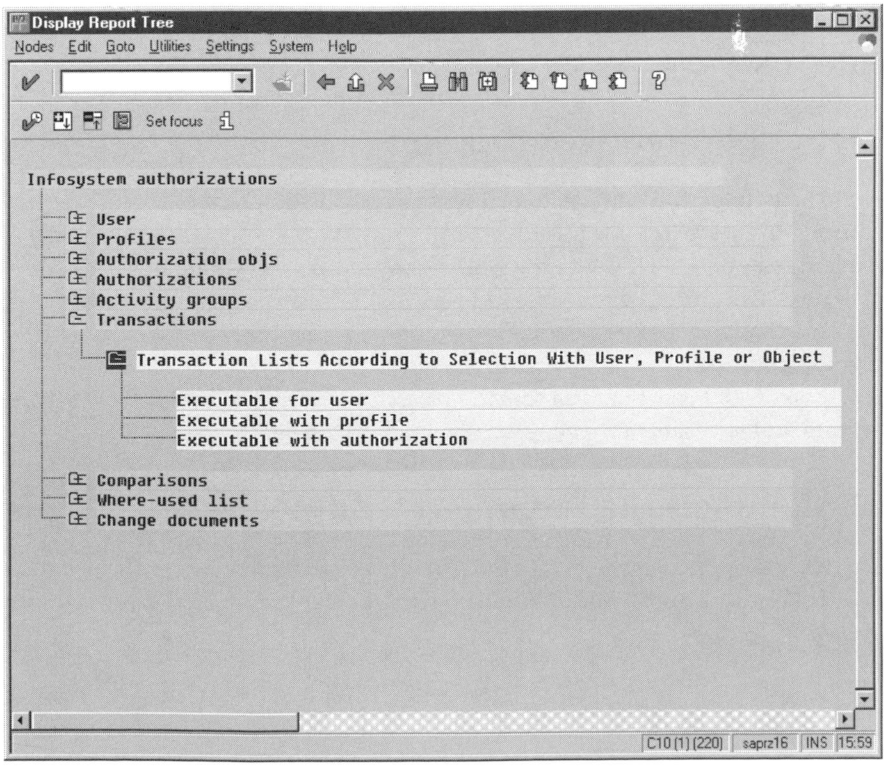

Figure 11.39   Information system for authorizations

11.4.3 Prepare for becoming productive

In this work packet, the existing system landscape was used as a basis to define the necessary hardware (e.g., application server, presentation server, network, printers, screens for the users, etc.) for the productive system. At the same time, a stress test checked whether all system components had been configured appropriately even under high system loading.

11.5 Phase 5: Implementation, live operation

11.5.1 Organize the system administration

The organization of the system administration concentrates on ensuring that the SAP R/3 system is permanently available with adequate performance.

This phase activity is DSDM-independent and contains the items:

- Define system administration.

- Train the system administrators.

11.5.2 Support for live operation

This phase activity permits (in the DSDM sense) the consideration of change requests and determining any potential for improvement. This plays a special role because several independent subprojects follow in the DSDM-based procedure model. These subprojects offer the possibility immediately, i.e., in the next DSDM pass, processing the change requests and changed requirements. Thus, support of the live operation also represents planning the optimization of system use.

The activity itself takes the form that the project members are initially with the user, to support him and so ensure a friction-free transition to the new system.

11.5.3 Complete the subproject (DSDM pass)

The final workshop held at the end of the fifth phase clarifies whether the set goals were attained. It should also be noted what knowledge can be gained from the previous DSDM pass.

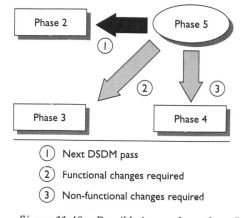

① Next DSDM pass

② Functional changes required

③ Non-functional changes required

Figure 11.40   Possible jumps from phase 5

Furthermore, either as part of the workshop or later during productive operation, it must be clarified whether a return to a previous phase must be made or whether a new DSDM pass can be started. A return is made to the fourth phase should there be problems with non-functional requirements, such as performance or security. A return to the third phase is made should there be problems with functional requirements, such as errors in the customizing settings or incorrectly represented business processes.

In the case study shown, the transition was made to the next DSDM pass.

12 The second DSDM pass

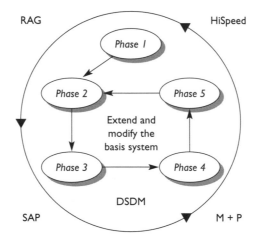

Figure 12.1   Extension and modification of the basis system

12.1 Phase 1: Feasibility study

Because the first phase of the DSDM-based procedure model is performed only when a new project is to be started, this phase is not repeated in the second DSDM pass.

Because the phases described in the following sections contain only those activities that are of particular importance for modification and extension of the basis system, the SAP and ASAP activities are not described here. If the reader wishes to study this chapter in detail, perhaps because an extension or modification of the SAP R/3 systems is pending at his company, he is recommended not to avoid reading the first part of the case study, because the fundamentals of the DSDM ideas are described there in detail.

12.2 Phase 2: Business study

- Even in this DSDM pass, risk analysis is always continued as an inter-phase activity.

- The *consulting requirement* was determined anew for every DSDM pass. The central point here was the question of whether the consulting company from the previous DSDM pass is also familiar with the subsequent subproject, how many tasks the internal employees can perform themselves and what consultancy requirement is still needed for the next pass. M+P was also commissioned for the second subproject. The only difference was that the individual consultants were scheduled to be present for just two days per week on average.

- The teams and the *project organization* were largely retained. There were no changes to the case study under consideration.

- The training for *Contextual Inquiry* was not repeated. In the first DSDM pass, this method was experienced by all the members involved; role behaviour and the various principles were considered. Communication did not represent any problem during business process analysis.

- Because no new employees were added to the project team, no new *determination of the training requirement* was needed.

- The phase activity of the general *business process description* again took place in a workshop. In addition to the requirements still to be realized, it was also necessary to determine which business processes had changed or had been added. The changed 'Stock transfer' business process should be considered for the MM team in the next section. The added 'Overhead surcharge costing' business process is considered for the CO team.

- Thus, the *MM general business process description* covered:
  - Returns from the sales personnel
  - Stocktaking
  - Subcontracting
  - Return of old goods
  - Destruction
  - Stock transfer

- The CO *general business process description* has the following screen:
  - Profit analysis
  - Standard costing with quantity structure
  - Overhead surcharge costing

- With regard to the creation of *EDI interfaces in SD*, this had already been considered in the first DSDM pass relatively independently of the actual case study. This topic should be completely ignored in the second DSDM pass.

- The MoSCoW rules were again used in the second DSDM pass as the *priority setting rule*, where subdivision into individual groups plays no further role in the following pass. Thus, a priority list with attributes like 'Must' or 'Could' was the initiator for the processing of the business processes. However, time planning should take account of all the business processes still to be handled. Important here was the position in the priority list and not the question of whether the individual business processes still belong in the 'Should' group or are already in the 'Could' group.

- The *MM priority list* had the following form, where the most important entry, namely the request to be processed first, was at the top:
  - Stock transfer
  - Subcontracting
  - Stocktaking
  - Returns from the sales personnel
  - Return of old goods
  - Destruction

  The time estimate for processing these requests was set at three weeks.

- The CO *priority list* is shown below. The most important request is also at the top here.
  - Profit analysis
  - Standard costing with quantity structure
  - Overhead surcharge costing

It was estimated that the processing of these three items would take two weeks.

- The *preliminary concept* from the first DSDM pass was updated.

- The *definition of the timebox for phase 3* in the second DSDM pass required that the PP, SD and FI areas should not exceed a duration of three weeks in their time planning. Thus, the global timebox for the third phase was defined with the aim of realizing all outstanding requirements within three weeks.

- The *quality plan* created in the first DSDM pass was updated.

- The *test management* from the first DSDM pass was updated in the usual manner.

- The same applies to *configuration management*, which was organized in exactly the same way as the configuration management from the first DSDM pass.

12.3 Phase 3: Function model iteration

- The *determination of the individual timeboxes* for the third phase produced the result that two timeboxes should be used. Whereas eight workdays were estimated for the first timebox, only seven workdays were estimated for the second timebox. Despite the small number of business processes still to be considered, to ensure goal-oriented teamwork it was important to provide clear planning details to avoid the teams continuously delaying completion of the work. The planning details for the MM team for the first timebox were as follows:
  - Stock transfer
  - Subcontracting
  - Stocktaking

  The following requirements were specified for the CO team:
  - Profit analysis
  - Standard costing with quantity structure

- The processing of the *business processes in the MM team* proceeded as usual. The entries in the general concept were refined, Visio graphics were created for the individual business processes, iterative prototyping management was used and finally CATT procedures were created for the consolidated prototypes. However, during the processing of the 'subcontracting' business process, the requirement arose in the productive system from the first DSDM pass that changes also needed to be made in the 'stock transfers' business process. Because the changes to the 'stock transfers' business process were considered to be more important to the business benefits, these changes were made first before continuing with the processing of the 'subcontracting' business processes.

- The *business processes of the CO team* were again performed on the basis of IPP. CATT procedures were also recorded on completion of the processing of each business process.

- The *tests were performed* similarly to the test execution in the first DSDM pass.

- The same applies to the tests that were performed using *AutoTester*.

- The *user documentation* was always expanded as soon as a business process prototype had attained 'consolidated' status or when a final agreement was reached in the IPP workshop.

- *User training* was performed stepwise after the completion of the individual business processes.

- A test was made in the *milestone meeting* at the end of the timebox to determine the extent to which the individual teams could satisfy the tasks planned for the timebox. All teams managed to meet the planned tasks completely. Statements about the quality of the timebox and which questions were also discussed in the milestone meeting can be taken from the first DSDM pass.

- It was determined in the *determination of the next timebox* step that the original planning could be retained and the timebox would therefore have a length of seven workdays. The planned details for this timebox specified that all outstanding requirements must be completely processed.

- The *extension of the report system* was performed in parallel to the complete second DSDM pass.

- The *quality review* performed at the end of the timebox of the third phase was only used to summarize the results of the individual milestones at the end of the 'short' timeboxes of the third phase.

- A further session for the *topic-centred interaction* was not performed.

- Thus, an extended SAP R/3 system appropriate for the changed requirements was available at the *end of the global timebox* of the third phase. The integration test determined the extent to which the changes made in the third phase had an effect on the basis system already in production.

12.4 Phase 4: System design and system build iteration

- It was of particular importance for the *integration test* that CATT procedures for all business processes had already been recorded in the first DSDM pass. These CATT procedures provided the capability to investigate simply and quickly whether the changed and extended SAP R/3 system still provided the required functionality. The test of the business processes did not show any errors. The same applied to the integrated business processes of the second DSDM pass. In this way, it was very easy to prove the integration capability of subsystems developed completely independently of each other.

- In addition, the *authorization concept* was extended and modified in the fourth phase.

- This phase ends with the *preparation for productive operation* of the extended or changed SAP R/3 system.

12.5 Phase 5: Implementation, live operation

- If necessary, the system administration may need to be modified or additional training provided in this phase, but this was not required in the case study.

- In addition, support had to be provided for *live operation*. This was done in a similar manner as in the first DSDM pass.

- The '*Close subproject*' phase activity is of particular importance for SAP R/3 projects that use the DSDM-based procedure model. Here, in addition to the activities described in the first pass, the next DSDM pass, namely the extension or modification pass, must be planned or, if necessary, a release-change project initiated.

13 The third DSDM pass

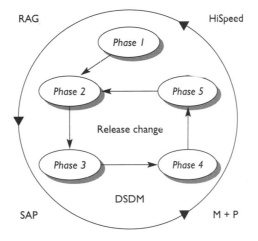

Figure 13.1   Release change

13.1 Phase 1: Feasibility study

The technical coordinator reported that SAP had delivered a new Release 4.0B. This new release has implemented many important functions that were still on the list of items still open for the project. The project manager then made the recommendation to initiate a new DSDM pass and so convert the existing productive system to this new release. The executive sponsor agreed to this suggestion.

Because the determining factors had not changed and the DSDM-based procedure model still applied, the feasibility study was not repeated.

13.2 Phase 2: Business study

The workshop moderator/organizer was given the task of organizing a workshop to determine whether and how the company should react to this new release of the SAP R/3 system.

During the workshop an external SAP specialist in Release 4.0B presented an overview of the more important changes. These included not only many changed dialogues in the individual transactions, but also an extended functionality. Every user had to be provided with a new version of the client software (SAPGUI).

As result of the workshop, the workshop sponsor received a report that contained the following decision: the production system should be converted from Release 3.1H to Release 4.0B.

- The highest priority was given to the actual release change while retaining the same functionality as previously.

- The end-users should learn to operate the new system.

- The functional extensions made available in Release 4.0B should be implemented as a second priority.

- The risk for the company resulting from the release change together with extended functionality was assigned a very high rating.

- The minimum goal: a pure release change with the same functionality as previously.

- A team was formed with representatives from the existing teams, consultants, end-users and SAP experts. The team consisted of six people.

The project manager specified the following list of requirements with priorities:

Timebox 1

Priority 1:   Create a test system from the development system with Release 4.0B

Priority 2:   Create a test system that exhibits all functionality of the existing development system

---

Timebox 2

Priority 1:   Create a test system that exhibits all functionality of the existing development system

Priority 2:   Create a test system that exhibits all functionality of the existing productive system

Priority 3:   Check and update the documentation

Timebox 3

Priority 1:   Create a test system that exhibits all functionality of the existing productive system

Priority 2:   Check and update the documentation

Timebox 4

Priority 1:   Check and update the documentation

Priority 2:   Convert the productive system to the new Release 4.0B

Priority 3:   Implement the new functionality of Release 4.0B

13.3 Phase 3: Function model iteration

Because no new functions were to be implemented as priority 1, the functional iteration phase was not performed. Rather, the goal was to provide a solid foundation on which additional functional iterations could build. Because the non-functional requirements had more importance in this pass, this phase should be started only when there is sufficient time to process the new functions from SAP R/3 Version 4.0B.

13.4 Phase 4: System design and system build iteration

13.4.1 The first timebox

As a first step, a development system should be built on the basis of Release 4.0B. To achieve this goal, the existing development system using Release 3.1H was copied to another computer (refer to Figure 13.2).

Before the actual release change could take place, the Oracle database system, which in this special case was technically located outside the SAP system, also needed to be converted. The conversion from Oracle Version 7 to Oracle Version 8 was made without any major problems.

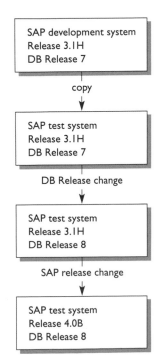

Figure 13.2   Mirrored development system

This converted system then needed to be tested. A regression test was performed with Version 3.1H from SAP and Oracle Version 8 to find any errors caused by the Oracle version change.

To achieve this goal, the complete test catalog of the existing systems could be re-executed. The result was that all test runs behaved exactly the same under Oracle Version 8 as under Oracle Version 7. Thus, the Oracle conversion provided no major problems.

The new client software had to be installed on the workplace computers before the team could use the new SAP version. All the prerequisites for the release change were satisfied after this installation.

The actual SAP release change from Version 3.1H to Version 4.0B was just as successful. The result of this work step was an untested SAP system with Version 4.0B.

Because the first timebox had not yet expired, the team decided to organize a seminar for Release 4.0B in which all team members would become acquainted with the new user interface and the new technology of the SAP R/3 system, Release 4.0B. A consultant who was already particularly well acquainted with this new release provided the teams with training tailored to their exact requirements.

Because the first timebox had now expired, a review was performed. The requirements of priority 1 had been achieved and part of the requirements of priority 2 – namely the training of the teams – had also been realized.

13.4.2 The second timebox

In order to document the project, a release project in accordance with the SAP specifications was first created in the next timebox. The project could be managed and documented in this release project.

To avoid unnecessary activities, the team had to test which actions were actually required for the pure release change. These were retained, and the others removed from the project (refer to Figure 13.3).

The actual regression test could be started now that all preparations had been made. For this purpose, the existing test catalog was extended with a branch titled 'Release Change 4.0B'. All previous test procedures were copied into this branch of the test catalog, and then a test plan with the goal of testing the release change was generated from this branch. This test plan now provided the basis for a test packet that was given to the team especially for this regression test. The complete test packet was started on completion of generation and all test procedures then tested for the absence of errors.

The analysis of the test logs of the individual test runs revealed many errors. As predicted during training, closer examination showed that many transactions had changed.

For this reason, all CATT modules that contained the changed transactions had to be recorded again. The users performed this task; after all, they had learnt to operate the new transactions during the course of the project and so they could also record them in CATT. Because the structure of the business processes had not changed, the existing data could still be used as test data. Thus, it was sufficient just to change the test modules and not the test procedures.

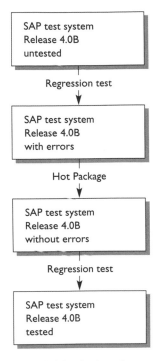

Figure 13.3   Activities during the second timebox

Even after modification to the new release, the test procedures still produced positive test situations (i.e., they indicated errors).

When errors occurred in a transaction, the team searched in OSS from SAP to find descriptions of the errors and correction suggestions. Information on the problems could be found in all cases. The associated repair measures for the existing ABAP/4 programs resulted in error correction. Requests could be sent to SAP for those problems not known in the OSS; however, all errors were found on this occasion.

A new test had to be performed now that the SAP R/3 system had been changed. This new regression test was to ensure that the repair and the new version had not introduced any new errors into the system.

Now that the complete test plan had succeeded in running correctly, one could assume that the existing functions also ran correctly in the development system SAP Release 4.0B.

The timebox had expired. A system was delivered that had the same functionality as the development system.

13.4.3 The third timebox

It was first determined in the next timebox that the release change times needed by system engineering were too long for the users working productively. Consequently, in order to avoid excessive downtimes, the team decided to perform the release change over two weekends. The work steps were:

- Over weekend 1, version change of the database system to the productive system

- During the following week, productive operation with the new version of the database system

- Over the next weekend, version change of SAP R/3 to the productive system

- Productive operation

In order to be able to perform the release change on the productive system within this short time period without risk, the complete run had to be subjected to a regression test on the consolidation system.

To achieve this, the current production system (Oracle Version 7–R/3 Version 3.1) was copied to the existing consolidation system. Because the copied system was a copy of the productive system, it did not have any test catalog. In order still to be able to use the CATT procedures, the complete test packet had to run on the development system. which then made a remote connection to the consolidation system.

The Oracle Version was converted first. The regression test did not show any errors in this constellation (refer to Figure 13.4).

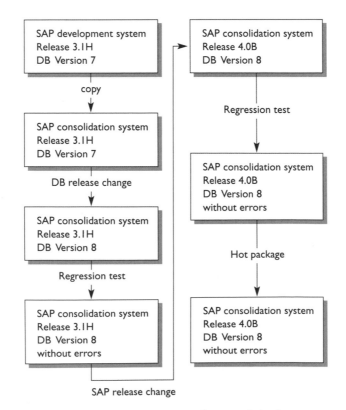

Figure 13.4   Activities in the second timebox

Then the SAP release change was performed, after which a 'Hot-Package' from SAP was loaded so that manual repair of the individual objects was unnecessary.

The new CATT procedures of the development system were used in the following regression test; no serious errors occurred.

Because this test ran without error, it could be assumed that no known errors had occurred during conversion to the productive system.

An additional test series was concerned with validating the authorizations for all user groups that could not yet be tested in the development system. Although the tests could be managed in the test plan tool, they could not be executed in CATT because CATT requires that a user has already been logged on. For this reason, the AutoTester product was used: AutoTester automatically creates test users with specific profiles, uses these to test the authorizations and then deletes the associated users.

The result of the authorization test was that some user profiles were no longer permitted to execute those transactions that they required for their work.

The third timebox was finished and the resulting system exhibited the functionality of the test system.

13.5   Phase 5: Implementation, live operation

The fourth timebox lay in the implementation phase and began with the validation of the release-dependence of the existing documents:

- The quality assurance plan for the project was changed because the official version of the SAP R/3 system was now Version 4.0B.

- The seminar notes were updated because they contained many screenshots from Version 3.1.

- The existing user's guide was updated.

- Because the business process descriptions had been created to be release-independent, they did not need to be updated.

All users could be trained in the use of the new user interface once the seminar notes had been updated.

The workplace PCs were converted to the new SAPGUI in the next step.

The existing productive system was now converted to Version 4.0B over two weekends, with no problems (refer to Figure 13.5).

Because correction of the documents took more time than planned, no additional functionality could be included. Although the original goal was achieved on time, the inclusion of the new functions from SAP 4.0B was postponed to subsequent DSDM passes.

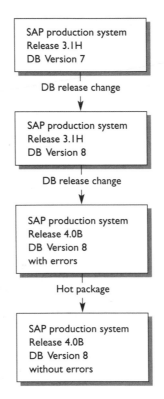

Figure 13.5   Production change

Part D
Appendices

A The DSDM Consortium

The DSDM Consortium was founded in 1994 by 17 companies with the goal of developing a public domain method for rapid system development. The first version of the DSDM manual was published in 1995, following by the second and third versions in 1996 and 1997, respectively. There are now over 1,000 member companies with international branches.

The initial contact for additional information on the DSDM method is the Secretariat of the DSDM Consortium. You can also obtain the manual here. Purchasing the manual automatically makes you an Associate Subscriber to the consortium, and you also receive regular newsletters, invitations to local user groups and summaries of White Papers.

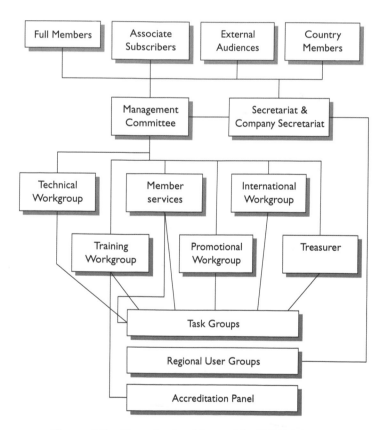

Figure A.1   Organizational form of the DSDM Consortium

If a company wishes to work more intensively in the consortium and receive all information, it can obtain Full Membership.

The organizational structure of the consortium was chosen so that three requirements were met:

- Usefulness to members

- Responsibility for development of the method

- Flexible in order to adapt to changing requirements

Various workgroups are concerned with the following topics: Internet/intranet applications, implementation of business process changes using DSDM, project estimation and metrics.

The consortium's homepage provides an initial introduction:

http://www.dsdm.org

The address of the Secretariat is:

DSDM Secretariat
DSDM Consortium
Kent House
81 Station Road
Ashford
Kent TN23 1PP, UK
Telephone: +44 (0) 1233 661003
Fax: +44 (0) 1233 661004

B The SAP procedure model

The following list contains all the work packets of the SAP procedure model. The SAP help file contains a comprehensive guide for every work packet.

Phase 1: Organization and Conceptual Design

Project Preparation
    Initialize Project
    Define Company Objectives for Using R/3 System
    Define 'As Is' Situation
    Introduce Team to R/3 Processes/Functions
    Define Business Processes
    Compare Your Functional Requirements with the R/3 System
    Establish Model for Organizational Structure
    Define Aims and Scope for Standardization
    Determine Implementation Strategy
    Determine Hardware Requirements
    Define Project Structure
    Define Project Standards and Procedures
    Define System Environment
    Create Preliminary Project Plan
    Approval of Report on Project Preparation
    Create and Issue Project Charter
    Kick Off Implementation Project

Set Up Development Systems
    Set Up Systems and Clients
    Set Up User Master Records for Project Team Members
    Set Up Client Management and Correction/Transport Service
    Set Up Printers and System Environment
    Set Up Remote Service
    Change Country-Specific Settings
    Create Enterprise IMG
    Create Customizing Projects

Train Project Team
    Carry Out Formal Project Team Training
    Familiarize Trainees with R/3 Functionality

Define Functions and Processes
    Specify Processes/Functions Against R/3 Reference Model
    Define Responsibility for Processes/Functions
    Check Input/Output Data Objects
    Determine Reporting Requirements
    Define Interfaces and Enhancements
    Define Your Enterprise Structure
    Prototype Selected Processes/Functions
    Create Technical Design
    Agree Process Design and Technical Design

Design Interfaces and Enhancements
    Create Detailed Definition of Interfaces
    Create Detailed Definition of Enhancements
    Create Detailed Definition of Data Transfer

Quality Check Conceptual Design
    Validate Project Organization
    Verify Compliance with Project Standards
    Validate System Environment
    Validate Conceptual Design
    Validate Detailed Interface and Enhancement Definitions
    Validate Project Plan
    Create Validation Report
    Agree to Proceed to Next Phase

Phase 2: Detailed Design and System Set-Up

Establish Global Settings
    Inform Team About Global Settings
    Amend Global Settings if Necessary

Establish Company Structure
    Check and Adapt R/3 System Organization Units

Establish Master Data
    Define Number Ranges and Basic Structures
    Determine Master Data Fields and Content
    Configure Master Data Settings
    Test Master Data Settings
    Detail Master Data Transfer

Establish Functions and Processes
    Determine Process/Function Fields and Content
    Configure Process/Function Settings
    Test Process/Function Settings
    Present Selected Processes to User Departments
    Detail Data Transfer
    Establish Forms and Messages

Define Screen Control
Make Technical and Graphical System Settings

Create Interfaces and Enhancements
Prepare Data Transfer Fields
Create Data Transfer Programs
Create Interfaces
Create Enhancements (User Exits)
Test Data Transfer Programs
Test Interfaces
Test Enhancements

Establish Reporting
Determine Information Requirements
Determine Extent of Information Requirement Coverage
Define Solutions for Information Gaps
Define Reporting System
Test Reporting System

Establish Archiving Management
Design Archiving Management
Configure Archiving Management
Test Archiving Procedures

Establish Authorization Management
Create Authorizations Design
Create Authorizations
Test Authorizations

Perform Final Test
Create Test Design
Create Test Plan
Perform Test Activities
Report on Final Test
Carry Out Final Review with User Departments

Quality Check Application System
Validate Project Organization
Verify Compliance with Project Standards
Validate Implementation of Conceptual Design
Validate Implementation of Interfaces and Enhancements
Validate Reporting
Validate Archiving Management Concept
Validate Authorizations Concept
Validate Final Test
Validate Project Plan
Create Validation Report
Agree to Proceed to Next Phase

Phase 3: Preparations for Going Live

Create Go-Live Plan
Finalize Live System Configuration
Procure System Equipment
Create Master Data for Users
Create Plan for Data Transfer

Create User Documentation
Define Structure, Content and Presentation Formats
Prepare Creation of User Documentation
Create Change Concept
Create User Documentation

Set Up Live Environment
Install Network
Install Hardware and Software for Users
Install R/3 on Live System

Train Users
Create Training Program
Prepare Training
Deliver Training

Establish System Administration
Define System Administration
Train System Administration Staff

Transfer Data to Live System
Transfer Customizing Settings and Development Objects
Carry Out Data Transfer
Carry Out Manual Data Entry
Have Data Transfer Accepted

Quality Check Live System
Verify User Documentation
Validate Live Environment
Validate User Training Delivered
Validate Organization of System Administration
Validate Data Transfers
Validate Project Plan
Create Validation Report
Agree to Proceed to Next Phase

Phase 4: Live Operation

Support Live Operation
  Support Users at Start of Live Operation
  Establish Permanent Support for Users (Help Desk)

Optimize System Use
  Monitor and Improve System Utilization
  Make Changes as Appropriate
  Formally Close Project

Project Management
Carry Out Detailed Planning
Determine Project Status
Take Steps to Correct Variances
Hold Project Discussions

System Maintenance and Release Upgrade
Carry Out System Upgrade
Carry Out Release Customizing

Glossary and Abbreviations

ABAP
Advanced Business Application Programming

Change order
Grouping of those SAP objects that a specific team changed during an iteration.

ASAP
AcceleratedSAP

AutoTester
External test tool from AutoTester that operates at the presentation level.

Base configuration
Grouping of those software elements that form a configuration and then may no longer be changed.

Baseline
refer to Base configuration

Big Bang
Complete analysis and description of all business processes before the actual implementation project is started in which all these business processes are implemented.

BSI
British Standards Institution

CATT
Computer Aided Test Tool; SAP R/3 system tool used for the automatic testing of the implemented R/3 system.

CCT
Concept Check Tool

CM

Configuration Management; management of configurations and the organization of change scenarios.

CM champion

The team member in a DSDM project who is responsible for configuration management.

CMM

Capability Maturity Model

Configuration

Bill-of-materials for those software elements with their associated version numbers that match each other at a specific time.

Configuration hierarchy

The description of the software elements that form a configuration.

Configuration identification document

refer to Configuration hierarchy

Configuration management

refer to Configuration hierarchy

Contextual Inquiry

Interview method in which the person questioned is interviewed in his work context.

CTO

Change and Transport Organizer; SAP R/3 functionality for the administration, transfer and control of changes in several SAP R/3 systems.

Customizing

Customizing and setting in accordance with company-specific requirements.

DSDM

Dynamic Systems Development Method

DSDM pass

A subproject, i.e., the processing of all phases of the DSDM-based procedure model.

DSDM iteration

Cycles within a phase of the DSDM-based procedure model.

DMS

Document Management System; SAP R/3 functionality for the administration and control of documents.

Element structure plan

List with those software elements that belong in a software version.

IDES

Industrial Demonstration and Education System

IEEE

The Institute of Electrical and Electronics Engineers

IMG

Implementation Guide; refer to Implementation guide

IPP

Iterative Process Prototyping

ISO9000-3

International Organization for Standardization; guideline for the development, supply and maintenance of software.

MoSCoW rules

Prioritization rules used to assign requirements in accordance with their importance into Must, Should, Could, and Would groups.

Network plan

Time-related description of the activities and their inter-relationships within a project.

OSS

Online Service System; support system from SAP AG used to search for error information.

Prioritization

Sorting of the requirements into a sequence according to their importance (measured against the business benefits).

Project structure plan

Hierarchical structuring of a project into subprojects and work packets.

Prototype

refer to Prototyping

Prototyping (DSDM)

Set a part of the system to be implemented that is not thrown away but developed or further developed iteratively and then used as part of the new system. This is a technique to determine and refine functional and technical requirements.

Prototyping (SAP R/3)

SAP R/3 prototyping permits the user to view or run individual business processes within an executable system.

Prototyping (software development)

Software development prototyping permits the contracting party to use his first image to make his ideas more precise and possibly correct. This first image is normally 'thrown away', namely not further developed.

QFD

Quality Function Deployment

QAP

Quality Assurance Plan; base document of quality management that lists all quality assurance measures for a project.

Quality assurance plan

refer to QAP

Q&A Database

Question & Answer Database

R/3

Realtime/3

RAD

Rapid Application Development

Reference configuration

refer to Base configuration

Risk analysis

Grouping of all possible dangers that could endanger a project.

Roadmap

Designation for the procedure model in the ASAP strategy.

SAP

Software Application Products

SAP implementation guide

Guide for configuring the SAP R/3 system.

SAP classification system

SAP R/3 functionality to classify objects using various attributes.

SAP office

SAP R/3 functionality for message exchange and the storage of documents.

SAP project system

SAP R/3 PS module for the management of projects.

SAP procedure model

Waterfall-based guide that describes the activities needed for the implementation of the R/3 system.

SEI

Software Engineering Institute

TB

Timebox; predefined time window in which as many requirements as possible are processed (in accordance with a prioritized sequence). The length of this time window remains unchanged under all circumstances.

Test procedure

Sequential arrangement of test modules in CATT.

Test module

Sequence of automatic calls and tests for SAP R/3 transactions.

Test catalog

Hierarchical structuring of all test runs in CATT and also the manual external test cases of a project.

Test packet

Part of a test plan required for a concrete test, assigned to a tester.

Test plan

Part of a test catalog in CATT that is required for a specific test task.

Testplan Tool

SAP R/3 functionality to manage and document a test scheme.

Test variant

Test procedure with changed import parameters.

Topic-centred Interaction, TCI

Psychological method to introduce a team to a topic.

Transport system

SAP R/3 functionality to transfer software changes from one SAP R/3 system to another.

TQM

Total Quality Management

VoC

Voice of the Customer

VoCA

Voice of the Customer Analysis

Workshop

Method used to make decisions, to develop ideas, to exchange knowledge and to solve business problems.

References

Balzert, H. *Die Entwicklung von Software-Systemen – Prinzipien, Methoden, Sprachen, Werkzeuge.* Mannheim, Spektrum Akademischer Verlag, 1992.

Balzert, H. *Lehrbuch der Software-Technik Band 2.* Heidelberg, Spektrum Akademischer Verlag, 1998.

Beyer, H. and Holtzblatt, K. *Contextual Design – Defining Customer-Centered Design.* San Francisco, Morgan Kaufmann Publishers, 1998.

Boehm, B.W. *Software Engineering Economics.* Englewood Cliffs, NJ, Prentice Hall, 1981.

Brand, H. *R/3-Einführung mit ASAP – Technische Implementierung von SAP R/3 planen und realisieren.* Bonn, Addison-Wesley, 1998.

British Standards Institution. *The Dynamic Systems Development Method and TickIT – Guidance to assist software developers using DSDM to meet the requirements of ISO 9001.* London, 1997.

Cohn, R. *Von der Psychoanalyse zur Themenzentrierten Interaktion.* Stuttgart, Klett Cotta, 1977.

Dräeger, E. *Project Management with SAP R/3.* London, Addison-Wesley, 2000.

DSDM Consortium. *Dynamic Systems Development Method, Version 2.* Farnham, 1995.

DSDM Consortium. *Dynamic Systems Development Method, Version 3.* Farnham, 1997.

Frese, M., Prümper, J. and Solzbacher, F. Eine Fallstudie zu Benutzerbeteiligung und Prototyping. In: F.C. Brodbeck, M. Frese (eds) *Produktivität und Qualität in Software-Projekten – Psychologische Analyse und Optimierung von Arbeitsprozessen in der Software-Entwicklung.* Munich, Vienna, 1994, 135–143.

Gladden, G.R. Stop the Life-Cycle, I want to get off. In: *Software Engineering Notes,* No. 2, 1982, 25–39.

Hesse, W., Merbeth, G. and Fröhlich, R. *Software-Entwicklung – Vorgehensmodelle, Projektführung, Produktverwaltung.* Munich, Vienna, 1992.

IEEE (ed.) *Standard for Software Configuration Management Plans.* IEE Std. 828–1990. New York, 1990.

IEEE (ed.) *IEEE Standard for Quality Assurance Plans.* IEEE Std. 730-1989. New York, 1990.

Jalote, P. *An Integrated Approach to Software Engineering.* New York, Springer-Verlag, 1991.

Keller, G. and Teufel, T. *SAP R/3 prozessorientiert anwenden – Iteratives Prozess-Prototyping zur Bildung von Wertschöpfungsketten.* Bonn, Addison-Wesley, 1997.

Martin, J. *Rapid Application Development.* New York, 1991.

Mazur, G.H. Voice of the Customer Table. A Tutorial. In: QFD-Institute (ed.) *Transactions from the Fourth Symposium on Quality Function Deployment.* Novi, Michigan, 1992, 105–11.

Mazur, G.H. and Zultner, R.E. Voice of the Customer Analysis Tutorial. In: QFD-Institute (Hrsg.): *Tutorials from the Eighth Symposium on Quality Function Deployment*. Novi, Michigan 1996, 1–27.

Mellis, W., Herzwurm, G. and Stelzer, D. *TQM der Softwareentwicklung – Mit Prozessverbesserung, Kundenorientierung und Change Management zu erfolgreicher Software*. Wiesbaden, 1996.

Enid Mumford, E. and Welter, G. *Benutzerbeteiligung bei der Entwicklung von Computersystemen – Verfahren zur Steigerung der Akzeptanz und Effizienz des EDV-Einsatzes*. Berlin, 1984.

Nagel, K. *Erfolg durch effizientes Arbeiten, Entscheiden, Vermitteln und Lernen*. 4. Munich, 1990.

Paulk, M.C., Weber, C.V., Curtis, B. and Chtissis, M.B. *The Capability Maturity Model: Guidelines for Improving the Software Process*. Munich, Addison-Wesley, 1995.

Stapleton, J. *Dynamic Systems Development Method – The Method In Practice*. Harlow, Addison-Wesley, 1997.

TickIT. *The Dynamic Systems Development Method and TickIT*. DISC TickIT Office, London, 1997.

Wallmüller, E. *Software-Qualitätssicherung inder Praxis*. Hanser-Verlag, Munich, 1990.

Index

Systems Consult.

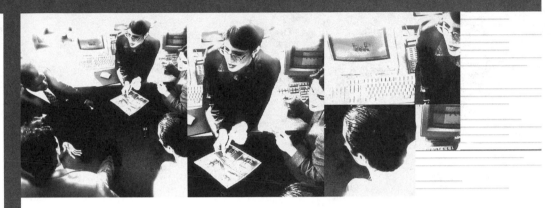

Listen to people. Structure technologies.
On the following pages we would like to give you an
introduction to our technological consulting mission.
The topics should not be considered as being services
that are strictly distinct, but rather as integrative
consulting modules from our overall consulting concept.

Mummert + Partner

Systems Consult: how we lead companies through the world of technology.

Mummert + Partner offers consultancy products and technology solutions to companies and industries based on the status quo that technological developments and innovations are the way to local and global competitiveness. The decisive success factor of our technology mission is provable and lasting commercial benefit for our contracting partners. Mummert + Partner technology projects lead to business success, because they are performed parallel to the benefits of our complete consulting value-added chain: starting at the process and organization consulting through to outsourcing. Technological problems are merely specific commercial weaknesses that cannot be repaired with just a little software or hardware.

Consequently, we provide consulting and technological support for our customers to the envisaged goal and beyond.

Our consultancy concept is always independent of manufacturers: Mummert + Partner supplies exclusively 'best-of-breed' solutions. Our partnership with market and technology leaders and the product evaluations from our software laboratories provide us with the capability to implement technology solutions. Our message is quite clear: to understand companies as complete commercial systems and to be at the customer's side with our complete consulting competence and experience.

'Sociologists, politicians, philosophers – they all envisage
the future omnicultural world society without limits.
Yesterday my daughter showed me the latest e-mails from
her Internet friends in Rio de Janiero and Moscow.'

**The relationship between technology and
people.**

Technology as a progress factor is still highly
regarded in people's sensitive areas. Companies
are founded and managed by people. Although
technology makes companies faster and more
effective, it changes the familiar work processes and organization structures. It is clear
that although change is the main idea behind
any progress, it would not be developed
without society and the market place.
However, we also appreciate that change must
be a process when new technologies are used,
particularly those in which people play the
major role. This is a responsibility that
confronts us every day: the art and science to
combine interpersonal communication and
consulting with a technological product and so
improve the economic potential of our
customers.

The difference between SAP R/3 and SAP R/3.

Without doubt, SAP's journey to SAP R/3 has brought worldwide companies to the highest level of standardized IT technology that is currently available. However, because SAP R/3 users are neither naive nor short-sighted, they also know that SAP R/3 and its modules do not provide one hundred per cent customized IT solutions for their own company processes. But this is rather the first and second step to an optimized IT environment.

Optimize, that is also the key that we discuss here. The interfaces identify where further testing is required, and where reports and functions must be brought to a true one hundred per cent solution.

Optimize also means not only correcting small errors but also providing prerequisites for continuous adaptation to changing requirements.

Efficient working is the stated goal. With new tools, which, for example, can be used to supply support as part of the supply chain management. Improved reporting, or just user satisfaction, and so increase the acceptance of the R/3 system? There are enough areas where SAP R/3 can be significantly optimized!

'An associated company told one of our new customers: "Without doubt you need SAP!" We have convinced him that he needs SAP consulting.'

Talk is good, but action is better.
With experienced SAP specialists and our broad industry know-how, we work together with our customers to produce concepts that permit to optimize the use of their SAP R/3 system. Our continuing success is based on a tailored customizing of the SAP R/3 system for the envisaged business and user-specific requirements of our customers.

We use components for processing and successful realization of these concepts that combine innovative methods and also represent the most up-to-date techniques. Stated briefly, this is the difference between SAP R/3 and SAP R/3.

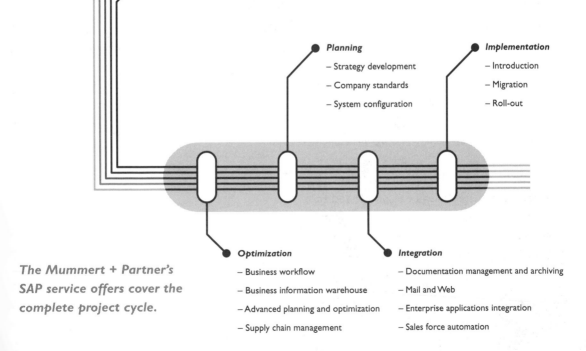

Logistics

Human Resources

Finances

IS Retail

IS RE

Planning
– Strategy development
– Company standards
– System configuration

Implementation
– Introduction
– Migration
– Roll-out

Optimization
– Business workflow
– Business information warehouse
– Advanced planning and optimization
– Supply chain management

Integration
– Documentation management and archiving
– Mail and Web
– Enterprise applications integration
– Sales force automation

The Mummert + Partner's SAP service offers cover the complete project cycle.

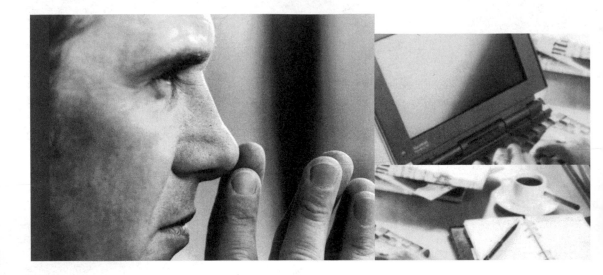

From idea to success.

Modern company consulting means shaping the future.
Nowadays, the art of providing objective and good consulting for companies and institutions lies in the capability of developing solutions appropriate for the market place and marketing. Mummert + Partner has always felt obliged to meet this demand. A consulting company which was founded in 1960 and which has more than 1,000 employees, has developed to one of the most renowed addresses in Europe. Mummert + Partner's specialization in banks insurers, public service providers/energy utilities and telecommunications industries – together with the intra-industry technology consulting in the Systems Consult business division – is the important prerequisite for developing tailored consulting products.

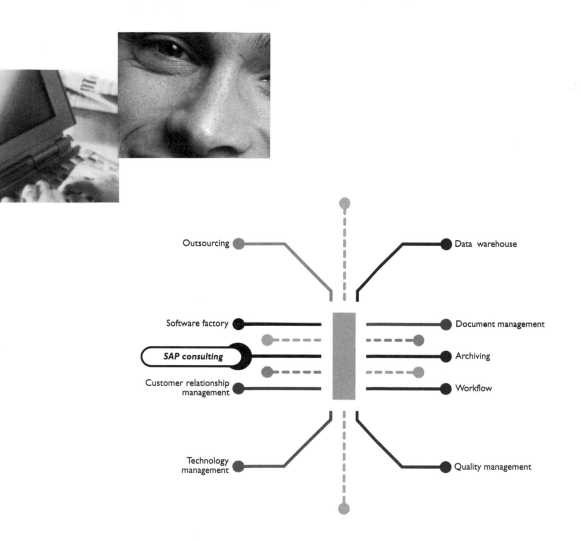

The branches we have in Germany, Europe and the USA lay the geographical basis for our proximitiy to customers in the most important markets. The principle of integrated consultancy has formed an important guarantee for our successful work in the past decades and is a very significant part of our company philosophy. We are not satisfied with half-complete solutions, but rather we accompany our customers right to the end – starting with the concept and finishing with the success. In this context, for example, the development of expandable information processing strategies, while taking account of tight cost/benefit aspects, adopts an important role. Namely, modern information systems are now decisive factors in the implementation of new controlling models and the realization of efficient business processes. These are the only ways of ensuring competitiveness through better information – and the best-possible marketing success.

Mummert + Partner Unternehmensberatung AG

Hans-Henny-Jahnn-Weg 9 · 22085 Hamburg · Germany

Tel: +49 (0)40 227030 · Fax: +49 (0)40 22703186

e-Mail: SystemsConsult@mummert.de

Internet: www.mummert.de

Berlin · Cologne · Düsseldorf · Frankfurt · Hamburg · Leipzig · Munich · Münster
London · Milan · New York · Vienna · Zurich

G5 10^{oc}

JAPAN'S MILITANT TEACHERS

THE EAST-WEST CENTER—formally known as "The Center for Cultural and Technical Interchange Between East and West"—was established in Hawaii by the United States Congress in 1960. As a national educational institution in cooperation with the University of Hawaii, the Center has the mandated goal "to promote better relations and understanding between the United States and the nations of Asia and the Pacific through cooperative study, training, and research."

Each year about 2,000 men and women from the United States and some 40 countries and territories of Asia and the Pacific area work and study together with a multinational East-West Center staff in wide-ranging programs dealing with problems of mutual East-West concern. Participants are supported by federal scholarships and grants, supplemented in some fields by contributions from Asian/Pacific governments and private foundations.

Center programs are conducted by the East-West Communication Institute, the East-West Culture Learning Institute, the East-West Food Institute, the East-West Population Insitute, and the East-West Technology and Development Institute. Open Grants are awarded to provide scope for educational and research innovation, including a program in humanities and the arts.

East-West Center Books are published by The University Press of Hawaii to further the Center's aims and programs.

Japan's
Militant
Teachers

A History of the Left-Wing Teachers' Movement

BENJAMIN C. DUKE

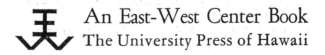 An East-West Center Book
The University Press of Hawaii

Honolulu

Copyright © 1973 by The University Press of Hawaii
All rights reserved
Library of Congress Catalog Card Number 72-88025
ISBN 0-8248-0237-3
Manufactured in the United States of America
Designed by Roger J. Eggers

To Noriko Susan and Kimiko Ann, our Japanese daughters

Contents

Foreword

In the development of educational policy in postwar Japan, the significance of the roles of the Ministry of Education and Nikkyōso (Japan Teachers Union) cannot be disputed. Their functions differ, of course, with one representing the government and the other the teachers. The Ministry of Education draws up the national curriculum, approves the textbooks, and recommends teaching methods. The power Japan's central government thus maintains over teachers, comparable to that of other highly centralized governments, is a legacy from prewar Japan, and shows the influence of French and Prussian practices.

Following World War II, the central government's influence over education was sharply curtailed as a result of the American Occupation policy, which was designed to decentralize educational administration. After the American interlude, the Ministry of Education recovered much of its prewar control and influence. But the government was confronted with an unprecedented situation brought on by the rise of Nikkyōso, a stronghold of opposition to the government.

Prior to World War II, the majority of teachers were represented by the Dai Nippon Kyōikukai (Great Japan Education Association), a quasi-government organization under strong influence of the Ministry of Education. A dissenting minority of teachers endeavored to organize the teaching body into an opposition force but was quickly suppressed by the government. Shortly after the war, prewar activists were able to reorganize a teachers' movement that crystallized into Nikkyōso in 1947, when the power of the Ministry of Education was curtailed by the American Occupation.

Nikkyōso, like its prewar predecessors, was initiated as an independent, militant organization. It derived its strength and power from the general political and social upheaval within the labor movement during the period of democratization after the war. Consequently, even after the Ministry of Education regained much of its prewar influence in the mid-fifties, the union continued as a formidable opposition force. Indeed, the period from 1955 to 1960 was marked by a series of anti-Nikkyōso measures undertaken by the Ministry of Education to restrict that power.

The union may well be considered at the present time to have been forced into a defensive position by the Ministry. Nevertheless, in certain instances such as Nikkyōso's appeal to the International Labor Organization and several successful legal cases, the Ministry itself seems to be on the defensive. This much is certain: the Ministry of Education can no longer make any decision concerning the educational policy for the nation without taking Nikkyōso's reaction into consideration.

Nikkyōso is a national federation of prefectural unions of teachers whose members include the large majority of elementary and junior high school teachers, as well as groups of teachers in other sectors. The Ministry refuses to recognize it at the national level, and consequently negotiations occur only between local education authorities and local teachers' unions. However, the union's national policy on wages and working conditions influences local negotiations; it also has its effect on the labor movement as a whole. Nikkyōso is, in fact, one of the most powerful labor unions in Sōhyō (General Council of Trade Unions), the largest labor confederation in Japan.

As is the case with most labor organizations in Japan, Nikkyōso is deeply involved in politics. It openly supports the opposition Socialist party, bringing it into confrontation with the ruling conservative party. The platform of Nikkyōso's annual conventions includes political slogans opposing American involvement in Vietnam and the United States–Japan Security Pact. As a union of teachers, though, the union is deeply concerned with educational problems.

The different aspects of Nikkyōso's activities, including teacher welfare, politics, and education, have received varying degrees of emphasis during the course of the union's development. Shifts of emphasis have occurred in parallel with changes in leadership of the union, while changes in leadership can be seen, in turn, as a reflection of the educational, political, economic, and social circumstances surrounding it. It is thus necessary to understand the problems of Nikkyōso within the whole context of Japanese society, and such an understanding requires not only a familiarity with Japanese education itself but also a knowledge acquired from related disciplines. This makes the study of Nikkyōso a difficult but challenging task, and, accordingly, few serious studies on the topic have ever been made either within Japan or elsewhere.

Professor Duke's work is an ambitious attempt by a non-Japanese scholar to take the lead in this field. Using the historical approach, he sets out to trace the origin and development of the left-wing teachers' movement through Nikkyōso's first twenty years. His work is based on his own first-hand observations in Japan, supplemented by published and unpublished works of Japanese scholars on the subject. Readers will find this a good introduction to, and analysis of, the problems of organized movements of Japanese teachers, as well as Japanese education as a whole.

UNESCO Institute of Education   KOBAYASHI TETSUYA
Hamburg, Germany   *Director*

Preface

Ever since I came to Japan in 1959 to teach in a university in Tōkyō, I have been keenly interested in the activities of the Nihon Kyōshokuin Kumiai (Japan Teachers Union), better known as Nikkyōso. From its inauguration in 1947, climaxing the chaotic movement among rival left-wing teachers' organizations immediately after the war, Nikkyōso has pursued a highly controversial policy involving strikes, demonstrations, sit-ins, mass vacations, and other forms of physical and verbal militancy, which at times attained violent proportions.

The hostile relationship between the Japanese Ministry of Education and Nikkyōso is reflected in the latter's militancy. Shortly after I undertook an intensive study of Japanese education, it became manifest to me that this mutual antagonism provides, in fact, the key to an understanding of developments within postwar Japanese education. Consequently, I concluded that without a knowledge of Nikkyōso and its militant policies and programs it is virtually impossible to grasp the significance of postwar educational policies that were carried out by the Japanese government and the Ministry of Education.

Although a knowledge of the role of Nikkyōso is essential for the comprehension of postwar Japanese educational developments, and although this union represents not only the largest union in Japan but also one of the largest unions of teachers in the world, Nikkyōso is virtually unknown outside Japan. A perusal of the literature revealed a dearth of material concerning this union published in languages other than Japanese. Based on this set of circumstances, I rather boldly set out to rectify the situation by undertaking a study of the evolution of the left-wing teachers' movement in Japan, which culminated in the birth and growth of Nikkyōso in 1947.

As a non-Japanese researcher approaching the extremely bitter controversy between the Japanese government and teachers' unions, I decided early on that I would make no attempt to judge the propriety of either side. Rather, my object was to analyze the continuing series of disputes by seeking out those individuals from both camps who were directly involved in the disputes. I then proceeded to present both points of view without evaluating either one. Primary sources were utilized to the fullest, since most of the original Japanese participants were living in the greater Tōkyō area when this research was carried out between 1968 and 1970.

In addition to interviewing individuals who were directly involved in the disputes and consequently highly critical of the opposition, I sought out certain informants who were totally familiar with the disputes but who were not directly involved themselves. In this manner additional light was shed on the progression of developments. The gratifying feature of it all was the openness and frankness with which each respondent, without exception, explained his position and attitude. Ironically, perhaps only a non-Japanese could be accepted with such confidence by both camps.

I am indebted to so many people for assisting me in this research that I hesitate to list them. Nevertheless, I would be totally lacking in gratitude if I did not express my appreciation to the following people for their assistance. I am deeply indebted to Ichikawa Shōgo, assistant professor of educational administration, Hokkaidō University, who happened to be studying at the University of London in 1969, when I was writing a doctoral dissertation on Nikkyōso. He rendered much help by reading each chapter, offering criticisms and advice.

From the union's side, I am particularly grateful to Nikkyōso's historian, Mochizuki Muneaki, who spent many hours with me discussing past events. His incredible memory of details, particularly of Nikkyōso's conventions and internal conferences, proved to be invaluable. The leader of the initial postwar movement, the Honorable Iwama Masao, currently Communist representative, clarified from the left-wing position many of the issues of that hectic period. The Honorable Kobayashi Takeshi, formerly Nikkyōso chairman and currently Socialist party representative, was most helpful with events during his tenure in the decade of the 1950s. And, finally, Chairman Miyanohara Sadamitsu met with me as often as I needed, to clarify Nikkyōso's monumental reorientation under his tutelage during the 1960s. I cannot adequately express my appreciation to Nikkyōso leaders for their full cooperation.

From the side of the Ministry of Education, I am most indebted to former Minister of Education, the Honorable Araki Masuo, long-term Liberal-Democrat representative and director of the National Security Agency, for analyzing his position during the violent period when he attempted literally to break Nikkyōso's power. Two former Vice-Ministers of Education, the Honorable Naitō Takasaburō, currently Liberal-Democrat representative, and Hidaka Daishirō, my former dean and now professor of education at the Gakushūin University, were most helpful in explaining the government's position during their tenures extending from the 1940s through the 1950s. Sagara Iichi, former ministerial secretary shortly after the war, devoted one whole day to me when I visited him at the Kyōto University campus, where he is dean of the College of Education; he described for me the minister of education's position between 1946 and 1950 under the American Occupation, when the left-wing teachers' movement developed so rapidly.

For the American Occupation position, I was most fortunate to have Professor Ronald S. Anderson from the University of Hawaii—and former SCAP Education Officer—as my neighbor in Tōkyō during his sabbatical year at the initial period of this study. His recollections of the years from 1948 to 1951, when he served within SCAP, cogently revealed the attitude of the Occupation during that momentous reorientation of policy commonly referred to as the "reverse course," when the Americans began to restrict the Communist-influenced labor movement, in which Nikkyōso played an integral role.

At the very beginning of this study, it was necessary to ask some person influential in the Japanese education world to serve as a go-between for me with the many individuals I wanted to interview. Itō Noboru, distinguished education critic and a member of the Tōkyō School Board, served that role by introducing me to most of the informants from both sides to arrange the initial interviews. He played a key role in this research, as expected by Japanese tradition.

I am most grateful to my assistants at the International Christian University who aided in translations, interviews, and various research details during the several years of the study: Tominaga Junichi served at the beginning; Tōyama Mariko and Yamamura Satoshi, now Mr. and Mrs.

Yamamura, served during the middle period; Hayakawa Eiichi, trusted assistant, worked diligently and with great precision throughout the project.

Various people read the entire manuscript or selected chapters and offered suggestions, advice, and encouragement. From the University of London, professors Joseph Lauwerys, Brian Holmes, and Ronald Dore provided invaluable support and advice for the initial version. Dr. Narita Katsuya from the Japanese National Institute of Educational Research reviewed the chapter on the prewar movement. Dr. Kobayashi Tetsuya, my former division chairman at the International Christian University and a distinguished Japanese scholar and authority on Japanese education, now serving in Hamburg, Germany, as director of the UNESCO Institute of Education, graciously read the manuscript and prepared the Foreword. I appreciate his interest in my work. In addition, I am indebted to Dr. Edwin O. Reischauer, former ambassador to Japan, who read the manuscript and encouraged me to seek publication of it.

Finally, I am eternally grateful to my wife, June, who expertly typed the manuscript in two foreign, but most hospitable, lands, a first draft in England and the final version in Japan.

A note about Japanese names used in this book. Japanese names are presented in the order in which Japanese use them, that is, the last name first, simply because it is more natural that way. The title of the book, incidentally, was inspired by a book entitled *Japan's Militant Buddhists*, written by my colleague, Noah Brannan.

International Christian University   BENJAMIN C. DUKE
Tōkyō

PART I

Origins of the Left-Wing Teachers' Movement, 1919–1947

The Prewar Movement

The Birth of
Left-Wing Traditions

Several weeks after Japan accepted the provisions of the Potsdam Declaration, which terminated the Pacific war in mid-1945, a left-wing teachers' movement spontaneously emerged through the debris of Japanese cities. Reacting to the strict prewar and wartime government control of the teaching profession and the pitiful economic conditions existent within a defeated land, the movement rapidly gained momentum. By the end of the year, thousands of teachers were organized into a variety of unions and associations, independent of the government, struggling to improve teachers' livelihood and to construct a new image of the Japanese teacher. A year and a half later, the initial postwar teachers' movement culminated in the formation of the one great organization, the Nihon Kyōshokuin Kumiai (Japan Teachers Union), better known as Nikkyōso, encompassing nearly a half million teachers and directed by a combination of Socialist and Communist leaders.

Although Nikkyōso was institutionalized after World War II, its roots lie embedded in prewar Japan. A direct relationship can be traced to the decade of the twenties and early thirties, when activist teachers endeavored to unify the teaching corps through left-wing organizations, independent of government control. And even though their fledgling attempts were crushed by the government, the prewar efforts, marked by both individuals and ideology, laid the foundation for the postwar left-wing teachers' movement and the ultimate formation of the militant, anti-government Nikkyōso.

The struggles to organize teachers in the prewar twenties and the postwar forties were aimed at repudiating the traditional image of the Japanese teacher, which successive governments had so effectively utilized to produce one of the most dedicated and self-sacrificing teaching corps in the world. The ideal image of the Japanese teacher had already been firmly established by the time of the Meiji Restoration in 1868. Originating from the fifteenth and sixteenth centuries—when Buddhist priests preserved the literary arts in their temples during the prolonged period of civil strife—and from the Tokugawa era (1603–1867)—when fief schools and schools for the commoners were taught mostly by individuals from the samurai (warrior) class, which was imbued with education based on "ethical training through study of the Confucian classics,"[1]—a unique combination of the two traditions merged into the ideal image of a Japanese teacher. On the one hand, teaching was considered as a holy profession (*seishoku*), resembling a religious order in which teachers worked with the poor and the illiterate as a mission of love. At the same time, the teacher was regarded as a moral disciplinarian, commanding a formal classroom environment similar to a pious military order. Student-teacher relations were summarized in the adage, "Let not the pupil tread within seven feet of his teacher's shadow."[2]

Inherent in the ideal image of the Japanese teacher was the notion that teachers taught as a service to mankind. The rewards were intrinsic rather than pecuniary. Close but formal personal relationships between the teacher and his small circle of students forged a bond that continued throughout life. The teacher was customarily consulted by his students for advice on life's important decisions, including career and marriage. The teacher's prestige was uncommonly high, even though his financial return was exceedingly low; his students, their parents, and the community at large held the teacher in high esteem because he personified the most prestigious calling of learning and because he performed his duties without regard for his personal well-being.

The pre-Meiji relationship is described thus by one historian:

> . . . The relation between pupil and teacher and parent was more than an economic one. Learning was too much respected to be treated simply as a commodity, and the tradition of the scholar who simply fulfilled a duty to mankind by passing on his scholarship was still sufficiently strong, and still played a real part in the motives of a high enough proportion of teachers, to prevent those who did rely on teaching for a living from lowering their dignity to the point of setting too explicit a price on their services.[3]

As long as the teacher remained a priest or a samurai with altruistic convictions, there was no inconsistency in the life of a venerated but unpretentious teacher. In other words, teaching was viewed as a heavenly mission conducted by special classes of people who assumed the responsibility of teaching through hereditary processes. But such a traditional concept was not to be upheld forever. Even as early as more than one hundred years ago, a transition was taking place from the concept of teaching as a heavenly mission to that of teaching as a regular occupation. The transitional sequence originated with the priestly class dominating the arts in pre-Tokugawa times, followed by the warrior class during the Tokugawa era, and succeeded by the commoner during the Meiji period; the final stage took place after World War II when teachers were organized into unions.

With the inauguration of the Meiji government in 1868, a new era in the history of Japanese teachers was ushered in, the background of which lies in the broad social and political changes that were carried out under the new regime. After the feudal Tokugawa military regime finally disintegrated in the 1860s before the twin threats of superior Western naval forces, which demanded access to the previously isolated nation, and the internal revivification of the then effete imperial institution, Japan experienced a most severe domestic crisis. The feudal clan leaders divided their allegiance, aligning themselves behind either the emperor or the general, thus provoking civil war. The imperial forces ultimately triumphed and were thrust into the unenviable position of ruling a divided and enfeebled nation while confronting the powerful naval forces of the several Western nations that were competing for Asian colonies, trade concessions, and diplomatic privileges.

The new government, in the name of the boy-Emperor Meiji, endeavored to consolidate its position and chart a new course with the proclamation of the famous 1868 Charter Oath to the gods. One of its most important provisions, shortly thereafter to exert an inordinate influence on Japanese education, proclaimed that "knowledge shall be sought from throughout the world so that the welfare of the Empire may be promoted."[4] Accordingly, emissaries were dispatched to Europe and America to investigate the variety of Western systems of education and government.

In 1871, following the closing of the old Tokugawa schools, all matters concerning education became the responsibility of a Department of Education, which immediately proceeded to formulate the first scheme for a national school system to take effect in 1872. The purpose of this plan was to break the shackles of feudalism; to unite the petty feudal states behind the emperor, following the enervating internal revolution that was reestab-lishing the emperor's political authority; and to overtake the West in sci-ence and military technology. The school system was to be the means. The goal was an independent Japan under Emperor Meiji.

The new Department of Education launched its program in 1872 by undertaking what must be one of the most daring attempts to apply comparative educational analyses in a cross-cultural situation. The depart-ment patterned the nation's new educational administrative structure after the French design, implanting ultimate control at the central govern-mental level. The plan, only partially effected because of its enormity, included the districting of the country into eight university regions. Under each university were to be thirty-two middle-school regions, each of which was to include 210 elementary schools, for an immense total of well over 50,000 educational institutions. The system involved an eight-year elementary school, with the lower four years recommended for all, followed by a six-year middle school and a three-year university.[5] The major educational goal of this grandiose scheme was to produce mass literacy and, in the process, mass acceptance of the new government and a carefully selected elite leadership to control the nation's destiny.

The Meiji government then began the importation and adaptation of many educational practices, including method and content, from the United States, which, ironically, had one of the most decentralized systems of education in the world. The American common school, instrumental in unifying early America and ideally bringing into one classroom all chil-dren in the community regardless of their diverse backgrounds, was par-ticularly attractive to the Japanese government endeavoring to unify Japan under Emperor Meiji. To the Japanese, America appeared the most suc-cessful nation in the world in solving the problem of universal education at that time.

Of necessity the Meiji government launched Japan's first national school system on the foundation of Tokugawa education, which had attained a remarkable rate of school attendance: by 1867[6] more than 40 percent of the boys and 10 percent of the girls were estimated to have had some form of schooling. Oftentimes, the new compulsory common ele-mentary schools for the masses were merely the old Tokugawa schools, that is, primarily the private *terakoya,* which was originally a temple school for local children but which later included almost any local school that taught the basic skills of reading, writing, and arithmetic. Because of the large number of *terakoya* available in the land, local governments henceforth recognized many of them as state schools, transferring their students and teachers to the new schools as they became available.

In the beginning, the preponderance of teachers for the new state schools had taught in the *terakoya* schools and had had no formal training. Many carried with them the traditional image of the ascetic but revered teacher. Those teachers from the samurai class, who considered monetary matters distasteful, running counter to the austerity of the warrior code had, by definition, little interest in financial rewards. This was indeed an auspicious legacy from the feudal past since the burden of financial support for the new schools was placed at the local level where adequate funds for a mandatory school were neither readily available nor forthcoming from many communities. A corps of loyal, dedicated, self-sacrificing, and experienced teachers thus formed an ideal ingredient for the Meiji government's monumental plan to unify the many feudal states behind the new emperor. The teachers proved to be one of the more stabilizing elements in this transitional society, encountering an experiment in modernization in the 1870s.

Although many of the experienced teachers from the schools of the Tokugawa period were adept at inculcating Confucian teachings of filial piety and loyalty, certainly a requisite of the new government, it was obvious to government officials that these same teachers were ill prepared to teach the imported Western learning to large classes of children, derived from all levels of society, in the new common compulsory elementary schools. Consequently, in 1872, the same year the first national education plan was inaugurated, a normal school was established in Tōkyō whose master teacher was Marion Scott, an American elementary school principal from California. Equipped with textbooks from home and a Japanese translator, Scott taught his pupils to teach a class of Japanese children the way he had taught American children in California.

Graduates of the Tōkyō Normal School were dispersed into the provinces to set up provincial normal schools for the training of a new class of teachers trained in Western methods of teaching using Western textbooks. And so the process went, and with it were planted the seeds for later discord between those teachers and government leaders who considered teaching as an altruistic, sacred mission and those of the newly trained teachers who considered it as an occupation by which one lived a normal life in the community, supporting a family with an adequate income.

The first normal school graduates were dominated by former samurai and their dependents from the Tokugawa era. Teaching attracted them not only because many were inclined to reject business and commercial work after losing their privileged warrior-class status but also because teaching offered them permanent work and appealed to their sense of duty to serve the government. However, by the end of the Meiji period in 1912, teachers and students at the normal schools originated mostly from non-samurai families. Examples from the Kumamoto Normal School and its training school are indicative of the trend, as shown in Tables 1 and 2.

By the 1880s, less than a decade after the establishment of the first normal school, which reflected strong foreign, mostly American, influence,

Table 1. Family Background of Students from the
Kumamoto Normal School

| Years | Class Origin | |
	Samurai	Commoner
1878–1887	80%	20%
1888–1897	67	33
1898–1907	50	50
1908–1917	34	66

Source: Data from Karasawa Tomitarō, *Kyōshi no Rekishi* (A History of Teachers) (Tōkyō: Sōbunsha, 1955), p. 86.

Table 2. Family Background of Teachers at the Training School
of the Kumamoto Normal School

| Years | No. of Teachers | Teachers from Samurai Families | |
		Number	Percentage
1878–1887	25	20	80
1888–1897	15	10	67
1898–1907	34	17	50
1908–1917	47	16	34

Source: Data from Nikkyōso (Japan Teachers Union), *Nikkyōso Jūnenshi* (Ten-Year History of the Japan Teachers Union) (Tōkyō: Nikkyōso, 1958), p. 432.

a reactionary movement engulfed Japanese education. Emperor Meiji himself set the stage for a return to more conservative and traditional principles in his 1879 Imperial Instructions on Education; he did so by criticizing those who, "in their eagerness to adopt Western ways make light of the virtues of humanity, justice, loyalty and filial piety." Education, he proclaimed, must inculcate the true teachings of Confucianism.[7] A year later, with the passage of the Assembly Act and the Primary School Teachers' Regulations, political restrictions enveloped the teachers. Under these provisions, "it became impossible for teachers to talk about political matters or even to listen to political speeches, virtually becoming isolated from social and political controversy."[8]

An even more conservative leadership gained control of Japan as the emperor came under the increasing influence of Motoda Eifu, a Confucianist who promoted the view that "the Emperor should be the model of virtue for the entire people as the recipient of the ancestral precepts transmitted from the Sun Goddess through the unbroken lineage of the of the Imperial Family."[9] Motoda endeavored to impose his ideas as a basis of the morals course in schools. His plans were temporarily delayed with the appointment in 1885 of Mori Arinori as the first minister of education.

It was Mori Arinori, who vigorously promoted national education for the development of Japan as an independent nation. Known as the father of Meiji education, Mori, who traveled widely in Europe and represented Japan in Washington for more than a year, believed that the advancement of the State depended upon education whose policies must be firmly established on the policies and purposes of the State.

In 1886 Mori rewrote the educational code into four separate education orders: the Primary School Code, the Secondary School Code, the Imperial University code, and the Normal School Code—all firmly based on the principles of nationalism. These codes continued in essence until 1945. Perhaps the most important of Mori's ideas, with unusual ramifications for the later years, was that concerning normal schools (*shihan gakkō*), for, according to Mori's first article of the 1886 Normal School Code, "pupils must be trained to cultivate the spirit of Obedience, Sympathy and Dignity. They must be filled with the spirit of loyalty and patriotism and made to realize the grandeur and obligations of loyalty and filial piety, and to be inspired with sentiments proper to our nationality."[10]

The normal schools under Mori's influence were administered as quasimilitary institutions, scrupulously designed to indoctrinate the principles of nationalism through a strict program of physical, moral, and mental training of the future elementary school teachers, who were, in turn, to inculcate these ideals in the young during compulsory school classes. Since all graduates were liable to military service, it was deemed proper that military gymnastics and drill on the German model should be taught for three to six hours a week. A high-ranking military officer was assigned to administer the Tōkyō Higher Normal School.

There were two types of normal schools. One type trained elementary school teachers; there were two such schools in each prefecture, one for men and one for women. The other type, known as the higher normal school, trained secondary school teachers. Both types gained wide recognition. The competition to enter these normal schools intensified when they attracted bright local students who were seeking a means of social mobility since there was only one university, Tōkyō University, at that time. Graduates became statesmen, scholars, poets, and writers, as well as teachers, all gradually replacing the warrior class as a new class of commoners. Offering free room, board, tuition, clothing, and an allowance, plus assurance of a teaching position upon graduation, the normal schools held a unique position in the Japanese educational world in the latter half of the nineteenth century, and produced a confident corps of teachers.

American ideals of education, shaped by Christian traditions and the Western frontier and emphasizing individualism, humanism, and local control, were no longer considered appropriate for an Oriental country experiencing the painful transformation from a feudalistic base of Tokugawa times to a modern state under Emperor Meiji. The Japanese leaders in the late 1880s thus made one of the most crucial decisions in the history of Japan: The model for Japanese education, as well as for many other institutions of the nation, including the 1889 Constitution, would henceforth be German, not American. The Herbartian educational ideal employed in Germany, a nation whose history, literature, and traditions formed the foundation of the country's educational curriculum and moral teachings, appealed to the Japanese leaders as an ideal combination of moral training and the acquirement of knowledge.

At the same time, Confucian nationalists, by promoting the mythical origins of Japan and the emperor, exploited the previous efforts of Mori, assassinated in 1889, who had endeavored to unify and strengthen the nation through a strong and unified school system. The culmination of the movement to traditionalize was finally attained in 1890 with the proclamation of the most important educational document in prewar Japan, the Imperial Rescript on Education.

Know ye, Our subjects:

Our Imperial Ancestors have founded Our Empire on a basis broad and everlasting and have deeply and firmly implanted virtue; Our subjects ever united in loyalty and filial piety have from generation to generation illustrated the beauty thereof. This is the glory of the fundamental character of our Empire, and herein also lies the source of Our education. Ye, Our subjects, be filial to your parents, affectionate to your brothers and sisters; as husbands and wives be harmonious, as friends true; bear yourselves in modesty and moderation; extend your benevolence to all; pursue learning and cultivate arts, and thereby develop intellectual faculties and perfect moral powers; furthermore advance public good and promote common interest; always respect the Constitution and observe the laws; should emergency arise, offer yourselves courageously to the State; and thus guard and maintain the prosperity of Our Imperial Throne coeval with heaven and earth. So shall ye not only be Our good and faithful subjects, but render illustrious the best traditions of your forefathers.

The Way here set forth is indeed the teaching bequeathed by Our Imperial Ancestors, to be observed alike by Their Descendants and the subjects, infallible for all ages and true in all places. It is Our wish to lay it to heart in all reverance, in common with you, Our subjects, that we may all thus attain to the same virtue.[11]

[Imperial Seal]

The Imperial Rescript represented a unique composite of ideals—ideals that are firmly embedded in Japanese tradition—and manifested the restoration of Motoda's prestige. At the same time, the Rescript combined filial piety with patriotism and industriousness in the Japanese version of the Protestant ethic. It could aptly be described as the embodiment of a "Japanese ethic," which provided a major motivating influence underlying Japan's transformation into one of the world's leading nations today. Unfortunately, this document was exploited by Japanese militarists in transforming the nation into one of the most aggressive nations in modern times. Therein lies the Rescript's uniqueness.

From the day of the Imperial Rescript's issuance until the end of World War II fifty-five years later, Japanese teachers inculcated in their students an awe and reverence for the hallowed proclamation, honored as each school's sacred treasure, along with the picture of the emperor and the empress. Through the Rescript, the youth underwent indoctrination by a dedicated teaching corps that lived by the simple precept that it was the duty of the individual to perform his role in society, no matter how great or humble, with complete devotion and energy for the welfare of Japan and the Imperial Throne, coeval with heaven and earth.

The Imperial Rescript on Education provided the moral, philosophical, religious, and patriotic foundation of Japanese education; the pattern of education was thus determined until the end of World War II. It was to be a highly centralized system based on the principles of elementary education for all and secondary and higher education for the intellectually able, with technical streams being added later in separate schools as Japanese industry developed. It was to emphasize Western technology and science, and Japanese culture and traditions based on Confucian hierarchal relationships. Its teaching methods were based on the Herbartian five-step process, which appealed to teachers seeking the most efficient means of teaching systematically a great deal of information and factual knowledge in the shortest possible time.

The purpose of prewar Japanese education was to modernize Japan industrially and technologically so that she could attain equality with Western countries, thereby enabling her to remain independent. At the same time, it was to cultivate Japanese culture and traditions in the name of the emperor, who represented the true Japanese spirit from his ancient ancestral lineage, to be taught in the morals course based on the Imperial Rescript which assumed a predominant position in the curriculum. To accomplish these multiple aims less than a century ago, Japanese education became a tool of nationalism and servant of the State, eventually fulfilling many of the goals originally set for it.

During the entire Meiji period, the government regarded teaching as a duty and service to the State, consistent with the emperor's appeal for each citizen to perform his role in society selflessly for the welfare of all. Teachers, however, were considered to be in a special category. Even though they were paid from local revenues, they were treated as quasi-national officers, paid not for their labor but for their loyalty to the emperor as his officers. Moreover, as civil servants serving the emperor, their honorable position was of such proportion that to protest the very low financial rewards was considered beneath the dignity of an individual in such a distinguished position.[12] This attitude continued into the twentieth century.

Another interesting phenomenon developed during the latter part of the Meiji period. Increasingly, farmers sent their eldest sons to the prefectural normal schools, reasoning that the son could later hold a teaching post, although poorly paid, while continuing to manage the farm. A male normal school graduate often became a local elementary school principal, a prestigious position in the community, which also allowed early retirement at about age fifty. In other words, an elementary school principal, in addition to owning land, retired in the most enviable circumstances, with a double income from his pension and the farm. This type of teacher never had to rely solely on his salary and was satisfied with the conditions of teaching that brought him the all-important prestige within the community.

Following the Sino-Japanese and Russo-Japanese wars at the turn of the century and upon the death of Emperor Meiji in 1912, which marked the end of the Meiji period, a new era was ushered in. By then the industrial revolution had started. With the new era came the first independent teachers' organization.

Japanese industry advanced rapidly, profiting considerably when European countries were cut off from their Asian markets during World War I. Without otherwise becoming involved in the fighting, except for minor skirmishes, Japan was able to remain secure from attack while reaping profits because of the war. Income buildup was substantial, leading to unprecedented economic prosperity and concomitant social disruption; spending and imports increased sharply, bringing about a spiraling inflation.

Salaries of teachers, as civil servants with fixed incomes, fell markedly behind industrial and commercial salaries and price increases, which led to a hopeless situation for teachers. For example, to support a family with five members in 1919 required at least 2,000 yen a year, but the average annual salary of teachers was 581 yen. The low teachers' salaries undermined the social prestige of the teaching profession and the self-respect of teachers.[13] The situation had already been aggravated by the growing unpopularity of the normal schools. Brighter students from the higher economic classes were increasingly attracted to the rapidly expanding middle schools leading to the broadening university system. Normal schools consequently were attracting more students from poorer homes, especially farming families, who were willing to take low-paying teaching positions upon graduation, often on a scale lower than apprenticeships.

By 1920, a fresh wave of liberalism was influencing Japan, affecting the role and image of the teacher. World War I stimulated a humanistic movement in many countries of the world, including Japan. Meiji men were being succeeded by a new class of commoner-bureaucrats during the reign of Emperor Taishō (1912–1926). Government leaders were chosen from the class of commoner-politician, rather than the aristocratic class; and the overestimated phrase Taishō Democracy was coined in response to the victory of Western democracy over German totalitarianism. Hara Takashi became the first commoner premier in 1918, marking the beginning of party government.

Liberalism and euphoria were spreading. Those few who had opposed the traditional heavenly-mission concept of the teacher moved into the forefront of the movement to reform education by establishing progressive schools, including the Jiyūgakuen (Liberty School) founded by Hani Motoko and the Seijō Elementary School by Sawayanagi Masatarō, still famous for their progressive methods of education. John Dewey visited Japan to introduce his philosophy of education. Progressive ideas from America, Pestalozzian theory, and Marxist teachings were all competing with Herbartian theories from Germany now losing popularity in Japan. With Pestalozzian theories as the central force of the new education movement, emphasis was placed on self-activity in contrast to cramming under Herbartian methods. A new era in Japanese education and society appeared imminent.

From 1919 to 1921, the beginning of the so-called proletariat period, the influence of Marx-Leninism within Japan was pronounced. A multitude of Marxist societies, journals, and activities emerged. Student organizations were ventured at Waseda and Tōkyō universities for the study of Marxism. Intellectuals were awakening to the new foreign ideology. A flood of socialist literature circulated throughout the country, mostly in the form of translated Western materials, keeping Japanese readers abreast of the progress of world socialism.

In 1919, in response to the liberal trends of the time and the hardships of the destitute teachers who were left behind in the sudden prosperity, the first independent organization of Japanese teachers was founded. Shimonaka Yasaburō, a teacher at the Saitama Prefectural Normal School, organized a movement called the Nihon Kyōin Kumiai Keimeikai (Japan Teachers Union Enlightenment Association), or Keimeikai. Keimeikai established an office in Tōkyō and held its first official meeting on August 4, 1919, with 200 members, at the Kanda Seinen Hall. They set themselves the following three goals: stabilizing teachers' livelihood, elevating teachers' positions, and securing their independence of thought. Their organ was the periodical *Keimei* (Enlightenment), serving at its peak a membership of 1,500 teachers throughout the nation. Their initial declaration, a curious assortment of moderate ideas, included the following:

> Our ideal is to attain a just life based upon human rights. We acknowledge the basic rights of human beings and respect their inalienable social rights.
> We are Japanese. We assert our sincerity as Japanese citizens and our desire to be loyal to the just and great principles of Japan. Therefore, we reject all irrational and unnatural laws, conventions and thoughts contrary to these principles.
> We are educators. We are conscious of our vocation and will devote ourselves to the education of all people in friendship.[14]

In 1920 Keimeikai discussed a proposal for public election of school principals, a recurring theme of many of the subsequent teachers' organizations, which objected to the role of the school principal as a puppet of the government. Saitama Prefectural authorities shortly thereafter dismissed or transferred leaders of Keimeikai within their jurisdiction. The government then banned Keimeikai's journal after an edition carried an article entitled "Kokka Seikatsu no Gōrika" (Rationalization of Our National Way of Life), concerning the hardships of life in Japan. A few intrepid members ventured to participate in Japan's first May Day celebration in 1920, an act totally counter to the traditional image of a Japanese teacher. Pressure by the government was increased until Keimeikai was forced to disband, terminating the first attempt to organize Japanese teachers independently of government control.[15]

Social unrest and rice riots continued to plague the nation, and the catastrophic Tōkyō earthquake of 1923 added to the misery of the people. In such an environment malcontents were readily attracted to opposition movements. By this time the Soviet Union had indicated an interest in Japan, and a tiny Japan Communist party was organized in 1922 under Soviet aegis. For the next several years, the party faithful worked within the labor movement. Acts of violence broke out, providing the police with a timely reason to crack down on the Communist party and dissolve it. Apparently, very few teachers were directly involved in the Communist movement at this time.

In the late 1920s, disaster again fell upon the nation when the effects of the Great Depression reached Japan, a land depleted of raw materials, totally dependent upon international trade, and faced with prohibitively high import tariffs among its traditional trading countries. Teachers, already poorly paid, suffered further deprivation and denigration. Farmers' incomes, however, fell below that of teachers, placing the local teacher in the unique position of struggling to maintain a minimum standard of living while witnessing the struggles for survival of his students' families. Socialist and Communist activities increased in response to these conditions, only to be more vigorously condemned by the government.

In 1929, the Shōgakkō Kyōin Renmei (Primary School Teachers League) was formed in Tōkyō, the first Communist teachers' association in the nation; it took a leading role in the class struggle by joining an international movement of teachers sponsored by the Soviet Union. In 1930, forty-five members were arrested under the 1925 Law for the Preservation of Public Order, and the organization disbanded.[16] In the same year, the Ministry of Education issued instructions for the appointment of active military officers to give military instruction in all public normal schools, middle schools, technical schools, and higher schools. Although Mori's code of 1886 had stipulated similar regulations, their enforcement had become haphazard during the Taishō Democracy era.

Several of the remaining activist teachers from the dissolved left-wing Shōgakkō Kyōin Renmei, led by Yamashita Tokuji, then formed in 1930 the underground Nihon Kyōiku Rōdō Kumiai (Japan Educational Labor Union), or Kyōrō, which had a distinctly proletarian platform. Kyōrō is considered the prewar spiritual predecessor of the postwar Nikkyōso and the originator of the concept of "educational laborer" (*kyōiku rōdōsha*), which became a major issue of contention after the war. Kyōrō distributed a publication entitled the *Kyōrō Panfuretto* (Educational Worker's Pamphlet) as a struggle guide and established illegal Kyōrō branches in eighteen prefectures. For a short time it joined the Nihon Rōdō Kumiai Zenkoku Kyōgikai (National Council of Japanese Labor Unions) as its educational division. Kyōrō thus came under the direct influence of one of the most active organizations controlled by Communists, which instigated local and national strikes that brought on the wrath of the police and the early disbandment of the parent body.

In the same year that Kyōrō was established, a recognized cultural organization called Shinkō Kyōiku Kenkyūjo (Institute for Proletariat Education), or Shinkyō, was also organized under the leadership of Yamashita Tokuji from Kyōrō. Shinkyō was used by Kyōrō leaders as a legal research body for the dissemination of left-wing literature through a journal called *Keimei*, which appealed to the young impoverished teachers experiencing the difficulties of teaching in a nearly bankrupt nation.[17] Shinkyō was distinctly leftist, criticizing contemporary bourgeois educa-

tion while promoting an educational system for the children of the proletariat. Readers of the journal formed a small network of left-wing
teacher cells throughout the nation until the group was forced to disband.

Shinkyō never attained a mass base among teachers because of its
theoretical and political tendencies. It represented an urban-based, rather
sophisticated, ideological group remote from the day-to-day life of the
average teacher. The leaders were influenced by international movements
and formal theories of which the ordinary teacher working under adverse
conditions was unaware. The following excerpts from Shinkyō's platform
illustrate its political and ideological persuasion and reveal its interpretation of the role of the teacher as an educational laborer:

DUTIES AND FUNCTIONS
1. To satisfy the desire for basic education to meet the daily needs of
   laborers, farmers, and other workers
2. To struggle against bourgeois and fascist educational principles
3. To struggle for satisfactory material conditions in order to provide
   for the full educational desires of proletariat children
4. To struggle against imperialistic education
5. To protect socialist education
6. To train leaders for the proletariat education movement

ACTIVITIES AND PLATFORM
1. Opposition to militaristic and religious education
2. Promotion of general educational activities for the proletariat
3. Opposition to any disciplinary measures against children of the
   working class
4. Consolidation of technical and professional education on socialist
   principles for children of the working class
5. Opposition to education emphasizing examination preparation which
   neglects children of the working class
6. Establishment of night schools and nurseries at factories financed by
   factory owners but managed by factory committees
7. Opposition to Seinen Gakkō (Youth Schools established by the
   government)
8. Elimination of school fees and provision of free educational materials
   for children of the working class
9. Adoption of educational principles and techniques based on a careful interpretation of Marx-Leninism
10. Cooperation with international proletariat movements
11. Promotion of freedom of revolutionary materials and movements
12. Promotion of freedom of speech, press, and association
13. Opposition to imperialistic wars[18]

Shinkyō's platform, blatantly anticapitalist and antibourgeois, was the overt basis of all left-wing teachers' organizations in the 1920s and the 1930s. They could operate on this basis usually with impunity, since the government was not much concerned with antibourgeois propaganda. However, any criticism of the emperor, the imperial institution, the national entity of Japan (*kokutai*), the military, or the government inevitably invited the wrath of the police. Implicit in the proletariat propaganda was a criticism of these sacrosanct institutions, but in order to avoid reprisals the emphasis was placed on opposition to capitalistic bourgeoisie. When the government decided these boundaries were violated, it simply closed down the organization.

During the early 1930s, the Communists and Socialists bickered among themselves for hegemony of the working-class movement, thus further confounding and inhibiting proletariat movements. The Communists, operating under strong influence from the Soviet Union, attacked the role of the emperor in Japanese society, an attack which provoked the full wrath of the police. The Socialists refrained from supporting such a radical position and, conversely, during the darkening thirties assumed a somewhat cooperative policy with the government based on "national socialism," which brought them into conflict with the Japan Communist party. The prewar split was a major underlying factor in the division between the Communist and Socialist parties after the Pacific war ended in 1945, when their respective leaders resumed the struggle for hegemony of the burgeoning postwar labor movement.

The period of the early 1930s, when the depression took its appalling toll in Japan, was of extreme importance to the postwar teachers' movement. During these several years of national economic distress, when the military began its inexorable drive to control the State, the teaching corps underwent one of the most excruciating periods in its history. Teachers' salaries were reduced. In 1931, about a thousand towns and villages were in arrears of teachers' salaries. The teaching profession had reached its nadir.[19]

The critical factor about this period is that every president and nearly every other leader of the postwar Nikkyōso underwent his teacher training in the normal schools of the late 1920s and early 1930s and went out to teach in their first positions during this time of extreme national tribulation. The relationship between normal school training and the teaching experiences of postwar union leaders in the depression years of the early 1930s, especially in impoverished rural Japan, and the left-wing attitudes and positions these leaders assumed after the war in organizing

Nikkyōso were of critical significance to the initial postwar attitude assumed by Nikkyōso.

In 1932, as the militarists sought to strengthen their grip on the government, Premier Inukai was assassinated, ending fourteen turbulent years of party government. In the same year the Ministry of Education issued an ordinance on April 8 stipulating that teachers were expected to fulfill their duties as *tenshoku,* literally, a heavenly occupation or mission. One of the contemporary normal school textbooks stated that "the goal of education is for others. Therefore true education is attained when the teacher sacrifices himself for his students. Herein lies the reason why teaching is called a holy profession (*seishoku*)."[20] The pendulum once again, as in the 1880s, swung back to the traditional image of a Japanese teacher, as progressive ideals in education were branded as foreign inspired and inimical to Japanese traditions.

Under the militarists, Japanese teachers were indoctrinated with nationalistic and quasi-religious concepts through a highly disciplined normal school curriculum, which was oriented toward the martial arts and in which normal school students participated in military maneuvers as part of their preparation for teaching. At the Okayama Prefectural Normal School, for example, there were three army officers on the faculty, who taught three to five class hours a week in weapons firing, marching, and military leadership.[21] Graduates from 1927 on had to serve a five-month tour of duty in one of the miiltary services in order to understand the "military spirit." Only then were they considered fit to educate young people. After their tour of duty, they were expected to regard the military spirit as the spirit of education.[22]

The moral code in both the normal schools and the imperial forces was founded on loyalty to the emperor and service to the State. The normal schools, once again achieving increased popularity during the mid-thirties as a means of attaining job security during the depression and as an alternative to prolonged compulsory military duty, became so closely aligned with the military that the transition from normal school to the military and on to the teaching post was a natural process. Several basic sectors of the society became inextricably intertwined in the single purpose of accomplishing the mission of the government.

As long as the teacher trainees were protected from the harsh realities of a destitute society while remaining within the confines of the normal schools and the military, where the State provided all amenities including a monthly stipend, the scheme operated efficiently. However, when some of the graduates, upon finally reaching their first teaching assignment, were sickened by the abject poverty, particularly of their rural students, reaction set in. The inconsistencies of the normal school teachings, where concepts of Japanese superiority and greatness were inculcated, were exposed when the new teachers encountered the actual condition of the poorer masses of Japanese.

Under these conditions, a few teachers influenced by Marxist literature tried to organize a "Pioneer Movement" patterned after the Pioneers in the Soviet Union. Posters ostensibly depicting the life of happy young Pioneers in a Communist land, contrasting sharply with life in Japan at that time, adorned a few classroom bulletin boards, as activist teachers hopelessly endeavored to organize like-minded teachers in a protesting proletariat movement. They were ruthlessly dealt with by the government, which branded all teachers' protest movements as Communist-inspired. From 1926 to 1935, the government arrested 748 teachers on ideological grounds and punished 649 of them. In Nagano Prefecture in 1933 alone, 131 teachers were arrested, of whom 58 were removed from their teaching posts by dismissal or compulsory early retirement, discouraging a radical teachers' movement through fear of reprisals and arrest.[23]

During this period, the one teachers' movement that persisted with a limited degree of success was the loosely termed Seikatsu Tsuzurikata Undō, which meant the creative-writing association or the life-in-education movement. The form and nature of this protest was such that it was extremely difficult for the authorities to suppress it. Although somewhat formalized in several different sections of the country, the movement was essentially amorphous. Teachers could participate, in most instances, without exposing themselves to any punitive action. In contrast Shinkyō, this movement was simple, devoid of theoretical premises, and based on the native life and daily activities of the ordinary teacher. Accordingly it had a much broader appeal than organizations such as Shinkyō.

The creative-writing or life-in-education movement was conducted mostly by teachers in Japanese language classes who oriented their composition lessons toward the daily life of their students. Since there were no prescribed lessons or teachers' manuals for composition classes, teachers were free to plan their own lessons. The movement originated when language teachers had their students compose essays on self-reflection, a subject dear to every Japanese. From criticizing one's own weaknesses, followed by earnest soul-searching to correct one's foibles, the next step was to reflect on life in general—that is, on Japanese society—by criticizing the evils and by seeking solutions to correct them. During the years of the depression, it was not a difficult task indeed for students to witness the ills of Japanese society.

Teachers as well as students were affected by the lessons. One teacher, Iwama Masao, who at this time found Marxism attractive and who was ultimately to become the major leader of the early postwar teachers' union movement, recalls: "My eyes were awakened to the evils of our society through compositions of my pupils in which their sufferings at home were revealed under the pressure of poverty."[24] The movement became political when teachers such as Iwama, who were themselves critical of the economic conditions and the harsh political restrictions the government placed upon them and the public at large, led the students to conclude that the Japanese government was the major source of the evils confronting Japan.

The life-in-education movement was less political and more humanitarian as practiced by the Hoppō Kyōikusha Undō (Northern Teachers Movement), founded by Narita Tadahisa, from the northern prefecture of Akita. Since northern Japan was traditionally considered the least developed area of the nation, teachers in this rural movement endeavored to show the rest of Japan that such movements could succeed under the most adverse conditions. Similar groups were begun in other rural areas, such as Shikoku, but most of the formal organizations did not long survive.

In 1934 the government sponsored a national convention of teachers in which it promoted a spiritual enhancement of education, demanding that teachers be purveyors of militaristic education. Shortly thereafter, the Thought Bureau was established. As the government increased its restrictive measures, the leader of the Hoppō Kyōikusha Undō was arrested in 1935. The government charged that teachers involved in this movement were organizing peasants' children to attack Japanese society in critical essays, and that this was done through proletariat methods to accomplish the purposes of the Comintern and the Japan Communist party.[25] The formal movement then ceased to exist.

The role of the creative-writing movement and the more politically inspired teachers' organizations must not be overestimated, for the preponderance of teachers, including language teachers, accepted the course toward militarism, using the classroom to support the government's aims throughout the war. Most of them did so because they had been thoroughly indoctrinated during their own schooling and thus zealously believed in the cause. Teachers used every course they taught as a means to instill "acceptable" concepts into the young. In particular, history, geography, and morals (*shūshin*) courses were used for these purposes. Teachers in morals education emphasized the themes of *bushidō* (the way of the warrior), stressing loyalty, filial piety, bravery, and honor in addition to the general theme of militarism, ultranationalism, and State Shintō.

An example of the role of the teacher in Japanese society during the 1930s can be seen in the prewar career of the fourth president of Nikkyōso, Miyanohara Sadamitsu, who exemplifies the depth of indoctrination of teacher candidates during the normal school training. When interviewed, Miyanohara recalled that upon graduation from the Kagoshima Normal School in southern Japan in the mid-thirties he was a confident young teacher imbued with concepts of Japanese superiority and love of the emperor. After graduation he entered the Japanese imperial navy for five months; upon release, he became an elementary school teacher in rural Kyūshū.

Miyanohara firmly believed in the militaristic education then being promoted by the government, as Japanese armies moved onto the Asian mainland. As a teacher in the upper elementary school, handling boys fourteen to fifteen years of age, he earnestly endeavored to develop among these boys a sense of service to the Japanese empire. In particular, he recruited volunteers for Manchuria in a special organization of young people organized to help develop the newly conquered territory. At that time he took especial pride in being able to persuade many of his rural students to join this governmental undertaking. Unfortunately, fewer than half his students lived to return home from Manchuria at the war's end, resulting in an ideological reversal within Miyanohara, from the right in the prewar era to the left in the immediate postwar period. This was ultimately to be reflected in his left-wing leadership of Nikkyōso from 1962.[26]

Those teachers who did not believe in the government propaganda were nevertheless compelled to teach the materials prescribed by the Ministry of Education, or lose their jobs or, in extreme cases, face arrest. Certain teachers who sympathized with their poverty-stricken students joined movements to help alleviate these conditions merely on humanitarian grounds. Although the government branded all suspect teachers' movements as Communist and ruthlessly intervened to stamp them out, there was, nevertheless, a fringe sector of teachers who were willing to sacrifice themselves for a liberal cause. Sometimes the motives were humanitarian, sometimes, political, and frequently, a blend of the two. Such teachers' movements were to be totally suppressed during World War II.

After 1935, as far as can be ascertained, no independent teachers' organization functioned until the formation in 1939 of two groups called the Nihon Seinen Kyōshidan (Japan Young Teachers' Association) and the Kyōiku Kagaku Kenkyūkai (Association for the Scientific Study of Education), or Kyōkaken. The Nihon Seinen Kyōshidan was a short-lived organization of activist teachers based in Tōkyō. Because of government pressure, it was unable to form a sustaining movement. Kyōkaken originated from the publication in the early 1930s of the most authoritative prewar encyclopedia of education, entitled *Kyōikugaku Jiten,* published by the Iwanami Company. The editors continued the work by publishing a series of relevant lectures which led to the publication of a journal called *Kyōiku* (Education). Promoters of the journal, Kido Mantarō, professor of psychology at Hōsei University, and Tomeoka Kiyō, formerly from the same department, decided to form an organization to further their ideals. They based their position on the reform of education through scientific research and study.

Initially, the movement grew out of an interest in psychology as it pertained to education; hence, it was not ideologically oriented. Nevertheless, inherent in this approach was a criticism of contemporary Japanese education as obsolete and inadequate to support a modern nation. There was an implicit criticism of the Ministry of Education that normally would have brought on the wrath of the police. The Ministry of Education did not suppress Kyōkaken for the following reasons: (1) Kyōkaken did not overtly question the war or the military regime, and (2) its leaders promoted the scientific reform of education for the advancement of Japan. Not even the military government could bring itself to ban such an organization that endeavored to improve the quality of Japan's war machine.

Kyōkaken attacked normal school training, the center of ultranationalism, as antiquated and anachronistic in its pedogogical methods based on the Herbartian five-step process, which encouraged rote memory when applied in the Japanese context. It also established local branches of Kyōkaken consisting of regular teachers. The plan was to reeducate teachers both in training and in service who would reconstruct education scientifically. In turn, the schools were to reform and reconstruct Japanese society, thereby enabling the government to wage modern warfare for the preservation of the Japanese nation.

.. Kyōkaken's recommendations for educational reform were originated mostly by Professor Abe Shigetaka of Tōkyō University, who was influenced by his lengthy visit to the United States in 1925, and after his death in 1939 were promoted by his student Munakata Seiya, who exerted considerable influence on the postwar teachers' movement. Among the recommendations were the following: decentralization of educational control, a 6–3–3–5 articulated system, curriculum reforms, teaching-methods reform, an extension of compulsory education from six to eight or nine years, and the integration of the various secondary schools into a unified or comprehensive school. The significance of these prewar progressive ideas lies in the fact that nearly all of them were included in the American Occupation's reforms of Japanese education after World War II.

Presided over by Kido Mantarō and Tomeoka Kiyō, Kyōkaken attracted a number of scholars who joined the movement because its scientific approach to education appealed to them intellectually. It also attracted a number of dissidents from the several left-wing organizations disbanded by the government who had no other formal organization to join. As a result, there was within the organization a mixture of conservatives, moderates, and leftists, all criticizing contemporary education while promoting a new education for Japan.

Kyōkaken had no direct relationship with the military government or the Ministry of Education. However, its contacts with Prince Konoe, who became prime minister in 1938, afforded it security. Prince Konoe financed a brain trust called the Shōwa Kenkyūkai (Shōwa Research Association), which included distinguished progressive scholars, several of whom belonged to another private organization called the Kyōiku Kaikaku Dōshikai (Educational Reform Society), which also included educationists and politicians of progressive leanings interested in promoting education. Among the members of the Kyōiku Kaikaku Dōshikai were Abe, Kido, and Tomeoka from Kyōkaken. Through this network of contacts and the meetings of the Kyōiku Kaikaku Dōshikai and the Kenkyūkai, the theories formulated by Kyōkaken were made known to politicians and to Prince Konoe himself.

Kyōkaken served a unique blend of purposes by providing the military regime with ideas for educational reform and new teaching methods to improve the manpower quality of the war machine, a continuing demand the military government placed on the Ministry of Education. At the same time Kyōkaken provided a base for left-wing activists to continue their antigovernment activities during the war in the guise of improving education, under the protection of their indirect association with Prince Konoe, who was related to the imperial family. Kyōkaken was finally dissolved by the government in 1944, when the military regime, facing continual battlefield reversals, dissolved any organization under the slightest pretext. With the arrest of Kido and Tomeoka, the government ended all movements having any semblance of a teachers' movement.[27]

Activist teachers in prewar Japan never posed a real threat to the military regime. They were merely annoying. Their activities, however, sustained the tiny ray of protest throughout the dark thirties and early forties. When the American Occupation authorities were seeking a liberal Japanese element in the aftermath of the war, they found it in these leftist teachers who had unsuccessfully attempted to organize prewar associations. The Americans and the Japanese left wing thus aligned themselves in their opposition to the military regime, initially by having the protesting teachers of the thirties forming the nucleus of the teachers' movement and later by having Nikkyōso as the nucleus.

The lone teachers' association recognized throughout the prewar and wartime periods was the Teikoku Kyōikukai (Imperial Education Association) founded in 1883 to unite teachers for the improvement of national education in support of the government's educational policy. The fortunes of this association were curious. Basically, they followed the alternations of the government. During the Meiji period, the Teikoku Kyōikukai was theoretically a federation of autonomous local and prefectural educational and cultural associations. Governmental influence was strong. During the period of the Taishō Democracy (around 1920), however, it transformed its image under the presidency of the educational reformer, Sawayanagi Masatarō, founder of the progressive school Seijō Gakuen. During this period the Teikoku Kyōikukai not only sent Japanese teachers to the West to study Western philosophies of education and modern teaching methods, but it also invited progressive educators of the West to come to Japan. In addition, it labored for increased national expenditures on elementary education and the payment in full of teachers' salaries that were in arrears because of the depression.

When the military embarked upon its aggressive expansionist campaign, the Teikoku Kyōikukai, along with all other cultural and social organizations, became submerged in the quagmire of ultranationalism and militarism. In 1944 it changed its name to Dai Nippon Kyōikukai (Great Japan Education Association). All teachers were asked to join the Dai Nippon Kyōikukai, thereby eliminating the autonomy enjoyed by local and prefectural associations. Nearly all teachers joined because to do otherwise stigmatized one as unpatriotic during the most dangerous period of the war, when the government was facing continual military reverses.[28]

Tanaka Kōtarō, a distinguished postwar minister of education and later chief justice of the Supreme Court, described the Dai Nippon Kyōikukai as obviously nationalistic, functioning as virtual agent of the Ministry of Education, which appointed the association's president and vice-president, who, in turn, chose the director and counselors. Many of the association's staff were ultranationalists and retired high officials of the Ministry of Education. As an official teachers' organization, its purposes were "to promote the educational ideal of the Japanese people on the fundamental principle of the national policy, encourage the indefatigable assiduity of its members, and render loyal service to national education. The government considered the association all the more worthy of its subsidy of a million yen per year because of its nationalistic tendency."[29]

During the later war years, no teachers' organization of consequence was recognized except this association. The others had already been either disbanded or effectively suppressed by the government through arrests and intimidation. Teachers lost their political rights, their freedom of thought, and their freedom of association, in common with the rest of the populace. However, teachers, as promoters of militaristic education and leaders of a new Japan, were viewed in a special way by the government. Their whole life was imbued with ultranationalistic militarism from their elementary schooling, their normal school training, and their mandatory period of military duty. Under these circumstances, the Japanese teaching corps became one of the most militaristic groups of people in Japanese society, perhaps next only to the military itself, perpetuating ultranationalism by faithfully sending forth their students to the battlefields for the Japanese Empire and the emperor. When the war finally ended in 1945, a regenerated teachers' movement was, to a substantial degree, a spontaneous reaction to these prewar circumstances.

NOTES

1. Ronald Dore, *Education in Tokugawa Japan* (Berkeley: University of California Press, 1965), p. 34.
2. Ikeda Susumu, *Gendai no Kyōshi* (Modern Teachers) (Tōkyō: Daiichi Hōki, 1968), p. 21.
3. Dore, *Education in Tokugawa Japan*, p. 260.

4. Kikuchi Dairoku, *Japanese Education* (London: John Murray, 1909), p. 45.
5. Mombushō (Japanese Ministry of Education), *Gakusei Kyūjūnenshi* (Ninety-Year History of the Education System) (Tōkyō: Mombushō, 1962), pp. 10, 583.
6. Dore, *Education in Tokugawa Japan*, p. 321.
7. Herbert Passin, *Society and Education in Japan* (New York: Teachers College Press, Columbia University, 1965), pp. 226–228.
8. Karasawa Tomitarō, "A History of Japanese Teachers," *Paedagogica Historica* 6, no. 2 (1966):402.
9. Marius B. Jansen, ed., *Changing Japanese Attitudes toward Modernization* (Princeton: Princeton University Press, 1965), pp. 236–237.
10. Kikuchi, *Japanese Education*, p. 283.
11. Ibid., p. 3.
12. Nikkyōso (Japan Teachers Union), *Nikkyōso Jūnenshi* (Ten-Year History of the Japan Teachers Union) (Tōkyō: Nikkyōso, 1958), pp. 432–433.
13. Karasawa, "A History of Japanese Teachers," p. 409.
14. Ibid., p. 411.
15. Karasawa Tomitarō, *Kyōshi no Rekishi* (A History of Teachers) (Tōkyō: Sōbunsha, 1955), pp. 165–167.
16. Ibid., p. 173.
17. Mochizuki Muneaki, *Nikkyōso Nijūnen no Tatakai* (Twenty-Year Struggle of the Japan Teachers Union) (Tōkyō: Rōdō Junpōsha, 1967), pp. 22–23.
18. Karasawa, *Kyōshi no Rekishi*, pp. 183–184.
19. Karasawa, "A History of Japanese Teachers," p. 410.
20. Ikeda, *Gendai no Kyōshi*, pp. 17–18.
21. Interview with Hashimoto Kyōzō, graduate of Okayama Prefectural Normal School, class of 1932, Tōkyō, April 14, 1968.
22. Karasawa, "A History of Japanese Teachers," p. 414.
23. Karasawa, *Kyōshi no Rekishi*, p. 179.
24. Iwama Masao, *Hitosujini* (In One Direction) (Tōkyō: Japan Communist Party Publications Department, 1967), p. 112.
25. Nikkyōso, *Nikkyōso Nijūnenshi* (Twenty-Year History of the Japan Teachers Union) (Tōkyō: Rōdō Junpōsha, 1967), pp. 22–23.
26. Interview with Miyanohara Sadamitsu, Nikkyōso chairman, Tōkyō, July 21, 1968.
27. Ichikawa Shōgo, "Senji Kyōiku Saisaku no Tokuhitsu to Kyōiku no Ron" (Character of the Education Policy during the War and the Theory of Educational Science), *Hokkaidō Daigaku Kyōiku Gakubu Kiyō* 8 (1962):1–62.
28. Supreme Commander for the Allied Powers (SCAP), *History of the Non-Military Activities of the Occupation of Japan* (Tōkyō: SCAP, 1949), 11:35.
29. SCAP, *A History of Teachers' Unions in Japan*, Tōkyō, March, 1948, pp. 1–4.

2

The Postwar Rebirth (1945)

Freedom of Association

On July 26, 1945, eleven days before the atom bomb obliterated a major part of Hiroshima, the Allied Powers issued the Potsdam Declaration, demanding that Japan either surrender unconditionally or face the "utter devastation of the Japanese homeland." The terms of the Potsdam Declaration read in part as follows: "The Japanese Government shall remove all obstacles to the revival and strengthening of democratic tendencies among the Japanese people. Freedom of speech, of religion, and of thought, as well as respect for the fundamental human rights, shall be established. The occupying forces of the Allies shall be withdrawn from Japan as soon as these objectives have been accomplished and there has been established in accordance with the freely expressed will of the Japanese people a peacefully inclined and responsible government."[1]

On August 14, Emperor Hirohito announced acceptance of the terms of the Potsdam Declaration. Acknowledging the threat of annihilation by further use of the new bomb and the rapidly deteriorating war situation, the emperor surrendered his nation to the Allied Powers. The final paragraph of the Potsdam Declaration paved the way for the cooperative attitude on the part of the Japanese toward the occupying forces, a monumental reversal that mystified many of the foreigners who participated in the comprehensive project. There is no doubt that Emperor Hirohito was instrumental in this regard since he declared, in a decree reminiscent of the 1890 Imperial Rescript: "Beware most strictly lest any outbursts of emotion, which may engender needless complication . . . lead you astray. . . . Devote your united strength to construction of the future . . . work with resolution so that you may enhance the innate glory of the Imperial state and keep pace with the progress of the world."[2]

At the end of hostilities on August 15, 1945, teachers in Japan were exhausted, sick, hungry, and demoralized. Many had lost their homes in the relentless bombings of the cities, which had destroyed over four thousand schools. Those who had moved to the suburbs spent hours each day commuting because of the unreliable transportation system. Married teachers were compelled to forage for food through the countryside in order to keep their families from starving. Blackmarkets proliferated overnight. Clothes, valuables, and personal belongings were bartered for rice, the most important commodity. Teachers parted with their few remaining precious books to obtain food and shelter.

Records of teachers' activities during these days of confusion immediately following the war's end are sketchy, to say the least. Personal accounts are somewhat conflicting. What can be concluded is that, sporadically, bewildered teachers found themselves returning to those schools that had escaped the bombings to meet with their colleagues. At these impromptu sessions, surviving teachers who had participated in prewar movements spoke more frequently than the others, consequently being looked upon more and more as leaders in a leadership vacuum. The teachers who had, so to speak, pursued the wrong cause during the war constituted a disenchanted silent majority. Leadership at many such school gatherings fell naturally to the more liberal element of the faculty. The one overwhelming problem confronting all teachers concerned rice. There simply was not much available food of any nature in Japan. Conversation invariably turned to the subject of food shortage and the lack of money, fundamental issues underlying the teachers' movement from the very beginning in the immediate postwar period.

On August 26, General MacArthur arrived in Japan with a skeleton force to sign the instruments of surrender on September 2 on board the U.S.S. *Missouri* in Tōkyō Bay. He received his orders for the conduct of the military occupation of Japan in the Initial Post-Surrender Policy of Japan, radioed to him from Washington on August 29 and announced in Japan on November 8. Under the provisions of this document, General MacArthur was appointed Supreme Commander for the Allied Powers (SCAP) with full authority to effectuate the provisions of the Potsdam Declaration.[3] He did, in fact, assume the position of commander of American occupying forces with token representation from the other Allied Powers. For all intents and purposes, it was an American occupation of Japan, and will be considered as such in this study.

General MacArthur was instructed not to establish direct military government but to exercise his powers through the emperor of Japan or the Japanese governmental machinery, national and local. The policy was to use the existing form of government, not to support it. The supreme commander was entrusted with the broad mandate to foster conditions for the greatest possible assurance that Japan would never again become a menace to world peace. This was to be accomplished by abolishing militarism and ultranationalism, by strengthening democratic tendencies, and by encouraging liberal political inclinations. Finally, in a notably brief section on education, General MacArthur received instructions to reopen the schools as soon as possible, replace teachers who were active exponents of militant nationalism, abolish military training in the schools, and ensure that curricula acceptable to him would be followed in all schools.[4]

As it became evident that the conquering soldiers did not intend to pillage the land, tensions among the Japanese people were somewhat alleviated. Activist teachers gained new courage. Schools, closed since April, were reopened in the cities in mid-September, even though many of the students were still in the mountains—students who had been evacuated there during the war because of the city bombing raids. Gradually, an emerging leadership, replacing the discredited principals at various schools, organized teachers into small study groups. Activist teachers got in touch with like-minded friends or fellow graduates of a particular normal school on teaching staffs of other schools. In a few cases, local prewar educational associations or societies regrouped. Unplanned, unauthorized, and uncoordinated, teachers began slowly banding together to cope with the exigencies of a defeated nation occupied by foreign soldiers.

On October 2, the official organization of General Headquarters, Supreme Commander for the Allied Powers (GHQ, SCAP), was created by General MacArthur's General Orders, thereby abolishing the interim military government. One of the special staff sections within SCAP—the Civil Information and Education Section (CI & E)—included the Education Division which alone had direct jurisdiction over educational matters dealing with the Japanese Ministry of Education. Its primary duty was to advise the supreme commander about "policies relating to public information, education, religion and other sociological problems . . . to effect the accomplishment of the information and education objectives."[5] The Education Division was responsible for removing militarism and ultranationalism from the schools and for developing patterns of democratic education.

On October 4, SCAP dispatched the Directive to the Japanese Government for the Removal of Restrictions on Political, Civil, and Religious Liberties, abolishing the detested Preservation of Public Order Laws. On October 11, General MacArthur forwarded a letter to Prime Minister Shidehara, ordering that policies be carried out which would open the schools to more liberal education and that unionization of labor be encouraged. With the restrictions on political liberties abolished and with the subsequent release of Communist political prisoners, some incarcerated for many years for their implacable opposition to the wartime military government, a new factor was introduced. The long-suffering Communists suddenly acquired respectability, admired by many for their courage during the war in upholding their beliefs. The Americans welcomed them back into the mainstream of Japanese social and political life as allies in the cause of demilitarizing Japan. The American Occupation and the Japan Communist party thus realized an initial affinity in their common purpose to eradicate ultranationalism and militarism from Japanese education and society.

With the legalization of the Japan Communist party and the encouragement of the unionization of labor, the Communists energetically focused their limited resources on the organization of a united labor movement under their aegis. A few Communist organizers were sent out to the local schools where teachers were meeting in support of the new liberal leaders. Marginal contacts were established between emerging leaders at individual schools and the resurgent Communist party, which was striving to establish a coordinated movement. The Communists, however, were still regarded with suspicion by the average teacher as revolutionaries opposed to the emperor, though they were accepted by many left-wing liberals because of their wartime antigovernment activities.

The first stage of the basic policy of the Occupation designed to demilitarize education was begun during the last two months of 1945 and completed within the first four months of the Occupation. On October 30, SCAP ordered the removal of all teachers "known to be militaristic, ultranationalistic, or antagonistic to the objectives and policies of the Occupation."[6] On December 15, a directive was issued separating religion and the State by abolishing State Shintō and all religious acts in the schools, in addition to the doctrines that taught the superiority of the Japanese people and the Japanese emperor.[7] Finally, on December 31, 1945, the concluding directive in this troika of denial suspended the courses in morals (*shūshin*), history, and geography.[8]

One particular group of individuals meeting informally in Tōkyō within weeks after the war played a special role in the birth of the postwar teachers' movement. It all began at the Tōkyō home of Ono Shunichi, son of a former president of the Bank of Japan. Ono, who had reluctantly accepted the chairmanship of the board of the wartime Japan Children's Cultural Association, an organ of the military government, had been active in the late thirties in organizing left-wing teachers, many of whom had belonged formerly to such organizations as Kyōrō, Shinkyō, Seikatzu Tsuzurikata Undō, and Nihon Seinen Kyōshidan, which no longer existed. In 1939 Ono attended a special meeting planned and sponsored by some of these young teachers of Tōkyō. Deeply impressed by the sincerity and beliefs of these teachers in their fight for democratic education, he made a substantial financial contribution to help their cause, although these teachers could not organize themselves officially for fear of punishment by the militarists who were then in control of Japan. Be that as it may, the point is that Ono, through such teachers' activities, had made prewar contacts with a number of individuals such as Hasegawa Shōzō, a progressive elementary school teacher from the Nihon Seinen Kyōshidan, who, after the war, became chairman of the central executive committee of the Tōkyō Municipal Teachers Union.

Several weeks after the war ended, Ono and a few of his friends sent letters to several other prewar activists they had known during the late thirties, inviting them to come to Ono's home in Tōkyō to discuss the plight of the teacher amidst the postwar chaos. At the first informal meeting, this coterie of prewar activists considered the problems of reconstructing Japanese education. Included in the initial group, most of whom eventually became leaders either within the teachers' movement or the Socialist and Communist parties, or both, were Kitamura Magomori, a member of the radical Kyōrō of 1930, and Inagaki Masanobu and Irie Michio, both prewar Communists. At a subsequent meeting, these men named their group the Kyōiku Saiken Renmei (Education Reconstruction League), proclaiming their commitment to revolutionizing Japanese education by awakening a new educational consciousness within the school, home, and society for the construction of a peace-loving Japan.

During the first several meetings at Ono's home in September 1945, the discussions centered around the need for educational reform through research activities independent of the government. The participants concluded that the foundation for a peaceful Japan must be rooted in education. By the end of October, however, the general attitude began to change. Workers were organizing unions after political restrictions were lifted by the SCAP directive. In witnessing these activities and in the hope of revolutionizing education in Japan, the participants in the discussions at Ono's home concluded that teachers must be organized into a union that would strive to alleviate the terrible living conditions then being experienced by teachers.

The meetings in Ono's home rapidly expanded as word about the plan spread among like-minded friends and acquaintances of the original group, some of whom had only recently returned to Tōkyō after being evacuated because of bombing raids during the war. To accommodate the growing attendance, the meeting place was moved to an elementary school in Kanda, Tōkyō, where, on November 18, 1945, it was unanimously agreed that the formation of a teachers' union was the next step to be taken. Having the participation of former members of Kyōrō, Shinkyō, Kyōkaken, Nihon Seinen Kyōshidan, and other organizations from the prewar teachers' movement, this group of teachers represented a broad spectrum of beliefs and political inclinations.[9]

Included in the group by now were two figures to become prominent in the teachers' movement, Hani Gorō and Iwama Masao. Hani, a left-wing historian, had been recuperating from his most recent wartime prison sentence for having spoken out against the war at the Tōkyō YWCA in early 1945, when several of the original organizers, including Inagaki, prevailed upon him to join their group.[10] Hani was to become one of the early theoreticians within the movement. The other individual, Iwama Masao, who had been a protagonist at the progressive Seijō School in the thirties, found a natural attraction to the movement.[11] He soon became the leader of the radical wing of the teachers' movement.

Some of the original organizers, it should be noted, were no longer regular school teachers; others, having been associated with universities or professions such as journalism, never were regular school teachers; still others had been dismissed from their teaching positions during the war. Certain leaders strongly advocated support of political movements, which to most of the people in attendance meant communism since the Communist party was actively interested in the group through its participant members. Others, mostly regular teacher-participants who leaned toward the Socialist party, warned against becoming associated with any political party, especially the Japan Communist party. The extreme leftists and the moderates were thus quickly making known their divergent political positions within the same group.

Simultaneously, a plan was afoot in Tōkyō for organizing another group of teachers. This group, which also played a significant role in the postwar teachers' movement, was organized by Kagawa Toyohiko, a famous Christian Socialist in Japan. On December 2, 1945, Kagawa invited thirty members from among his friends in Tōkyō and seventy-five volunteers from other prefectures to an inaugural meeting of what became known later as the Nihon Kyōikusha Kumiai (Japan Educators Union), or Nikkyō, at the Kuramae Industrial Hall, Shimbashi, Tōkyō. Kagawa's purpose in calling this meeting, according to his secretary, was to initiate an organization to "accomplish educational reform without violating the cultural pattern of Japan."[12]

Nikkyō included some well-known progressives of a moderate political nature including Ouchi Hyōe, a distinguished economist; Kawasaki Natsu, well-known champion of women's rights; and Hani Setsuko, wife of Hani Gorō, from the distinguished Christian family that founded the prewar Jiyūgakuen (Liberty School) in Tōkyō. Nikkyō exhibited more of the characteristics of a cultural society than those of a labor union. Although membership was open to all, most of the officers of Nikkyō were affiliated with, or sympathetic to, the Socialist party and were elected by the initial committee members appointed by Kagawa, who was immediately elected president of the group.

The two main objectives of Nikkyō concerned salary increases and security of position for teachers. The day after Nikkyō was founded, its representatives handed a resolution to Minister of Education Maeda Tamon, with the following demands: the immediate reappointment of teachers illegally dismissed during the war, the public election of educational administrators and school principals, and the establishment of autonomous rights of schools. Shortly thereafter, Nikkyō placed before the Tōkyō municipal education authorities two demands: a 600-yen monthly salary increase to offset inflation and the abolition of the plan to dismiss redundant primary school teachers. A Nikkyō spokesman also made known Nikkyō's decision to join the Nihon Rōdō Kumiai Sōdōmei (Japan Federation of Labor Unions), or Sōdōmei, a council of moderate labor unions endorsed by the Socialist party.[13]

Learning that Kagawa's Nikkyō had set December 2 as its inaugural meeting, the rival group of prewar activists, mentioned earlier, hurriedly agreed to organize formally on December 1 at the Kanda Education Hall under the name of Zen Nihon Kyōin Kumiai (All Japan Teachers

Union), or Zenkyō.[14] The promoters of this group energetically circulated throughout Tōkyō and nearby prefectures seeking members sympathetic to their union. Since many of the evacuated students had not yet returned to their reopened schools in Tōkyō, there were a number of teachers who had time to proselytize for the movement.

Zenkyō, at its inaugural meeting on December 1, 1945, issued to teachers throughout the nation the following appeal embodying its fundamental purpose of uniting the nation's teachers into an antigovernment union:

> The war which has been fought over these many years since the Manchurian incident by our misguided leaders has come to a terrible end. Our cities and towns are in ruin and we face severe food and housing shortages. What is the teacher's role in this situation?
>
> Each one of us entered the teaching profession with high ideals and a love for young people. And then this catastrophe took place. We must not allow it to happen again. We are not afraid of poverty, but if we suffer from hunger and our children are left without shelter, we cannot fulfill our educational ideal. Our feudalistic leaders filled us with fear, placed us in straitjackets, forced militarism upon us, and drove us and our students into this most unhappy state of affairs.
>
> Never again will we be misled by the deception of our government leaders. We must accomplish our educational ideal and love of children regardless of authority from above. In order to accomplish this goal, we must unite. By forming a united front we can protect our livelihood, educational administration can be reconstructed, our social positions can be heightened, and we can attain our high educational ideals. If we do not unite now, government affiliated unions will be organized to suppress our free movement. They are even now spreading an administrative network of a police nature to locate teachers responsible for the war. This is to avoid the Ministry of Education's responsibility for its wartime activities. Therefore we must unite and welcome anyone from any political party or ideological disposition. Then the union can accommodate all of the 400,000 teachers throughout the country.[15]

Zenkyō promoted the following demands, combining economics, politics, and ideology: increase teachers' pay by five times, establish the right of collective bargaining, establish union control of school administration, eliminate school inspectors to free the teachers from feudalistic control, abolish textbook approval by the Ministry of Education, establish a system to publicly elect school principals, abolish the Dai Nippon Kyōikukai, punish those educators responsible for the war, eliminate militaristic and nationalistic teachers, reappoint progressive teachers who were dismissed illegally during the war, establish a single union for all teachers, and form a common front with the workers of Japan.[16]

The first two independent teachers' organizations founded after the war in late 1945, Zenkyō and Nikkyō, were based on platforms with fundamental differences of extreme importance. Essentially, Nikkyō was a moderate Socialist organization while Zenkyō was a left-wing group which was under Communist influence and assumed a militant stance. Precisely in this difference was the underlying antagonism that existed between the moderates and the radicals in the teachers' movement from 1945 onwards. According to Hani Gorō, individuals of all political persuasions from ultranationalists to communists were welcomed into Zenkyō, which was then seeking members on an individual basis.[17] Apparently, no nationalists joined this obviously left-wing group supported by the Communist party, while many leftist teachers who had been discharged by the government during and prior to the war found an ideological home in Zenkyō. Nikkyō, on the other hand, mainly encouraged membership of moderate socialists sympathetic to Kagawa's principles of cooperatives, receiving tacit Socialist party support, in part from an anti-Communist position.

Another crucial difference between the two organizations involved the role of the emperor, an issue reflecting a deep ideological divergence. Zenkyō leadership in a manner similar to that taken by the Japan Communist party, adamantly opposed the imperial institution. Kagawa, the founder of Nikkyō, who was a leader of the Christian Socialist movement from the early twenties, would not consider a united front with Zenkyō because of Zenkyō's implacable stand against the continuation of the emperor system. The conflict over this issue between the Socialist and Communist parties was exacerbated when the Socialist party included the emperor, albeit powerless, in its January 1946 proposals for a revised constitution. Kagawa's attitude toward Zenkyō also perhaps reflected his opposition as a Christian to atheistic communism operating within Zenkyō leadership. Kagawa's unyielding position on this issue of the emperor eventually led to the loss of some of Nikkyō's leading members.

Zenkyō and Nikkyō differed in other ways as well. Zenkyō, in the first edition of its weekly journal, *Nippon Kyōiku Shimbun* (Japan Education Newspaper), on December 1, 1945, attacked Emperor Hirohito for his failure to acknowledge war guilt. The article was written by Hani Gorō, who had become influential in developing Zenkyō's ideological position. Nikkyō, in contrast, prepared a publication on democratic education centering around the emperor system. Zenkyō promoted a common front with workers to democratize Japan against the present government and against the alleged despotic and corrupt Ministry of Education. Nikkyō aimed at democratizing education by erecting a cooperative form of society based on the teaching of love and of a forever peaceful world. Zenkyō did not reject strike action by teachers, while Kagawa denounced it.

Despite these differences, the two organizations had some basic similarities. Both were organized at the top administrative level first, followed by appeals for rank-and-file support. Both championed democratic education and opposed militarism in the school; both demanded the discharge of ultranationalist teachers and favored the reinstatement of liberal teachers dismissed during and prior to the war; both attacked the Dai Nippon Kyōikukai as a reactionary organization and called for the public election of local school administrators. Above all, the major immediate concern of both groups, regardless of their political dissimilarities, was the economic conditions of the teacher in the period immediately following the war.

The teachers' plight in postwar Japan of 1945 was most acute. A study of teachers' salaries and expenses undertaken by SCAP in December 1945 produced the results shown in Table 3.

Table 3. Average Income and Expenses of Teachers,
          December 1945 (in yen)

Income and Expenses	Primary School	Middle School
Monthly salary	90	103
Yearly bonus	630	2,040
Monthly income	143	217
Monthly expenditure	450	600
Monthly deficit	307	383

Source: Data from Supreme Commander for the Allied Powers, *A History of Teachers' Unions in Japan*, Tōkyō, March, 1948, p. 58.

By comparison, according to the *Mainichi Shimbun*, in 1945 an office boy made 250 yen a month, and a taxi driver earned as high as 1,500 yen a month.[18] In another daily paper, it was reported that an elementary school teacher's monthly salary of 93 yen (the year-end bonus was not calculated in this figure) could purchase only two large cans of sweet potatoes on the black market.[19] A SCAP officer reported that a waitress in an officers' mess could earn a salary of 250 to 900 yen a month, a place to sleep, and two meals a day, while the monthly salary of a university professor was equal to the black-market price of a carton of cigarettes.[20]

Meanwhile, the cost of living soared. Using June 1937 as a base index of 100 for the average retail price of food in Tōkyō, the index that stood at 241 in September 1945 jumped to 1,897 by June 1946. In the same period, clothing prices rose from a base of 192 in September 1945 to 1,528 in June 1946.[21] SCAP's surveys showed that the ordinary working man was unable to provide himself and his family with the necessities of life out of his current earnings. Ministry of Education officials asserted that earnings of teachers, ranging from the elementary school level to the university level, barely could pay for one-third of their need.[22]

In order to survive under these circumstances, teachers resorted to unusual means for supporting themselves and their families. Absenteeism was rampant as teachers who were heads of households literally foraged for food in the countryside. Many took on extra jobs. Some shined shoes in distant wards so that their students would not witness their destitution. Others became seriously ill with diseases such as tuberculosis aggravated by malnutrition, and were permanently disabled. A newspaper reported that the daily caloric intake of a Tōkyōite averaged a disabling low of 881.[23] These were the reasons why Zenkyō and Nikkyō, as newly formed teachers' organizations, had as their major demand a basic living wage of 600 yen a month for all teachers, with higher salaries according to rank.

Two additional organizational developments taking place at this time compounded the overall confusion of the teachers' movement. On October 16, 1945, in the city of Musashino at the edge of Tōkyō, a group of local teachers who had been holding meetings to discuss their problems organized the Musashino Kyōshidan (Musashino Teachers Group), led by Jitsukawa Hiroshi, who was experienced in the left-wing prewar teachers' movement. This organization was the first group of teachers to be formed at the grass-roots level to become prominent eventually in the overall teachers' movement. On November 18 this group, whose membership had grown to about one thousand, changed its name to Kitatama Kyōin Kumiai (Kitatama Teachers Union), representing a larger district in the northwestern part of Tōkyō.[24]

Teachers in other areas of Tōkyō were also organizing themselves. On December 17, 1945, two hundred teachers in Toshima-Ku of Tōkyō formed the Toshima-Ku Kyōin Kumiai (Toshima Teachers Union).

Finally, on December 23, with the two organizations from Kitatama and Toshima as its nucleus, a new union was created called Tōkyō-To Kyōin Kumiai (Tōkyō Municipal Teachers Union) or Tokyō.[25] (The abbreviated name Tokyō comes from the *To* [capital] of *Tōkyō-To* and the *Kyō* of *Kyōin* [teachers].)

The demands of the newly formed Tokyō were almost identical with those of the leftist Zenkyō, consistent with the similar backgrounds of the leaders of both organizations during the prewar movement. From the moment of its formation, Tokyō began coordinating its activities with Zenkyō. Within a very short time, Tokyō, serving as the Tōkyō municipal branch of Zenkyō, was powerful enough to act as an independent organization in its struggles with the Tōkyō municipal authorities, while uniting with Zenkyō in their common struggles against the Ministry of Education and the national government.

The fourth and final group of importance during the last four and one-half months of 1945 after the war's end was the Dai Nippon Kyōikukai, (Great Japan Education Association) reorganized on November 14, 1945. Taking the position that labor unions work purely for the improvement of economic conditions, the Dai Nippon Kyōikukai strove for the spiritual improvement of teachers, maintaining that strong cooperation with the government was essential for raising the level of cultural life in Japan.[26] Its initial demand was a 500-percent increase in a teacher's monthly salary. As in the past, this association received a subsidy from the Ministry of Education. The other three teachers' organizations were opposed to the Dai Nippon Kyōikukai on ideological and historical grounds from the date of its postwar reorganization until its near demise in August of 1947, when the Ministry withdrew its subsidy at the urging of SCAP.

Thus, by January 1, 1946, the framework for a much larger and lasting postwar teacher's movement was constructed. It included, on the one hand, the left-wing organization Zenkyō and its subordinate, Tokyō, both led by prewar activists who opposed the government with the support of the Japan Communist party. Their ideological stand placed them in the mainstream of the class struggle of the proletariat movement wherein teachers and workers labored together for a new democratic Japan. The workers' methods became the teachers' methods. Collective bargaining and the right to strike were fundamental to the cause. On the other hand, there was Nikkyō, consisting of teachers of a moderate persuasion opposed to Zenkyō's ideological proclivities. Nikkyō was supported by the Socialist party, which aimed at achieving harmony through cooperatives and peaceful negotiations with the Ministry of Education. Conservatives and apolitical teachers could return to the Dai Nippon Kyōikukai.

During this unprecedented four-month period immediately after the war, when Japanese teachers originated their initial postwar organizations, the American Occupation authorities and the Japanese Ministry of Education had remarkably little direct contact with the various teachers' organizations. The major contributions of the American Occupation to the teachers' movements at this time were the decrees of October 4 and October 11, which authorized the unionization of labor, the renewal of civil liberties, and the release of political prisoners, in addition to the proclamations to demilitarize and democratize Japanese education. A highly significant deduction that can be made about this crucial period, then, is that prewar Japanese activists spontaneously grouped themselves into teachers' organizations without directive, without guidance, and without direct participation of American Occupation authorities.

Why were the American Occupation authorities not participating actively in the fledgling teachers' movement during the first several months after the war? One major reason is that they were preoccupied with their own peculiar problems. They were still maneuvering through the complex web of the Japanese social, political, and cultural institutions, striving to understand their intricacies. Concurrently, they were undergoing the process of organizing themselves administratively to carry out their broad mandates. The direct influence exerted by SCAP on the postwar teachers' movement came after the beginning of 1946. By that time, the fundamental attitudes of the teachers' organizations were already firmly established.

The Japanese Ministry of Education at this time was likewise in no position to intervene actively in teachers' organizations because it, too, was undergoing the trauma of adjustment to the new situation. The Ministry, months later, in April 1946, made an attempt to organize all teachers' organizations into a new union led by Ministry officials called the Zenkoku Kyōiku Shokuin Kyōgikai (National Council of Educational Personnel Unions), but this council failed at its first meeting, when it encountered strong opposition from left-wing representatives from Zenkyō.[27]

What happened, in short, was that an independent teachers' movement, which began in private homes and teachers' rooms, evolved, for the most part indigenously and undisturbed by the Ministry of Education and the American Occupation. It can be said, in retrospect, that the undercurrent of resistance found in prewar and wartime Japan could not be destroyed despite the harsh social, political, and cultural restrictions exercised by the military government. The prewar resistance was strong enough so that at war's end it was able within several weeks to generate a surprisingly effective movement. The Americans played the role of catalyst.

Several important conclusions can be made concerning this brief but momentous period between mid-August and December of 1945, and how it affected the entire postwar teachers' movement. First, the movement developed in direct response to the conditions that existed in Japan before 1945 and to the economic chaos of a defeated and destitute nation immediately after the war. Second, the movement was originated by the Japanese for the Japanese, with almost no direct involvement by the American Occupation. The Americans, so to speak, had removed the lid of suppression, thus enabling those prewar activists to emerge and resume independently their movement in the new environment of postwar Japan. Third, the movement was initiated at the top administrative level primarily by prewar left-wing activists because the average teacher, confronted with the enormous problems of obtaining food and shelter, was in no position to consider the problems of uniting teachers, and because there was a leadership vacuum created when educational administrators were discredited for their role during the war. Finally, the Ministry of Education, historically the major influencer of Japanese teachers' organizations, was itself under criticism by both the teachers' organizations themselves and the American Occupation, rendering the Ministry powerless to intervene in the movement. Consequently, at the end of 1945, for the first time in the history of Japan, the welfare of the classroom teacher became of paramount concern to several independent teachers' organizations vying for his allegiance.

NOTES

1. Supreme Commander for the Allied Powers (SCAP), *Education in the New Japan* (Tōkyō: SCAP, 1948), 2:6–8.
2. David James, *The Rise and Fall of the Japanese Empire* (London: Allen and Unwin, 1952), pp. 347–348.
3. Edwin M. Martin, *The Allied Occupation of Japan* (New York: American Institute of Pacific Relations, 1948), pp. 122–150.
4. Ibid.
5. SCAP, *Education in Japan*, 2:57–58.
6. Ibid.
7. Ibid., pp. 31–35.
8. Ibid., pp. 36–37.
9. Sawada Fumiaki, *Nikkyōso no Rekishi* (History of the Japan Teachers Union) (Tōkyō: Gōdō Shuppan, 1966), pp. 96–99.

10. Interview with Hani Setsuko, Hayama, Japan, June 2, 1968.
11. Interview with the Honorable Iwama Masao, Japan Communist party representative, Tōkyō, May 10, 1968.
12. SCAP, *A History of Teachers' Unions in Japan,* Tōkyō, March, 1948, pp. 18–19.
13. Ibid., pp. 3–4.
14. Iwama Masao, ed., *Kyōin Kumiai Undōshi* (A History of the Teachers' Movement) (Tōkyō: Shūkan Kyōiku Shimbunsha, 1948), pp. 9–10.
15. Mochizuki Muneaki, *Nikkyōso Nijūnen no Tatakai* (Twenty-Year Struggle of the Japan Teachers Union) (Tōkyō: Rōdō Junpōsha, 1967), pp. 25–27.
16. SCAP, *Teachers' Unions in Japan,* pp. 16–18.
17. Ibid., p. 15.
18. *Mainichi Shimbun* (Mainichi Newspaper), February 2, 1946.
19. *Nippon Times,* May 30, 1946.
20. Robert King Hall, *Education for a New Japan* (New Haven: Yale University Press, 1949), p. 7.
21. SCAP, *Teachers' Unions in Japan,* p. 62.
22. Ibid., p. 12.
23. *Nippon Times,* June 27, 1946.
24. Mochizuki, *Nikkyōso Nijūnen,* pp. 28–29.
25. Ibid.
26. SCAP, *Teachers' Unions in Japan,* pp. 4–5.
27. Ibid., p. 27.

3

Struggles for
Economic Survival (1946-1947)

Champions of
Democratic Education

On January 1, 1946, when Emperor Hirohito made his famous declaration of mortality—that "the ties between us and our people . . . are not predicated on the false assumption that the Emperor is divine"[1]—the several teachers' organizations faced the new year with two immediate goals. One concerned the improvement of the livelihood of the destitute teachers, and the other, the organization of the teaching corps throughout the nation. The two were inseparably linked since the organization capable of improving the plight of teachers could attract the rank and file into its membership.

Competition began immediately among the radical Zenkyō (All Japan Teachers Union) with its affiliate Tokyō (Tōkyō Municipal Teachers Union), the moderate Nikkyō (Japan Educators Union), and the conservative Dai Nippon Kyōikukai (Great Japan Education Association). The major goal for all was to improve teachers' living wages. Table 4 reveals the magnitude of the problem of price increases the Japanese people faced in 1946.

Zenkyō sponsored its first national convention in Tōkyō on January 19 to deliberate the formation of a united front with Kagawa's Nikkyō group. Its demands were as follows: (1) a 500-percent increase in salary to keep up with the rampant inflation; (2) the abolition of the plan to dismiss as redundant 30 percent, or 9,600, of Tōkyō municipal teachers; and (3) the reinstatement of 800 surplus teachers already dismissed.[2] On January 23 Zenkyō held a demonstration at the Imperial Palace Plaza, the first of its kind, to send off a petition containing the demands to the Ministry of Education. The reply from the Ministry, representing a gov-

43

ernment with limited resources, was far from satisfactory to Zenkyō, although teachers' salaries were slightly increased in January and the plan to dismiss redundant teachers was shelved shortly thereafter under union pressure.

Table 4. Tōkyō Price Index for Wholesale and Retail Items for Selected Periods (in yen)

Items	Selected Periods			
	June 1937	Sept. 1945	May 1946	June 1946
Wholesale Average				
All items	100.0	228.7	1,054.2	1,084.4
Retail Average				
All items	100.0	253.3	1,491.5	1,650.9
Food	100.0	241.1	1,660.1	1,897.9
Fuel	100.0	260.1	1,305.8	1,305.8
Clothing	100.0	192.4	1,528.2	1,528.2
Others	100.0	294.6	1,267.0	1,428.6

Source: Data from Supreme Commander for the Allied Powers, *A History of Teachers' Unions in Japan*, Tōkyō, March, 1948, p. 62.

Tōkyō, with Zenkyō support, held a mass meeting of teachers on January 28 at Hibiya Park to publicize and promote its local demands. About three thousand teachers participated in the meeting and later marched through the streets to the municipal office of education to present a petition; this march was the first of a series of teachers' street demonstrations in postwar Japan.

In response to the ideological controversies engulfing the Japanese teachers at this time, less than six months after the war, the minister of education clarified his position concerning what he called "the present period of confusion." He stated during a press conference that teachers as individuals had the right to join the political party of their choice, including the Japan Communist party, according to their political beliefs; but that, once the teacher entered the classroom, he must maintain political neutrality in his teachings.[3] This declaration was of vital significance, for it not only granted official approval to Communist teachers within the radical Zenkyō but also pleased the non-Communist teachers sympathetic to the Communist cause. It was also consequential because the press conference called attention to the Japan Communist party, which had by then become the most active political party; as a result, it received more press coverage than did all other parties combined.

In reaction to the public demonstrations sponsored by the Zenkyō-Tokyō combine of left-wing unions, two major developments were taking place within the overall teachers' movement in the first several months of 1946. Within Zenkyō a more moderate element of teachers was beginning to make itself heard against Communist influence among the leaders and against the rather unfavorable image of teachers being spread by the noisy street demonstrations. Many teachers in this opposition group sincerely believed that the teachers' plight could be mitigated only through a united teachers' movement, and they recognized that Zenkyō represented by far the major organization in the movement. But they could not go along with Zenkyō's militant action. Although the Zenkyō-Tokyō combine continued under an increasingly radical leadership, it is notable that within the organization there was an early split between the radical and moderate factions, with the Socialist party providing support for the latter.

At the same time, several new organizations of moderate teachers were in the making within Tōkyō in reaction to Zenkyō's militancy and its close association with the Communist party. In March and April, the Tōkyō-To Seinen Gakkō Kyōin Kumiai (Tōkyō Municipal Youth School Teachers Union), the Tōkyō-To Chūtō Gakkō Kyōshokuin Kumiai (Tōkyō Municipal Middle School Educational Personnel Union), and the Tōkyō-To Kukumin Gakkō Kyōin Kumiai (Tōkyō Municipal People's Primary School Teachers Union) were formed. Having similar objectives, the three groups united into a new, moderate, nonpolitical organization on April 26, 1946, called the Tōkyō-To Kyōshokuin Kumiai Kyōgikai (Council of Tōkyō Municipal Educational Personnel Unions), referred to as Tokyōkyō.[4]

Tokyōkyō attracted many of the moderate and conservative teachers in the Tōkyō area who were either anti-Communist or simply apolitical but who believed that the only path to higher salaries was through the organization of teachers. In addition, many of the teachers who had become disenchanted with Kagawa's Nikkyō, which clung to pro-imperial principles and whose leadership remained distant and somewhat closed, dropped out and joined the new Tokyōkyō. This shift from one moderate organization to another was a natural development because the average teacher found a more hospitable atmosphere in Tokyōkyō, an amalgamation of teacher-led unions. Kagawa's Nikkyō, which had served as a moderate alternative to the radical Zenkyō from the very beginning of the postwar teachers' movement and which had reached a peak of five thousand members by mid-1946, dwindled rapidly and was no longer functioning actively by the end of 1946. Its centrist role was assumed by Tokyōkyō.

The arrival of the First United States Education Mission (USEM) to Japan in March 1946 signaled the direction in which the American Occupation was planning to move with respect to the democratization of Japanese education. Shortly after the declaration of the Imperial Rescript on January 1, 1946, General MacArthur initiated step two of the Occupation—the formulation of the policy of educational reforms to democratize Japanese education and, in turn, Japanese society. The supreme commander asked the United States government to send to Japan an education mission of distinguished American educators, to be given the challenging task of recommending basic reforms of Japanese education so that never again would it contribute to a military imperialistic regime. At the same time, he requested the Japanese government to appoint a committee of qualified Japanese educators, which became the Japan Education Reconstruction Committee (JERC), to work with the United States Education Mission. Specifically, the Mission was assigned the four following tasks:

1. To study how education for democracy may be best achieved in Japan and to make recommendations regarding content of courses and curriculum
2. To make a study of psychology in the reeducation of Japan and to advise on educational methodology, language training, timing and priority of educational reforms, development of student initiative and critical analysis, and the reorientation of teachers
3. To study the administrative reorganization of the educational system, including the reorganization of the Ministry of Education and the problems of centralization
4. To survey higher education and to advise on methods of obtaining more active participation in the life of the community and nation by the students[5]

The teachers' unions welcomed the Mission's arrival since fundamental reforms of a positive nature had not yet been effected because of SCAP's initial negative phase during the last four months of 1945. Indeed, teachers who had been strongly identified with the wartime militarists were legally untouched, although many had already voluntarily resigned in fear of reprisals in addition to those who left the teaching profession out of a sense of guilt for their wartime activities. Moreover, the Ministry of Education was still staffed with many of the same bureaucrats from the war period. This situation was deplorable to the teachers' unions, particularly when the Ministry initially approved a subsidy for the reorganized Dai Nippon Kyōikukai, which promptly elected Minister of Education Abe as president; he declined the post.[6]

The Mission immediately began working with the special committee of Japanese educators, JERC, appointed by the minister of education at the request of SCAP. In effect, the Mission was working through the Ministry of Education, the object of criticism by the left-wing Zenkyō-Tokyō unions, and, ironically, the object of reform by SCAP. In other words, the Ministry of Education was to be inextricably involved in drastically curtailing its own power. The minister of education made no provision for appointing any teachers' union representative to JERC until more than a year after the Mission returned home.

The United States Education Mission, which played a central role in the reformation of Japanese education, had very little contact with organized teachers' associations. Zenkyō sent a message prepared by Hani Gorō attacking Ministry of Education personnel and offering to send a committee of teachers to advise and assist the Mission. The offer was not accepted. Hani met briefly with the Mission and explained in characteristic terms that success in democratization of Japanese education depended not on the Ministry of Education but on the activities of the teachers' union.[7]

Subsequently, the Mission met with many individual classroom teachers on school tours during its four-week investigation. Apparently, the Mission members were deeply impressed with the teachers' opinions, for the Mission's final report concerning teachers read in part as follows:

> Mistrust engenders mistrust. The Ministry of Education through its apparent lack of confidence in the intelligence of teachers at all levels has succeeded in producing a lack of confidence on the part of teachers in its power for leadership. The teachers of Japan, in so far as their views have been represented to the Mission, are critical and restless and are looking for leadership outside the Ministry of Education. This unrest among teachers is not wholly due to their pitiable economic status. It arises out of a genuine desire for guidance and for the opportunity to help in building the new Japan. Despite control and repression, there are teachers who are thinking for themselves and who are growingly aware of the direction that Japanese education must take. Such teachers are waiting expectantly for the stimulus and encouragement of the right kind of leadership.[8]

The Mission gave its stamp of approval to the organizing teachers without referring to unions per se. They felt that teachers should "organize into voluntary associations on local, prefectural, and national levels"; and that "teachers' organizations must be free to act with initiative and vigor and to work closely with other organizations."[9] The teachers' unions welcomed the Mission's recommendations.

The United States Education Mission, in addition to the suggestions concerning the organization of teachers, made major recommendations to General MacArthur for a fundamental reformation of Japanese education, summarized as follows:

1. The Ministry of Education should "not prescribe content, methods of instruction, or textbooks, but should limit its authority in this area to the publication of outlines, suggestions, and teaching guides." Curricula and course of studies "would thus result from the cooperative action of the central authority and the teachers." "It is essential that teachers, school principals, and local heads of schools be free from domination and control by higher-ranking school officials." School inspectors, who compelled regimentation, "should be replaced by a system of consultants."
2. A coeducational articulated system, including a six-year elementary school, a three-year lower secondary school, and a three-year upper secondary school, should replace the old 6–5–3 system.
3. The multiplicity of secondary schools should be united into comprehensive schools.
4. Prefectures, cities, and other subdivisions "should establish an elected education commission," which "should have general charge of public schools" within its jurisdiction.
5. Ethics should become a "part of the social studies course." Moral behavior and ethical attitudes can also be developed in other school institutions such as drama clubs, sports, and musical organizations.
6. Normal schools should become colleges.
7. General education "must be integrated into the regular curriculum" of the universities.[10]

The report of the United States Education Mission, following very closely the educational system of the United States, proposed a revolutionary reform of Japanese education. As a result there was enormous significance in the report for the teachers' unions. They, too, were demanding a complete reformation of Japanese education. And even with little direct contact between the unions and the Mission, by the very nature of the situation, the unions got the support they wanted. The Japanese teachers' unions, and particularly the radical Zenkyō, supported by the Communist party, fully endorsed the Mission's recommendations for the reform of Japanese education and carried them out enthusiastically a year later when their implementation became official. The unions believed that a new era in Japanese education had finally arrived.

The United States Education Mission's recommendations for reform elicited varying degrees of enthusiasm from the three powers that played an important role in their implementation. The teachers' unions accepted the reforms as their very own because the reforms coincided with their overall demands and because these reforms could only strengthen the positions of teachers and unions. SCAP, the originator of the reform proposals through the United States Education Mission, committed itself to their implementation. General MacArthur described the report as a "document of ideals high in the democratic tradition."[11] The Ministry of Education accepted the reforms in general but showed reservations about the feasibility of some of them, and particularly about the speed with which they were to be effected. SCAP and the unions thus had more in common at this time than did SCAP and the Ministry, although SCAP carried out the reforms through the Ministry of Education. When the Ministry, which was responsible for carrying out the drastic measures in a bankrupt and defeated nation, balked at certain reforms, the unions attacked the Ministry as reactionary. SCAP agreed on occasion. The reforms nevertheless brought together the teachers' unions and the Ministry of Education, for the first time in the postwar period, to work together for the common goal of carrying out the United States Education Mission's recommendations.

Throughout 1946 the living conditions of teachers deteriorated as did the general economic conditions within Japan. The SCAP education officer who claimed shortly after the war that a black-market carton of cigarettes cost the equivalent of a university professor's monthly salary reported six months later that a carton cost five months' salary for the same professor.[12] The threat of rice riots prompted warnings against demonstrations from both the emperor and General MacArthur. Unemployment reached 4.5 million. SCAP reported that 2 million people were destitute.[13]

Circumstances led the Ministry of Education to issue the following warning to the nation's educational administrators in April 1946.

> We hear that consequent to the worsening of the food situation, some teachers and officials of schools have recently been demanding foodstuffs from the pupils or their parents. It is a matter of deep regret since it will

become a menace to the home life of children who are under the same ration system as everyone else, including teachers. You are therefore requested to take the measures necessary immediately to prohibit strictly such illicit activities on the part of teachers of the schools.[14]

Teachers' salaries were increased several times during the year, but inflation absorbed the increases. Even within the civil service, a typical government employee earned about 80 percent more than a teacher of the same age. Employees of private industry earned from three to five times more. In addition, because the national treasury was bankrupt, it could not pay teachers' salaries on time after June 1946. Teachers received their July and August pay in September.[15]

With the continuing economic crisis, the first half of 1946 in Japan was marked by the unprecedented proliferation of labor unions with concomitant labor disputes. Tables 5 and 6 illustrate the increase in number of Japanese trade unions, including the teachers' unions, during this period.

Table 5. Spread of Unionization

Date	No. of Unions	Union Membership
December 1945	508	379,631
January 1946	1,516	901,705
February 1946	3,242	1,536,560
March 1946	6,537	2,567,467
April 1946	8,530	3,002,933
May 1946	10,540	3,413,653
June 1946	12,006	3,677,771

Source: Data from Ayusawa Iwao, *A History of Labor in Modern Japan* (Honolulu: East-West Center Press, 1966), p. 258.

In anticipation of the first free May Day celebrations since the war's end, scheduled for 1946, Zenkyō held a mass meeting of teachers in April to plan for the event. The meeting also considered teachers' grievances, which led to the inevitable dispatch of a delegation to the Ministry of Education on April 26 to submit complaints to the minister. Union representatives forced their way into the minister's office, where a boisterous meeting took place when they demanded that May Day be declared a a holiday and that teachers control the schools. The vice-minister, who

Table 6. Labor Disputes

Month (1946)	No. of Cases	No. of Participants
January	74	42,749
February	81	35,153
March	103	83,141
April	109	60,917
May	132	58,978
June	104	33,554

Source: Data from Ayusawa Iwao, *A History of Labor in Modern Japan* (Honolulu: East-West Center Press, 1966), p. 259.

met the representatives, was forced to flee the building. This incident was the first of a series of unconventional meetings between Zenkyō and the Ministry of Education.

May Day celebrations took place in an orderly manner. Approximately one million people throughout the nation participated. Among them were five thousand teachers from both Zenkyō and its Tōkyō affiliate, carrying red flags and placards bearing slogans such as, "Prevent Teachers from Starving—Establish a Salary Based on the Cost of Living."[16] Children carrying red flags also paraded despite the Ministry's disapproval of the participation of school children in the event. As far as can be determined, the moderate Tōkyōkyō was not officially represented.

SCAP's attitude toward Japan's first postwar May Day of 1946 is important because it is indicative not only of SCAP's overall favorable attitude toward the union movement but also of a very serious difference of opinion between SCAP and the Japanese government concerning teachers' unions. For example, the minister of education most reluctantly approved teachers' participation in the May Day demonstrations while rejecting student involvement on grounds that May Day was not a school holiday.[17] In contrast, SCAP's records of the event exude pride, reporting that "May Day celebrations were unprecedented. They demonstrated the new freedom which the Occupation has given to the Japanese people and the political vitality of the working class which, when properly guided, can be a potent force in the democratic reconstruction of Japan."[18] Only three weeks later, General MacArthur issued a stern warning against mass violence led by Communists, as the number of public disturbances increased in protest over the shortage of rice and the general living conditions. The immediate provocation was the so-called Food May Day of May 19, when 150,000 people paraded through Tōkyō.

A member of SCAP's Labor Division summed up the Occupation's policy toward the labor movement as follows:

> Labor policy, like so many others, had first to be improvised. After some confusion a fairly clear and consistent policy was eventually formulated in Tōkyō. . . . This was based on a working philosophy evolved by Labor Division which assumed that the working classes constitute, potentially, the strongest if not the only reliable base for a democratic regime in Japan. Democracy must, therefore, offer to Japanese workers freedom of expression and action. . . . Japanese labor holds the key to success or failure in the attempt to convert Japan from a dangerous enemy into a good neighbor.[19]

This attitude revealed sharp differences between the Occupation's approach to the democratization of Japanese education and society and that of many officials within the Ministry of Education and the Japanese government in general during 1946 and much of 1947. From late 1947 onward, the two powers converged, paradoxically, not because SCAP had reformed the Ministry's attitude but because SCAP had realigned itself more closely with the Ministry's original position vis-à-vis the teachers' unions. There can be no doubt, however, that in 1946 SCAP was encouraging labor unions.

In mid-1946 the chief of SCAP's Labor Division supported labor leaders, when he told them during a convention, "The response of the Japanese workers to the opportunities opened to them by SCAP . . . has exceeded my most optimistic expectations."[20] During informal contacts between SCAP officials and individual labor unions, encouragement was continually given to the labor leaders. For example, Iwama Masao, chairman of the communist-influenced Tōkyō, by this time the one most active group within the radical Zenkyō leading the teachers' left-wing movement, stated unequivocally that SCAP officials from the Civil Information and Education Section urged him and his group to unionize all teachers.[21]

In contrast, Education Minister Abe met with fifty Zenkyō representatives on May 4, 1946, and questioned the right of school teachers to unionize, rejecting all of their demands. Later, he issued a statement confirming teachers' right to organize into unions but restricting their activities to matters concerning wages, work hours, and working conditions; teachers were forbidden to participate in political activities or to interfere with school management and educational policy. The unionists countered with a sit-down demonstration in the Ministry hallway.[22]

It was natural for Ministry officials to be chary of the radical wing of the teachers' movement. On a number of occasions, Zenkyō-Tōkyō delegations had invaded the Ministry's offices, demanding interviews with the minister and staging sit-down strikes inside the building which at times extended for several days and nights. The unions also scurrilously attacked the Ministry in print and in public speeches. Hidaka Daishirō, a division chief of the Ministry at that time and later permanent vice-minister of education, charged that SCAP not only encouraged the radical teachers' unions but also prevented the Ministry from taking action to curtail what the Ministry considered as obvious excesses.[23] The Ministry, he recalled, did everything in its power to encourage the moderate Tokyōkyō group while SCAP secretly brought pressure on the Japanese government in certain cases to modify its resistence to union demands.[24]

A peculiar development, in fact, was underway within SCAP and the Ministry of Education: both were divided internally in their attitudes toward the left-wing teachers' unions. Many of the bureaucrats within the Ministry who had continued in their positions since prewar days, along with some of the new appointees who were responsible for carrying out SCAP's extensive reforms without the necessary resources, were aghast at the militancy of the Zenkyō-Tōkyō combine. Others among the new appointees, however, who were of the liberalist tradition of prewar Japan, were more in sympathy with the teachers' movement. Such a divided attitude was understandable since some of the ministers of education themselves during the period from 1945 to 1951 were liberal while others were more conservative, though all were from the academic world. Within SCAP were also two factions. There were, on the one hand, the American officials, including many civilians thrust into the military government, plus some of the officers, who were imbued with progressive ideas and committed to the task of reforming Japanese society through freedom. There were others, on the other hand, mostly career military officers, who found it naturally difficult to allow unbridled freedom to the Japanese so soon after the Pacific war. This ambivalence within both governing bodies, particularly SCAP, made it difficult at times for leaders of the teachers' movement to determine the extent of official approval of their policies. For all intents and purposes, throughout 1946 the left-wing union leaders operated on the assumption that SCAP approved of their activities and that the Japanese Ministry of Education was hostile toward them.[25]

To fulfill SCAP's original mandate for the demilitarization of Japanese education, Imperial Ordinance Number 263 of May 6, 1946, was issued for the removal, exclusion, and reinstatement of teachers and educational officials. Under the provisions of this edict, all 400,000 teachers were to be examined to "eliminate militarists, ultranationalists, and individuals hostile to Occupation policy, and to provide for the preferential treatment of persons previously dismissed for anti-militarism or similar reasons."[26] The plan for carrying out the purge was devised by the Ministry of Education with SCAP approval. Minister of Education Tanaka Kōtarō, who was the official responsible for devising the machinery, assumed a favorable attitude toward the purge, but some Ministry officials opposed it in fear of being purged themselves.[27] The teachers' organizations, notably Zenkyō, led by leftists, enthusiastically approved the long-awaited purge of right-wing teachers.

The Ministry of Education, responsible for carrying out the purge, had a committee created in each prefecture, consisting of a teacher, a school principal, a representative from the educational staff, and two members from outside the education sector.[28] All but the teacher were appointed by the prefectural governor, who was a government appointee himself. The teacher was selected, moreover, by the reorganized Dai Nippon Kyōikukai of prewar fame, provoking the charge by the teachers' unions that the Ministry was continuing a reactionary policy by favoring this organization. Zenkyō took strong issue, claiming that it was not appropriate for this association to have a hand in purging undemocratic elements.[29]

Every Japanese teacher completed a questionnaire in private concerning his prewar and wartime publications, speeches, memberships, and other activities related to militarism and ultranationalism. These questionnaires were then screened by the appropriate prefectural committee. Membership in certain wartime organizations meant automatic expulsion. Only teachers whose credentials were in doubt appeared in person before the committee. At the next level, each university set up its own purge committee, appointed by the university president, to examine the faculty. At the top level, officials of the Ministry of Education themselves underwent examination by a special committee of seven members from various areas of public life appointed by the minister of education. This committee also served as a committee of appeal for those teachers who objected to the prefectural committee's decision. Although the final court of appeal for all cases was ostensibly the Ministry of Education, in reality, it was SCAP.

The purge of ultranationalist teachers was particularly important to the teachers' movement because in effect it could remove the hard-core rightists who would have been in natural conflict with the unions. Accordingly, the unions cooperated to the fullest possible extent with the examining committees. Wherever possible the unions submitted evidence against certain teachers, creating sensitive situations among the local teaching body. Anonymous letters were used on occasion to submit evidence with incriminating charges. Admittedly, injustices by both sides were committed.[30]

In addition, some of the prefectural purge committees were attacked as unrepresentative of the public at large on the charge that they were dominated by the old conservative establishment of landowners and businessmen. The unions and even members of SCAP complained that certain committees were investigating teacher's questionnaires perfunctorily, paying little heed to suspect activities of the more conservative teachers. SCAP headquarters apparently agreed, because orders were sent out to include representatives of labor and women on the committees to attain a better cross-section of society.[31]

The results of the right-wing purge were impressive, not because of the number of teachers removed by the committees—only about 1 percent of all teachers—but because of the total number of teachers who voluntarily resigned from the teaching profession because of the purge threat. By May 1947, when the purge was completed, 120,000 teachers or 22 percent of the entire teaching corps had been removed, most of them choosing the path of voluntary early retirement rather than subjecting themselves to the purge.[32] What could have been a competitive force, or at least a hindrance to the teachers' unions, was effectively removed as right-wing elements withdrew, leaving the field in the hands of left-wing activists. Surprisingly, very few progressive or leftist teachers dismissed prior to 1945 applied for reinstatement.

While the purge was underway, an attempt to unite the major teachers' unions was initiated once again. In May 1946 the moderate Tōkyōkyō and the radical Zenkyō, the latter having changed its name on May 3 to Zen Nihon Kyōiku Rōdō Kumiai (All Japan Educational Labor Union), known as Zenkyōrō, agreed to cooperate in demanding a basic monthly salary of at least 600 yen. The first joint mass meeting was scheduled for June 1 at the broad Imperial Palace Plaza. Thousands attended. The understanding on the part of the moderate Tokyōkyō was that no Japan Communist party officials would be invited. For some as yet unexplained reason, however, Nosaka Sanzō, head of the Japan Communist party, was invited by the militant Zenkyōrō to address the convention. As he spoke, Tokyōkyō representatives shouted criticisms and walked out, throwing the meeting into general confusion. The Communist leader finally completed his speech in which he pledged the support of the Japan Communist party for the teachers' struggles.[33]

Although reports of the ensuing events differed considerably, it is clear that the departing moderates sent a delegation to the minister of education, claiming that the tumultous meeting was not representative of teachers' unions. Following Nosaka's speech, Zenkyōrō, led by Iwama Masao, also sent a delegation to the Ministry and demanded a 600-yen monthly salary and the abolition of the Dai Nippon Kyōikukai. The minister of education set a thirty-minute time limit on the clamorous meeting, which was abruptly cut off. The delegation left embittered.[34]

The breach between the moderate and radical streams of the organized teachers' movement was deepened when the radical Zenkyōrō, hoping for wider support, once again changed its name, on June 26, to Nihon Kyōiku Rōdō Kumiai (Japan Educational Labor Union), or Nikkyōrō, deriving its name from a radical prewar teachers' organization.[35] Nikkyōrō launched a nationwide campaign for membership from the growing ranks of independent prefectural unions, which were springing up throughout the country. In addition, the newly named Nikkyōrō decided to join the labor council Sanbetsu, distinguished for its close ties with the Japan Communist party. (Sanbetsu is the short form for Zen Nihon Sangyōbetsu Rōdō Kaigi [Congress of Industrial Unions of Japan].) Sanbetsu had been established specifically to counter mass dismissals of redundant government employees in a general reorganization of government-run industries such as the railroads, where reduction of workers by 130,000 men was planned. Nikkyōrō, by declaring for Sanbetsu, made no secret of its extreme left-wing ideological proclivities.

The moderate Tokyōkyō, up to now appealing primarily to teachers in the Tōkyō area, also decided to broaden its foundation of nonradical unions on a nationwide basis. Accordingly, on July 21, 1946, Tokyōkyō changed its name to Kyōin Kumiai Zenkoku Renmei (National Federation of Teachers Unions), known as Kyōzenren. Kyōzenren promptly announced its decision to join the moderate labor council Sōdōmei, a smaller rival of Sanbetsu organized by the Socialist party.

Once again the hiatus between the moderate and radical streams of the teachers' movement was brought sharply into focus. Until mid-1946 the movement within both streams was centered primarily in Tōkyō, the seat of the national government. Because of the large number of teachers in the capital city, Tōkyō provided a natural arena for the teachers' unions to confront the Ministry of Education directly. By the latter half of 1946, new prefectural unions of teachers were forming in various areas of the country, though most groups calling themselves prefectural unions had little support outside the major cities. In other words, activist teachers within major cities who were aware of the movements in Tōkyō formed the driving force behind the formation of prefectural or local teachers' organizations.

One reason that the rural areas lagged far behind the urban centers in organizing the teaching profession was that teaching was the only avenue open to a commoner in the rural areas who wanted to elevate his social status, for teachers were regarded as members of the rural elite that included priests and landowners. Those teachers from families without privileged status who entered the rural elite were initially reluctant to join a common labor union because to do so was tantamount to forfeiting their preferential status. Prefectural cities thus had to lead the way. The competing national unions encountered the problem of gathering the many small local unions into the fold, then broadening their memberships.

Along with the kaleidoscopic revision of names of the two rival Tōkyō-based unions, the competition between them spread throughout the nation for the membership of the growing prefectural unions. Since affiliation with a national teachers' organization meant an automatic relationship with either the Communist-dominated Sanbetsu or the Socialist-dominated Sōdōmei, the decision of each local union clearly reflected the ideological persuasion of its leadership. In some prefectures teachers were divided in their support, splitting the local movement in a manner similar to that at the national level.

The popularity of the rapidly expanding teachers' unions at this time stemmed not only from the economic conditions of the time, but also from the status held by the unions under the Occupation. Teachers' unions attained more importance than teachers' associations because unions were endorsed by the new labor-union laws and by SCAP, Education associations, especially the discredited Dai Nippon Kyōikukai, whose assets were systematically taken over by local militant unions and which did not have union status, received only tacit approval of the Ministry of Education. Thus many of the proliferating teachers' organizations preferred the title of union, associating their memberships *en bloc* by uniting with a national teachers' union at the expense of the education associations.

Another important development during the American Occupation had its beginning also in the last half of 1946: the militant campaign to increase salaries of government employees, which led to the first direct confrontation between Japanese labor and SCAP. The struggle was conducted mainly in Tōkyō by the Zenkoku Kankō Shokuin Kumiai (National Public Employees Union), or Zenkankō, through the Communist-dominated Sanbetsu, whose membership of more than 2.6 million civil servants was fighting the Japanese government for higher salaries and opposing the dismissal of redundant railroad workers.[36] The radical Nikkyōrō, whose demands were generally ignored by the government, led the struggle for teachers' salaries in conjunction with the campaign for increased salaries for all civil servants.

On October 18 the militant Nikkyōrō held a national conference to plan the "struggle campaign." It was decided to suspend temporarily all activities of Nikkyōrō and its Tōkyō municipal subordinate, Tōkyō, and to elect a special committee called the Struggle Committee (Tōsō Iinkai) to lead the entire teachers' movement for a 600-yen basic monthly salary. Katō Masao was elected chairman; Iwama Masao, then chairman of Tōkyō, secretary general; and Higashitani Toshio, Ogasawara Fumio, and Akiyama Tadao, committee members.[37]

The Struggle Committee immediately proceeded to take its demands to Minister of Education Tanaka Kōtarō, at both his office and his private residence. Minister Tanaka declared that he would not meet with the teacher representatives because of their violent methods, and that a union of teachers should not be controlled by any political ideology.[38] It should be noted that Tanaka was a devout Catholic, fundamentally opposed to the Communists within the teachers' unions.[39]

The Struggle Committee retorted that their demands pertained to economic issues, not political issues, and that Tanaka's illegal refusal to meet with teachers revealed his insincerity in his relations with teachers. According to Iwama, the Struggle Committee was infuriated at Tanaka's refusal to grant legitimate teachers' representatives an interview.[40] On October 22 Tanaka was forced to use police protection to escape the Strug-

gle Committee's insistent representatives. The government then, on November 1, announced a pay raise for teachers, raising, for example, the
basic monthly salary for teachers with three years' experience to 460 yen.
This was still well below the 600 yen demanded by Nikkyōrō.

On November 6 the Struggle Committee met again, changed its name
to Zenkoku Kyōin Kumiai Saitei Seikatsuken Kakutoku Kyōgikai (Council of All Japan Teachers Unions to Secure a Minimum Standard of
Living), or Zenkyōso, and elected Iwama Masao chairman. Zenkyōso
proceeded to the office of the minister of education, who had finally
agreed to meet them; they threatened him with a resolution to call a
general teachers' strike, a tactic yet to be employed, if the government did
not grant the full pay increases as demanded. The reply came from the
Ministry of Finance, explaining that a 600-yen basic salary for all teachers
would require a general tax increase, something that simply could not
be carried out then.[41] It might be added here for comparative purposes
that, according to the figures published by *Asahi Shimbun,* the average
monthly salary of coal miners in 1946 was 900 yen.[42]

The moderate Kyōzenren, which had decided in mid-October to base
its demands on a 600-yen net monthly income, in contrast with the radical Nikkyōrō's demand for a 600-yen basic income plus allowances, could
not approve of the threatened teachers' strike being planned by Nikkyōrō's Struggle Committee, Zenkyōso. The moderate council of unions,
Sōdōmei, of which Kyōzenren was an affiliate member, supported the
government workers' struggles but rejected the planned general strike as
politically motivated. The two organizations, Nikkyōrō and Kyōzenren,
characteristically promoted similar economic demands but employed dissimilar tactics to achieve them, being unable to form a joint struggle
movement.

By November, Zenkyōso, assuming complete leadership of the radical
teachers' movement, claimed a membership of 200,000 teachers in twenty-
nine district affiliates. The moderate Kyōzenren listed 130,000 members
from thirty-one districts.[43] As charges and countercharges between Zenkyōso and the Ministry of Education were exchanged, maximum efforts
were expended to increase Zenkyōso's membership for the inevitable
showdown with the government. Zenkyōso dispatched speakers to local
meetings of teachers and PTAs, seeking their understanding and support
against the Ministry. Once again, on December 22, the radical stream
changed its name, from Zenkyōso to Zen Nihon Kyōin Kumiai Kyōgikai
(Council of All Japan Teachers Union), better known as Zenkyōkyō.[44]

At nearly every national conference, the radical stream changed its name when it formally accepted more prefectural units into the fold. In one sense, it meant a new beginning with a new membership each time. It also indicated an attempt to win new members or to placate the less radical teachers by encouraging them to remain within the union. Their numbers were essential. However, as the left-wing union increased its membership, it was, in the process, enlarging the moderate wing of the union since leftists were already members and only moderate teachers were left to be recruited. (See Figure 1, which shows the evolution and relationship of the variously named teachers' unions.)

During the conference on December 22, Zenkyōkyō reported that 320,000 members were on the rolls. At this conference, those who were opposed to the extreme radical leadership and the plans to carry out a general strike united to elect as chairman a moderate, Araki Shōzaburō, a Socialist from Osaka, along with a slate of moderates from the Socialist party. All of the candidates from the so-called Leftist League (Saha Rengō) from the Communist party were defeated.[45] By this time, the Socialist party was placing increasing support behind the Araki wing of Zenkyōkyō in an effort to offset the Communist wing behind Iwama.

The election results threw the conference into an uproar when the Communist group that supported Iwama refused to accept the verdict. After much confusion, the conference finally decided that the election results would be respected but that the new executive would not function until the old Struggle Committee under Iwama completed its campaign for higher salaries. In effect, the old Struggle Committee was temporarily revived to resume its leadership of the campaign for a living wage. Iwama's Struggle Committee immediately decided to cooperate with the Struggle Committee of the Public Employees Union under Yashiro Ii from the Japan National Railways, which had decided on December 18 to conduct a nationwide strike against the Yoshida cabinet. This pact marked the first national struggle in which a teachers' union cooperated with other unions in a joint campaign.

On December 23 Zenkyōkyō held a national meeting of twenty thousand teachers at the Imperial Palace Plaza. Once again, the members voted to send a delegation led by Iwama to the Ministry of Education with twelve demands along their previous line. A time limit was set for the minister's reply, and the Ministry was threatened with a possible nationwide teachers' strike if the reply came late or proved unsatisfactory. The plan for the strike, of course, had been in the making throughout

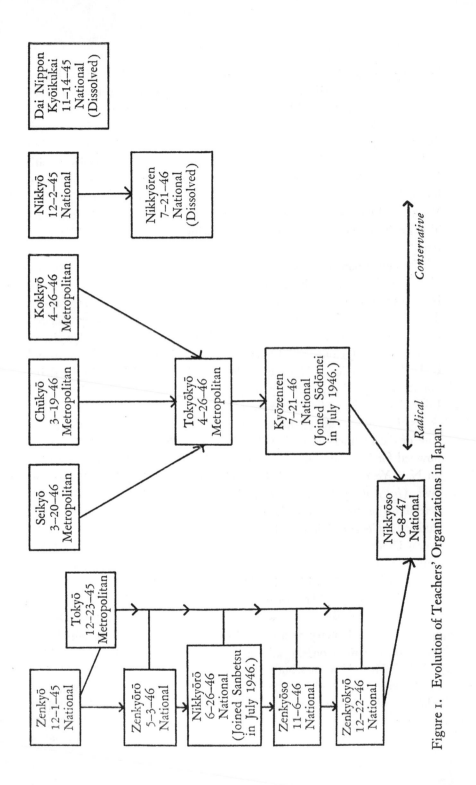

Figure 1. Evolution of Teachers' Organizations in Japan.

December. It is unclear who provoked whom, but the delegation clashed with police at the Ministry of Education, and Iwama and seven other leaders were arrested. Although they were released after lengthy questioning while their delegation demonstrated in front of the police station, the incident was the first serious clash between the radical teachers' union and the police. Ironically, the moderate Kyōzenren met quietly with Minister Tanaka on the very same day and won a signed agreement from him to have the teachers' salaries increased to 600 yen as soon as possible. When Zenkyōkyō learned about this agreement between Kyōzenren and Tanaka, it charged that Tanaka was showing favoritism toward Kyōzenren.

The newly named Zenkyōkyō, under instructions from Iwama's Struggle Committee, transmitted orders on December 29 to all prefectural branches to prepare for a general strike since their demands were not met. The plan was as follows: On the first day the strike would be declared and classes would be held for only two hours; on the second day classes would be held for only one hour; and on the third day no classes would be held. The moderate Kyōzenren decided not to participate in the strike but to continue in an orderly manner its demands on the Ministry of Education for the early attainment of the agreed-upon salary increase.

As the nation entered its second new year after the war—the target date of the planned general strike—Prime Minister Yoshida Shigeru, renowned for his Meiji-like determination, in a radio address to the nation on New Year's Day branded those who were planning the strike as outlaws (*futei no yakara*).[46] Enraged, the labor leaders intensified their determination to carry out the strike plans. On January 11, the National Public Employees Union, including the Union of National Railways, the Postal Union, the teachers' union of Zenkyōkyō, the tobacco and mining unions, and the union of workers for the Occupation Army met and set the date of the nationwide strike for February 1, with the express purpose of toppling the Yoshida government.

On January 15 some concessions were granted, and the prime minister apologized. On January 22 a salary increase of 150 yen was granted government employees on the advice of SCAP, which had been working quietly behind the scenes but taking no public role in the crisis developing between organized labor and the Japanese government. According to a labor spokesman, union leaders did not anticipate action by SCAP since they were operating within the legal framework established by SCAP, empowering unions with the right to strike. Moreover, their object of protest was not SCAP but the Japanese government.[47] Hence, when General Marquat from SCAP's Economic and Scientific Section summoned labor leaders to his office on January 22 and advised them not to strike, warning them that SCAP would intervene if they did, he was not taken seriously.[48]

Activist teachers within Zenkyōkyō feverishly prepared their students for the strike, explaining that because the Yoshida government had failed to bring prosperity to the Japanese people the teachers could not fulfill their duty to their students. Teachers seeking parental support visited students' homes to explain their position. As February drew near, last-minute mediatory attempts between the National Public Employees Union and the government failed. Finally, on January 31, 1947, General MacArthur dramatically intervened with the following famous statement:

> Under the authority vested in me as Supreme Commander for the Allied Powers, I have informed the labor leaders, whose unions had federated for the purpose of conducting a general strike, that I will not permit the use of so deadly a social weapon in the present impoverished and emaciated condition of Japan, and have accordingly directed them to desist from the furtherance of such action.
>
> It is with greatest reluctance that I have deemed it necessary to intervene to this extent in the issues now pending. I have done so only to forestall the fatal impact upon an already gravely threatened public welfare. Japanese society today operates under the limitations of war, defeat, and allied occupation. Its cities are laid waste, its industries are almost at a standstill, and the great masses of its people are on little more than a starvation diet.
>
> A general strike, crippling transportation and communications, would prevent the movement of food to feed the people and of coal to sustain essential utilities, and would stop such industry as is still functioning. The paralysis which inevitably would result might reduce large masses of the Japanese people to the point of actual starvation, and would produce dreadful consequences upon every Japanese home regardless of social strata or direct interest in the basic issue. Even now, to prevent actual starvation in Japan, the people of the United States are releasing to them quantities of their own scarce food resources.
>
> The persons involved in the threatened general strike are but a small minority of the Japanese people. Yet this minority might well plunge the great masses into a disaster not unlike that produced in the immediate past by the minority which led Japan into the destruction of war. This in turn would impose upon the Allied Powers the unhappy decision of whether to leave the Japanese people to the fate thus recklessly imposed by a minority, or to cover the consequences by pouring into Japan, at the expense of their own meager resources, infinitely greater quantities of food and other sup-

plies to sustain life than otherwise would be required. In the circumstances, I could hardly request the Allied peoples to assume this additional burden.

While I have taken this measure as one of dire emergency, I do not intend otherwise to restrict the freedom of action heretofore given labor in the achievement of legitimate objectives. Nor do I intend in any way to compromise or influence the basic social issues involved. These are matters of evolution which time and circumstance may well orient without disaster as Japan gradually emerges from its present distress.[49]

On the evening of January 31, Yashiro Ii, over a nationwide radio broadcast, instructed local union officials to call off the strike. In tears, he made his famous statement about taking one step backward, then two steps forward. Iwama, as chairman of the teachers' Struggle Committee involved in the strike, hesitated until the early morning of February 1 before canceling the teachers' strike amidst general confusion.

General MacArthur's proclamation caught the restless labor movement by surprise. Labor leaders were aware of SCAP's regulation that "strikes which are inimical to objectives of the military occupation were prohibited,"[50] but SCAP had also maintained an attitude of encouragement toward Japanese labor, then laissez-faire. Hence the new policy of direct negative intervention by SCAP bewildered labor leaders. To the average laborer, SCAP was their liberator from the oppressive wartime military government. The restrictions on their right to strike by the American military were reminiscent of suppression by the Japanese military.[51]

The radical Tokyō, the Tōkyō branch of Zenkyōkyō under the chairmanship of Iwama, which served as the core of the Struggle Committee's campaign, then took up the challenge by circulating a document which charged that the proclamation of February 1 was oppressive, undemocratic, and discriminatory against labor. It intimated that American policy in Japan was a form of economic invasion by American imperialism, a charge later to be hurled over and over again as the Occupation wore on. In this instance, the charge was presented in guarded terms, because of Occupation censorship, by suggesting that General MacArthur, technically carrying out the Far Eastern Commission's policy in Japan, perhaps did not represent only the United States. Moreover, the charge ultimately was focused on the Yoshida government as the real oppressor of Japanese labor.[52]

The immediate effect of the Occupation's ban on the general strike was to quiet the labor unions as General MacArthur, only a week after the incident, called for general elections. Conditions within the land were still deplorable in the continuing aftereffects of the war. The food situation had deteriorated so badly that General MacArthur had to appeal to the United States Congress for emergency food shipments. Even the empress began raising chickens within the palace grounds to provide food and to save on the limited imperial household budget. A famine holiday was declared at Kyōto University to avert a food crisis.

The unions experienced a period of self-reflection after the debacle of February 1, unable to judge the extent of freedom of action that was allowed them. Within the unions there was a general reaction against the radical leadership that had led them to the brink of direct confrontation with the Occupation forces. Moderates within Zenkyōkyō shortly thereafter quietly moved Iwama and his group out of their all-powerful positions, with a word of gratitude for their efforts. Several unions within Sanbetsu withdrew from the organization amidst criticism of its Communist leadership and its emphasis on strike tactics. Nevertheless, the leadership of Sanbetsu remained firmly under Communist control.

Rather curiously, the traumatic effect of the incident of February 1 prompted a more ameliorative attitude on the part of the Ministry of Education. Takahashi Seiichirō, the new minister of education appointed on January 31, was a long-time teacher himself. Unexpectedly, he agreed to a salary increase and to negotiations with Zenkyōkyō over a labor contract for teachers. According to a high Ministry official, the major reason for the minister's abrupt modification of the government's position was directly related to the appraisal of the balance of power within the radical union. Ministry officials presumed that the moderate wing of Zenkyōkyō was in the ascendency following reaction to the strike episode. The Ministry consequently wanted to strengthen that position vis-à-vis the rank-and-file membership.[53]

The first teachers' union contract, signed by Minister Takahashi and Zenkyōkyō President Araki on March 8, 1947, recognized the left-wing Zenkyōkyō as the official bargaining agency for its members with the Ministry of Education. The following provisions were included: a forty-two-hour work week; specified holidays; twenty free study days a year; establishment of a Personnel Affairs Committee, with members from both sides to consider the appointment, discharge, transfer, and punishment of teachers; sickness and maternity provisions; security for teachers to participate in the union movement; the right of a specified number of union officials to work full time for the union while holding a teaching post; the use of school buildings for union activities; agreement of the Ministry not to apply the Administrative Order if a dispute should arise between the two parties; that the Ministry would not interfere with the political interests of union members; that the Ministry would make efforts to unite all teachers in the country into one single agency, namely, Zenkyōkyō; and that the duration of the agreement would be six months.[54]

The negotiated contract between Zenkyōkyō and the Ministry of Education appeared as a great victory for the union after the crisis of February 1. The Japan Education Reconstruction Committee (JERC) immediately criticized the agreement as violating the principles the Committee had developed for the reform of Japanese education, and it recommended the establishment of a teachers' association along the lines of the Nihon Kyōikukai (Japan Education Association), which was the old Dai Nippon Kyōikukai under a revised name.

Ironically, after a year of protest demonstrations, Zenkyōkyō had obtained the bulk of its demands without demonstrating. Kyōzenren, the moderate union, immediately negotiated a similar contract for its members, bringing the majority of all teachers in the country under a labor agreement that granted teachers' unions the right to bargain collectively and an implied right to strike. And, of extreme importance, the contracts provided for an agreement to unite all teachers into one union, hastening the efforts already underway to find a common ground for uniting the two major unions.

Several weeks after the signing of the extraordinary contracts between the unions and the Ministry of Education, the basic education reforms recommended by the United States Education Mission a year previously were finally ready for implementation. During that intervening year, the Japan Education Reconstruction Committee (JERC) had diligently and in good faith carried the reform work forward after the United States Education Mission had left, laboring between the Japanese Ministry of Education and SCAP's Civil Information and Education Section officials in an effort to carry out the recommendations of the Mission to the mutual satisfaction of both sides. The final results were the School Education Law, March 29, 1947, and the Fundamental Law of Education, March 31, 1947. Significantly, the new Japanese Constitution, which proscribed the emperor from assuming any political role, became effective shortly thereafter on May 3, 1947.

The two education laws together were designed to replace finally the 1890 Imperial Rescript on Education as the legal and philosophical basis of Japanese postwar education and to carry out the recommendations of the United States Education Mission. Obviously American inspired, both in content and tone, with strong similarities to the American version of The Revision of the Japanese Education System released earlier the same week, the purposes of the new education emphasized democratic education for world peace and individual dignity for the welfare of the country and mankind. Academic freedom, the development of personality, equal educational opportunities, and the separation of State and Church were the pillars upon which the new education was being established.

The critical passages from these documents, which ever since have been the center of the political and ideological controversies over postwar education and the teachers' movement, include the following:

THE FUNDAMENTAL LAW OF EDUCATION

Article 6 (School Teachers)
Teachers of the schools prescribed by law shall be servants of the whole community. They shall be conscious of their mission and endeavor to discharge their duties. For this purpose, the status of teachers shall be respected and their fair and appropriate treatment shall be secured.

Article 8 (Political Education)
The political knowledge necessary for intelligent citizenship shall be valued in education. The schools prescribed by law shall refrain from political education or other political activities for or against any specific political party.

Article 10 (School Administration)
Education shall not be subject to improper control, but it shall be directly responsible to the whole people.[55]

THE CONSTITUTION

Article 9. Aspiring sincerely to an international peace based on justice and order, the Japanese people forever renounce as a sovereign right of the nation the threat or use of force as a means of settling international disputes. In order to accomplish the aim, land, sea, and air forces, as well as other war potential, will never be maintained. The right of belligerency of the state will not be recognized.

Article 19. Freedom of thought and conscience shall not be violated.

Article 21. Freedom of assembly and association as well as speech, press, and all other forms of expression are guaranteed.

Article 23. Academic freedom is guaranteed.

Article 26. All people shall have the right to receive an equal education correspondent to their ability.

Article 28. The right of workers to organize and to bargain and act collectively is guaranteed.[56]

As a result of the two laws of March 1947, essentially following the United States Education Mission's recommendations, Japanese education finally entered the period of the new education, nearly two years after the end of the war. The following basic reforms were initiated: a coeducational articulated system including a six-year elementary school; a three-year lower secondary school; a three-year comprehensive upper secondary school, amalgamating the various types of schools into one as soon as possible; and a four-year university system. Compulsory education was extended to nine years, scheduled for full implementation by 1949. A separate course in morals education was proscribed from the curriculum.

Meanwhile, the political parties were preparing for general elections, called by General MacArthur following the strike incident of February 1, "to obtain another democratic expression of the people's will on the fundamental issues with which Japanese society is now confronted."[57] The strike ban became a central issue in the election. Labor unions, which had given up their plans to strike because of General MacArthur's intervention, seized upon the elections as an opportunity to attain through the ballot box what they had hoped to gain by the strike. Switching their primary tactics from demonstrations and strikes to the political processes approved by SCAP, they threw themselves into the election campaign.

On March 26, 1947, the Ministry of Education published a directive that clarified the political rights of teachers. Teachers were declared free to run in the forthcoming general elections but were not allowed to retain their teaching positions if they entered the Diet (Parliament). Teachers were free to run for local assemblies and could retain their teaching posts if elected. Teachers elected as prefectural governor or local mayor could not concurrently continue teaching. Teachers' unions were declared free to carry on an election campaign so long as its goals did not deviate from the essential aims and status of a labor union.[58]

The election of April 1947 brought the first postwar nationwide victory, although a qualified one, for the Socialist party. Socialists gained 143 seats in the Lower House, to become the largest single party. However, the two major conservative parties, the Liberals and the Democrats, polled 131 and 121 votes respectively, continuing the conservative political hegemony. Winning only four seats, the Communist party fared badly during the Socialist swing. A similar result obtained in the Upper House election, with the Socialist party winning forty-seven seats.

The teachers' unions moved into national politics for the first time in the April elections. Iwama Masao, a Communist sympathizer running independently, receiving both criticism from union moderates and praise from the leftists for his role in the February 1 strike campaign, was selected to run for a seat in the Diet as a way of moving him out of union leadership while rewarding him for his indefatigable efforts. Zenkyōkyō won three other seats, in addition to Iwama's, in the Upper House and five in the Lower House on the Socialist ticket. Sympathetic Hani Gorō also won election to the Upper House, supported by a quasi-independent educational organization. The moderate Kyōzenren ran three successful Socialist party candidates in the Upper House, including their chairman, Kōno Masao.[59]

This election marked a turning point both in national elections and in the teachers' movement. A coalition government was formed by Katayama Tetsu, the first postwar Socialist prime minister, who selected Morito Tatsuo, a Socialist scholar, as minister of education. At the same time, Zenkyōkyō, the radical teachers' union, turned from the primary tactics of street demonstrations and protest movements to those of parliamentary processes, launching a two-pronged movement to attain its demands, with the threat of strikes and demonstrations supported by political power in the Diet.

During April and May 1947, the rival unions Zenkyōkyō, now under the more moderate leadership of Socialist Araki Shōzaburō, and the smaller, moderate Kyōzenren, with strong Socialist party ties, held a series of meetings to discuss merger of the two groups. There were several compelling reasons for uniting the two that finally made their alliance inevitable. First, their basic aims—to improve teachers' welfare, to democratize Japanese education, and to unionize all teachers—were similar, although their tactics to attain them were dissimilar. Second, by this time, the issue concerning the role of the emperor, a stumbling block for unity in the earlier period, had been eliminated as a source of contention since the emperor was declared a symbol of the State in the new Constitution. Third, the two groups were also convinced that they could never overcome the power of the Ministry of Education, then threatening them with a new teachers' association, backed by the American Occupation, as long as teachers were divided. Unity was essential.

Unity was also necessary for the successful implementation of the new education plan and the 6–3 system legislated weeks previously, both of which each union supported avidly. In addition, their combined power was needed to confront a threat to the twenty-eight thousand teachers who had been hastily recruited during the war and who had no teacher certification, thus failing to meet the minimum qualifications for teachers as stipulated in the pending revision of the licensing of teachers. And finally, Socialist party members were now leading both unions, so that a rapprochement was not only possible but inevitable.

An agreement reached by a joint committee on May 8, 1947, concluded the plan to form a merger of Zenkyōkyō, the militant Council of All Japan Teachers Union, and Kyōzenren, the moderate National Confederation of Teacher Unions. At the last minute, another organization of teachers, the small Daigaku Kōsen Kyōso (Teachers Union of Universities and Specialized Colleges), agreed to join the merger of the larger unions. An inaugural convention was scheduled for June 8, 1947, at Nara, ancient capital of Japan, unscathed during the war because of its irreplaceable historical treasures; in fact, Nara was one of the very few cities in Japan in 1947 that could accommodate a large conference. The name of the organization was decided upon simply as the Japan Teachers Union (Nihon Kyōshokuin Kumiai), better known today as Nikkyōso.[60]

NOTES

1. *Nippon Times*, January 1, 1946.
2. Iwama Masao, *Kyōin Kumiai Undōshi* (A History of the Teachers' Movement) (Tōkyō: Shūkan Kyōiku Shimbunsha, 1948), p. 13.
3. *Asahi Shimbun* (Asahi Newspaper), February 22, 1946.
4. Mochizuki Muneaki, *Nikkyōso Nijūnen no Tatakai* (Twenty-Year Struggle of the Japan Teachers Union) (Tōkyō: Rōdō Junpōsha, 1967), pp. 31–32.
5. *Nippon Times*, January 6, 1946.
6. *Asahi Shimbun*, January 26, 1946.
7. Iwama, *Kyōin Kumiai Undōshi*, p. 29.
8. *Report of the [First] United States Education Mission to Japan, Tōkyō, March 30, 1946* (Washington: United States Government Printing Office, 1946), p. 8.
9. Ibid., p. 27.
10. Ibid., p. 8.
11. Supreme Commander for the Allied Powers (SCAP), *History of the Non-Military Activities of the Occupation of Japan* (Tōkyō: SCAP, 1949), 11:93.
12. Robert King Hall, *Education for a New Japan* (New Haven: Yale University Press, 1949), p. 7.
13. SCAP, *Summation of Non-Military Activities in Japan and Korea*, Tōkyō, June, 1946, p. 21.
14. SCAP, *A History of Teachers' Unions in Japan*, Tōkyō, March, 1948, p. 83.
15. Ibid., pp. 13, 59.
16. Iwama, *Kyōin Kumiai Undōshi*, p. 29.
17. SCAP, *Teachers' Unions in Japan*, p. 34.

18. SCAP, *Summation*, May, 1946, p. 29.
19. Miriam S. Farley, *Aspects of Japan's Labor Problems* (New York: John Day Co., 1950), p. 28.
20. Ibid., p. 48.
21. Interview with the Honorable Iwama Masao, Japan Communist party representative, Tōkyō, August 5, 1968.
22. SCAP, *Summation*, May, 1946, p. 171.
23. Interview with Hidaka Daishirō, former vice-minister of education, Tōkyō, August 17, 1968.
24. Farley, *Japan's Labor Problems*, p. 51.
25. Interview with Iwama Masao, August 5, 1968.
26. SCAP, *Summation*, May, 1946, pp. 233–234.
27. Interview with Sagara Iichi, former secretary of the Ministry of Education, 1946–1949, Kyōto, July 29, 1968.
28. Sagara Iichi, *Kyōshokuin Tekikaku Shinsa Kankei Hōki to Kaisetsu* (Analysis of the Regulations Concerning the Qualifications of Teachers) Tōkyō: Ministry of Education, 1948), p. 108.
29. SCAP, *Teachers' Unions in Japan*, p. 3.
30. Interview with Sagara Iichi, July 29, 1968.
31. Interview with Ronald Anderson, former SCAP education officer, Tōkyō, June 5, 1968.
32. SCAP, *Summation*, May, 1947, p. 232.
33. Nikkyōso (Japan Teachers Union), *Nikkyōso Nijūnenshi* (Twenty-Year History of the Japan Teachers Union) (Tōkyō: Rōdō Junpōsha, 1967), p. 35.
34. *Yomiuri Shimbun* (Yomiuri Newspaper), June 2, 1946.
35. *Asahi Shimbun*, June 6, 1946.
36. Farley, *Japan's Labor Problems*, p. 138.
37. Mochizuki, *Nikkyōso Nijūnen*, p. 34.
38. *Asahi Shimbun*, October 26, 1946.
39. Interview with Sagara Iichi, July 29, 1968.
40. Interview with Iwama Masao, August 5, 1968.
41. *Asahi Shimbun*, November 9, 1946.
42. Ibid., November 30, 1946.
43. Mochizuki, *Nikkyōso Nijūnen*, p. 35.
44. Ibid.
45. Ibid., pp. 35–36.
46. *Asahi Shimbun*, January 2, 1947.
47. Mochizuki, *Nikkyōso Nijūnen*, p. 38.
48. Farley, *Japan's Labor Problems*, p. 148.
49. Foreign Affairs Association of Japan, *Contemporary Japan* 16 (1947):103.
50. SCAP, *Summation*, December, 1946, p. 1121.
51. Interview with Mochizuki Muneaki, Nikkyōso historian, Tōkyō, May 25, 1968.
52. Mochizuki, *Nikkyōso Nijūnen*, pp. 40–41.
53. Interview with Hidaka Daishirō, Tōkyō, August 17, 1968.
54. SCAP, *Teachers' Unions in Japan*, pp. 68–72.
55. Mombushō (Japanese Ministry of Education), *Education in Japan* (Tōkyō: Mombushō, 1968), p. 13.
56. John Maki, *Government and Politics in Japan* (New York: Praeger, 1962), pp. 245–258.

57. Foreign Affairs Association of Japan, *Contemporary Japan* 16 (1947):9.
58. SCAP, *Education in the New Japan* (Tōkyō: SCAP, 1948), 2:205–206.
59. Nikkyōso, *Nikkyōso Jūnenshi* (Ten-Year History of the Japan Teachers Union) (Tōkyō: Nikkyōso, 1958), p. 55.
60. Mochizuki, *Nikkyōso Nijūnen*, p. 47.

PART II

The Japan Teachers Union:
Twenty Years of Militancy, 1947-1967

The Rise and Fall
of Communist Leadership (1947–1951)
SCAP's Reverse Course

On June 8, 1947, in the outer gardens of the Kashihara Shrine near Nara, where the legendary Jimmu was crowned the first emperor of Japan in 660 B.C., 900 delegates purporting to represent 500,000 teachers approved the formation of Nikkyōso, the Japan Teachers Union. SCAP reported that Nikkyōso embraced nearly all of the 400,000 teachers in the country, with 278,500 members from the more militant Zenkyōkyō and 98,500 from the moderate Kyōzenren.[1] Daigaku Kōsen Kyōso (Teachers Union of Universities and Specialized Colleges), the union unaffiliated with either Zenkyōkyō or Kyōzenren, accounted for the remainder. The following officers, all from or sympathetic with, the Socialist party were elected: Chairman: Araki Shōzaburō (former chairman, Zenkyōkyō); Vice-Chairmen: Iwasaki Kyūzō (vice-chairman, Kyōzenren), and Tsuruoka Shinzō (chairman, Daigaku Kōsen Kyōso); Secretary General: Ogasawara Fumio (vice-chairman, Zenkyōkyō); Vice-Secretaries General: Narita Yoshihide (vice-chairman, Kyōzenren), and Konami Kintarō (secretary general, Zenkyōkyō).[2]

The first convention of Nikkyōso adopted the following slogans as the union's goals:

1. Reconstruct education and build a new Japan.
2. Implement the new 6–3 education system (elementary and lower secondary schools) with national funds.
3. Assure the freedom and democratization of research activities.
4. Establish a living wage.
5. Stabilize the cost of living.
6. Promote nursery schools with national funds.
7. Liberate women and youth.

8. Promote the nationwide unification of teachers.
9. Strengthen the unity of the working class by cooperating with labor groups and peoples' organizations.
10. Destroy fascism by expelling war criminals from education.

The major structural decisions approved at the inaugural meeting included the following: (1) Nikkyōso will be organized as a federation of prefectural unions; (2) the body that has the final approval over policy matters will be called the Central Committee, whose delegates will each represent 4,000 members; (3) the Central Executive Committee, made up of members from the Central Committee, will formulate policy.

The final ceremony of the opening convention of Nikkyōso concluded with the following oath:

> We have now formed the Japan Teachers Union through the combined will of 500,000 teachers with great expectations. We will endeavor to establish a new democratic order for the creation of a new Japanese society. We hereby swear that we will promote the social and economic status of teachers through the united power of our 500,000 members. We will earnestly struggle against the poor conditions experienced by our teachers. And we will cooperate with workers and farmers not only in Japan but throughout the world.[3]

Nikkyōso's initial policy reflected the moderate socialist leadership that had gained supremacy over the two former unions by the time of their merger. Only two members of Nikkyōso's first Central Executive Committee were members of the Communist party. The remaining sixty members were considered Socialist.[4] A variety of factors explain this imbalance. There were strong latent feelings against the Communist faction which had become influential under Iwama Masao during the strike fiasco of February 1. Many local teachers were still opposed to Communists as revolutionaries. The Socialist party remained opposed to communism, refusing to cooperate with the Japan Communist party in the formation of a united labor front. Furthermore, the leader of the radical left within Nikkyōso, Iwama Masao, who had entered the Upper House of the Diet after the April general elections, was no longer available in the day-to-day union activities. The fact that Nikkyōso, although recognizing organized strikes as a weapon for labor unions, nevertheless assumed the position that its use was to be avoided as far as possible was considered a victory for the moderates.

Regardless of the moderate persuasion of the national leaders of Nikkyōso at the time of its formation, the union's historian estimates today that in 1947 the ratio of the influence of the non-Communist faction to that of the Communist faction was about 6 to 4.[5] No exact figures are available, but this rough estimate is revealing. The Communist strength lay in the influence of a small number of activists who had been instrumental in organizing the early locals. Thus they occupied positions of power at the branch level far out of proportion to their actual numbers. Within a year, the Communist faction was able to project itself into the dominant position of influence within Nikkyōso.

The dominance of moderates within the top leadership was particularly evident at the inaugural convention in that the designation of labor union (*kyōin kumiai*) was omitted from the official union name and the concept of teachers as educational laborers (*kyōiku rōdōsha*) was avoided in the declarations. Both issues were fundamental to the Communist movement. Moreover, the left-wing faction was confronted with the generally prevailing attitude that teachers were different from ordinary laborers. Public sentiment would neither approve nor support the concept of teachers as laborers. But of perhaps even greater importance was the fact that the average teacher did not consider himself a common laborer. The rank and file thought of themselves simply as members of a mass movement of teachers attempting to improve their livelihood—not as educational laborers.

During the summer of 1947, following the formation of Nikkyōso, feelings of accomplishment and anticipation permeated the teachers' movement. The vast majority of teachers were united in one organization. Their union was recognized as the bargaining agent for the average teacher. Their rights were embodied in a legal contract with the government. Prime Minister Katayama, although heading a coalition cabinet, was a Socialist whose minister of education, Morito Tatsuo, was a Socialist sympathetic to Nikkyōso's program. And the new 6–3 system supported by the union had recently gone into effect with the opening of the school year in April.

The exigencies of the day, however, proved to be overwhelming. The Japanese government was not only depleted of financial resources but also diminished in authority since it was functioning under the rule of an occupying army. For example, there simply were not enough funds for extending compulsory education to the seventh year—the first year of the new lower secondary school—or for raising teachers' salaries. In addition, the minister of education, whose office traditionally holds a lesser position in the cabinet, witnessed the budget for the new school system being sharply curtailed. In short, Prime Minister Katayama governed from a position of weakness, at the mercy both of the conservative members in his coalition cabinet and of SCAP, the ultimate authority in Japan.

This combination of frustrating circumstances provoked the labor unions, including Nikkyōso, to oppose the Socialist prime minister and his minister of education within a relatively short time. The government was incapable of alleviating the terrible conditions of the working classes since an annual three-fold increase in the cost of living in Tōkyō was reaping its toll. When a completely inadequate budget, though a budget nonetheless, to carry out plans for the new lower secondary schools received reluctant approval by the minister of education—while many children attended the compulsory lower secondary schools in warehouses, barracks, temples, and even in the open air—Nikkyōso unreservedly criticized the Socialist government. In total disarray, the Katayama cabinet resigned on February 9, 1948, ending more than eight months of disastrous Socialist leadership of the Japanese government, the only period since the war when a Socialist served as prime minister.

The year 1948 was a milestone in the history of the American Occupation of Japan, with repercussions greatly affecting Nikkyōso. Internationally, Soviet–United States relations were rapidly deteriorating—this was the time of the Berlin Blockade. The American-supported government of Chiang Kai-shek was retreating across the Chinese mainland, pursued by a Communist army under Mao Tse-tung. Communist plots were being discovered within the United States government. Throughout the world, American policy toward the Communist block hardened. Accordingly, the policy of the American Occupation of Japan entered a period of transition greatly influenced by the increasingly tense international atmosphere between Communist and non-Communist blocs.

Internally in Japan, the first half of 1948 witnessed growing discontent among labor unions as critical economic conditions continued. In February 1948 the postal workers' union planned a strike, which was banned by SCAP in March. The Osaka Teachers Union, a local branch of Nikkyōso, went on strike for higher wages. Teachers from Gumma Prefectural Union planned a fifteen-day strike. Shortly thereafter, Nikkyōso and the Ministry of Education negotiated a settlement whereby Nikkyōso won an average monthly salary of 2,920 yen, in common with other government employees, on the condition that further strike plans be suspended. Thus labor unrest was calmed for the moment.

Within a few weeks, however, certain local unions became dissatisfied with the salary-increase agreement. In May teachers in Kyōto and Hyōgo prefectures struck for twenty-four and forty-eight hours, respectively, for higher salaries. Other nationwide strikes planned by unions of government employees threatened the nation once again. Indicative of the trend were statistics from December 1947 which showed that, of the 1,794,000 workers involved in disputes, 1,670,000 were government employees, who had fared the most poorly during the period of ceaseless price rises and growing inflation.[6] A SCAP official estimated that salaries of government employees had increased 20 to 80 percent since the end of the war while wages in private industry had gone up 200 to 400 percent and in commerce, 400 to 800 percent.[7]

Faced with numerous strikes, General MacArthur once again dramatically intervened. On July 22, 1948, he sent a letter to Prime Minister Ashida, informing him that his government should revise the National Public Service Law so that:

> No person holding a position by appointment or employment in the public service of Japan or in any instrumentality thereof should resort to strike or engage in delaying or other dispute tactics which tend to impair the efficiency of governmental operations. . . . all government employees should realize that the process of collective bargaining, as usually understood, cannot be transplanted into the public service.[8]

This famous letter, instigating what Nikkyōso considers the most restrictive legislation for teachers in the entire postwar period, was based on the American pattern of civil service regulations. General MacArthur borrowed freely from President Franklin D. Roosevelt's rationale for the prevention of strikes and collective bargaining by American civil servants —ironically, in his support of the 1935 Wagner Act, granting industrial unions broad powers. SCAP reasoned that the purpose of the National Personnel Authority, the quasi-independent governmental agency responsible for the welfare of civil servants, was:

> to provide for the installation of a democratic and efficient public service in the government of Japan. The plan envisages a modern type of personnel system which recruits public employees from the entire public by competitive tests and promotes them on the basis of merit, providing scientific supervision over their classification, compensation, training, evaluation, health, safety, welfare, recreation and retirement. The system provides a grievance procedure for the fair and equitable treatment in administration.[9]

SCAP's letter made frequent reference to the differences between the public and private sectors of employment. Arguing that, historically, trade unions have translated their increasing economic power into political power through support of duly constituted political parties, General MacArthur wrote that:

> It would be violative of the democratic concept for the trade union movement to usurp the function of the duly elected representatives of the people as a whole by superimposing union judgment upon legislation and administration. . . . There is a sharp distinction between those who have dedicated their energies to the public service and those engaged in private enterprise. The former are the very instruments used for the exercise by government of the people's sovereign power . . . for upon them rests . . . the obligation to serve the whole people. . . . A strike of public employees manifests nothing less than intent on their part to prevent or obstruct the operations of government until their demands are satisfied. Such action, looking toward the paralysis of government by those who have sworn to support it, is unthinkable and intolerable.[10]

With the "paramountcy of the public interest as the foremost consideration," the intent of the letter from General MacArthur to Prime Minister Ashida was carried out through Cabinet Order 201 on July 31, 1948, and legislated in an amendment to the National Public Service Law, December 1948. In one stroke, the new law superseded the right to strike and bargain collectively that had been granted by the Ministry of Education to the two competing teachers' unions in early 1947, prior to the formation of Nikkyōso. These formal contracts of 1947, applicable to Nikkyōso, had remained in force without modification until the spring of 1948, when the Ministry of Education and the union expressed a desire for a new agreement. Failure to reach an accord resulted in the union's decision in July to ask for mediation by the Labor Relations Board. General MacArthur's letter was written before the Board acted. Without prior consultation or the right of appeal, the Ministry of Education notified Nikkyōso that the agreement was unilaterally repealed, transforming Nikkyōso into a union of teachers devoid of the usual instruments of unionism.

As a result of having teachers teach under the provisions of the regular national civil servant regulations rather than under those of the former contracts, all teachers were now bound by strict laws concerning political activities. According to the 1947 National Civil Service Law, Article 102, employees of the national government were restricted from participating in any political activities except that of voting.[11] Teachers, who had enjoyed broad political rights under their former contracts, came under these new restrictive regulations because of the letter written by General Mac-Arthur.

Once again, as in the abortive strike of February 1947, teachers as civil servants were affected by a government act overtly designed to curtail the strength of other government unions, primarily in transportation and communications, whose strikes were threatening to disable the country. In both instances, the crisis faced by the country was not brought on by teachers, but it can be assumed that the Ministry of Education welcomed the restrictive provisions affecting the hostile Nikkyōso as well. But to Nikkyōso, in which by now one-fourth of the Central Executive Commitee members were Communists or fellow travelers,[12] this was naked oppression by the American Occupation, violating the fundamental rights of Article 26 of the Constitution, which granted workers the right to bargain collectively.

Both sides were hardening their positions. An officer of the Government Section of SCAP revealed the occupying army's changing attitude toward union leaders based on the new law. The chief of the Government Section explained as follows:

> Leadership of certain organizations has been taken over by men who have not been devoted to the welfare of Japan and her people and a situation has been created dangerous to the future of the nation. Despite the critical need for national recovery, this pattern of labor relations recently on several occasions has led Japan to the brink of a general strike of government services. A national disaster has only been prevented by the decisive action on the part of the Supreme Commander for the Allied Powers.[13]

Within SCAP, however, there was a sharp division of opinion toward the conflict created by the new law. The Government Section viewed it simply as a problem in creating an efficient, modern, civil service system. The Labor Division regarded it as part of the larger problem of labor relations. When the Government Section prevailed, James Killen, chief of the Labor Division and a vice-president of the International Brotherhood of Pulp, Sulphite, and Paper Mill Workers, resigned in protest. The American Federation of Labor promptly criticized SCAP on the grounds that by denying collective bargaining rights to government employees, SCAP was not weakening communism but was driving Japanese workers into its arms.[14]

The unions of Japanese government employees reacted bitterly toward their new status under the National Public Service Law. Communist influence, gradually intensifying within the hierarchy of public service unions, was strengthened when the Communists led a determined resistance against the newly imposed strike ban. Acts of violence broke out throughout the land. There were many arrests and convictions of militant unionists within the public service sector.

Shortly after this frustrating episode for government employee unions, in which their political activities and labor rights were sharply curtailed, preparations for the first elections of the new school boards got underway, causing further deterioration of the already strained relationship between SCAP and Nikkyōso. The principle of a locally elected school-board system was based on the recommendations of the United States Education Mission made two years previously that "each prefecture should establish an elected educational committee to take general charge of public schools within the prefecture"; that "in each city or other prefectural subdivision, there should be a lay educational agency elected by the people to administer the local education program."[15] SCAP's purpose in supporting the school boards was quite clear. A spokesman declared at a press conference that "the schools of Japan, long under the domination of the Ministry of Education, are being placed in the hands of the people themselves."[16]

A disagreement developed among SCAP, the Japanese Ministry of Education, and the Japan Education Reconstruction Committee (JERC) over the school-board system itself and over the question of the lowest feasible administrative level suitable for having the new boards. SCAP at first proposed that they extend down to the grass-roots level (the town and village), whereas the Japanese government recommended having them only at the prefectural and large-city level. JERC had misgivings about direct public election and proposed an indirect system of selection.[17] SCAP finally agreed to a compromise restricting the first school-board elections to the prefectural level and the five largest cities, thus postponing school-board elections at the smaller-city and town and village levels until 1950 because of budgetary difficulties. In addition it was agreed that six members would be elected at large and one appointed by the local assembly to the prefectural school boards; and four members would be elected and one appointed to the municipal school boards.[18]

Nikkyōso, completely ignoring the new political restrictions placed upon teachers as a result of General MacArthur's letter, heartily approved of school boards and set out vigorously to have their representatives elected to the boards by following the democratic procedure prescribed by the American Occupation. At first, the union supported school boards down to the local level. However, as the election drew near and the "true nature of the powers of the boards were fully understood in that local laymen could restrict teachers' activities," Nikkyōso altered its position and supported only the prefectural boards. Nikkyōso's policy was based on the concern that local conservative landowners and politicians would dominate the elections by assuming a hard line against the leftist teachers' union.[19]

SCAP took a personal interest in the school-board elections, perhaps because the boards were considered a traditional American institution and because SCAP placed an abiding faith in them to accomplish a truly democratic reform of Japanese education. Consequently, the school boards were to be run as the American officers knew them in America. But Nikkyōso leaders had their own ideas about the boards, considerably different from those of SCAP and contrary to SCAP's plan. The confrontation between SCAP and Nikkyōso on the school-board issue was most pronounced in Tōkyō where SCAP's Tōkyō Military Government Team challenged the Tōkyō branch of the teachers' union. SCAP's officers showed films and spoke in every ward of the city, explaining the American tradition of having laymen—not educators—control educational policy through the school boards. The antagonism between SCAP and Nikkyōso was publicly exposed when Colonel Hollingshed, commander of the Tōkyō Military Government Team, addressed a meeting of Tōkyō teachers in these words:

> On September 10, we requested that you submit a statement about whether or not you would endorse as candidates any members of your union. Statements were requested from each chapter. To date only one has declared endorsing Narita. Yet we know that the Itabashi Chapter is endorsing Kaneko, and others are planning to back candidates. It is high time you realize that your union is being severely criticized in opposing and obstructing every measure to improve education in Tōkyō. Now is the time to redeem yourself in the eyes of the public by issuing a clear-cut statement that the Tōkyō Federation of Teachers Union and its chapters will neither select nor sponsor any teacher or members of the union as a candidate for the board of education. Such a statement should result in the immediate withdrawal of those candidates whom you have already selected. . . . Public school teachers in the United States which had experience with boards for 150 years are never permitted to serve on boards because it is an accepted principle that no one in public service should determine policies under which he works.[20]

In spite of SCAP's demands, Nikkyōso members, including Kaneko Reigaku, supported by the Communist party, and Narita Yoshihide, vice-secretary general of Nikkyōso, who was affiliated with the extreme left-wing faction of the union, ran for the Tōkyō school board. Throughout the country, more than one hundred candidates from Nikkyōso entered the race for the 296 seats in Japan's first postwar attempt to democratize education through popularly elected school boards.

The first school-board election on October 5, 1948, resulted in a conservative victory, according to the *Nippon Times,* with 72 percent (213) of the winners considered conservative, 26 percent (76) progressive, and 2 percent (7) radical.[21] Although both Narita and Kaneko lost in the Tōkyō election, Nikkyōso claimed that out of the 95 seats won by active teachers, 54 had been endorsed by the union. In addition 23 others had been sponsored jointly by Nikkyōso and by various local organizations.[22] Regardless of the exact number of teachers elected to the boards, the results indicated that a significant number of Japanese voters did not view Nikkyōso negatively.

From the vantage of hindsight, it can be concluded that the elective school-board system did not place education in the hands of the people nor did it render the Ministry of Education simply an advisory agency, as originally intended by the United States Education Mission. Certain conditions precluded such a radical decentralization: (1) SCAP held ultimate authority. (2) The Ministry of Education was the agency responsible for carrying out the new 6–3–3 educational system. (3) The Ministry of Education set teachers' minimum qualifications. (4) Fifty percent of teachers' salaries were subsidized by the Ministry, enabling the government to determine the number of teachers who could qualify for the subsidy—in effect, setting a quota. Prefectural superintendents of education frequently traveled to Tōkyō to appeal for funds to build the new schools required for the extension of compulsory education. The optional courses of study formulated by the Ministry of Education were considered mandatory by many teachers because of the long tradition of local subservience to the Ministry. Consequently, the schools still looked to Tōkyō for direction, where the all-powerful SCAP continued to operate through the Ministry of Education.

The Ministry of Education in 1948 thus maintained a considerable amount of influence over Japanese education, augmented by the conservative dominance of the new school boards. Predictably, many Nikkyōso affiliates launched a general campaign of a hostile nature to bring pressure on the school boards to meet the aggressive demands of the union for higher salaries and for greater control of educational affairs by teachers. On many occasions, Nikkyōso militants disrupted school-board meetings when their demands were not met. In the face of strong teacher opposition, some boards yielded, in particular where former teachers were serving as board members.

American Occupation officials, reacting to both the international climate and internal developments in Japan, finally reached, by late 1948, the stage of a full "reverse course" policy for Japan from the initial "heady" period of democratization. Japan was considered ripe for communism, with a high unemployment rate, runaway inflation, low production, chronic food shortages, and general labor unrest plaguing the land. With worldwide communism posing what was interpreted as an international threat to the non-Communist world, Japan was thought to be similarly threatened. The American government then made the important decision that Communist advances in Japan, as well as throughout the world, must be repulsed. Concurrently, it was decided that the Japanese economy must be placed posthaste on a viable basis, regardless of the consequences to the original Occupation policy of strengthening the democratic institutions related to the labor movement.

The American Occupation moved forcibly to counter the internal Communist threat and to place the stagnant Japanese economy on a viable basis. Industrial production was still at a standstill with a production rate in 1949 only 60 percent of that during the years between 1930 and 1934.[23] A radically new approach to the chronic economic problem, announced in December 1948, was to have serious repercussions on Japanese education and Nikkyōso policies. General MacArthur, on December 20, declared that one of the primary goals of the Occupation was the prompt economic stabilization of Japan.[24]

An American banker named Joseph Dodge, who had played an important role in German currency reform, was brought to Japan in February 1949 to plan the financial rehabilitation of Japan. The Dodge Plan, a nine-point program, involved drastic measures to balance the budget, reduce inflation, and stabilize prices. An immediate curtailment was imposed on government expenditures and subsidies; printing of new money was sharply reduced; and a program to rationalize labor was instituted to unravel a "rigged economy," perpetuated, Dodge believed, on the twin stilts of American aid and large Japanese government subsidies.[25]

The effects of the Dodge Plan were dramatic. On February 20, 1949, a law concerning the rationalization of government employment was passed by the Diet, and 258,543 civil servants were dismissed.[26] The unions of government employees, particularly those most affected—the national railroads and the post office—were thrown into confusion. Violence broke out. The president of the Japan National Railways, who had dismissed 95,000 employees, was found dead on the railroad tracks near Sendai on July 6. An empty train, released from its moorings in Mitaka, Tokyo, on July 14, crashed into crowded steps, killing eight persons. Many Communists were arrested and charged in connection with the violence.

The Dodge Plan perforce had a severe impact on the school-expansion program legislated in 1947, which was to complete by 1949 the extension of compulsory education through grade nine. National funds allocated for this project were reduced in the general retrenchment of government spending, exacerbating the already severe shortage of school buildings for the new junior high schools. Under the Dodge Plan, the educational share of the national budget was reduced from 8.1 percent for the 1948–1949 academic year to 6.3 percent for the following year.[27] This contrasted with 9 percent in the early 1930s.[28]

Chairman Araki of Nikkyōso testified forcefully before a Diet Committee, charging that since there was already a shortage of 52,416 classrooms, an increase in the education budget to sustain the new 6–3–3 educational system was mandatory.[29] He was referring to conditions that prompted the resignation of 683 village heads, several of whom committed suicide because of their failure to fulfill promises to build lower secondary schools. At that time more than 350 lower secondary schools were conducting classes in barns and other buildings with similar poor facilities.[30]

The initial effects of the Dodge Plan played into the hands of the growing number of Communist teachers who were appealing to the disillusioned non-Communist teachers for support against the policies of the Japanese government and the American Occupation. SCAP became deeply concerned about the steadily increasing number of Communists; party membership had grown from 1,000 in 1945 to 70,000 by 1947.[31] The general public, experiencing the third straight year of impoverishment following the bombing holocausts of the last years of the war, looked with more favor than at any other time in Japan's history on the Communist plan to reform Japanese industry and society in 1948 and 1949. The Communists had also effectively capitalized on the American Occupation's more conservative policies from 1948 by appealing to the liberal inclinations of students, intellectuals, labor leaders, and others who had become disenchanted with the Socialist party after its misadventure at running the government. Liberals disappointed with the Socialist party had little choice but to turn to the Communist party.

By election time in 1949, the Socialists had lost much of their previous popularity, receiving only 13 percent of the votes for 49 seats. It was during this election that the Japan Communist party made its strongest bid for political power in the postwar period, polling 9.6 percent of the votes (2,900,000) for 35 seats, up from 3.7 percent, or 4 seats, in the previous general elections in 1947. The conservatives, with 264 seats, however, gave Prime Minister Yoshida his first majority government.[32] That the Communist party and the Conservative party won great numbers of votes was an indication of the public's general dissatisfaction with the centrist Socialist party.

Within Nikkyōso a similar trend was underway. Teachers were extremely dissatisfied with their deplorable living conditions. SCAP reported that by April 1948, out of the average monthly salary of 2,156 yen of an unmarried teacher living alone in a single room in Tōkyō, 1,500 to 2,000 yen was used for room and board.[33] Communist influence within Nikkyōso had consequently been gaining strength throughout 1948 until it had finally attained dominance among the leadership by the beginning of 1949.

At the fourth national convention of Nikkyōso, convened in the southern resort city of Beppu in February 1949, the internal struggle between the Communists and Socialists disrupted the proceedings as a reaction to Communist domination emerged. A non-confidence motion was submitted by the moderate wing, charging that the Central Executive Committee had "followed a mistaken wage policy and had cooperated with the wrong political party,"[34] referring to the committee's efforts on behalf of the Communist party. A bitter floor debate ensued. As an open attack on Communist supremacy within the union, the motion finally lost by a vote of 465 to 425, revealing the relative strengths of the two factions.[35] This vote was the first open break between the Communists and Socialists, turning the tide against Communist dominance of Nikkyōso, which was not to be equalled for a decade.

The convention at Beppu also attained notoriety for the Communist declaration of a bloc of Nikkyōso's members. Iwama Masao, left-wing leader of the teachers' movement through 1946 and 1947 and Independent representative in the Diet since 1947, representing the union's interests, declared his allegiance to, and membership in, the Japan Communist party. Seventy other members of Nikkyōso, mostly Iwama's colleagues from the old radical Tōkyō Municipal Teachers Union, stood with him in the joint declaration, giving substance to the public's general impression that Nikkyōso was dominated by Communists. Because of the rapid increase of Communist influence both within labor unions and at the polls in 1948 and 1949, Iwama and his followers had the feeling that the Communist revolution was at hand.[36]

Following the dramatic confrontation at Beppu, the moderates redoubled their efforts to unify their ranks against Communist control of Nikkyōso. The significance of Communist control of the union's Central Executive Committee and other administrative positions was not underestimated in the antagonism between the two factions. The Japan Communist party held direct control over the Communists within Nikkyōso through its Education and Culture Department (Kyōiku Bunka-Bu) and its Labor Department (Rōdō-Bu). The Communist faction was in constant touch with the Communist party headquarters in Yoyogi, Tōkyō, for instructions.[37]

Amidst such Communist advances, SCAP finally moved directly against the Japan Communist party in 1949 by systematically carrying out a program to discharge active Communists from government, politics, labor, and industry in what became known as the Red Purge. As an integral part of a general suppression of left-wing activists, the education sector, too, underwent its own Red Purge. On July 19, 1949, Dr. Walter Eells, SCAP's advisor on higher education in the Civil Information and Education Section, spearheaded the attack on Communist teachers with one of the most famous speeches in postwar Japan. Although he referred specifically to university teachers, the effect of his speech permeated the entire school system. Dr. Eells, speaking at the opening ceremony of Niigata University, declared that:

> Freedom of teaching and freedom of research are the most widely held and jealously guarded functions of a university. In our country, the American Association of University Professors has published carefully prepared and widely influential statements of principles to assure academic freedom. . . . One sentence from one of its statements reads as follows: "No teacher may claim as his right the privilege of discussing in his classroom controversial topics outside his own field of study." . . . This means that a mathematics teacher, for example, has complete

academic freedom to study or teach his own field of mathematics but does not have freedom to teach such a subject as communism.

In the past few years the question has come up in the United States, as it has recently in Japan and in other countries, whether in a democracy a member of the Communist Party should be discharged from his position as a university professor because he is a communist. . . . Communism is a dangerous and destructive doctrine since it advocates the overthrow of established democratic governments by force. Must those who may believe in this dangerous doctrine be allowed to teach such doctrine to the youth of the country?

In the United States we have an important organization known as the Educational Policies Commission, composed of the leading scholars of the country. . . . The Commission only a few weeks ago issued a document which advocates and defends the discharge of proved communists from the schools of America. Do the recommendations of this document violate the long and jealously guarded academic freedom of the university? By no means. The basic reason for advising exclusion of communist professors is that they are not free. Their thoughts, their beliefs, their teachings are controlled from the outside. Communists are told from headquarters what to think and what to teach. In the very name of academic freedom, therefore, the most important right and duty of a university, we dare not have known communists as university professors because they are then no longer really free to teach or carry on research. . . . Therefore they cannot be allowed to be university professors in a democracy.[38]

Predictably, Dr. Eells' speech set off a storm of protest. When he further expounded his thesis at other universities, students heckled his speeches, forcing him off the stage at Tōhoku and Hokkaidō universities. His name became synonymous with anticommunism. His position on communism became SCAP's basis for purging Communist teachers from the entire school system in one of the most controversial acts of the American Occupation of Japan.

On September 7, 1949, prefectural superintendents of education were summoned to Tōkyō by the minister of education for a secret meeting. The superintendents were notified that the purge of Communist teachers was ordered by SCAP and must be complied with. However, the minister explained that, since this action could possibly violate the constitutional rights of teachers, the official reason for dismissing such teachers must not be membership in the Japan Communist party.[39]

The superintendents returned to their prefectures and began the systematic dismissal of the most active left-wing teachers within their jurisdictions. Personnel officers had dossiers on all local activists. It was not difficult for the superintendents to select the activist teachers and prosecute their cases before the prefectural school boards, usually on the legal grounds that these teachers were obstructing the normal operations of the school system or that they were redundant over and above the quota set by the Dodge Plan. The school board alone voted for their dismissal; the Red Purge of teachers was thus accomplished. In certain cases it is known that the list of teachers to be purged submitted by the prefectural SCAP education officer to the school board usually coincided with the list drawn up by the superintendent's office.

Teachers implicated in the Red Purge were not cross-examined, were not present for any of the deliberations, and had no right of appeal except through the civil court, where decades later several cases remained in litigation. They merely received their notice of dismissal. An American researcher, evaluating the Occupation in process, concluded that "there is evidence that proper safeguards have not been observed by the Japanese authorities in some areas and that a considerable number of teachers not proved communists have been dismissed."[40]

The Red Purge of teachers was a direct attack on Nikkyōso, which by this time, in common with many labor unions, had come under the dominant influence of Communists, particularly at the prefectural and the large-city administrative levels. The Communists were filling the vacuum created by the waning Socialist influence, following the disastrous attempt at Socialist government between 1947 and 1948. At the prefectural and local levels, these Communist leaders were carrying out frequent demonstrations and acts of intimidation against the local school boards—activities that were indeed legal grounds for dismissal. Some school boards were forced to relocate repeatedly and secretly the site of their meetings to elude picketing and general harassment.

The school boards themselves were most reluctant to punish left-wing leaders of teachers, because they realized that such action would result in widespread reprisals by teachers and in further deterioration of relations between teachers and the school boards. In addition, the school boards, in operation for only a year, were theoretically models of democracy. To discharge leaders of their teachers was felt to be an undemocratic act by a democratic institution. Under these circumstances, it can be assumed that many school-board members approved the Red Purge, since they had no recourse but to follow SCAP's desires, but they placed the responsibility for the purge primarily at SCAP's doorstep.

The effect of the Red Purge on Nikkyōso was serious. First of all,

1,010 teachers were fired,[41] many of them prefectural and local leaders of Nikkyōso. They were among the 20,997 Communists and fellow travelers who lost their jobs in government, information media, and industry.[42] In Tōkyō alone, 246 Communist or allegedly Communist teachers were purged.[43] Consequently, although the national leadership of the union was not directly affected since the purge of teachers was carried out by prefectural authorities at the local level and not at the national level by the Ministry of Education, the ranks of Nikkyōso at the local level were severely depleted of the left-wing activists.

Nikkyōso protested the purge when representatives met with the minister of education during the dismissals, charging that it was illegal to dismiss teachers simply on the basis of their personal ideological beliefs. However, the union was not able to organize coordinated nationwide protests because the purge took effect rapidly throughout the nation, especially after the Korean War broke out in 1950. At that time SCAP had Communist leaders arrested on a number of occasions and banned their newspaper, the *Akahata*. Nikkyōso itself, moreover, was in a weakened condition due to internal instability because of the Communist-Socialist confrontations. As a result of the purge, Communist influence within the union dropped from a high in 1949 to its lowest level ever in the years 1950 and 1951. This was, of course, the very result SCAP had desired.

The second highly significant result was that the moderate element within Nikkyōso, gaining strength thanks to the Red Purge, began to exert increasing influence against Communist domination. This movement was first seen in the non-confidence motion against the Communist-dominated Central Executive Committee during the February convention in Beppu. It won the day when Nikkyōso's President Araki, during the sixth national convention in November 1949 at Shiobara, recognized the problem and declared in his address that the union "has shifted between right and left wings during the past two and a half years of struggles, leading to much misunderstanding of us. Now, the 500,000 members of the union must reunite, eliminate leftist unionism in order to strengthen the union, and establish policies to protect the actual interests of all our members."[44]

The Red Purge of leftist teachers in the 1949–1950 period contrasted sharply with the purge of right-wing teachers during 1946 and 1947, illustrating the "reverse course" of the American Occupation between 1947 and 1949. And when the "depurge" of thousands of individuals convicted during the right-wing purge was carried out concurrently with the Red Purge, the timing made the public feel that the American Occupation was no longer concerned about the democratic process in Japan but thought only of the international cold war.[45]

The Red Purge also illustrated the peculiar predicament into which the Occupation had worked itself by infringing upon legally instituted democratic rights, promulgated by SCAP, in the name of academic freedom. The inconsistency was evident in the fact that certified teachers who were card-carrying Japan Communist party members, such as Iwama, were eligible to become members of the Diet, representing hundreds of thousands of constituents, but were ineligible to teach in the schools within their constituencies. Dr. Eells himself recognized this paradox when he later wrote that the "situation admittedly had some elements of difficulty since the Communist Party is legalized in Japan and has elected many members to the Diet, and academic freedom is guaranteed in the Constitution of the country."[46]

Under these conditions, even Minister of Education Takase, according to his secretary, had reservations about carrying out the wishes of SCAP. Takase felt that relations between Nikkyōso and the Ministry of Education were not particularly bad at this time, calling it the honeymoon period, as the Ministry and the union were both striving to realize the reforms of Japanese education legislated in 1947. He also felt that there was no legal basis for dismissing Communist teachers. Takase's position was explained to the Government Section of SCAP by the Secretariat, but the decision to purge Communists from all sectors of Japanese society had apparently already been made somewhere within SCAP and in Washington. No compromise was permitted.[47]

Nikkyōso's convention at Shiobara on November 11, 1949, after the Red Purge had been initiated, marks the official turning point of the leadership away from Communist dominance toward a more moderate Socialist position. Communist influence within the entire union movement waned during late 1949 and 1950, with the emergence of an anti-Communist movement called Mindō (Democratic League) within union affiliates of the Communist-dominated Sanbetsu (council of unions). Sanbetsu membership declined from a high of 5 million in the 1947–1948 period to 1.5 million by the end of 1949, as the Red Purge took its toll.[48]

Simultaneously, Nikkyōso was playing a major role in organizing unions of government employees into a united association of unions. At that time, Nikkyōso's president was also president of Kankōrō, a council of civil servant unions, known officially as Nihon Kankōchō Rōdō Kumiai Kyōgikai (Japan Council of National and Local Government Workers' Union). Because the railway and postal unions were split over the Red Purge, Nikkyōso, which remained intact, became by far the largest union in Kankōrō, taking a leading role in unifying the moderate factions from other unions into a movement to organize a new council of unions. SCAP worked behind the scenes to promote such a development.

The result was the formation in July 1950 of Sōhyō, known officially as Nihon Rōdō Kumiai Sōhyōgikai (General Council of Trade Unions in Japan). Consisting of three million members, Sōhyō, an amalgamation of moderate, mostly civil servant unions, supported the Socialist party from an essentially anti-Communist position.[49] Sōhyō was shortly to become the most powerful federation of unions in postwar Japan. Nikkyōso voted to join Sōhyō at its seventh national convention in May 1950. The vote was 321 in favor to 130 opposed,[50] indicating the relative strengths of the Socialist and Communist factions within the union leadership at that time.

During the Red Purge and during the realignment of labor unions leading to the birth of Sōhyō, the second of the two most important postwar legislative acts relating to teachers was passed. The first one, discussed above, was the 1948 act which brought teachers under national civil servants' regulations, resulting in the forfeiture of the teachers' rights to strike, to bargain collectively, and to participate in any political activities except voting. The second, a combination of two laws planned for later enactment at the time the 1948 act was hastily passed, included the Special Law for Public Service Education Personnel (Kyōiku Kōmuin Tokurei Hō) of 1949 and the Local Public Service Law (Chihō Kōmuin Hō) of 1950.

The Special Law for Public Service Education Personnel stipulated in Article 3 that henceforth teachers in national schools would be classified as national public servants and those in locally maintained schools would be classified as local civil servants. This differentiation of teachers, the vast majority of whom were in public schools and only a minority in the several national schools, required a new law for local civil servants, which followed in 1950. However, Article 21 of the 1949 Special Law stipulated specifically that, for the time being, that is, until a local civil service act could be prepared, teachers who were newly classified as local civil servants were still bound by Article 102 of the National Public Service Law, which prohibited all political activities except voting.[51]

In 1950 the Local Public Service Law was passed consisting of regulations for local public servants, with minor exceptions written into the Special Law to provide for matters unique to the teaching profession. The following crucially significant clauses were included in the bill for all local government employees, including teachers:

ARTICLE 36 (Political activities)
  1. Local public service personnel may not contribute to the formation of political parties or become officers in them. They also may not induce others to become members of any political party.
  2. Local public service personnel may not participate in any of the following activities in support of, or opposition to, a particular political party, person, or event in a public election: (*a*) engage in soliciting votes, (*b*) participate in a signature campaign, (*c*) engage in fund raising campaigns, (*d*) use or allow others to use public funds or public buildings.

ARTICLE 37 (Dispute tactics)
  Local public servants may not resort to strikes, slowdown, or other acts of dispute against their employer, who is the local people as represented by the agencies of the local public body, or to conduct such idling tactics as will deteriorate the functional efficiency of the local public body, or to instigate others to do so.

ARTICLE 52 (Organization)
  Public servants' organizations whose purpose is to promote the improvement of working conditions will be recognized. Local public servants may join such an organization.

ARTICLE 55 (Negotiations)
  Local public servants' organizations may negotiate with the local public body concerned with regard to compensation, work hours, and other working conditions of their personnel. However, such negotiations do not include the right of collective agreement with the authorities of the local public body.[52]

Nikkyōso made a determined effort through nationwide meetings to block passage of this bill, claiming that the basic rights of workers set forth in Article 26 of the Constitution—"the right of workers to organize and bargain collectively is guaranteed"—would be violated. After a short postponement of the deliberations, a compromise clause pertaining to the matter of political activities contained in Article 36, was added by the government because of Nikkyōso's opposition. In the revised version, political restrictions were to be enforced only in the district in which the local civil servant was employed.[53]

As a result of these laws, in which teachers were classified as local civil servants, Nikkyōso lost its official status as a national union. Thus it became virtually a voluntary organization in the eyes of the law since teachers are hired by the prefectural school boards rather than by the Ministry of Education. In other words, whereas to Nikkyōso, the prefectural teachers' organizations recognized by the prefectural government under Article 52 continued as federated members of Nikkyōso, to the prefectural governments, the teachers' organizations were not recognized as Nikkyōso affiliates. In a sense, the prefectural teachers' organizations were operating simultaneously in two capacities, depending on whom they were dealing with. In practice, they functioned as prefectural units of the national union Nikkyōso, regardless of what the prefectural governments called them.

The effect of the new laws was the elimination of all legal basis for Nikkyōso's claim to negotiating rights with the Ministry of Education on behalf of the vast majority of teachers in the country. There seems little doubt that such an anticipated outcome was one of the major purposes behind the formulation of the laws in the first place. What the laws failed to do, however, was to restrict the political activities of Nikkyōso's national leadership, which, after all, was directing the union's political program. Since members of the national executive were working at the Tōkyō headquarters away from the local districts, where each was technically employed on the teaching staff but on leave at the national office, they were not affected by the political restrictions on teachers in the district of employment.

For the next decade, the Ministry of Education refused any formal negotiations with Nikkyōso on grounds that teachers' organizations are recognized only at the prefectural and local levels where teachers are employed, and that only at that level can teachers and their employers negotiate under the law. Representatives of Nikkyōso, however, continued to meet with those ministers of education who were receptive to their incessant demands for consultation until later ministers finally ceased all contact between the Ministry and the national executive of Nikkyōso. At this point their relationship deteriorated to abysmal depths.

The Local Public Service Law also established a quasi-independent local organ similar to the National Personnel Authority, whose purpose it is to make recommendations to the local public body concerning compensation, working conditions, and welfare of the local public servants. Nevertheless, because the salaries of local public servants are based on the standards recommended by the National Personnel Authority for national civil servants, for all intents and purposes, the major target of pressure for Nikkyōso in raising teachers' salaries remained the national government.

The year 1950, in addition to being the year when the Local Public Service Law was passed, also was the beginning of a monumental transition period in the postwar history of Japan. The focal point was the outbreak of the Korean War. Communist armies by 1950 had sent the U. S.-supported Nationalist Chinese fleeing to the island of Formosa. The new Communist People's Republic of China entered into a thirty-year alliance with the Soviet Union on February 14, and Communist North Korean troops moved south on June 25 and took the South Korean capital of Seoul. On June 27 the Security Council of the United Nations asked member nations to aid South Korea. By July, General MacArthur, Supreme Commander for the Allied Powers in Japan, was commanding the United Nations forces sent to aid South Korea. Commuting between Korea and Japan, MacArthur used Japan as a forward supply base for military operations on the Korean Peninsula.

With Communist armies controlling the whole of China and sweeping south with Soviet support through Japan's nearest neighbor only tens of miles away, the earlier Occupation policy of Japan became anachronistic to the American government. Article 9 of the postwar Constitution, proscribing a Japanese army, rendered Japan a military vacuum, precisely as originally intended. The international situation prompted the American government to seek a new policy for Japan.

During January of the same year, the Cominform under the influence of the Soviet Union issued its famous rebuke to the Japan Communist party and its leader Nosaka Sanzō, attacking the moderate policies followed by the party in its relationship with SCAP. The Japan Communist party hesitantly accepted the criticism as valid and initiated a militant policy of internal violence, training cadres of young Communists that attacked police stations with bombs. SCAP retaliated by cracking down on the Japan Communist party, forcing it underground. At a time when South Korea was nearly overrun with North Korean Communist armies, SCAP found itself harassed by Communist militants within Japan, the forward supply and marshaling base for the Korean War.

The American Occupation and the Japanese government then resorted to a unique measure to meet the internal Communist threat by approving a new National Police Reserve of 75,000 men to maintain peace and order and to guarantee public welfare. Heavily financed and technically advised by SCAP, the National Police Reserve called upon 800 experienced

World War II officers of the Japanese imperial army to fill the officers' ranks and train the new recruits. The initial recruitment produced 203,000 applicants.[54] Leftists considered the National Police Reserve to be the first step toward the rearmament of Japan.

Then, in September 1950, the Second United States Education Mission to Japan arrived to evaluate the results of the first mission's recommendations made in 1946. Five members who had served on the first mission returned. The second mission's report had little impact on Japanese education since it merely praised the steady progress made by the earlier American reforms, though calling for more funds for education. Its notch in history, however, was achieved through a simple statement deep within the text of its report: "One of the greatest weapons against communism in the Far East is an enlightened electorate in Japan."[55]

Opposition forces branded SCAP's policy for Japan as imperialistic exploitation of the nation asserting that Japan was being used as an Asian bulwark against communism, thus providing America with its farthest Pacific outpost in the struggle against international communism. Nikkyōso interpreted the Second United States Education Mission's controversial statement concerning an enlightened electorate as an attempt by the Americans to mold the Japanese people to serve America's interests.[56] When the initial negotiations began for a treaty to terminate the American Occupation of Japan, leftists became alarmed that SCAP would harness Japan with a treaty that would bind the nation to America militarily.

At its seventh national convention, convened in May 1950, Nikkyōso reflected the national and international political currents, indicating that a new direction was imminent. Oka Saburō, a Socialist from Osaka, succeeded the first Nikkyōso president, Araki Shōzaburō, who was elected in 1950 to the Upper House, along with Secretary General Ogasawara Fumio and six other Nikkyōso candidates.[57] Under the military threat prevailing in 1950, with the Korean War at Japan's southern doorstep, and the probability of a peace treaty in which American military forces would remain on Japanese soil after independence, the issue of peace became for the first time a major concern of Nikkyōso.[58]

The convention of 1950 thus marks an important turning point in the development of the left-wing Japanese teachers' movement. Since the end of the war, Nikkyōso's struggles had been focused on teachers' salaries and teachers' rights and on the reform of Japanese education through the implementation of the School Education Law and the Fundamental Law of Education. Moreover, the major emphasis of the organized teachers' movement until then had been primarily on national affairs. But as Japan became deeply enmeshed in the international currents of the cold war, the teachers' movement rearranged its priorities accordingly. In response to the concern for peace in 1950, the union expanded its activities into the international realm as well. A new era in the development of Nikkyōso was imminent.

NOTES

1. Supreme Commander for the Allied Powers (SCAP), *A History of Teachers' Unions in Japan,* Tōkyō, March, 1948, p. 54.
2. Mochizuki Muneaki, *Nikkyōso Nijūnen no Tatakai* (Twenty-Year Struggle of the Japan Teachers Union (Tōkyō: Rōdō Junpōsha, 1967), p. 50.
3. Nikkyōso (Japan Teachers Union), *Nikkyōso Jūnenshi* (Ten-Year History of the Japan Teachers Union) (Tōkyō: Nikkyōso, 1958), pp. 48–50.
4. Correspondence with Mochizuki Muneaki, Nikkyōso historian, Tōkyō, December 28, 1968.
5. Interview with Mochizuki Muneaki, Tōkyō, June 1, 1968.
6. SCAP, *Summation of the Non-Military Activities in Japan and Korea,* Tōkyō, February, 1948, p. 191.
7. Miriam S. Farley, *Aspects of Japan's Labor Problems* (New York: John Day Co., 1950), pp. 137–138.
8. *Nippon Times,* July 24, 1948.
9. Ibid.
10. Ibid.
11. Mombu Hōrei Kenkyūkai (Educational Law Research Association), *Shin Kyōiku Roppō* (Revised Edition of the Fundamental Education Laws) (Tōkyō: Daiichi Hōki Shuppansha, 1969), p. 924.
12. Nikkyōso, *Nikkyōso Jūnenshi,* p. 120.
13. Foreign Affairs Association of Japan, *Contemporary Japan* 17 (1948):34.
14. Farley, *Japan's Labor Problems,* pp. 191–192.
15. *Report of the [First] United States Education Mission to Japan, Tōkyō, March 30, 1946* (Washington: Government Printing Office, 1946), pp. 28–29.
16. Press conference statement by Mark Orr, chief of SCAP's Education Division, Civil Information and Education Section, Tōkyō, September 9, 1948.
17. Japanese Educational Council, Report of the Council, *Educational Reform in Japan,* Tōkyō, 1950, p. 20.
18. Hidaka Daishirō, "The Aftermath of Educational Reform," *The Annals of the American Academy of Political and Social Sciences* 308 (1956):147.
19. Interview with Mochizuki Muneaki, June 1, 1968.
20. *Nippon Times,* September 18, 1948.
21. Ibid., October 8, 1948.
22. Nikkyōso, *Nikkyōso Nijūnenshi* (Twenty-Year History of the Japan Teachers Union) (Tōkyō: Rōdō Junpōsha, 1967), p. 100.
23. Farley, *Japan's Labor Problems,* p. 10.
24. *Nippon Times,* December 21, 1948.

25. Robert A. Fearey, *The Occupation of Japan, Second Phase: 1948–50* (New York: Macmillan Co., 1950), p. 129.
26. Mochizuki, *Nikkyōso Nijūnen*, pp. 62–63.
27. SCAP, *History of the Non-Military Activities of the Occupation of Japan* (Tōkyō: SCAP, 1949), 11:128.
28. Fearey, *Occupation of Japan*, p. 38.
29. Nikkyōso, *Kyōiku Shimbun* (Education Newspaper), April 18, 1949.
30. *Nippon Times*, November 2, 1949.
31. Robert A. Scalapino, *The Japanese Communist Movement, 1920–1966* (Berkeley: University of California Press, 1967), p. 67.
32. Evelyn S. Colbert, *The Left Wing in Japanese Politics* (New York: Institute of Pacific Affairs, 1952), pp. 283–284.
33. SCAP, *History of Non-Military Activities*, 11:120.
34. Nikkyōso, *Nikkyōso Nijūnenshi*, p. 102.
35. *Asahi Shimbun*, February 5, 1949.
36. Interview with the Honorable Iwama Masao, Japan Communist party representative, Tōkyō, August 5, 1968.
37. Interview with Mochizuki Muneaki, Tōkyō, June 1, 1968.
38. *Nippon Times*, July 26, 1949.
39. Interview with Kojima Gunzō, former superintendent of Gumma Prefecture, 1948–1952; Tōkyō, June 1, 1968; and with Sagara Iichi, former secretary to the Ministry of Education, 1946–1949; Kyōto, July 29, 1968.
40. Fearey, *Occupation of Japan*, p. 58.
41. Nikkyōso, *Nikkyōso Nijūnenshi*, p. 179.
42. Hans Baerwald, *The Purge of Japanese Leaders under the Occupation* (Berkeley: University of California Press, 1959), p. 77.
43. Munakata Seiya, *Nihon no Kyōiku* (Japanese Education) (Tōkyō: Iwanami Shoten, 1967), p. 6.
44. Nikkyōso, *Nikkyōso Nijūnenshi*, p. 129.
45. Baerwald, *The Purge*, p. 79.
46. Walter Eells, *Communism in Education in Asia, Africa, and the Far Pacific* (Washington, D.C.: American Council on Education, 1954), p. 29.
47. Interview with Sagara Iichi, Kyōto, July 29, 1968.
48. Colbert, *The Left Wing*, p. 206.
49. Allan Cole, *Socialist Parties in Postwar Japan* (New Haven: Yale University Press, 1966), p. 32.
50. *Asahi Shimbun*, May 4, 1950.
51. Mombu Hōrei Kenyūkai, *Shin Kyōiku Roppō*, p. 863.
52. Ibid., pp. 871–903.
53. Nikkyōso, *Nikkyōso Nijūnenshi*, pp. 155–158.
54. *Nippon Times*, August 10, 1950.
55. *Report of the Second United States Mission to Japan*, Tōkyō, September 1950.
56. Nikkyōso, *Nikkyōso News*, November 15, 1962.
57. Nikkyōso, *Kyōiku Shimbun*, May 18, 1950.
58. Nikkyōso, *Nikkyōso Nijūnenshi*, pp. 141, 169, 290.

5

Obsession with
Ideology (1951–1956)

Government Revisions and a
Reemergence of the Radical Left

The priorities of Nikkyōso were undergoing a definite transition by late 1950 and early 1951. In addition to the international influences, several crucial domestic factors also influenced the union to move in a new direction. First of all, the terrible depression years were finally over. The Japanese economy was gaining momentum. The war in neighboring Korea brought in substantial sums of foreign currency for military spending in support of American forces engaged in the conflict. Factories were beginning to hum again, supplied with new equipment through American aid, replacing that destroyed during the Pacific war. A boom was expected. Labor strikes were no longer a constant national concern. Food shortages were over. A new atmosphere was replacing that of a defeated nation. Japan was moving forward again.

Teachers' salaries, although still low, no longer constituted the overriding concern of the individual teacher, for they had been increased to a level comparable to those of other government employees and thus were now tolerable. The *Asahi Shimbun* reported in March 1951 that the average monthly salary of elementary school teachers was 7,027 yen; that of high school teachers, 9,160 yen; and that of industrial workers, 9,133 yen.[1]

The postwar educational reforms were essentially in effect by 1951. The new educational system, including the six-year elementary school, the three-year lower secondary school, and the three-year upper secondary school, followed by a four-year university, was in operation. Elected school boards at the prefectural level and in the five large cities, to be automatically extended to the remaining cities, towns, and villages in 1952, were making certain educational decisions, a function that was previously the prerogative of the Ministry of Education. Morals education was proscribed from the curriculum. The struggles concerning the implementation of the initial postwar educational reforms were almost at an end, as were the struggles for a living wage.

Nikkyōso, by early 1951, had substantially realigned its priorities away from the original ones of economics and education to meet the exigencies of the rapidly changing conditions. For example, at the beginning of January, U. S. Secretary of State John Foster Dulles arrived in Japan to discuss a peace treaty with the Japanese government. He offered Japan a military defense alliance with the United States. More than six thousand teachers purged as rightists in 1946 and 1947 were "depurged" in May 1951. More than 20,000 former military men were also "depurged" shortly thereafter; from these 20,000 men were recruited 800 former military officers to become officers in the new 75,000-man police reserve.[2] Simultaneously, at the fifth national party conference of the Japan Communist party, a decision was made to follow a militant policy, sparking acts of violence and government suppression, as the Japan Communist party was once again purged of all its leaders by SCAP. Police entered university campuses and sought Communist student instigators threatening university autonomy.

It is within this context that Nikkyōso shifted its emphasis from economics and education to politics and education. Faced with the threat of rearmament of Japan and with the conservative policies of the Japanese government, as the ruling party inevitably reacted to the sweeping educational reforms enacted during the American Occupation, Nikkyōso leaders became obsessed with a movement for peace and peace education. Nikkyōso's new orientation became official policy at its national convention held in May 1951, which adopted the following Four Principles of Peace as the union's fundamental platform: (1) total peace—Nikkyōso objected to the San Francisco Peace Treaty Conference, scheduled for September and boycotted by the Soviet Union, China, and North Korea; (2) complete neutrality of Japan—Japan should have no special relationship with any country; (3) opposition to military bases in Japan, referring to the planned continuation of American military bases on Japanese soil after the signing of the peace treaty; (4) opposition to rearmament— Nikkyōso reacted to the new police reserve force of 75,000 men and to a threat to revise the Constitution to permit Japan to have an army.[3] The

Four Principles of Peace were to be reaffirmed at each successive convention.

At the same convention, Nikkyōso adopted a slogan that has been repeated at each successive convention. "Never send our students to the battlefield again" perpetually reminded delegates of the role of wartime teachers who zealously prepared their students to fight courageously and die for the honor of the Japanese empire. Since a significant number of teachers who had been involved in this indoctrination process had latent feelings of guilt, Nikkyōso's peace movement during the Korean War appealed to many, especially those who were becoming less interested in economic issues than in the political issues of the day. In the process, the foundation was being laid for a long series of events that took place between 1951 and 1956, during which time Nikkyōso and the Ministry of Education gradually polarized their positions until they reached an inevitable confrontation.

The strained relationship between the Ministry and Nikkyōso worsened with the signing of the San Francisco Peace Treaty on September 8, 1951; this treaty set the terminating date of the American Occupation of Japan for April 28, 1952. The Americans had carried out their mandate to demilitarize and democratize Japanese society and education to the best of their ability and were ready to withdraw the machinery of the Occupation government. However, because the Korean War was still being fought and because the Chinese Communists were supporting North Korean Communists with massive ground forces, the Americans qualified their withdrawal from Japan: they positioned a string of military bases throughout the land to defend Japan against external aggression—that is, the threat of communism—as provided in the United States–Japan Security Pact, which took effect the same day as the Peace Treaty.

With the near termination of the American Occupation in 1951, the Japanese government under conservative Prime Minister Yoshida Shigeru, a stout anti-Communist, began to originate policies for Japan independently of foreign control. The initiative came from the successor to General MacArthur, General Matthew Ridgeway, the new Supreme Commander for the Allied Powers. He suggested on May 1 that the Japanese government should officially evaluate American Occupation reforms. SCAP felt that the time had arrived for the Japanese to determine for themselves which Occupation reforms were essential and which ones should be revised, in an atmosphere free from the fear of censorship should there be criticism of the Occupation. This was the first time since the end of the war that the Japanese enjoyed this immunity. The purpose of the suggestion was to smooth the transition from occupation to independence.

Responding to General Ridgeway's invitation, the Japanese government, in mid-May 1951, appointed the Committee for the Examination of Occupation Reform Policy (Seirei Kaisei Shimon Iinkai) to evaluate the American Occupation reforms in all sectors of society, including education. The committee consisted of Ishizaka Taizō, president of Tōshiba Electrical Manufacturing Company and the most influential businessman in postwar Japan; Itakura Takuzō, chairman of the Board of Directors of the Jiji Shimpō Newspaper Company; Obama Ritoku, adviser to the *Nihon Keizai Shimbun* (Japan Economic Newspaper); Hara Yasaburō, president of Nihon Kayaku Company (Japan Chemicals); Kimura Atsutarō, former minister of justice; Maeda Tamon, former minister of education; and Nakayama Ichirō, president of Hitotsubashi University.[5]

A statement in the introduction to the committee's report of July 1951, concerning the revision of the education system, laid the framework for ensuing Japanese reforms of the American Occupation education reforms:

> The reforms of education after World War II significantly revised the old education system and promoted a democratic system. These revisions, however, were patterned after foreign systems of education, disregarding differences in fundamental characteristics among countries. Accordingly, the occupation reforms must be examined in order to establish a rational education system which meets the prevailing needs of Japan based upon present conditions and characteristics of the nation.[6]

The report made the following recommendations:

1. The 6–3–3–4 system should be maintained in principle but more flexibility must be provided to meet the needs of the country. Increased provisions for vocational education should be introduced by dividing each level of schooling at the lower and upper secondary schools and the universities into two separate types of institutions, general and vocational.
2. A five-year vocational secondary school should be established including three years of lower secondary and two years of upper secondary school, and/or a five- or six-year vocational college of three years upper secondary school and a two- or three-year college course.
3. The course of study should not be uniform but must be revised for general schools and technical schools.
4. The government should prepare the textbooks.

5. Every prefecture and each city with a population over 150,000 should maintain a school board of three members to supervise local education, appointed by the head of the local government with consent of the assembly.

6. The Minister of Education should be made responsible for educational matters.

7. A Central Advisory Council should be appointed to advise the Minister of Education in the conduct of Japanese education.[7]

The recommendations were accepted by the government as recommendations only. They were important because they represented the first official recommendations by the Japanese government to reform the American Occupation reforms of Japanese education. Throughout the decade of the 1950s, the Japanese government carried out nearly every one of the committee's proposals, a policy that became a major factor underlying the growing antagonism between the Ministry of Education and Nikkyōso. To the Japanese left wing, it symbolized the "reverse course" of the Japanese government.

While the special committee was making its recommendations to reform the American Occupation reforms, the last of the postwar scholar-ministers of education, Amano Teiyū, became the center of a very serious controversy concerning morals education. Amano, a distinguished Kantian scholar, was attacked for having recommended the reintroduction of morals education into the curriculum, with the emperor as the "center," setting off a major reaction throughout the leftist camp. In personal correspondence, Amano explained the controversy as follows:

> It is true that I favored the reintroduction of morals education. My position was based on the understanding that the purpose of education is to develop human beings. The core of humanity is morality. So it goes without saying that morals education is essential. And in Japan, in particular, where most people are atheistic, morals education is even more important. That is why I urged the reintroduction of morals education into the curriculum.
>
> But it is not true that I advocated the Emperor as the center of morals. This misunderstanding was caused when I replied to the question, "Is there any center for the Japanese people?" (*Nihon kokumin ni chūshin ga aru ka?*) at a plenary session of the House of Councillors. I answered that the Emperor was an integral part of morals (*dōtokuteki chūshin*) meaning that he was no longer the political or authoritative center. The reporters wrote that I said the Emperor should be the center of morals (*dōtoku no chūshin*). I never said that.[8]

The semantic problem did not blur the fact that the government was contemplating the reintroduction of morals education which had been banned by the American Occupation in 1945 as a course that could be used to inculcate militaristic and ultranationalistic ideology. In reaction to Minister Amano's policy on morals education and to the special report by the government's select committee to reform the Occupation reforms, Nikkyōso countered with the following position paper entitled Principles for Japanese Education:

1. The present 6–3–3–4 system should be maintained.
2. The revival of morals education should be opposed.
3. A common curriculum should be continued through the elementary and lower secondary school. Vocational education should be strengthened in regular upper secondary schools only to meet the needs of nonmilitary industry.
4. Members of a Central Advisory Council on Education should be elected at large to reflect the will of the public.
5. Elected boards of education should be established only at the prefectural level and in the five largest cities.
6. Admission tests to upper secondary schools should be abolished and all who desire to enter must be accepted.
7. Textbook screening should be entrusted to the prefectural boards of education, not the Ministry of Education.
8. Eighty percent of compulsory school education expenses and 100 percent of kindergarten and upper secondary school expenses should be borne by the national treasury.[9]

As it became manifest by 1951 that the government was planning significant changes in educational policy, even though the outburst of criticism against Amano's plan to reintroduce morals education forced the Ministry of Education to delay action, the extreme left-wing faction within Nikkyōso, which had been sharply reduced but not eliminated during the Red Purge of 1949–1950, reasserted itself. Its first opportunity came unexpectedly when Nikkyōso, at its convention at Kinosaki in May 1951, decided to join the World Confederation of Organizations of the Teaching Profession (WCOTP). Shortly thereafter, WCOTP invited its member organizations to prepare a teacher's code of ethics for consideration at its 1951 convention, to be held on Malta. Nikkyōso accepted the invitation and asked four scholars sympathetic to the union's activities to prepare an initial draft of the code. The four chosen were Miyahara Seiichi, associate professor at Tōkyō University, and Katsuta Morikazu, professor at Gakushūin University, both left-wing activists in the prewar Kyōkaken movement; Sugo Hiroshi, professor at Ochanomizu University;

and Yanagida Kenjūrō, formerly from Kyōto University. Several others were consulted later.[10]

According to Miyahara, this group of scholars accepted Nikkyōso's request on the condition that the code would be used not merely for the WCOTP Convention but would also be presented to Nikkyōso's next national convention as the way of life for the Japanese teacher. Upon Nikkyōso's acceptance of these terms, the scholars devoted their attention primarily to two problems: the "increasingly reactionary policies of the government since the beginning of the Korean War, and the gap between the ideological position of Nikkyōso leaders and [that of] the rank-and-file membership.[11]

The problem of the hiatus in the political sentiment between Nik-kyōso's leaders and its rank and file had plagued the union executive ever since the founding of Nikkyōso. Miyahara commented on this rift as follows:

> One of the major defects of the Union at the beginning was that it was organized primarily at the top by individuals who were politically oriented, rather than from below by the rank and file. Before the Union leaders could instill into the membership the necessary political awareness, that is, that they are educational laborers (*kyōiku rōdōsha*), the government conducted the Red Purge of local leaders and initiated its reactionary policies. Consequently, the politically aware Union leaders decided to utilize this opportunity in preparing a code of ethics to promulgate the concept that teachers are laborers throughout the entire teaching corps. This was the background of the Code of Ethics.[12]

The Code of Ethics drawn up by the four scholars contained a short introduction and ten brief articles with explanations. Nikkyōso declared in a lengthy foreword to the code that:

> Conservatives and reactionaries are discussing the reform of the present system of education. Needless to say, the Union and working people are opposed to such a reactionary tendency. It becomes necessary to suppress the teachers if the reactionary forces want to enforce their plans. Nevertheless, we must defend freedom of learning, thought, and education against this dishonest tendency and secure peace and prosperity for our younger generation by guarding the nation against the risk of war. For this we need to have a definite outlook on life and on scientific views of society, and a righteous moral doctrine. . . . Such terms as "holy profession" . . . impede our progress as modern citizens. An outmoded Confucian creed of life still remains as a motto observed by teachers. So long as we adhere consciously or unconsciously to the old morality and ways of thought, we cannot "revolutionize ourselves" if we wish to fulfill our mission. Therefore,

we have drawn up this Code of Ethics to lay the foundation for teachers' actions.[13]

The code's ten articles are:

1. Teachers shall work with the youth of the country in fulfilling the tasks of society.
2. Teachers shall fight for equal opportunities in education.
3. Teachers shall protect peace.
4. Teachers shall act on behalf of scientific truth.
5. Teachers shall allow no infringement on freedom in education.
6. Teachers shall seek after proper government.
7. Teachers shall fight side by side with parents against corruption in society and shall create a new culture.
8. Teachers are laborers.
9. Teachers shall defend their right to maintain a minimum standard of living.
10. Teachers shall unite.[14]

The article that received major attention was the eighth, which stated that teachers are laborers or educational workers (*kyōiku rōdōsha*). The history of this concept in Japan is interesting. It extends back to the proletariat organization of the thirties called the Nihon Kyōiku Rōdō Kumiai (Japan Educational Laborers Union), an illegal left-wing group under Communist influence. After the war, when the organizing unions were seeking rank-and-file support, even the most radical Zenkyō hesitated to use the term *educational laborer* or *labor union* (*rōdō kumiai*) as part of its name, although the leaders employed the concept in their speeches ad infinitum, because of the feeling that the average teacher did not yet approve of the political implications.

The first time that the leadership of a teachers' union felt secure enough to include in its name the term *labor union* was in May 1946, when the radical Zenkyō changed its name to Zen Nihon Kyōiku Rōdō Kumiai (All Japan Educational Labor Union), better known as Zenkyōrō. As the left-wing Zenkyōrō attempted to broaden its membership in order to appeal to a wider clientele, it changed its name again— to Zenkyōso, omitting the word *labor* (*rōdō*). Finally, in June 1947, the several unions merged into the one great union, and the omission of the term *labor union* from the name was conspicuous when the simple designation Nihon Kyōshokuin Kumiai (Japan Teachers Union) was selected by the moderate faction then in control.

Four years later, when Nikkyōso's famous Code of Ethics for teachers was prepared, the leadership capitalized on the opportunity to declare officially that teachers are educational laborers, in contrast to the prewar ideal concept of teaching as a heavenly mission. Leaders of the union had been proclaiming this ideologically left-wing concept for years, but the specific clause had never been included in any of its declarations. Hence, Nikkyōso's open identification with it in the Code of Ethics did not come as a surprise to pro-Nikkyōso people. But those opposed to the union pounced upon it as indicative of the unprofessional persuasion of Nikkyōso and of the ideological proclivities of its leaders. Article 8 thus became a symbol of the dispute between the union and the Ministry of Education, which claimed that teaching was a "profession" and that teachers must act accordingly.

During the code-of-ethics controversy, Nikkyōso held its first annual National Education Research Convention (Kyōiku Kenkyū Zenkoku Taikai), in November 1951 at Nikkō. The theme of the meeting was education for peace under the slogan, "Never send our students to the battlefield again," consistent with the union's major emphasis at that time. This convention, with three thousand teachers in attendance, many of whom presented papers before section meetings, resembled a labor union convention rather than an educators' convention, because regular activists present dwelt on topics remote from the day-to-day activities of the classroom teachers.

The research meetings were developed by the union into annual events, eventually attended by about ten thousand teachers, where full emphasis was placed on topics directly related to education. The regular Nikkyōso convention was then free to give full attention to union matters, which happened to be concentrated on political issues of the day. In effect, the union was sustaining interest on two fronts. The union also established the tradition of inviting a group of twenty to thirty scholars sympathetic to Nikkyōso, called Kōshidan, to serve in an advisory capacity for the education research conventions. This lent a certain degree of academic respectability to Nikkyōso's entire movement.[15]

At the regular national convention at Niigata City, in June 1952, Nikkyōso approved the Code of Ethics and firmly established its new orientation, moving more to the left under the slogan, "Fighting Nikkyōso." It was at this convention that the union adopted its inflexible attitude against a revision of the Constitution to permit rearmament, the presence of any American military bases in Japan, extension of school boards below the prefectural level, and revision of the school-board law. A program of demonstrations, hunger strikes, and sit-ins was planned to support the campaign. By advocating the overthrow of the Japanese government's dictatorship and the establishment of a government for the workers, this convention got Nikkyōso more deeply involved in political controversy.

The American Occupation of Japan came to an end on April 28, 1952, after a total of six years, eight months, and fourteen days. The victorious American army had entered Japan in 1945 amidst a calm but tense atmosphere following the collapse of the Japanese military government. They departed more than six years later, leaving a nation run by a democratically elected government but in the throes of internal agitation and violence. The degree of violence and the number of strikes and demonstrations had turned upward beginning in 1951, ironically coinciding with general economic improvements. The culmination came on Bloody May Day, in 1952, four days after the Occupation ended. Nevertheless, the Americans considered their interlude in Japan successful, trusting that democratic roots had been planted sufficiently deep so that dissent could be expressed without destroying the democratic forms of society and government.

One of the very first episodes between the government and Japanese labor during the transition period from Occupation to independence concerned the Subversives Activities Prevention Law (Hakai Katsudō Bōshi Hō), a bill to replace the American Occupation's Organizations Control Ordinance, originally aimed at controlling Communist violence. Sōhyō, the new moderate General Council of Trade Unions, which was originated in 1950 to offset Communist hegemony of the labor union movement, led the opposition to this bill. The government claimed that the purpose of the bill was to "prescribe necessary actions to control organizations which shall have carried on any terroristic subversive activities, thereby contributing to the securing of public safety."[16] Sōhyō, heavily influenced by Nikkyōso, interpreted the bill as an attempt to "revive the old detested Peace Preservation Laws which suppressed all democratic activities in prewar Japan."[17]

Two people were killed and dozens wounded in the Bloody May Day demonstrations of 1952, as police fired on thousands of angry demonstrators surging around the Imperial Palace Plaza in Tōkyō, overturning and burning cars. Coming only several days after Japan achieved independence, this incident prompted the government to press for the bill's enactment. At the very time of the debate, there were riots all over the country, led by left-wing protestors against the United States–Japan

Security Pact and the American military bases in Japan. Police were entering university campuses, searching for leaders of Zengakuren, the left-wing student association, thus thrusting campus autonomy as an additional issue into the controversy over the bill. Nevertheless, the Subversive Activities Prevention Law was finally pushed through the Upper House on July 3, 1952.

Hostility between the government and the labor movement over this episode resulted in a hardening of attitudes by Sōhyō and its intellectual leaders from Nikkyōso, quickly turning Sōhyō's orientation from an anti-Communist organization, its original purpose, into a left-wing antigovernment labor council. At the same time, the government called for the first general elections since independence for October, three months after the controversial Subversive Activities Prevention Law was passed. The two conservative parties won a resounding victory, with a combined total of nearly 70 percent of the seats, while the Communist party, which was generally blamed for the violence, lost all of the 22 seats it previously had held in the Diet.[18]

The first major direct confrontation between Nikkyōso and the Ministry of Education after independence involved the 1952 school-board elections. The original plan in 1948 was to extend gradually the school-board system from the level of prefectures and large cities down to the village level; such an extension meant an increase of nearly ten thousand boards. Nikkyōso, which initially supported this plan in 1948, opposed it just prior to the school-board elections in 1952 because the leaders concluded that the local conservative establishment would monopolize the boards. The Ministry of Education had opposed the extension in 1948 as representing a much too rapid decentralization of education.

The school-board extension to the local level had developed into a highly controversial issue by 1951. Nikkyōso, supported by the Socialist party, much of the press, and even some government officials, opposed the plan, which was scheduled to go into effect automatically based on previous legislation. During the union's ninth national convention in May 1952, at Niigata, a resolution was passed opposing school boards below the prefectural level.

Meanwhile, the Yoshida government pressed forward with the original plan, presumably, according to Permanent Vice-Minister of Education Hidaka Daishirō, "as a countermove against the Japan Teachers Union, believing that conservatives would dominate the new local boards and thus check the influence of the Union in the prefectural boards of education."[19] The Ministry of Education was particularly anxious to have local conservative forces control local appointments of teachers, thereby reducing the power of prefectural boards of education where Nikkyōso was notably successful in the 1950 school-board elections. The union assessed the extension of school boards to the local level in exactly the same way as did the government, that is, as a means to restrict union influence, much to the consternation of the Americans who had placed great faith in the boards to democratize Japanese education.

Nikkyōso conducted daily demonstrations in front of the Diet building when a bill to postpone the school-board expansion was under consideration. But the government elected to delay the vote until the next session of the Diet. During the interval, Minister of Education Amano Teiyū resigned on August 12, 1952, terminating the postwar tradition of having a succession of scholar-ministers. His successor, Okano Kiyotake, former president of Sanwa Bank, was appointed on August 26, just two days before Prime Minister Yoshida dissolved the Diet for new elections. The bill to postpone the extension of school boards to the local level was consequently not brought before the Diet. This turn of events opened the way for earlier legislation authorizing local school boards to take effect automatically. The nationwide school-board elections, involving 80 additional cities and 9,600 towns and villages, was set for October 5, 1952.

Let us go back two years to trace the development of the matter of school boards. The government's favorable attitude toward the principle of local school boards, where conservative forces could be a dominant factor, can be explained by an overall review of Nikkyōso's political successes. For example, in the 1950 prefectural school-board elections, Nikkyōso won a total of 66 seats,[20] a rather remarkable feat coming as it did during the Red Purge, when Nikkyōso was under attack for its left-wing activities. In the 1950 House of Councillors election, 8 Nikkyōso members made successful bids. Nikkyōso was also instrumental in electing 10 of the 46 governors and 150 candidates to the assemblies, including 84 union members in the 1951 prefectural elections.[21]

To promote Nikkyōso's political campaigns and to separate the union legally from a political organization, it formed the Nihon Kyōshokuin Seiji Renmei (Japan Teachers Political League), in April 1951, to manage its political campaigns. In July 1952, the organization was strengthened when the name was changed to Nihon Minshū Seiji Renmei (Japan

Democratic Education Political League), known as Nisseiren, and the first Nikkyōso chairman, Araki Shōzaburō, was appointed head of the organization.[22]

Nisseiren, with a branch located at each level of Nikkyōso's organization, managed the union's political campaigns from 1952. Its success in the 1952 general elections was pronounced. Eight of 15 candidates for the Upper House and 38 candidates for the Lower House, supported by Nisseiren and others sympathetic to Nikkyōso's policies, were elected, constituting a bloc of 46 representatives, all related to Nikkyōso in the nation's supreme legislative organ.[23] From the very beginning, only Socialists were endorsed. The growing success of the union at the polls, in part as a result of the zealous efforts by activist teachers to win the votes of parents of their students, caused much anguish in the ranks of the ruling conservative party of the government.

The school-board controversy was intensified when the government appointed Okano to replace Amano on August 12, 1952; Okano was the first postwar politician to assume the position of minister of education, breaking the tradition of having scholars as ministers of education. The contention between Nikkyōso and the Ministry of Education over this appointment became a major issue in the Japanese educational world for the next decade.

The government's position concerning Okano's controversial appointment was summed up years later by the then permanent vice-minister of education, the Honorable Naitō Takasaburō. He explained that, since education is part of the ruling party's overall responsibility to the nation, it was essential that a party man be responsible for carrying out the party's educational policy—not a scholar-minister who was unrelated to political parties—and that the minister should also be influential within the party in order to win approval of his policies. In addition, he should be capable of presenting effectively and forcefully the party's policies to the public. To support his point, Naitō mentioned Prime Minister Yoshida, who at first approved of scholar-ministers but very shortly came to realize that without a political base they were powerless within the party as well as before the public. For this reason, all ministers of education from Minister Okano on were selected from the ranks of party politicians.[24]

Such justifications notwithstanding, Nikkyōso escalated its campaign against the government, charging the conservative party with subverting education into the arena of partisan politics. The Communist group within Nikkyōso capitalized on these developments to exert gradually increasing influence. Even though Nikkyōso was administered during the transition from Occupation to independence by a moderate chairman, Oka Saburō, who, in his own words, "constantly strove to keep our movement away from Communist influence,"[25] the extreme left-wing faction strengthened its position within the union as the government escalated its opposition to Nikkyōso.

Minister Okano, the first minister of education to brand Nikkyōso as an enemy of the Ministry of Education, immediately plunged into the conflict by supporting the expansion of school boards to the local level and by proposing a plan in September 1952 to differentiate teachers' salaries according to three levels of schooling. Salaries of compulsory school teachers, that is, teachers of students up to and including the ninth grade, were to be set at a lower level than salaries of teachers of upper secondary school students. University teachers were to be paid at the highest level.

The announcement about salaries exacerbated a smoldering antagonism within Nikkyōso between the vast majority of compulsory school teachers and the minority of upper secondary school teachers, which had its beginning in August 1950 when the upper secondary school teachers from Hokkaidō, Akita, Yamanashi, and Iwate prefectures formed a splinter group in March 1951—the moderate Zen Nihon Kōtōgakkō Kyōshokuin Kumiai (Japan High School Teachers Union) called Zenkōkyō. The issue first revolved around the priorities of Nikkyōso, which emphasized economic demands primarily of compulsory school teachers to the neglect of those of the upper secondary school teachers, who came from the old prestigious upper middle schools. Nikkyōso's policy to unify all teachers into one body failed to distinguish the special role the old upper secondary schools and their teachers had played in prewar Japan.

Despite ill feelings, Zenkōkyō maintained formal contact with Nikkyōso through its left-wing faction. But the ministry's plan to differentiate teachers' salaries struck a sensitive chord in the already deteriorating relationship between Zenkōkyō and Nikkyōso. A moderate faction within Zenkōkyō shortly thereafter opposed maintaining any contacts with Nikkyōso, eventually splitting it into two separate hostile divisions. In 1952 Zenkōkyō approved Minister Okano's plan to establish a graduated salary system while Nikkyōso vehemently opposed it. Nikkyōso charged that the government was implementing a new salary scheme to divide the teachers' movement by appealing to Zenkōkyō and unaligned upper secondary school teachers in order to weaken Nikkyōso. When the new salary system went into effect in 1953, a total of twenty-five prefectural upper secondary school teachers' organizations, comprising a membership of about one-third of all the teachers at that level in Nikkyōso, split off from Nikkyōso to join Zenkōkyō. These teachers claimed that since their work was more specialized and they had more educational preparation than did the elementary and lower secondary school teachers, their salaries should be higher.[26]

Nikkyōso, finally accepting the inevitability of the school-board expansion, scheduled for October 1952, decided to coordinate sympathetic PTAs and other related organizations into a campaign to capture as many seats as possible in the elections so that "reactionaries cannot control the new boards."[27] Based on their success in the 1950 elections, the leaders realized that their best chance remained with prefectural boards of education. It was in the 1950 election that Nikkyōso candidates had won about one-third of the seats, provoking the Yoshida government to extend the school boards to the local level in the hope of curtailing Nikkyōso's strength at the prefectural level.

Nikkyōso's aim in 1952 was to gain as many seats as possible at the local level in an attempt to influence local school boards and local heads of government to entrust educational matters to the prefectural school boards where the union had significant representation and influence. The results of the 1952 school-board election further annoyed the government. Nikkyōso candidates won approximately 35 percent of the prefectural school-board seats,[28] including one seat out of five in Tōkyō,[29] and an estimated 30 percent at the local level.[30]

During the school-board controversy, the government was charged with a major revision of the Ministry of Education Establishment Law. Article 4 of the original law of 1949 stipulated that the Ministry of Education should be the administrative agency for providing professional and technical advice to boards of education, that it should prepare drafts of laws concerning minimum standards of education, and that it should prepare the budget for national funds for education.[31] On August 30, 1952, in addition to several internal administrative adjustments, Article 4 was changed to read that "the Ministry has the duty to promote school education, social education (adult), and culture, and assumes responsibility to carry out the administrative business concerning the above."[32] Nikkyōso attacked this revision as reactionary and reminiscent of prewar Japanese education. The revision in fact did not change the relationship between the Ministry of Education and the school boards, which could, and often did, ignore the wishes of the Ministry. In other words, the 1952 revision did not give the Ministry new compulsory powers as charged by Nikkyōso.

The years 1953 and 1954 can be looked upon as a period of rapid escalation in the struggles between the Ministry of Education and Nikkyōso, culminating in 1954 in the twin laws on the political neutrality of teachers. This controversy began with the appointment of the first Central Advisory Council on Education in January 1953, as provided for in the revision of the Ministry of Education Establishment Law of 1952. Nikkyōso took strong issue with several of the fifteen appointments, including Ishikawa Ichirō, president of the powerful Federation of Economic Organizations; Fujiyama Aichirō, president of the Japan Chamber of Commerce; and Moroi Kanichi, head of the Kantō Employers' Association.[33] The union claimed that the Central Advisory Council was biased, favoring Japanese capitalism. Nikkyōso also opposed the appointment to the council of Amano Teiyū, former minister of education, who was embroiled in the controversy over the return of morals education. The government argued that it had balanced the composition of the council with men like Dr. Yanaibara, distinguished president of Tōkyō University.[34]

Another matter that did not help the poor relationship between Nikkyōso and the Ministry was the Ministry's announcement on January 17, 1953, of the government's plan to alter the system of national subsidies for local teachers' salaries.[35] At that time, salaries originated equally from the national treasury and the prefectural treasury, although the Ministry of Education provided large subsidies to the prefectures through an equalization grant from the national treasury. Minister Okano drafted a bill providing that all teachers' salaries be paid from the national treasury, thereby changing the status of local civil servants to national civil servants; in effect, teachers were being returned to the status they had held prior to the 1950 Local Public Service Law. The Ministry of Finance objected to this bill on the grounds that it would place a heavy burden on the national budget. On the other hand, the National Association of Prefectural Governors supported it.

Naitō Takasaburō, then serving in the Ministry of Education as chief of the General Affairs Section, explained the reasoning behind Minister Okano's controversial proposal. He said that teachers in national schools were considered national public servants. As such, their political rights were severely restricted. In fact, the only political right national public servants enjoyed was the right to vote. The large majority of teachers, however, were local civil servants who could participate in political activities outside the district in which they were employed. Minister Okano's goal was to render all teachers national public servants (*kokka kōmuin*) by having their full salaries paid from the national treasury; teachers then would be subject to all political restrictions prescribed for national public servants.[36]

Nikkyōso planned massive demonstrations, including coordinated nationwide leave-taking for March 12, 1953, the final day for deliberating the teachers' salary bill in the Diet. Several days before that date, Prime Minister Yoshida, in a fit of exasperation over an unrelated issue, called a member from the opposition party a "stupid fool" (*bakayarō*) during a Diet session. A non-confidence motion was passed against Yoshida, then engaged in a struggle to retain the prime ministership; his position was threatened by former conservative leader Hatoyama Ichirō, who had been recently "depurged." Yoshida dissolved the session and called for new elections, upon which Nikkyōso called off the general strike. Nevertheless, 300 members of Nikkyōso began a hunger strike on March 11, and 15,000 teachers of the Tōkyō branch of the union walked out of their classrooms at 1 P.M. on March 12 to march in front of the Diet building to protest the pending bill.

In the general elections in April, Prime Minister Yoshida's party was returned to power but with a reduced margin due to the split with Hatoyama, while the number of successful Nikkyōso candidates dropped from 38 to 22.[37] The new cabinet, which decided not to bring the controversial salary plan before the Diet again, was installed on May 19. Among the new cabinet members was Odachi Shigeo, one of the most controversial ministers of education in postwar Japan.

Odachi, a former official of the prewar Ministry of Home Affairs (Naimushō), the most powerful segment of bureaucracy in pre-1945 Japan, controlling as it did local government, local education, and the national police, immediately came under attack for his wartime actions as mayor of Singapore during the infamous Japanese occupation of that city. Odachi was also accused of replacing with prewar Ministry of Home Affairs officials many Ministry of Education officials, who had been employed during the American Occupation to replace purged officials. In fact, it has been established that a number of officials resigned from the Ministry of Education around this period partly as a result of the moves to bring the Ministry under the control of the political party in power. But, according to the then chief of the General Affairs Section of the Ministry of Education, who also resigned in 1953, only two former Ministry of Home Affairs officials were brought in at this time, including Odachi's former assistant in Singapore and his permanent vice-minister of education. Most of the other replacements were former Ministry of Education officials who had been purged between 1946 and 1947 and "depurged" between 1950 and 1951.[38]

Odachi was now confronted with Kobayashi Takeshi, a quiet Socialist of moderate political persuasion, who was elected Nikkyōso chairman at the tenth national convention in Ujiyamada City. Kobayashi succeeded Oka Saburō, who was elected to the House of Councillors in the general elections of April 1953, in the tradition of the first Nikkyōso chairman, Araki Shōzaburō. In that election, Nikkyōso's candidates won a total of 9 seats in the Lower House and 13 in the Upper House, a marked reduction from the total of 46 in the previous election.[39]

The Nikkyōso convention at Ujiyamada revealed an open conflict between the left-wing and moderate factions within Nikkyōso. The radicals submitted several motions against the more moderate policies of the outgoing executive—Oka Saburō, chairman, and Miyanohara Sadamitsu, secretary general—protesting the moderates' relatively mild opposition to the Ministry of Education in recent campaigns. All non-confidence motions were defeated. However, the moderates' narrow margin of victory, less than two-thirds of the votes cast, provided new evidence that left-wing influence was growing, particularly as its leader, Hiragaki Miyoji, replaced Miyanohara as secretary general, balancing the moderate president, Kobayashi. The rivalry between Hiragaki and Miyanohara, which eventually shook Nikkyōso to its foundations, had its beginning in this election at Ujiyamada.

During the beginning of the new school year in April 1953, two events occurred which further revealed the growing strength of the leftist group within Nikkyōso in reaction to the government's attempt to curtail left-wing activities of teachers. Nikkyōso distributed a pamphlet at the beginning of the new semester in April entitled *To the New Teachers* (Atarashii Kyōin ni Natta Hitobito ni), in which the statement was made that 10 percent of the Japanese people were capitalists and that the remainder were poor. The imbalance was attributed to the prevailing social system. Nikkyōso then went on record as opposing Japanese capitalists and the ruling conservative party:

Because of the subservient relationship between the United States Government and the Japanese Government during the Occupation, the Japanese Government finds itself unable to break this dependency even after independence. A good example of this relationship is manifest in our government's agreement to produce military goods for the American–Korean War. The Japanese Government has become a death merchant. This policy is extremely dangerous.

In order to accomplish its policy, the government is attempting to restrict the freedom of the people by resorting to police force to suppress meetings, speeches and thought of those who understand the evils of the government's policies. Our government is deceiving the common people through newspapers and the mass media. In addition, the government is exploiting education to conceal this dangerous policy. We teachers who are members of the Union do not think the same way as Japanese capitalists. Accordingly we oppose the government from the standpoint of a class struggle.[40]

The government naturally took strong issue with the pamphlet. Shortly thereafter in 1953, before this controversy subsided, the *Yamaguchi Diary* case captured the nation's attention. The Yamaguchi Prefectural Teachers Union, a branch of Nikkyōso, had compiled and edited excerpts from students' summer compositions related to the union's peace education, a plank in the policy adopted at the Nikkyōso convention in 1952 in Niigata. The publications were in the form of workbooks with commentaries passed out to each elementary and secondary school student in Yamaguchi Prefecture at the beginning of the school year in April.

Several of the provocative passages from the workbooks are given in the following:

> Some Japanese compare the Soviet Union with a thief claiming that we must fasten our doors securely locking that country out in order to keep the thief away from the house. They argue that securing our doors is the same as rearmament. Is this really true? These people then spend more and more money buying a large lock on the front door but the burglars haven't yet come. While we concentrate on making the lock on the front door bigger and more secure, we left the back door wide open and a decent gentleman (the United States) came in wearing muddy shoes and took 806 valuables (American military installations in Japan) out of the house. But the Japanese people didn't even notice it. Now, who is really the thief?[41]

> North Korea and South Korea both wanted to unite their divided land into a unified Korean nation. Both governments wanted to become the head of the new government. Most people thought the workers' country, North Korea, was the better of the two but Syngman Rhee of South Korea did not agree. With American help, South Korea attacked North Korea

several times but was beaten back on each occasion. Finally, on June 25, 1950, North Korea chased South Korea deep into her own territory after the South had attacked the North. This is how the Korean War began.[42]

The first aim of socialism is to attain the happiness of laborers and farmers. It is diametrically opposite to capitalism. Capitalists who own the factories make their profits through exploiting laborers by paying them low salaries and paying low prices to farmers for their rice. Now, what is the difference between Russia, a socialist country, and Japan and the United States, capitalist countries?[43]

In June 1953, the Iwakuni Municipal Board of Education in Yamaguchi Prefecture banned the publications as "undesirable" on grounds that they were politically biased. The Yamaguchi Prefectural Board of Education supported the local board's decision and banned the publications throughout the prefecture. The Iwakuni Teachers Union immediately attacked the action by the prefectural board as suppression of Nikkyōso's peace-education policy. Nikkyōso was then in the midst of its tenth national convention. It was reported that the union's national leaders were unaware of the publications until the case came under public attack in Iwakuni.[44] Nevertheless, a resolution was quickly passed by the convention in support of the Iwakuni chapter. The school board's decision prevailed.

The tenth national convention revealed the extent to which Nikkyōso had become involved in political issues outside the field of education as the left-wing group inexorably strengthened its position. The convention concentrated on issues of Japanese rearmament, American imperialism, and American military bases in Japan. The *Iwakuni* incident fit neatly into the picture since Iwakuni was the site of an American air base under the provisions of the Japan–United States Security Pact. In addition to the decision to support the local Iwakuni teachers against the school board in the *Diary* case, the convention voted to launch a movement against all American bases in Japan and to sponsor the production of a film entitled *Hiroshima,* which turned out to be a controversial anti-American production.

The emphasis on political and ideological issues epitomized by the *Yamaguchi Diary* case proved to be costly for Nikkyōso. A large number of members withdrew from the Yamaguchi Prefectural Teachers Union, resulting in a reduction of membership from 10,000 to only 4,000, including the loss of many principals of elementary and lower secondary schools. A year later, those teachers who had rejected Nikkyōso formed a new union called the Prefectural Federation of Teachers, the first group of teachers to be formed in opposition to Nikkyōso since March 1951, when the upper secondary school teachers split off to form an independent organization. Similarly, smaller groups of teachers who had dropped out from the union, for example the 800 teachers from the Shimonoseki City branch, also formed independent local unions in opposition to the political activities of Nikkyōso.

The government became increasingly alarmed by the activities of left-wing teachers within Nikkyōso. At a press conference on August 30, Minister of Education Odachi expressed official concern, stating that if the government finds that political neutrality of education is being violated by teachers, countermeasures, including legislation, must be taken to maintain that neutrality.[45] A week later the government announced the preparation of legislation to prohibit political activities of teachers both in and out of the classroom. The proposed legislation for the preservation of political neutrality of education thus became the next major source of contention between Nikkyōso and the government.

Solidifying the government's determination to pass special legislation to curb the political activities of teachers was the *Asahigaoka* case, which received widespread publicity in late 1953 and early 1954.[46] On December 15, 1953, a delegation of parents from the Asahigaoka Lower Secondary School, Kyōto, submitted a formal complaint to the superintendent of education, charging that teachers were incorporating Communist-oriented material in their teachings. Specifically, they charged that mathematics and science teachers, during their regular classes, were opposing Japanese rearmament and the presence of American military bases in Japan by attacking the Peace Treaty, the Japan–United States Security Pact, and the Yoshida government. Teachers were accused of reading to their classes long passages from the *Akahata* (Red Flag), the Japan Communist party newspaper. The parents also charged that propaganda films emphasizing the atomic bombings of Hiroshima and Nagasaki were being shown at school. Children, it was claimed, were taught to sing the "Internationale."

The Asahigaoka area was a new middle-class suburb of Kyōto, where a number of white-collar workers, university professors, and intellectuals lived. Therefore, in the area there was a high proportion of families with progressive political views, to the extent that one of the local assemblymen had run successfully on the Communist party ticket. Supported by the Kyōto City branch of the Kyōto Prefectural Teachers Union, famous as one of the most militant organizations within the teachers' movement, the local progressive elite had united to make the Asahigaoka School a center for "peace education."

The Kyōto School Board of five members included two conservatives from the Yoshida party and two left-wing Socialists supported by Nik-kyōso. The fifth member, a conservative, was away on a grant in the United States at the time that the *Asahigaoka* case was first brought under review. The superintendent, also a conservative, was placed in a unique position since the board was deadlocked. The superintendent had already been involved in endless conflict on other matters with the powerful Kyōto City Teachers Union; the *Asahigaoka* case compounded his problems.

At the beginning of the new school year in April, the superintendent, acting within his prerogative, ordered that the three teachers who were leading the leftist campaign at the Asahigaoka Lower Secondary School be transferred to three other schools. This method of removing and dividing ringleaders was—and still is—a common method used by local education authorities in dealing with a hard core of leftist teachers in any school. In this case, the three teachers returned their orders to the superintendent's office and continued teaching at the Asahigaoka School. The superintendent, planning next to dismiss the three teachers, called the fifth school-board member home from America since it was necessary to get the full board's approval for outright dismissals. The case developed into a nationwide spectacle as both Nikkyōso and the Ministry of Education sent their representatives to Kyōto to investigate the case and support their respective sides.

On May 5, the full school board met and, predictably, in a vote of 3 to 2, approved the dismissals, which were in turn immediately rejected by the teachers. The superintendent officially closed the school. The three teachers and their supporters representing the majority of the faculty responded by raising red flags over the school and continuing to conduct classes. They confined the school principal to his office for the next two days amidst general confusion. Finally, at a mass meeting, the principal was forced to resign.

The superintendent then announced that classes would be held at a different location, and on May 11 temporary classes were begun in another building. Local public feelings ran very high as teachers and parents attempted to induce children to attend one of the two schools. On the first day 819 children were transported in twenty buses to the temporary school, while 893 attended the Asahigaoka School under teacher control.

On the second day, more than 1,000 students showed up for classes at the officially approved school. As more and more children left the non-official school, the local branch of Nikkyōso finally announced, at the end of a week, that their school was closing.[47]

The Asahigaoka Lower Secondary School was officially reopened shortly thereafter with an entirely new faculty. The three teachers had been formally dismissed. Nikkyōso appealed their case to the Kyōto District Court on the grounds that the superintendent had failed to give the teachers a full and complete hearing. The District Court upheld the school board's decision, and the Osaka Higher Court upheld the lower court's verdict. Nikkyōso then took the case directly to the Supreme Court, which referred it back to the Osaka Higher Court, where it lay pending.[48]

In the meantime, the government was maneuvering to restrict political activities of teachers. The process proved more difficult than expected. The first step involved an investigation of the political activities of teachers by the Ministry's Central Advisory Committee. Interpreting this move as another Red Purge, Nikkyōso accused the government of instructing police and superintendents of education to search for cases of politically biased teaching and report them to the government. The committee was divided over its findings. The majority of the committee members, claiming that Nikkyōso functioned like a political party, recommended legislative action; the minority, led by the president of Tōkyō University, Dr. Yanaibara, and by former scholar-minister of education, Maeda Tamon, opposed legislation, arguing that the new Japanese Constitution guaranteed freedom of political expression.[49]

Minister of Education Odachi approved the committee's majority opinion. The government subsequently drew up its so-called twin laws on political neutrality, designed to make it illegal to teach or incite to teach in any manner contrary to Article 10 of the Fundamental Law of Education, which states that "education shall not be subject to improper control, but it shall be directly responsible to the whole people." Supporting the government's position was Tanaka Kōtarō, one of the first postwar ministers of education and later chief justice of the Supreme Court. He reasoned that Article 6 of the same Fundamental Law provided the "legal framework for the ethics of the teaching profession." This article states that "teachers . . . shall be servants of the whole community," which he interpreted to mean that "the political neutrality of public servants will be maintained."[50]

One of the twin bills for the political neutrality of education was called

The Law to Revise the Special Law for Public Service Education Personnel (Kyōiku Kōmuin Tokurei Hō no Ichibu o Kaisei suru Hōritsu An). The Special Law under revision was originally passed in 1949; it classified teachers as either national or local public servants. Since there was no local civil service law to regulate the newly classified local teachers at that time, Article 21, Clause 3, of the 1949 law stipulated that "local civil servants, for the time being, would continue to be bound by Article 102 of the National Public Service Law," which restricted the political activities of national public servants to voting only.[51]

When the Local Public Service Law was finally passed in 1950, the clause "for the time being" in the 1949 bill was superseded, and local public servants then came under the provisions of the new law. Article 36 of the 1950 Local Public Service Law also restricted the political activities of local teachers to voting, but only within the district where they were employed. Outside the district of employment, teachers had the same rights to participate fully in all political activities as did the average citizen.

The bill introduced in 1954 was designed to revise Article 21, Clause 3, of the 1949 law to read: "Political activities of teachers in local schools, for the time being, and disregarding Article 36 of the Local Public Service Law, will be bound by the political restrictions of the National Public Service Law."[52] In other words, teachers of local schools would be subject to the same restrictions as teachers in national schools; that is, they would not be permitted to participate *anywhere* in political activities, except voting, even outside their districts. Thus, those teachers serving in the national executive of Nikkyōso in Tōkyō, away from their local districts, would no longer be able to participate in any political activities except voting.

The second of the twin bills was called the Law for the Temporary Measures to Preserve Political Neutrality in Compulsory School Education (Gimu Kyōiku Shōgakkō ni okeru Kyōiku no Seijiteki Chūritsu no Kakuho ni Kansuru Rinji Shochi Hō). This short bill contained five articles. The key clause was found in Article 3, which stipulated that "no one or no organization may instigate or incite teachers or students of compulsory education to support or oppose a political party or political activity." Article 4 set punishment at one year's imprisonment or 30,000 yen for violation of this law.[53]

Nikkyōso's Central Executive Committee met immediately to plan united action against the political neutrality legislation, which could destroy Nikkyōso's strikingly successful political machinery that functioned on all levels from the village school boards to the Diet. On February 24, the bills were introduced in the Diet and on March 1 the Education Committee began hearings. By this time, considerable interest had been generated over the bills, with a significant number of individuals and national organizations opposing them. For example, Rōyama Masamichi, one of the most respected political scientists in the nation, argued that the laws ignored the concept originally stated in the Fundamental Law of Education that education must be kept free of government control.[54]

The government placed before the Education Committee twenty-four examples of allegedly biased political teachings, including the *Yamaguchi* and the *Asahigaoka* cases. A third case involved the submission of a petition from parents at the Daishōgun Elementary School in Kyōto, claiming that teachers taught the students to despise the Japanese flag and the imperial family and advised them not to listen to the Japanese national anthem, which Nikkyōso claimed was a glorification of the emperor.[55] Nikkyōso charged that the evidence was fabricated and that, in certain cases, the schools mentioned in the examples did not even exist.

Nikkyōso then staged a most provocative act to focus nationwide attention on its opposition to the political-neutrality bills. The union decided to hold simultaneous Safeguard Education Rallies of all its members on Monday, March 15, 1954, to defend its peace-education program. In place of regular classes on Monday, Nikkyōso unilaterally declared that the nation's schools would be open on Sunday, March 14, for students and parents; and Monday would be a school holiday. The Ministry of Education immediately branded the action illegal.[56]

There was great confusion among parents throughout the nation whether children—and parents—should attend school on Sunday. Similar confusion was witnessed among rank-and-file teachers who were forced to decide whether to abide by Nikkyōso's plan or to heed the Ministry's warning. The day passed peacefully. Varying conclusions concerning the effectiveness of the union's scheme were reported. One newspaper estimated that 70 percent of all classes were called off on Monday, when teachers met to discuss the imbroglio.[57] The union claimed that in 5 of the 46 prefectures more than 50 percent of Nikkyōso members attended the rallies on Monday and held classes on Sunday. In 28 prefectures, more than 38 percent of the membership followed instructions. In the remaining 13 prefectures, Nikkyōso members conducted rallies on Sunday and held regular classes on Monday. The union claimed a great victory in "shocking the authorities, who were trying to control education, by demonstrating that educational initiative lay with the teachers."[58]

The union's claim was accurate. The government, incensed with Nikkyōso's Sunday classes, forced its legislation through the House of Representatives on March 26, by a vote of 256 to 137 amidst fistfighting in the chamber. The opposition was intensified by the United States–Japan Mutual Defense Assistance Agreement, which was being reviewed in the Diet at that time. Under this agreement, the United States was to provide significant aid for the purchase of military equipment for the Japanese forces.

The issue of Japanese rearmament had been magnified several months earlier when Richard Nixon as vice-president of the United States visited Japan and made the famous statement that the United States, miscalculating Soviet intentions, had erred in eliminating Japanese military forces after the war. He suggested to the Japanese that they should strengthen their military position.[59] Other bills were under consideration also in the Diet, such as the controversial bill aimed at changing the National Safety Force—the former Police Reserves—into Self-Defense Forces and bills aimed at strengthening the prefectural police system. Consequently, legislation concerning the political activities of teachers became inextricably involved in broader national and international issues.

Attention then turned to the Upper House of Councillors. Nikkyōso was divided in its plans for action because of some unfavorable reaction from among the membership over the Sunday-class episode. The left-wing demanded mass leave-taking while the moderate wing advocated a short hunger strike to publicize Nikkyōso's protest. The latter prevailed.

There was considerable political jockeying in the Upper House over the twin bills concerning the political neutrality of education. Fortuitously, the chairman of the Education Committee of the Upper House was a member of the Ryokufūkai, a club whose membership included over forty representatives. Some of them were independent from regular political parties, for example Tanaka Kōtarō and Takase Sōtarō, both former scholar-ministers of education during the American Occupation, and others were in the left wing of the conservative parties. In order to reduce the severity of the penal provisions, the Ryokufūkai, claiming that criminal punishment for teachers who were politically active was entirely too strong, attached an amendment to the bill revising the Special Law for Public Education Personnel. The amendment added a clause to Article 21 stipulating that teachers in public schools who violate the political

restrictions listed therein would not be subject to the regular penal provisions of imprisonment of less than three years or a fine of less than
100,000 yen.[60] This critical revision would automatically change criminal
punishment (*keijibatsu*)—that is, on the initiative of the police—to administrative punishment (*gyōseibatsu*); and it would thus eliminate
police initiative in local educational affairs.

In order to appreciate fully and clearly the simple but enormously
significant modifications proposed by the Ryokufūkai to the 1954 legislation, the pertinent clauses of the original and revised versions of the law
are juxtaposed in the following:

SPECIAL LAW FOR PUBLIC EDUCATION PERSONNEL

Article 21 [The Ministry of Education's Interpretation of the Original
Version, 1949]
  The political activities of teachers in public schools will be governed by
  the political restrictions contained in the National Public Service Law.
  [Article 102 of the National Public Service Law restricts political activities of national public servants to voting only, with penal provisions
  of less than three years' imprisonment and less than 100,000 yen in
  violation thereof.][61]

Article 21 Section 3, Part 1 [Revision proposed by the Japanese government
and adopted in 1954]
  The political activities of teachers in locally maintained schools, for the
  time being, and disregarding Article 36 of the Local Public Service Law
  [Restricts political activities of teachers exclusively to voting, within
  district of employment only] will continue to be governed by the political
  restrictions contained in the National Public Service Law.[62]

Article 21 Section 3, Part 2 [Amendment proposed by the Ryokufūkai
and adopted in 1954]
  The penal provisions in the National Public Service Law will not be
  applicable to teachers who violate the political restrictions contained in
  the National Public Service Law.[63]

A second last-minute revision maneuvered by the Ryokufūkai was to
add the words *for the purpose of* in Clause III of the Law for the Temporary Measures to Preserve Political Neutrality in Compulsory School
Education. The revised statement read: "No one or no organization may
take action for the purpose of instigating or inciting teachers or students
at the compulsory education level to support or oppose a political party
or political activity."[64] Again, the purpose of this amendment was to
soften the original provisions of the bill by changing the phrase "instigate

and incite to support or oppose a political party or political activity" to "for the purpose of instigating and inciting . . . ."

Although Nikkyōso and the government were opposed to the diluted versions of the bills, both sides eventually accepted both amendments; and the bills became laws at the end of May. The significance of the amendments is crucial, for the revised versions were ineffective from the point of view of the government. In fact, as far as can be determined, the provisions of these two bills have never been applied, even though their restrictions have been clearly violated on many occasions. Proving intent has made it so difficult to prosecute a case that no school board has ever undertaken the effort—the defendent can claim his "purpose" was not political but educational. And removal of the criminal penal provisions has rendered the other bill useless.

The first test of the political-neutrality laws came just over a month after their passage. On July 7, 1954, a journal of the Public Employees Union (Kankōrō), whose nominal publisher was a Nikkyōso teacher from a secondary school in Chiba Prefecture serving in the capacity of secretariat of Kankōrō, published statements such as "Let's overthrow the scandalous Yoshida cabinet and cause the Diet to dissolve immediately."[65] Minister of Education Odachi called the publication to the attention of the Chiba Prefectural Board of Education as a violation of the new political-neutrality laws. He publicly charged that "some if not all of the 500,000 teachers in the country are deliberately and systematically conducting such a type of education as to help destroy the present social order. Nikkyōso is utilizing every opportunity to conduct an education designed to destroy the existing social order as a necessary step toward an ultimate revolution."[66]

The Chiba Board of Education undertook an investigation and concluded that there was no justification for prosecuting this case under the political-neutrality laws. Nikkyōso interpreted the board's conclusion as proper, exemplifying democracy in action: a publicly elected board of education had withstood pressure from the reactionary Ministry of Education. Minister Odachi arrived at a different conclusion. He was angered by the prefectural school board's conclusion and charged that the case was a naked violation of the law. He complained that under the current administrative system in which there was collusion between leftist teachers and school boards under their influence, the minister of education was rendered helpless to carry out the provisions of the law. He indicated that the educational administrative system must be revised, as in his statement that "the school-board system has many faults and does not suit the conditions of the nation. We cannot abolish the boards of education outright but we must make necessary judgments."[67] His comments were a portent of the next stage in the escalating struggles between Nikkyōso and the Ministry of Education.

During the remainder of 1954 the ruling conservative party was beset with internal rivalry and scandal. After six years of one-man rule—from the end of the American Occupation into the period of independence and economic rehabilitation—the seventy-six-year-old Prime Minister Yoshida Shigeru finally resigned to be succeeded by Hatoyama Ichirō, who had been purged in 1946 and "depurged" in 1950. Hatoyama appointed a succession of ministers of education, each serving for only a few months as the prime minister periodically reshuffled his cabinet. The first was Andō Masazumi, who had also been purged as a rightist in 1946 and "depurged" in 1950. Andō immediately indicated to the prefectural boards of education, which had the final decision in curriculum matters, that it would be desirable to include ethics as a major subject at the upper secondary school level. It was clear where the new minister stood in the ideological conflict.[68]

General elections for the Lower House were held in February 1955. The Hatoyama party—the Democrats (Minshutō)—were returned as the dominant conservative party with 185 seats, while the Socialist party, by then divided into the right and left Socialist parties, gained 156 seats, giving them about one-third of the total number of seats. The other conservative party, Yoshida's, captured 112 seats, and the Communists 2.[69] Twenty-four Nikkyōso-supported candidates won in the election, including 19 from the left-wing and 3 from the right-wing Socialist parties plus 2 independents, in spite of the political restrictions the 1954 bills had placed on teachers.[70]

At the same time, the Japan Communist party was experiencing a structural change when the leaders who had been abroad or underground since the Red Purge of 1950 suddenly reappeared. The sixth Communist Party conference, held in July 1955, reflecting U.S.S.R. Prime Minister Khrushchev's coexistence policy, initiated a realignment of forces within the party; a program of peaceful, parliamentary revolution gained favor.[71] In effect, the Japan Communist party was renouncing violence for moderation, paradoxically, at a time when Communist members within Nikkyōso were pursuing an increasingly militant policy against the government.

During the same year, a realignment of the major political parties took place. In October the left-wing and right-wing Socialists reunited. But perhaps of even greater political importance was the merger in November of the two large conservative parties, the Liberals and the Democrats, into the one overwhelming party, the Liberal Democratic party (Jiyūminshutō), better known as Jimintō. The new party reelected Hatoyama as prime minister; he appointed Kiyose Ichirō, loyal party politician, minister of education.

The succession of conservative governments since independence had been frustrated in their attempts to restrict the political activities of Nikkyōso, which, they felt, were grossly biased to the left, thus corrupting Japanese youth at a time when the nation was making a dramatic economic recovery after the miserable years immediately following the war. The main emphasis of Nikkyōso was no longer economic but political, and the government was frustrated in dealing with the challenge.

The list of government failures in curtailing the left-wing teachers' movement is impressive. The attempt to bring all teachers under national civil servants' strict political regulations by paying their full salaries from national funds never got off the planning boards. The revised Ministry of Education Establishment Law of 1952 gave the Ministry of Education the responsibility for educational matters but not the power to compel boards of education to comply to the wishes of the Ministry. The special laws restricting the political activities of teachers, passed in 1954, were rendered ineffective at the last moment. The school boards, especially at the prefectural level, were heavily influenced by Nikkyōso through its hand-picked candidates, who had gained about one-third of the seats in the public elections. And the Ministry of Education was still operating under the basic guidelines of the Ministry of Education Establishment Law of 1949, drawn up originally during the American Occupation to decentralize educational control, and slightly revised in 1952.

The powerful conservative party, the new united Jimintō decided to undertake the single most important legislative revision following the American Occupation. The government announced a plan to revise the school-board system and the relationship between the boards and the Ministry of Education. This announcement initiated the next stage in the growing hostility between the Ministry of Education and Nikkyōso, engulfing virtually the entire educational arena in the conflict.

The planned school-board revisions embodied in the proposed Law for the Administration of Local Education (Chihō Kyōiku Gyōsei Hō) were relatively simple, though they had enormous consequences. School-board members were no longer to be elected by the public at large. Prefectural school-board members, reduced from 7 to 5 on each board, were to be selected and appointed by the prefectural governor, who was an elected official, with the consent of the prefectural assembly. Local school-board members, reduced from 5 to 3, were to be appointed by the local mayor or village head with the consent of the local assembly. The prefectural superintendents of education were to be appointed by the school board with the approval of the minister of education;[72] this was the first time since the end of the war that the national government held such influence over personnel at the prefectural level.

The permanent vice-minister of education serving at the time explained the government's purpose in revising the school-board system as follows: The original purpose of the school-board system was to avoid control of prefectural education by national politicians and bureaucrats as well as control of local education by local politicians. However, because candidates for the school boards required substantial funds to mount a successful electoral campaign, the ordinary citizen could not afford to participate as a candidate. Nikkyōso, having a large treasury, supplied funds to local hand-picked candidates for the campaign. As a result many Nikkyōso-supported candidates were elected to school boards. And, since Nikkyōso itself was supported by the Socialist and Communist parties, the school-board system inevitably became involved in politics. It was for this reason, the vice-minister explained, that the Ministry of Education viewed the school boards as agencies controlled by Nikkyōso and the Socialist and Communist parties. In conclusion he said that the major reason for revising the school-board system was the Ministry's desire to restore the political neutrality of the boards.[73]

The minister of education, in testimony before the Diet committee considering the bill, gave the following reasons for proposing the revisions: ". . . to insure the political neutrality of education and the stability of educational administration; to build a harmonious relationship between educational administration and local government; and to consolidate educational administration into one body consisting of the national, prefectural, and local educational agencies for more efficient administration of education."[74]

Also included in the proposed Law for the Administration of Local Education was a provision pertaining to the relationship between the Ministry of Education and the school boards. Under the proposed provision, mandatory compliance by the school boards with Ministry directives was to take the place of voluntary compliance. The law raised a semantic issue of crucial importance. Article 52 of the proposed law stated that the minister of education, if he determines that a local school board is not complying with education regulations or is violating the original purposes of education, has the authority to demand (*yōkyū*) necessary action for the board's compliance.[75] The difficulty in interpretation relates to the meaning of the term *yōkyū*, which can be defined as *demand* or *request*, depending on the context. Naturally, the Ministry of Education considered the meaning to be *demand*, and the opposition, *request*. Adding the provision of compulsion would give the Ministry authority to fulfill its responsibility for the conduct of Japanese education which it was granted in the 1952 revision.

A bill to revise textbook policies was also under consideration along the lines of the ruling party's pamphlet entitled *Deplorable Textbook Problem*, which charged that Nikkyōso teachers were bringing pressure on textbook publishers to approve leftist-oriented books before teachers would recommend purchase for their schools. The textbook bill proposed the following: to reduce sharply the number of textbooks requiring approval by the Ministry's Textbook Authorization Committee to about three in each subject area for each grade level; to have the prefectural school board establish selection committees to make the final selections from the approved list; to have one textbook used throughout the prefecture for a given subject for each grade level.[76]

Nikkyōso interpreted all of these revisions as an assault on the union itself in the Ministry's attempt to remove the labor movement from the schools. Nikkyōso thus claimed that school boards would become "just a channel through which the directions and orders of the Education Ministry are transmitted."[77] The government claimed there was more than an anti-Nikkyōso motive behind this first major change in the postwar administrative structure of Japanese education since independence. The Honorable Araki Masuo, one of the most powerful politicians of Jimintō involved in the revisions, explained the government's position as follows:

> The new postwar Constitution states in Article 26 that "All people shall have the right to receive an equal education correspondent to their ability, as provided by law." The Fundamental Law of Education reinforces this right in Article 3 that "The people shall be given equal opportunities of receiving education according to their ability, and they shall not be subject

to educational discrimination on account of race, creed, sex, social status, economic position, or family origin." The Ministry's position is based on this right which unequivocally states that from Hokkaidō to Kyūshū, in every prefecture, city, town and village, educational opportunities should be equal. But the Ministry and everyone else know that in reality educational opportunities vary greatly from one section of the nation to another, from one village to another, and from one classroom to another. And few will dispute that one of the major reasons for the distortion and imbalance in Japanese education related to the school board system whereby each individual board basically determined the educational opportunities and standards within its own particular area. The result was that every student in Japan did not have an equal opportunity for receiving an education commensurate with his abilities.

Furthermore, Articles 20, 38, and 43 of the School Education Law dealing with elementary, lower secondary, and upper secondary schools, state identically that "Matters concerning school subjects (kyōka) shall be decided by the competent authorities." The government considers that the competent authority (kantokuchō) is the Minister of Education. Therefore, in order for the competent authorities, i.e., the Minister of Education, to assume responsibility under the Constitution for assuring that each citizen obtains equal opportunities of education, the relationship between the Ministry and the school boards perforce had to be revised to enable the Ministry of Education to acquire the necessary authority to carry out its constitutional mandate.[78]

Nikkyōso immediately launched a nationwide campaign against the school-board revision. Other organizations and individuals joined the opposition. In particular, Dr. Yanaibara, president of Tōkyō University, and Dr. Nambara, former president of Tōkyō University, declared their objections before the Diet committee which was conducting hearings on the pending legislation. Dr. Yanaibara attacked the Ministry of Education for not consulting its own Central Advisory Committee, of which he was a member, before submitting the board-of-education bill to the Diet, brushing aside the minister's claim that he did not have sufficient time. Dr. Nambara claimed that the "government bills run counter to what we have been advocating since the war."[79] The Association of Boards of Education also opposed the revisions. Nikkyōso organized meetings throughout the nation to protest the bills.

On April 20, 1956, after reviewing an interim committee report, the House of Representatives passed the school-board bill, by a vote of 220 to 0; the opposition had refused to vote.[80] In May the textbook bill also passed the Lower House. All attention and protests then became focused on the House of Councillors. Nikkyōso held its fourteenth national convention in Kōfu on May 10 to plan united action against what it regarded as the intensified reactionary educational policies of the government.

Nikkyōso's mass demonstration began on May 18: half a million teachers walked out of their classrooms before the school day was over. They were joined in their protest that day by the National Association of Boards of Education, the Japan PTA, and the Federation of Housewives Association. Zengakuren, the left-wing student organization, and Sōhyō, the left-wing labor organization, conducted demonstrations around the Diet building, together with Nikkyōso delegations. Their protests were aimed at the deliberations of the Education Committee of the Upper House, for once a bill is reported out of committee, its passage is virtually certain. Their protests were finally overcome, and the bill was reported out of committee for a floor vote. By this time, the government had abandoned the textbook bill and was concentrating only on the school-board revision bill.

Members of the ruling Jimintō and of the opposition Socialist party with its block of Nikkyōso-supported representatives fought on the House floor on June 1 as tempers flared. Police were called in to restore order. Finally, on June 2, 1956, while five hundred policemen guarded the chambers, the Law for the Organization and Management of Local Education Administration (Chihō Kyōiku Gyōsei no Soshiki oyobi Unei ni Kansuru Hōritsu) was passed by a vote of 143 to 69.[81] The voting brought to a close one of the most important and turbulent sessions of the Diet in postwar Japan and in the process set the stage for the violent confrontation between the Ministry of Education and Nikkyōso that followed.

NOTES

1. *Asahi Shimbun* (Asahi Newspaper), March 2, 1951.
2. *Nippon Times,* January 2, February 3, May 4, August 28, September 14, 1951.
3. Mochizuki Muneaki, *Nikkyōso Nijūnen no Tatakai* (Twenty-Year Struggle of the Japan Teachers Union) (Tōkyō: Rōdō Junpōsha, 1967), p. 72.
4. *Asahi Shimbun,* May 2, 1951.
5. Ibid., May 7, May 9, 1951.
6. Kaigo Tokiomi, *Shiryō Sengo Nijūnenshi* (Materials on the Twenty-Year History of Postwar Japan) (Tōkyō: Nihon Hyōronsha, 1966), pp. 39–41.
7. Ibid.
8. Correspondence with former Minister of Education Amano Teiyū, Tōkyō, October 13, 1968.
9. Nikkyōso (Japan Teachers Union), *Nikkyōso Nijūnenshi* (Twenty-Year History of the Japan Teachers Union) (Tōkyō: Rōdō Junpōsha, 1967), pp. 284–286; *Asahi Shimbun,* October 20, 1952.

10. Nikkyōso, ibid., pp. 290–291.
11. Miyahara Seiichi, "Nihon no Kyōin Kumiai Undō to Rinri Kōryō" (Japanese Teachers' Union Movement and the Code of Ethics), *Kyōiku Hyōron* (Educational Review), November, 1960, p. 92.
12. Ibid.
13. Nikkyōso, *Ethical Code for Teachers with Explanatory Notes,* Tōkyō, July, 1951, pp. 1–3.
14. Nikkyōso, *A Code of Ethics for Teachers,* leaflet, Tōkyō, 1952.
15. Interview with Munakata Seiya, Tōkyō, August 22, 1968.
16. *Nippon Times,* June 20, 1952.
17. Mochizuki, *Nikkyōso Nijūnen,* p. 78.
18. Robert A. Scalapino, *Parties and Politics in Contemporary Japan* (Berkeley: University of California Press, 1962), p. 159.
19. Hidaka Daishirō, "Japan Since Recovery of Independence," *The Annals of the American Academy of Political and Social Science* 308 (1956):153.
20. Nikkyōso, *Kyōiku Shimbun* (Education Newspaper), December 1, 1950.
21. Hidaka Daishirō, *Sengo no Kyōiku Kaikaku no Jittai to Mondai* (Problems of Postwar Educational Reforms) (Tōkyō: Institute for Democratic Education, 1958), p. 55.
22. Tsukahara Kaheiji, *Nikkyōso* (Japan Teachers Union) (Tōkyō: Sōbunsha, 1959), pp. 129–130.
23. Ibid., pp. 130–132.
24. Interview with the Honorable Naitō Takasaburō, Liberal-Democrat party representative, Tōkyō, August 28, 1968.
25. Correspondence with Oka Saburō, Tōkyō, October 7, 1968.
26. Nihon Kyōiku Keiei Kenkyūkai (Japan Education Management Research Association), ed., *Kyōiku Keiei* (Educational Management) (Tōkyō: Nippon Bunka Kagakusha, 1961), 4:11.
27. *Asahi Shimbun,* September 18, 1952.
28. Muramatsu Takeshi, *Kyōiku no Mori* (Educational Forest) (Tōkyō: Mainichi Shimbunsha, 1965), p. 57.
29. Nikkyōso, *Kyōiku Shimbun,* October 10, 1952.
30. *Nippon Times,* June 3, 1956.
31. Supreme Commander for the Allied Powers (SCAP), *Postwar Developments in Japanese Education,* Tōkyō, April, 1952, pp. 2–3.
32. Mombu Hōrei Kenkyūkai (Educational Law Research Association), *Shin Kyōiku Roppō* (Revised Edition of the Fundamental Education Laws) (Tōkyō: Daiichi Hōki Shuppansha, 1969), p. 40.
33. *Asahi Shimbun,* January 6, 1953.
34. Interview with Naitō Takasaburō, Tōkyō, August 28, 1968.
35. *Asahi Shimbun,* January 18, 1953.
36. Interview with Naitō Takasaburō, Tōkyō, August 28, 1968.
37. *Asahi Shimbun,* May 11, 1953.
38. Interview with Naitō Takasaburō, Tōkyō, August 28, 1968.
39. Nikkyōso, *Kyōiku Shimbun,* May 1, 1953.
40. Nikkyōso, *Atarashii Kyōin ni Natta Hitobito ni* (To the New Teachers), Tōkyō, April, 1953, pp. 2–4.
41. Mochizuki, *Nikkyōso Nijūnen,* p. 96; "The Altered Image of Teachers," Summary translation by the editorial staff of the *Asahi Jānaru* (Asahi Journal), *Journal of Social and Political Ideas in Japan* 1, no. 3:107.

42. *Asahi Jānaru* (Asahi Journal), June 25, 1961, pp. 6–8.
43. Ishii Kazutomo, *Ushinawareta Kyōiku* (Lost Education) (Tōkyō: Hōbunsha, 1954, p. 45.
44. *Yomiuri Shimbun* (Yomiuri Newspaper), April 7, 1955.
45. Mochizuki, *Nikkyōso Nijūnen*, pp. 97–98.
46. Satō Tadao, ed., *Kyōiku no Shisō* (Educational Thought) (Tōkyō: Chikuma Shobō, 1969), pp. 181–182, 192; Lawrence Olsen, *Dimensions of Japan* (New York: American University Field Study, 1963), pp. 34–40.
47. *Asahi Shimbun*, May 12, 13, 19, 1954.
48. Correspondence with the Legal Affairs Department, Nikkyōso, Tōkyō, April 8, 1969.
49. *Nippon Times*, January 19, February 11, 1954.
50. "The Altered Image of Teachers," pp. 34–35.
51. Mombu Hōrei Kenkyūkai, *Shin Kyōiku*, pp. 863, 924.
52. Ibid., p. 863.
53. Ibid., pp. 35–36.
54. "The Altered Image of Teachers," p. 38.
55. Takase Sōtarō, *Kyōin no Seiji Katsudō* (Political Activities of Teachers) (Tōkyō: Meiji Tosho Shuppansha, 1954), p. 14.
56. *Asahi Shimbun*, March 13, 14, 1954.
57. *Nippon Times*, March 16, 1954.
58. Mochizuki, *Nikkyōso Nijūnen*, p. 110.
59. *Nippon Times*, November 20, 1953.
60. Mombu Hōrei Kenkyūkai, *Shin Kyōiku*, p. 930.
61. Arikura Ryōkichi, *Kaisetsu Kyōiku Roppō* (Interpretation of the Fundamental Laws of Education) (Tōkyō: Sanseidō, 1971), p. 487.
62. Suekawa Hiroshi, *Roppō Zensho* (The Complete Collection of Fundamental Laws) (Tōkyō: Iwanami Shoten, 1955), p. 1498.
63. Ibid.
64. Mombu Hōrei Kenkyūkai, *Shin Kyōiku*, p. 34.
65. *Nippon Times*, November 12, 1954.
66. Ibid., October 29, 1954.
67. Ibid., November 12, 1954.
68. Ibid., December 29, 1954.
69. Scalapino, *Parties and Politics*, p. 159.
70. Tsukahara, *Nikkyōso*, p. 129.
71. Robert A. Scalapino, *The Japanese Communist Movement, 1920–1966* (Berkeley: University of California Press, 1967), pp. 91–100.
72. Mombu Hōrei Kenkyūkai, *Shin Kyōiku*, pp. 112–133.
73. Interview with Naitō Takasaburō, Tōkyō, August 28, 1968.
74. Muramatsu, *Kyōiku no Mori*, p. 76.
75. Mombu Hōrei Kenkyūkai, *Shin Kyōiku*, pp. 126–127.
76. *Shūkan Asahi* (Asahi Weekly), October 23, 1955, p. 38.
77. Makieda Motofumi, *Japan Teachers Union*, leaflet, Tōkyō, n.d., p. 5.
78. Interview with the Honorable Araki Masuo, Liberal-Democrat party representative, Tōkyō, August 21, 1968.
79. *Nippon Times*, March 27, April 8, 1956.
80. Ibid., April 21, 1956.
81. *Mainichi Shimbun* (Mainichi Newspaper), June 3, 1956.

6

Violent Encounter with the Government (1957-1961)
The Battle for Union Leadership

Nikkyōso's direct confrontation with the Ministry of Education began in 1957. The struggles in which the two powers had been engaged since the end of the war had finally reached a climax. With the passage of the critical revisions of the school-board system and the modifications in the relationship between the Ministry of Education and the school boards legislated in 1956, the stage was set. The new school boards had more conservative than progressive appointees, precisely as the Ministry of Education had planned. And when Prime Minister Ishibashi resigned because of illness only two months after assuming office, Kishi Nobusuke, one of the most remarkable politicians in postwar Japan, who advanced from a Class A war criminal in 1946 to prime minister on February 25, 1957, became leader of the powerful Jimintō, the Liberal-Democrats.

Minister of Education Nadao Hirokichi, one of the strongest ministers of education in the entire postwar period, assumed a determined attitude against Nikkyōso. Nadao immediately came under attack by the union because of his assignment in the powerful Ministry of Home Affairs prior to 1945. Of all the ministers of education during the nine-year tenure of Nikkyōso Chairman Kobayashi Takeshi, it was Nadao whom Nikkyōso feared most; he was brillant and implacable.[1]

Confronted with a new and threatening situation after the 1956 educational administrative revisions, Nikkyōso published its own program for a democratic educational system. The statement is important as an outline of Nikkyōso's policies at that time. In the following are given Nikkyōso's major recommendations for Japanese education in the mid-1950s:

136

1. Basic Revision of the Education System.
   Abolishment of the position of minister of education, appointed by the prime minister representing a political party, and establishment of a Central Education Council whose members will be elected democratically. The Ministry of Education will be revised to become the Secretariat of the Central Education Council. A new board of education law will be enacted under which the board members will be chosen by public election. The board will be granted authority on personnel and financial matters.

2. Equal Opportunity for Education.
   The quality of senior high school education must be improved. Entrance will become compulsory. Special senior high schools for night students will also be established.

3. Elimination of Over-crowded Classrooms.
   Special emphasis will be given to restricting class size to fifty pupils or less. There should be no merging of schools for financial reasons. In order to lighten the parents' share of compulsory education expenses, the state treasury should meet 80 percent of compulsory education expenses.

4. Promotion of Science and Technological Education.
   The school curriculum will be revised so that pupils are taught to regard production as the basis of human activity. Revision of the school curriculum should be carried out voluntarily by teachers. Industrial training will be stressed and state subsidies will be drastically increased for this purpose. Establishment of senior high schools for vocational training will be opposed.

5. Promotion of Morals Education.
   Morals in the new age should be based on an awareness of human rights, love of independence, the education of an individual imbued with the spirit of peace, democracy and international friendship, and on respect for an individual who possesses practical knowledge and techniques and who has awakened to the principles of science. Morals education should be conducted at all times in the entire process of education. Morals education along this line should be conducted constantly at school, in the home, and in society, with full cooperation of teachers, parents, and the general public. Morals education would thus be conducted during the whole course of education. A special ethics course will not be established.

6. Democratization of School Textbook Authorization System.
   Enactment of a school textbook law will be opposed. Inspection of school textbooks should be democratic. Teachers will be given authority to select textbooks.[2]

Diametrically opposed to most of the recommendations of the union, the government, with a powerful prime minister, a strong minister of education, and a Ministry of Education having authority over the school boards, felt confident that it was at last in a position to restrict the activities of the left-wing Nikkyōso teachers. The opportunity was quickly seized with the Teacher's Efficiency-rating Plan (Kinmu Hyōtei), over which the two powers were locked in violent internecine conflict for the next several years.

The controversy over the Teacher's Efficiency-rating Plan began in Ehime Prefecture, a small, rather obscure rural prefecture located on Shikoku, one of the least developed of the four main islands of Japan. Ehime was incurring a huge financial deficit—460 million yen ($1,275,-000)—for 1955, a common situation among the poorer prefectures.[3] The prefectural education office of Ehime requested the Ministry of Education to suggest possible ways to reduce the prefecture's increasing educational costs. The Ministry recommended that the prefectural education office reduce the teachers' annual salary increments, half the cost of which was being borne by the prefecture. The method suggested by the Ministry involved a plan to rate the efficiency of teachers and award annual increments only to those who were accorded a good rating.[4] The plan was based on enforcement of Article 40 of the Local Public Service Law passed in 1950, which in theory applied to all regular employees of local governments, but which had not previously been applied to teachers. This article, on efficiency rating, read as follows: "The appointment officer of local public servants must conduct periodic efficiency ratings of all employees under his responsibility and must act according to the results."[5]

In August 1956 the Ehime Prefecture government issued directives for all school principals to conduct ratings of their teachers for purposes of awarding salary increments to two-thirds of them. A form was circulated which included nineteen items for evaluation, including cooperative attitude, planning ability, diligence, and the like.[6] In general, the school principals, most of them members of Nikkyōso at that time, objected to the plan partly because they were union members themselves and partly because some thought it was impossible to evaluate teaching in that manner. Since the new system for appointing school-board members had not yet gone into effect, the prefectural government withdrew the directive.

In October, however, the new appointive system became effective, and board members were from then on to be appointed by the prefectural governor or the local mayor. Accordingly, all of the Ehime Prefectural

School Board members except one woman member were promptly replaced by the governor. New directives were issued for evaluating teachers. They were to be given grades (A to D) on each of eleven rating items, including responsibility, teaching knowledge and technique, discipline, and reliability. The Ehime Prefectural Teachers Union, an affiliate of Nikkyōso, opposed the scheme, claiming that it could not work because of the nature of the teaching profession. The national union headquarters supported that opinion. The prefectural union held a general meeting of teachers in mid-October while seven officers began a seventy-hour hunger strike. After a mass negotiation session between teachers and education officials, it was agreed that the rating plan would not be carried out in 1956.

After Prime Minister Kishi and Minister of Education Nadao took office in February 1957, Saga Prefecture, a small prefecture on the southern island of Kyūshū, dismissed 259 teachers as a way of reducing educational expenditures, upon which the Saga Prefectural Teachers Union, an affiliate of Nikkyōso, called a three-day mass leave-taking; 30 percent of the members stayed away from school on the first day, 30 percent the next, and 30 percent on the final day. The prefectural union ultimately refused to recognize the dismissals and the Saga authorities promptly dismissed eleven union leaders on April 2, 1957. Nikkyōso took the case to court.[7]

At Nikkyōso's fifteenth national convention in Wakayama, in June 1957, commemorating the tenth year since the birth of the union, the executive apparently remained unaware of the significance of the controversies going on in Saga and Ehime prefectures, especially that in Ehime. Only one statement opposing the rating plan was approved at the convention. Instead, emphasis was placed on a nationwide appeal for more funds at the local, prefectural, and national levels for the enrichment of education, the raising of educational standards, and an increase in teachers' salaries. Nikkyōso established, moreover, the Peoples Education Research Institute (Kokumin Kyōiku Kenkyūjo), whose objective was to formulate, on the basis of scientific research, policies for the protection of democratic education from governmental influence.

Meanwhile, the rating plan had been enforced in Ehime Prefecture early in 1957, much to the indignation of the local branch of the union. Opposition was steadily increasing. The Ehime Prefectural Teachers Union pitched a tent in front of the prefectural education office. Alongside the tent was a lantern on which were the words, "For the complete fulfillment of our goals"; the union members were determined that the light would not be extinguished until victory. Union leaders conducted daily negotiations with prefectural authorities. Two thousand protesting teachers took leave en masse. In anticipation of a nationwide fight against the rating plan, Nikkyōso sent nearly three thousand members into Ehime from all over the country in support of the local branch.

In July 1957, the government made known its intention to enforce the rating plan throughout the nation, beginning later in the year, in conformity with Article 40 of the Local Public Service Law. Ehime was, in a sense, a test case.[8] Nikkyōso, interpreting the plan as a threat to its very existence, quickly held a series of meetings all over the country, endeavoring to build a unified front against the government's plan. The breakaway Upper Secondary School Teachers Union, recently reorganized into the Nihon Kōtōgakkō Kyōshokuin Kumiai (Nikkōkyō), pledged itself to cooperate with Nikkyōso's struggles against the rating plan.[9]

Nikkyōso's national executive protested to Ministry officials concerning the rating plan. In one incident, during a sit-in of five hundred members at the Ministry, the rivals, Hiragaki and Miyanohara, were both arrested. At the same time, the Ehime prefectural authorities, facing increased resistance by teachers, postponed until December 10 the deadline for submitting to the school boards the first teacher evaluation reports; by that date 434 of 767 principals had complied.[10] Some were forcibly prevented by Nikkyōso teachers from turning in the reports.

Finally, on December 15, a compromise was reached between Nikkyōso and the Ministry when the prefectural board of education agreed that the board would draw up a new rating form based on a broad range of opinions, including those from teachers, and that the protestors would not be punished. The first stage of the controversy over the Teacher's Efficiency-rating Plan thus came to an inconclusive end in late 1957.

The next stage developed quickly when the National Conference of Superintendents on December 20 drew up a draft of a rating form and announced its nationwide enforcement from the beginning of the next school year in April 1958. Since the appointments of prefectural superintendents required Ministry approval under the 1956 administrative revisions, it can be assumed that this conference of superintendents was carrying out the wishes of the Ministry of Education. Two days later Nikkyōso convened an extraordinary national convention in Tōkyō to draw up a "Declaration of the State of Emergency" in which the union vowed not to compromise until the rating plan was abolished. Union leaders felt that up to the time of the rating-plan controversy, the government had been attacking them only indirectly by suppressing Nikkyōso's influence on the school boards. The rating plan, however, was interpreted as a direct attack on the union, since the fear of being rated poorly would discourage the average teacher from participating in Nikkyōso's movement.[11]

Nikkyōso Chairman Kobayashi Takeshi explained the union's opposition to the rating system as follows:

> Our major concern is that the implementation of the rating plan will result in subservience to authority, characteristic of prewar Japan, thereby distorting education. Under the new system the local school principal must evaluate the teacher's performance. In this role the principal will become merely a representative of the controlling powers, that is, the boards of education and the Ministry of Education. The resulting disastrous effect will be an emotional struggle between the principal, representing the entrenched power structure, and his teachers. The principal will then be able to coerce his teachers through the implementation of the rating system. In addition, teachers will lose their identity as educators responsible to their students and to the country as a whole. Therefore we are resolutely committed to resisting all efforts to effect the Teacher's Efficiency-rating Plan which would sacrifice the students for the benefit of the ruling powers.[12]

A sample rating form was drawn up by the superintendents of education in consultation with the Ministry of Education; from it each prefectural school board was to draw up its own form. The following excerpts are taken from the sample:

A. Performance of Duties.
  1. Management of class.
     a. Is the management of the classroom in conformity with the basic principles of school management?
     b. Does the class act harmoniously as a group, and is order established?
  2. Lesson guidance.
     a. Are methods worked out to see that the guidance plans of the school are put into effective operation?
     b. Are steps taken to handle the difference in ability of the students?
  3. Guidance in living.
     a. Is guidance in living and morals education carried out with enthusiasm?
  4. Rating.
     a. Are the students graded properly?
  5. Research and training.
     a. Is research carried out regularly?
     b. Are research results properly applied to guidance?

6. Disposition of school duties.
   a. Are allocated duties carried out correctly?
   b. Is work carried out according to regulations?

B. Special Capabilities.
   1. Love of education.
      a. Is love for the students manifested?
      b. Is the teacher liked by the students?
   2. Knowledge, ability, and skills.
      a. Has the teacher acquired the knowledge and skills of a specialist?
      b. Can the teacher devise original ideas?
   3. Sincerity.
      a. Is the teacher honest and fair?
      b. Do the teacher's actions conform with his statements?
   4. Sense of responsibility.
      a. Does the teacher realize his responsibility to his work and his mission as an educator?
      b. Does the teacher carry out matters in line of duty on his own free will and responsibility?
   5. Impartiality.
      a. Does the teacher show partiality?
      b. Does the teacher have the courage to say or do what he believes is right?
   6. Dignity.
      a. Is he well mannered and clean in body and dress?
      b. Does he have a healthy attitude toward life?[13]

Each teacher was to be graded (from A to E) on these and other questions. A section for special notations and general comments followed. The evaluation report was to serve as a basis for determining whether the teacher deserved a salary increase; it was also to be used in determining the teacher's general career pattern. Each prefecture had to prepare its own form by April 1, 1958, and the first evaluation report was to be submitted to the boards of education by September.

Prior to April, the prefectural union affiliates of Nikkyōso campaigned against the rating plan on a prefectural basis, employing violent tactics in some instances. Because of the local nature of these campaigns, both the national union and the Ministry supported from a distance their respective sides in each prefecture. Moreover, because each prefecture campaigning against the rating plan was faced with conditions peculiar to its own location, different prefectures campaigned at different times. Consequently, Nikkyōso was unable to bring about a united, nationwide demonstration of force. A single target was needed to unify the movement.

From among all the districts campaigning, Nikkyōso chose Tōkyō as the rallying point for all prefectures; it then called upon its local affiliates for nationwide support in April, the beginning of the 1958 school year. The Tōkyō affiliate of Nikkyōso, Tokyōso, traditionally a strong, militant organization, decided on a policy of force by staging mass holidays. The plan called for all teachers to take a leave day en masse on the first day of the new school term in April if the local authorities enforced the rating plan. Daily mass negotiations with Tōkyō education authorities led to a postponement of the deadline for submitting evaluation reports from April 1 to April 23.

On April 23, 35,000 of Tokyōso's 37,000 members carried out a mass leave. Sōhyō, the largest council of labor unions in Japan, advised its members to keep their children home that day in sympathy with Nikkyōso's actions. About 80 percent of Tōkyō schools were disrupted.[14] Under the provisions of the Local Public Service Laws, Tōkyō police arrested nearly all of the union leaders, including Chairman Hasegawa Shōzō, who was one of the founding fathers of Nikkyōso. The case was taken to court. The rating system was officially adopted in Tōkyō on April 23 in spite of the strike.

The government instructed prefectural boards of education to carry out the rating program during April 1958. In reaction, Nikkyōso's prefectural affiliates in Fukuoka, Wakayama, and Kōchi followed Tōkyō's example and conducted strikes which resulted in police action and court cases. In spite of such protests, the rating program was put into effect in twenty-three prefectures during April. The opposing forces were strong in prefectures like Kōchi and Wakayama, but weak in others. The form of penalty placed upon protesting teachers varied as well from district to district. The mass daily newspaper, *Asahi Shimbun,* reported that, according to Nikkyōso, eighty thousand teachers had been transferred at the beginning of the school year because of their opposition to the rating plan.[15] Parents' organizations took sides.

In the midst of the growing turmoil, a general election for the Lower House was called in May, during which the new unified conservative party, Jimintō, campaigned as a united party for the first time. The conservative majority won 61.5 percent (287) of the seats, slightly less than the 63.6 percent it had won earlier; the reunified Socialist party gained 35.5 percent (166); and the Communist party won 1 seat.[16]

Also coming during the middle of the rating-plan conflict was the announcement by the Ministry of Education that the entire curriculum for compulsory education was being revised for compulsory implementation.

This revision was another of the critically important revisions of Japanese education since the American Occupation. Until 1958 the Ministry of Education published periodically the *Course of Study Guides,* which gave teaching guides but did not prescribe the course content, thus leaving the individual teacher a degree of latitude in developing course content independently. In fact, teaching was most heavily influenced, not by the *Course of Study Guides,* but by the examination preparation that any student wishing to enter the next higher level had to go through and by teachers' guides prepared by commercial publishers to accompany each textbook.

The last time the school curriculum had been revised was 1951. Since that time the Ministry of Education had become increasingly aware of the need for updated course content. Around 1954, during Minister of Education Odachi's term of office, there was a movement within the government and the Ministry of Education to have a mandatory school curriculum. But the government and the Ministry did not come forth with such a curriculum because they felt that the Ministry was powerless to enforce it under the prevailing laws.[17] When the relationship between the school board and the Ministry changed through the 1956 revisions, the Ministry finally gained the power to revise and standardize the curriculum. The Ministry justified the revision as a move in the direction of providing equal educational opportunities for all students. Few would deny, however, that what the Ministry hoped to accomplish by having a prescribed curriculum was to curtail the left-wing teachers' influence in the classrooms. Needless to say, Nikkyōso was not consulted in the planning of the new curriculum.

The Ministry of Education implemented the Revised Course of Study on August 28, 1958. The fundamental principle of the revision was "to strengthen morals education" by providing "an assigned weekly school hour in each grade for an organized program of morals education"; a curriculum embracing this principle was to become effective by September 1959.[18] To Nikkyōso, which had defended the educational reforms enacted during the American Occupation proscribing a mandatory curriculum and abolishing the morals course, the new measures were clearly reactionary. Coming as it did in the middle of the efficiency-rating controversy, Nikkyōso charged that the government was scheming to usurp total control over education through the revised mandatory curriculum that specified course content and through the Teacher's Efficiency-rating

Plan, which ensured adherence to the prescribed course content. To Nikkyōso, the revision thus meant a reversion to the conditions existing prior to 1945.

Those teachers protesting the mandatory revised curriculum, particularly the newly required course in morals, perforce merged forces with those involved in the rating-program fight already underway. Amid the voices of protest, the Ministry, during the later part of 1958 and early 1959, sponsored for teachers special courses and lectures concerning the new curriculum and the new morals course. Nikkyōso not only boycotted these courses and lectures but also attempted to block physically the scheduled events wherever possible. On a number of occasions, protesting teachers clashed with police, forcing the sponsors to cancel the meeting or change the meeting place secretly. With many districts already in near chaos over the rating program, the revised mandatory curriculum and the series of incidents involving the boycotting of the Ministry's special lectures only intensified the strain between the Ministry and Nikkyōso.

Organizations other than Nikkyōso that were concerned over the controversies were also involved in the turmoil. Parent-teacher associations loyal to Nikkyōso were opposing parents who protested the union's activities. Schools were being closed for a day or more throughout the country when teachers walked out en masse. Police raided many of Nikkyōso's local offices. The left-wing student organization, Zengakuren, joined local demonstrations. Fierce fighting broke out between police and demonstrators in several prefectures. The situation worsened rapidly.

Nikkyōso convened its seventeenth national convention at Kaminoyama City, in June 1958. It proved to be one of the most crucial meetings in the entire history of the union. It was at this meeting that the two major factions of Nikkyōso, the radical left behind Hiragaki Miyoji, supported by the Communist party, and the moderates behind Miyanohara Sadamitsu, supported by the Socialist party, clashed for hegemony of the union. The victor was destined finally to assume prolonged leadership of the union.

When the Kaminoyama convention convened on June 1, Nikkyōso was engaged in the most severe conflict in its history. Many prefectural affiliates of the union were locked in local pitched battles with the school boards. The Teacher's Efficiency-rating Plan was in operation in thirty-five prefectures in the nation, including the city prefecture of Tōkyō. Nikkyōso was totally preoccupied with its fight against the Ministry—

an involvement having deep political implications which annoyed some of the apolitical rank and file. Critical opinions were expressed during this convention against the union's militancy.

Nevertheless, the major discord during the convention concerned the method of opposing the rating program as advanced by Hiragaki and Miyanohara; the discord caused the union to be divided in the election contest of the two men for the position of general secretary, then held by Hiragaki. The basic issue at the root of the split had to do with one of the trade-union tactics employed by Sōhyō. During the phenomenal growth of the trade-union movement during 1946 and 1947, Japanese labor developed two kinds of struggle tactics. One was called the unified or vertical union struggle (*sangyōbetsu tōitsu tōsō*), and the other, the regional peoples' struggle (*chiiki jinmin tōsō*). Under the first approach, union members throughout the country joined in unified national action to achieve their goals even if a particular struggle concerned only one section or region. Under the second approach, maximum force was shown only in the region where there was a specific dispute.

The former secretary general of Sōhyō, Takano Minoru, leader of the radical left-wing and antimainstream faction within Sōhyō, adhered to the regional-struggle tactic, as did the Japan Communist party. Takano planned joint struggles with the Communist party because of their methodological propinquity. Hiragaki, a close personal friend of Takano, also favored the regional-struggle concept. Consequently, Hiragaki, as Nikkyōso's general secretary, adopted the Takano–Japan Communist party approach of regional struggles for Nikkyōso.[19]

The Communist group within Nikkyōso threw its full support behind Hiragaki, who became known as the leader of the Communists within the teachers' movement, although to this day he vehemently denies ever having been a Communist himself. He recognizes that he had a reputation as a radical leader of the Communist faction, but he feels that that was the result of his "uncompromising attitude toward the government's educational policy."[20] His obdurate position against the efficiency-rating system also attracted many non-Communist teachers who were equally opposed to the program and who voted for Communists in the Hiragaki faction. They believed that the hard-line posture of the Communists was the most effective one for them to take in their fight against the Ministry of Education.

The position of secretary general is the most powerful position in Nikkyōso when the chairman is a nonaggressive person. In 1958 the chairmanship was held by Kobayashi Takeshi, who was not an aggressive leader but a good mediator; the position of secretary general was held by Hiragaki, who was leader of Nikkyōso's Communist faction. Consequently, in 1958 Nikkyōso leadership once again came under the control of the union's Communist faction. This reemergence of Communist hegemony was the first since 1950, when the Red Purge decimated Communist ranks. What, in fact, had been developing since 1953, when Hiragaki first replaced Miyanohara as secretary general, was that, as Hiragaki moved more to the left in reaction to the government's restrictive policy toward Nikkyōso, the Communists were gradually gaining momentum by uniting with Hiragaki's forces to attain their objectives. As Hiragaki strengthened his influence, so did the Communists. The coalition gained strength through the control of powerful positions. For example, according to the estimates of the union's historian, the Communist group supporting Hiragaki controlled about 80 percent of the members on Nikkyōso's Central Executive Committee by 1958, attaining its pinnacle of power.[21]

Miyanohara followed the unified approach to labor struggles as practiced by Sōhyō Chairman Ota Kaoru, claiming, for example, that all teachers throughout the nation should have struck in protest when the rating program was first introduced in Ehime Prefecture. His reason was that local teachers in Ehime were too weak to oppose the entrenched conservatives alone and that an isolated protest movement would result in heavier punishment than would a mass protest movement. The moderates within Nikkyōso supported Miyanohara's position, while the extreme leftists pitted their support behind Hiragaki, crystallizing the intraunion disharmony into a contest between the Communist and the non-Communist factions.

Hiragaki was Nikkyōso's secretary general at the start of the Ehime case in 1956. He immediately went to Ehime to lead a concerted attack on the local prefectural government. His plan was to crush the rating program in Ehime before it could be introduced into other prefectures by bringing into Ehime nearly three thousand Nikkyōso members from all over the country. In other words, Hiragaki wanted to let the education authorities of the rest of the prefectures know through the Ehime example that enforcing the Teacher's Efficiency-rating Plan would invite disaster. When the Ehime Prefecture School Board enforced the rating plan in spite of Hiragaki's efforts, his tactics came under increasing criticism from union rank and file.

Nikkyōso's struggle tactics and strategy thus were of major importance and closely related to the intraunion rivalry between the Hiragaki and Miyanohara factions. As the union continually failed to block enforcement of the rating plan from prefecture to prefecture, the leadership in the person of Hiragaki, who was in charge of the union's campaign, turned defensive. The internal discord finally came to a head at the famous Kaminoyama convention, when Miyanohara opposed Hiragaki for the secretary generalship.

Meanwhile, certain Socialist party representatives in the Diet, reacting to growing public concern over the interminable disruptions at schools, began to exert pressure on Nikkyōso to modify its firm opposition to the rating plan. Despite rumors that both Sōhyō and the Socialist party were maneuvering to remove Hiragaki from the position of secretary general, Hiragaki continued adamantly to oppose both the rating plan and the Japan Socialist party executives' intervention in Nikkyōso's leadership affairs.[22]

The crucial voting for the position of secretary general at the Kaminoyama convention took place amid great confusion. The announcement was made on the floor that Miyanohara had won by a single vote and that Makieda Motofumi, in the Miyanohara faction, was elected vice-secretary general. The Hiragaki faction promptly walked out of the meeting, throwing the hall into confusion. The convention was abruptly adjourned. At an extraordinary national convention hastily convened a month later, a second vote was taken. This time Miyanohara won by an official vote of 261 to 226. Makieda's margin of victory was 19 votes.[23] However, even though the moderates had overturned the radicals on the convention floor, the Central Executive Committee remained in the hands of the Communists, which restricted the alternatives open to the new secretary general.

On June 20, 1958, Minister of Education Nadao reaffirmed the government's decision to enforce the rating plan throughout the nation.[24] By that time, thirty-eight of forty-eight prefectures had already adopted it. On July 4, the government passed an education bill, after violent struggles on the Diet floor, granting special allowances of 2,500 yen a month to school principals, who were thrust into the middle of the rating-plan controversy since nearly 80 percent of them were Nikkyōso members at that time. Those opposing the bill declared that the purpose of the special allowance was to induce school principals to leave the union and enforce the rating plan. Concern was expressed that the government would ultimately introduce a bill prohibiting principals from joining Nikkyōso. Sōhyō threatened a national strike if such action were taken.

While Nikkyōso remained divided at the national executive level by interfactional disputes, its local affiliates fought against the rating system. The situation in Wakayama and Kōchi prefectures became particularly severe when nearly all schools were shut down on several occasions as teachers walked out of their classrooms in protest, paralyzing the school system and inviting recriminations and further closing of schools. Sōhyō and the left-wing university student organization, Zengakuren, joined the daily demonstrations. The students became known as Nikkyōso's "shock troops" when they repeatedly clashed with police in street demonstrations against the rating plan. Violence broke out in Wakayama City in mid-August, when Sōhyō sponsored a rally of tens of thousands of workers and students against the rating plan. Many arrests were made.

Zengakuren gained notoriety in 1958 through its attempts to block the extension of runways into Sunagawa village from the huge American military air base at Tachikawa, on the edge of Tōkyō, to accommodate jet aircrafts. The *Sunagawa* incident, which led to a district court decision in 1959 that American forces in Japan violated the no-war-potential clause of the Constitution, shocked the nation, but it was only a prelude to the major battles of 1960 against the United States–Japan Security Pact. To the students, the Teacher's Efficiency-rating Plan was merely one in a succession of pernicious measures undertaken by the government to suppress democratic forces.

Chairman Kobayashi of Nikkyōso, during the rating plan struggles, unequivocally refuted the charge that Nikkyōso exploited students by enlisting their support in the union's campaign against the government. He explained that the students automatically participated in any anti-government movement whether they were invited or not. Kobayashi did seem to feel, however, that in areas where the union was weak and the local government strong, there could be little doubt that certain Nikkyōso officers welcomed the participation of Zengakuren students and coordinated the students' efforts with those of the union against the Kishi government.[25]

Nikkyōso's immediate goal was to stop the school principals from submitting to the school boards the rating forms due in September 1958. Making manifest Miyanohara's ascendency in power, Nikkyōso decided to employ the unified-struggle tactic; the plan was to have all union teachers boycott classes on the afternoon of September 15. In a notice of September

4, the government declared such action illegal.[26] Police warned that rightist groups, arch enemies of Nikkyōso, were planning to disrupt the boycott. Sōhyō appealed to its several million members not to send their children to school that afternoon. Shortly before September 15, Nikkyōso Chairman Kobayashi was arrested for having led a previous strike. To the great disappointment of the union, its first attempt at a nationwide unified strike against the rating plan resulted in compliance in only seventeen prefectures.[27] Few schools had to close. Nikkyōso was not yet capable of using effectively Miyanohara's tactic of unified struggle.

Prime Minister Kishi, in his policy speech before the Diet shortly after the strike fiasco, placed his government unequivocally behind enforcement of the rating plan when he said:

> The efficiency rating plan is indispensable to ensuring a fair and just personnel administration. It is a system already in force for public service personnel in general. There is no reason why teachers should be excepted. It is in the belief that the plan will serve to maintain fairness in personnel administration of teachers, and the government is determined to enforce it, as has long been decided, with the cooperation of all circles concerned.[28]

Nikkyōso convened its second consecutive extraordinary national convention in Tōkyō on October 14, 1958, to reconsider the dismal results of the September strike and to plan a renewed unified struggle. The convention voted to suspend classes at 2 P.M. on October 28 in conjunction with Sōhyō's national unified action day, in protest against the rating plan and the government's attempt to revise and strengthen the police laws. Thirty prefectures complied with short walkouts, and in two, Kōchi and Gumma prefectures, the membership took mass leaves. On November 26 and December 10, further unified action was conducted, though with decreasing degrees of success.

Violent clashes with police were erupting throughout the nation. Local left- and right-wing forces confronted each other in pitched battles, resulting in bloodshed and recriminations. Teachers and administrators were dismissed or suspended from their positions by the hundreds. As a result, defections of teachers and school principals from Nikkyōso became commonplace, running into the thousands as the intensity of the conflict increased. New organizations of local teachers were launched in many sections of the country in a negative reaction to Nikkyōso's militant actions. In the history of postwar Japanese education, there was never such chaos affecting the schools as that which took place during this direct confrontation between the union and the Ministry of Education for the control of schools.

The viciousness of the conflict was demonstrated, for example, on December 15, 1958, when Nikkyōso Chairman Kobayashi attended a rally in Kōchi Prefecture. He later described the incident as follows. While he was making a speech to parents in a local school assembly hall, a gang of local ruffians entered the hall from the back entrance. They switched off the lights and began throwing loose objects at the stage. Kobayashi was hit on the shoulder by a small stove (*hibachi*) used to heat the hall. He was knocked to the floor and lost consciousness. The intruders then apparently kicked his face because, when he regained consciousness in a local hospital hours later, he discovered that his front teeth were missing and his face was badly cut, requiring an emergency operation. When asked who, he thought, was behind the attack, he felt certain that the local boss, who was a conservative party leader, had hired thugs to break up the protest rally.[29] The *Asahi Shimbun* reported that Kobayashi was attacked by about two hundred angry parents who were opposed to Nikkyōso's activities. On the same day, fifteen other union members were assaulted and hospitalized in Kōchi City.[30]

The first sign of an end to the seemingly interminable conflict was seen in the so-called Kanagawa Formula, proposed in early 1959. The Kanagawa Prefectural School Board had been negotiating with the prefectural branch of the teachers union in an attempt to devise a plan whereby the board could comply with the Ministerial demand to enforce the rating plan without alienating the teachers. During the last six months of 1958, the board and the union in Kanagawa met a total of thirty-nine times, or more than once a week, trying to find a solution to the rating-plan controversy.

According to the Kanagawa Formula, each teacher was to evaluate himself by maintaining a Record of Educational Activities, which was to be submitted to the school principal. The principal, in turn, was to add his own comments to the report in consultation with the teacher and then submit the report to the school board, which theoretically was to use the results for the improvement of local education. When Nikkyōso's national executive considered the virtues and defects of this compromise plan in January 1959, the two rival factions once again disagreed with each other. Miyanohara cautiously approved the formula while Hiragaki adamantly opposed it. The Central Executive Committee voted in favor of

Hiragaki's position by a vote of 32 to 27,[31] indicating the relative strength of the Communist and non-Communist blocs, in spite of the fact that Miyanohara was now secretary general.

Miyanohara, with Chairman Kobayashi placing his support with the moderates, immediately called for a third consecutive extraordinary national convention to be held in mid-February 1959, in Tōkyō. At this convention, a local delegate from Iwate Prefecture criticized the uncompromising attitude of the union executive, opining that such an attitude if continued much longer would destroy what energy remained at the local level; and that such a consequence would drive a wedge between the national executive and the local unions. A vote was taken on the "Iwate Resolution," which advocated that each prefectural branch of the union should adapt the Kanagawa Formula to meet the conditions peculiar to that prefecture and then negotiate a rating plan with the school board. In a secret vote 241 ballots were cast in favor of the compromise and 218 against it.[32]

Secretary General Miyanohara had narrowly won the day. This victory signified the beginning of another historic transition for Nikkyōso. Gradually, the union turned away from the intractable, hard line of the Communist-supported Hiragaki faction, which had dominated Nikkyōso's activities from about 1955. The rank and file had become disillusioned with the hard-line tactic, holding Hiragaki responsible for the unsuccessful struggles. By the time of the next regular convention in June 1959, Miyanohara was returned to the position of secretary general by a vote of 264 to 219, while the Hiragaki faction remained barely in control of the Central Executive Committee by a count of 33 to 31.[33]

In 1959 Miyanohara began his move to purge Communist opposition on the Central Executive Committee and replace it with men aligned with his more moderate views. The process was to take him until 1962, when his faction finally gained indisputable control of the Central Executive Committee and elected him chairman of Nikkyōso. But between 1959 and 1962 many events deterred his plan.

Nikkyōso continued its opposition to the rating plan although in greatly modified form. The new policy was to negotiate locally a plan that would, in effect, be the least disadvantageous to the average teacher and, if possible, render it useless. The controversy over the rating plan in late 1959 became submerged in the greatest unified movement of left-wing forces in Japan during the entire postwar period—the opposition to the renewal of the United States–Japan Security Pact, which overshadowed all other movements for a year. But before we leave the discussion of the rating-plan conflict, an analysis of the effects of the controversy upon Nikkyōso and the rating plan itself is essential for an understanding of the subsequent period.

First of all, the rating plan had gone into effect in one way or another in all prefectures except Hokkaidō and Kyōto. School principals dutifully completed the evaluation reports and submitted them to the school boards. But because of the intensity of teacher opposition to the plan, the boards of education were reluctant to employ the results for determining salary increases as originally planned. In other words, although the rating plan was carried out widely, its prime objective remained unattained. An example is the Tōkyō School Board, which, to this day, has conducted the annual teacher's efficiency evaluation as demanded by the Ministry of Education but has never related the results to wages.[34] The relative impotence of the rating plan stemmed from the school boards' concern that the majority of teachers, both nonunion and union members, did not approve of the plan. Hence, to enforce the results of the evaluation would invite total opposition by the teaching corps; the results that could be obtained from the ratings did not seem worth the trouble that was sure to come. Moreover, many school-board members themselves were not convinced of the validity of the evaluation forms used as the basis in determining teachers' pay increases. Hence, because of Nikkyōso's efforts to undermine the plan, in addition to the inherent difficulties of evaluating teaching, the rating plan quickly turned ineffective.

The cost of the battle to Nikkyōso was extremely high. The three-year struggle from 1957 to 1959 debilitated the union, depleting its membership through arrests and withdrawals. For example, the Ehime Prefectural Union lost the majority of its members, at the rate of about two thousand a year, between 1957 and 1960.[35] The government estimated that eighty thousand teachers withdrew from Nikkyōso between 1957 and 1960, including fifteen thousand school principals.[36] The entire episode was one prolonged nightmare of internal and external struggles that threatened the very existence of the union.

Statistics shown in Tables 7 and 8 reveal the magnitude of the effects of the rating-plan struggles on the union treasury and on the membership. The rating-plan conflict took a heavy toll in other ways as well. Administrative punishment was carried out by local education authorities without litigation. Criminal punishment was carried out under the provisions of the following articles of the Local Public Service Law:

Table 7.   Expenditure by Nikkyōso for the Campaign against the
Teacher's Efficiency-rating Plan, 1957–1959 (in yen)

Year	Expenditure	Union Dues	%of Dues Spent on Campaign
1957	10,531,965	191,231,762	5.5
1958	118,841,196	400,497,617	29.6
1959	172,345,119	489,803,390	35.2

Source: Data from Nikkyōso, *Report to the International Labor Office in Geneva,* Tōkyō,
November 9, 1960, p. 9.

Table 8.   Punishment of Teachers during the
Teacher's Efficiency-rating Struggles, 1956–1960

Classification of Punishment	Type of Punishment	No. of Teachers Affected
Administrative	Dismissal	112
	Suspension	292
	Demotion	1,018
	Reprimand	3,076
	Salary reduction	52,273
Criminal	Indictment	108
	Arrest	208
	Subpoena	4,104

Source: Data from Nikkyōso, *Report to the International Labor Office in Geneva,* Tōkyō,
November 9, 1960, p. 37.

Article 37, Clause 1
Local public servants may not resort to strike, slowdown, or other acts
of dispute against their employer, who is the local people as represented
by the agencies of the local public body, or to conduct such idling tactics
as will deteriorate the functional efficiency of the local public body, or to
instigate others to do so.

Article 61, Clause 4
Violation of Article 37, Clause 1, is subject to punishment of imprisonment of less than three years or a fine of less than 100,000 yen.[37]

Recalling the thoughts he had during those chaotic years, Miyanohara
commented that he could feel that Nikkyōso was losing its foundation
because of its own intransigent policy that failed to recognize the strength

of the opposition and the weakness of Nikkyōso. As chaos continued year after year, the union's image had become disastrously tarnished both to the public and to the rank and file, who, having had enough of turmoil, were willing to accept a compromise simply to end the conflict. With the union executive assiduously dispatching orders to continue the struggle, Miyano-hara finally concluded that a policy change was necessary to salvage the teachers' union, which had taken so many years to develop.[38]

While the opposition to the Teacher's Efficiency-rating Plan was weakening, the most spectacular movement of left-wing opposition to the government in the postwar era was taking place against the extension in 1960 of the United States–Japan Security Pact, providing for the continuation of American military bases in Japan for another ten years. Nikkyōso, however, was just concluding a three-year period of the most enervating struggles in its history. Consequently, when the labor movement, the student movement, and other left-wing forces were reaching new heights in their unified struggle against the government, Nikkyōso was experiencing new lows in morale, unity, and energy.

When the People's Council for Preventing Revision of the Security Pact (Anpo Kaiteisoshi Kokumin Kaigi) was formed in March 1959, although Nikkyōso extended unqualified support, it was in no condition to mount another offensive, regardless of the urgency of the issues. Several prefectural affiliates of the union staged local demonstrations, and many teachers participated as individuals in the daily mass street demonstrations around the Diet building. A certain amount of doubling-up occurred when one teacher took charge of two classes to free a colleague to participate in the demonstrations. The one unified effort by Nikkyōso was the mass walkout against the Teacher's Efficiency-rating Plan, scheduled for 2 P.M. on September 8, 1959, to coincide with the day of unified action scheduled by the People's Council against the Security Pact. But this action was one of the dying gasps of Nikkyōso's struggles against the rating plan. The major action in 1960 against the Security Pact was led by Sōhyō, the Socialist party, the Communist party and the Zengakuren; Nikkyōso played only a small role.

Upon passage of the Security Pact after months of turmoil in and around the Diet building, Prime Minister Kishi on June 23 announced his decision to resign. On July 19 Ikeda Hayato from Kishi's Jimintō assumed the prime ministership. Ikeda's policy was essentially based on an economic concept of doubling the income in ten years, to be carried out in a "low-keyed" manner, that is, quietly and without causing antagonism. Ironically, Ikeda appointed Araki Masuo, one of the most provocative politicians in Jimintō, as minister of education.

Minister of Education Araki, who had never concealed his contempt for Nikkyōso, launched a concerted attack on the union and its proclivities for politics. Shortly after taking office, he declared unequivocally that he would not meet with any representatives of Nikkyōso because it functioned under the remote control of the Japan Communist party, which is related to a foreign Communist government. Araki particularly attacked the union's Code of Ethics, claiming that teachers influenced by the union's philosophy were brainwashing the students to believe in leftist ideology under the assumption that teachers are laborers. This concept, to Minister Araki, violated the Fundamental Law of Education, guaranteeing the political neutrality of education, because it pointed toward a social revolution based on left-wing ideology. Until Nikkyōso reoriented its policies, he would have absolutely no contact with its representatives.[39]

Minister Araki's charges struck a sensitive spot, as was demonstrated at the union's 1961 national convention at Miyazaki City. At this meeting, Nikkyōso became deadlocked over the issue of politics. The question basically revolved around the union's policies since the early 1950s, which emphasized politics and education to the neglect of the economic welfare of teachers. The point was made that the function of labor unions such as Nikkyōso was to strive for the improvement of the economic welfare of the union members, and therefore that labor unions should let political parties handle political issues. In order for both the labor unions and the political parties to succeed, it was considered necessary that there be a formal working relationship between the two so that they might mutually reinforce their efforts to obtain their respective goals.

There was a degree of ambiguity in Nikkyōso's actions during this convention, as witnessed by the general public. If the union wanted to endorse a new policy that gave priority to economic issues, why did it consider formalizing a relationship with a particular political party? The answer lay behind the scenes in the internal maneuvering for union leadership. The moderates behind Miyanohara believed that they had the majority of the rank-and-file convention delegates behind them. They also realized that the powerful Central Executive Committee was still under the influence of the Communist faction led by Hiragaki.[40] Although Hiragaki was no longer an executive of the committee, he remained on it representing Osaka Prefecture.

Miyanohara consequently found himself hampered by the Communist group at the policy-forming level (the Central Executive Committee), while holding strength at the policy-approving level, the convention floor representing the rank and file. In order to move Nikkyōso in the moderate direction away from the recent debilitating political struggles, he had somehow to curtail the Communist strength on the Central Committee in order to present his proposals to the whole union. His solution was to try to associate the union officially with the moderate Socialist party by going directly to the convention floor, over the heads of the Communist group on the Central Executive Committee.

The significance of having a formal relationship with the Socialist party lay in the fact that Nikkyōso up until then had overtly supported both progressive parties—the Socialist and the Communist—since each was an antigovernment organization. The Japan Communist party had traditionally exerted significant influence on the union through its activist members in the Nikkyōso hierarchy. In fact, the Communist party had played an integral role in Nikkyōso from the beginning even though the very top union executives and the rank and file traditionally aligned themselves with the Socialist party. A motion to support only the Socialist party obviously represented an important step, inviting strong reaction from the Communist faction. This maneuver was only one part of Miyanohara's grand scheme to salvage the union following its enervating confrontation with the government over the rating system.

The other part of Miyanohara's plan was to deemphasize political struggles to reduce their disastrous effects on Nikkyōso, dividing the membership between the moderate or apolitical rank and file and the minority of extreme left-wing political activists, who had worked themselves into influential positions on the local level. Political struggles had not only polarized the factions within the union but had also brought on fragmentation, resulting in the splintering off of large groups of disaffected members.

Miyanohara realized that the one concern that all members had in common, regardless of their political inclinations or disinclinations, was economics. Few could oppose a platform based primarily on the objective of improving teachers' salaries. On this assumption, Miyanohara set himself the task of reuniting Nikkyōso's membership by reorienting the platform away from the divisive policy of politics to the uniting policy of economics. To accomplish these long-range goals, his first task was to circumvent the power of the Communist bloc on the Central Executive

Committee, which opposed his plan, by having Nikkyōso align itself with only one political party, the Socialist party.[41]

The proposals to promote economic issues through deemphasis of political issues and to support only the Socialist party threw the 1961 convention into an uproar. The Communist bloc was fighting to retrieve its influence, which had been slowly eroded with the growth of the Miyanohara faction. Amid shouting, filibustering, and general confusion, a vote was taken; an undetermined majority supported the motion for a new economic orientation. When the vote was about to be taken on the matter concerning association only with the Socialist party, opposition radicals surrounded the chairman of the subcommittee, thrusting the convention into total chaos as fighting broke out. The convention was abruptly adjourned. The spectacle was given much publicity.

A month later the convention reconvened in Tōkyō, and a second vote was taken. Amid maximum opposition from the Communist bloc, the two original proposals were finally approved by a majority of the convention.[42] Even though Secretary General Miyanohara had won his battle on the floor of the convention, the policies he advocated had one final hurdle to cross—the nationwide achievement tests (*gakuryoku tesuto*).

The Ministry of Education had announced that it would conduct a battery of achievement tests in mathematics, social studies, science, English, and Japanese for all second- and third-year lower secondary school students throughout the nation on October 4, 1961. Achievement tests had been given annually for the previous six years, but only at selected schools. Minister of Education Araki Masuo later explained the purpose of the new compulsory-test plan:

> Based on Article 26 of the Constitution, which states that "all people shall have the right to receive an equal education correspondent to their ability" and the Ministry of Education's interpretation of Articles 20, 38, and 43 of the School Education Law, stating that "matters concerning school subjects shall be decided by the competent authorities," that is, the Minister, it became necessary for me as Minister to measure the effects of the curriculum for which I was responsible. In order to assure that every student from Hokkaidō to Kyūshū was receiving an equal educational opportunity, it was essential that the Ministry conduct nationwide achievement tests to obtain national standards for comparisons. Only by such a procedure could we determine exactly where students were not achieving at the national standard, enabling the government to undertake corrective measures to guarantee equal educational opportunities throughout the nation, according to the Constitution.[43]

Nikkyōso interpreted the achievement-test plan from a different point of view. It charged that the government was striving to grasp total control of the classroom by first standardizing the curriculum in 1958 and then conducting national achievement tests in 1961 to ascertain whether teachers were following the prescribed curriculum. The union considered the test plan as a direct intervention into the classroom by the government.

Nikkyōso's opposition to the achievement-test plan was the union's last stand against what it concluded were the government's reactionary education policies, completely reversing the earlier postwar democratic education reforms. Since the end of American Occupation in 1952, Nikkyōso had already experienced two defeats: (1) its endeavor to preserve the independence of the school boards and also the union's influence on them, and (2) its endeavor to preserve the autonomy of the school from the school board after the appointive system became effective in 1956, through sympathetic school principals who were mostly Nikkyōso members. The union's sphere of influence had been narrowing—at first from the school board to the school, and finally down to the classroom itself—as a result of government policies.

The last preserve of the union seemed to be the classroom where the government still could not supervise effectively, even with its mandatory curriculum. The achievement tests were thus viewed by Nikkyōso as a postwar surrogate for the prewar school inspector. Nikkyōso considered that the government's purpose in employing the achievement tests was to ascertain whether teachers were actually teaching in their classrooms the mandatory curriculum prescribed by the government. It was the teacher who was going to be tested, not the students.[44]

Nikkyōso objected to the tests for another reason—that they were means to exploit labor to develop Japan's economy, as part of Prime Minister Ikeda's economic policy. The union argued that the government's purpose was to encourage students to work for high grades in paper-pencil tests in certain subjects so that they could be classified later into such vocational categories as managerial or clerical, in a process similar to that used for sorting animals. Nikkyōso predicted that the test plan would reduce Japanese education to just a preparation-for-examination mill.

The Central Executive Committee, still under the influence of the Communist faction, proposed a nationwide strike for October 26, 1961, the first day of the examinations. Nikkyōso informed Minister of Education Araki that teachers are entrusted to test their students for educational purposes, not for administrative purposes to suit the government, and therefore that they do not have to cooperate with the government in conjunction with the achievement-test plan.

Minister Araki replied that teachers must indeed comply with the directives of the Ministry of Education, designed to enhance Japanese education. Araki claimed that under the 1956 revision of the relationship between the Ministry of Education and school boards, the minister acquired the power to conduct investigations such as the achievement examinations. He pointed out that under Article 54 of the Law for the Administration of Local Education, the Minister of Education had the power to demand school boards to conduct necessary investigations and to submit their results to the Ministry.[45] Again, the word *demand* (*motomeru*), which can also be interpreted as *request,* became a major point of contention.

Minister Araki accepted the union's challenge by going on a speaking tour of the country, urging parents and educators to oppose Nikkyōso because he alone could not dissolve the union, a voluntary body of federated prefectural associations, although he would have liked to. He estimated that during his lecture tour he publicly branded Nikkyōso activists as fools and outlaws approximately 150 times on the grounds that they tried to brainwash their students with leftist propaganda.[46] At a meeting before a group of national education administrators, Araki made one of his most famous speeches during his term of office when he told the administrators to "shut out" Nikkyōso because it aimed at a Communist revolution. To support his claim, he cited statistics published by the Public Safety Investigation Agency, which reported that 3,000 of the 500,000 union members belonged to the Japan Communist party. He charged that "these communist members are trying to work up a revolution by brainwashing the good teachers and children. Rascals as members of the Union could not be trusted to educate Japanese youth. There is no choice but to get rid of the Union in order to pass on to the generations to come our culture and virtues built up by the efforts of our forefathers."[47]

In light of Minister Araki's threat of harsh punishment if teachers went on strike, Nikkyōso altered its tactics against the achievement-test plan. The revised tactics called for teachers in those grades where the tests were to be given to teach their classes as usual and ignore the tests completely; strike action was not to be taken. Workshops for all teachers were scheduled during the first period of the day to achieve a united front and to negotiate with the school principals.

Nikkyōso claimed that on October 26, 1961, the tests were not given in 90 percent of the schools in Iwate Prefecture and 60 percent in Fukuoka,

Hokkaidō, and Kōchi prefectures.[48] Disruption of some schools in the majority of the remaining prefectures gave the union the small satisfaction that, contrary to the Ministry's plan, the achievement tests were not administered simultaneously in every school. It was a shallow feeling of satisfaction because the Ministry of Education was successful in administering the examination in a large majority of the schools in spite of Nikkyōso's determination to block it. In some districts, compromises were negotiated whereby the local administration agreed not to reveal scores for later employment purposes. Apparently the average teacher did not view the examination as constituting a serious threat to his independence; hence the teachers did not take mass action to block it.

Prompt measures were taken against activist teachers who either refused to give the tests or physically blocked test administrators. Sixty-one teachers were arrested and taken into custody; 15 of them were prosecuted in court for resorting to physical force. Twenty teachers were dismissed, 63 suspended, 652 reduced in salary, and 1,189 given official warnings.[49] The achievement-test controversy generated bad feelings not only between Nikkyōso and the Ministry of Education, but also between teachers and school principals, and among teachers themselves.

The achievement test was the major source of contention between the Minister of Education and Nikkyōso in 1961. Minister Araki was determined that the tests be given the following year, scheduled for July 11 and 12, 1962, at the lower secondary and elementary school levels. As the date for the second national achievement tests neared, Nikkyōso again modified its position to that of "prior struggles," that is, negotiating with school boards before the day of examinations in order to gain concessions in the hope of rendering the examination process ineffective. The examinations were carried out with minor concessions and difficulties.

Nikkyōso's decision in 1962 against striking, euphemistically referred to as mass leave-taking or mass holidays, was a momentous pronouncement. What it signified was that Miyanohara had finally gained control of the Central Executive Committee, which he had set out to do in 1958. It had taken him nearly four years of slow but determined effort to gain supremacy over the radicals in the national executive. He was at last ready to make his ultimate move.

Nikkyōso's twenty-fourth national convention was convened at Toyama City on July 23, 1962. Kobayashi Takeshi, chairman of the union since 1953, had won election to the House of Councillors several weeks prior to this convention in the tradition of former Nikkyōso chairmen, and therefore he was not running for reelection. Miyanohara Sadamitsu, former elementary school teacher from the southernmost island of Kyūshū, was elected chairman without difficulty. Once again, Nikkyōso was embarking on a new course under new leadership.

NOTES

1. Interview with the Honorable Kobayashi Takeshi, Socialist party representative, Tōkyō, August 12, 1968.
·2. *Asahi Jānaru* (Asahi Journal), October 26, 1957, pp. 7–14.
3. *Mainichi Shimbun* (Mainichi Newspaper), December 12, 1957.
4. Interview with Sagara Iichi, professor of educational administration, Kyōto University, July 29, 1968.
5. Mombu Hōrei Kenkyūkai (Educational Law Research Association), *Shin Kyōiku Roppō* (Revised Edition of the Fundamental Education Laws) (Tōkyō: Daiichi Hōki Shuppansha, 1969), p. 888.
6. Mochizuki Muneaki, *Nikkyōso Nijūnen no Tatakai* (Twenty-Year Struggle of the Japan Teachers Union) (Tōkyō: Rōdō Junpōsha, 1967), p. 141.
7. Ibid., pp. 147–148.
8. Interview with the Honorable Naitō Takasaburō, Liberal-Democrat party representative, Tōkyō, August 28, 1968.
9. *Asahi Shimbun* (Asahi Newspaper), October 16, 1957.
10. Ibid., December 11, 1957.
11. Mochizuki, *Nikkyōso, Nijūnen,* p. 166.
12. *Bungei Shunjū* (Literary Journal), September, 1958, pp. 10–14.
13. *Japan Times,* September 15, 1958.
14. *Tōkyō Shimbun* (Tōkyō Newspaper), April 24, 1958.
15. *Asahi Shimbun,* April 4, 1958.
16. Robert A. Scalapino, *Party and Politics in Contemporary Japan* (Berkeley: University of California Press, 1962), p. 160.
17. Interview with Naitō Takasaburō, Tōkyō, August, 28, 1968.
18. Mombushō (Japanese Ministry of Education), *Revised Curriculum in Japan* (Tōkyō: Mombushō, 1960), pp. 2–3.
19. Interview with Mochizuki Muneaki, Nikkyōso historian, Tōkyō, June 11, 1968.
20. Correspondence from Hiragaki Miyoji, Osaka, November 8, 1968.
21. Interview with Mochizuki Muneaki, Tōkyō, June 11, 1968.
22. Correspondence from Hiragaki Miyoji, November 8, 1968.
23. *Asahi Shimbun,* July 27, 28, 1958.
24. *Japan Times,* June 20, 1958.
25. Interview with Kobayashi Takeshi, Tōkyō, August 12, 1968.
26. *Asahi Shimbun,* September 6, 1958.
27. Mochizuki, *Nikkyōso Nijūnen,* p. 186.
28. Foreign Affairs Association of Japan, *Contemporary Japan* 25 (1959):715.
29. Interview with Kobayashi Takeshi, Tōkyō, August 12, 1968.
30. *Asahi Shimbun,* December 16, 1958.
31. Ibid., December 28, 1958.
32. Nikkyōso (Japan Teachers Union), *Nikkyōso Nijūnenshi* (Twenty-Year History of the Japan Teachers Union) (Tōkyō: Rōdō Junpōsha, 1967), pp. 411–416; *Asahi Shimbun,* February 18, 1959.

33. *Asahi Shimbun,* June 15, 1959.
34. Interview with Itō Noboru, member of Tōkyō Board of Education, Tōkyō, April 20, 1968; January 17, 1970.
35. International Labor Office (ILO), *Report of the Fact-finding and Conciliation Commission on Freedom of Association Concerning Persons Employed in the Public Sector in Japan,* Special Supplement to the ILO Official Bulletin, vol. 49, no. 1 (Geneva: ILO, 1966), p. 365.
36. *Shūkan Shinchō* (Shinchō Weekly), 1960, p. 7.
37. Mombu Hōrei Kenkyūkai, *Shin Kyōiku,* p. 888.
38. Interview with Miyanohara Sadamitsu, Nikkyōso chairman, Tōkyō, July 21, 1968.
39. Interview with the Honorable Araki Masuo, Liberal-Democrat party representative, Tōkyō, August 21, 1968.
40. Interviews with Miyanohara Sadamitsu and Mochizuki Muneaki, Tōkyō, July 21, 1968 and June 23, 1968, respectively.
41. Interview with Miyanohara Sadamitsu, Tōkyō, July 21, 1968.
42. Mochizuki, *Nikkyōso Nijūnen,* p. 207.
43. Interview with Araki Masuo, Tōkyō, August 21, 1968.
44. Interview with Mochizuki Muneaki, Tōkyō, June 23, 1968.
45. Interview with Araki Masuo, Tōkyō, August 21, 1968.
46. Interview with Araki Masuo, Tōkyō, August 21, 1968.
47. *Japan Times,* July 16, 1961.
48. Mochizuki, *Nikkyōso Nijūnen,* p. 213.
49. Ibid., p. 214.

7

Economic Struggles (1962-1967)

The Return to Original Goals

The newly elected chairman of Nikkyōso, Miyanohara Sadamitsu, faced with the major problems of reorienting the union's policies and of reversing the alarming rate of membership withdrawals, unveiled his program at the 1962 national convention at Toyama City. The new orientation focused on teachers' salaries and teachers' rights,[1] which had been the fundamental issues in the teachers' movement from 1945 to 1950. But from 1951 to 1961, Nikkyōso was preoccupied with national and international political controversies as they related directly, and frequently indirectly, to education. After a decade of ideological struggles that had destroyed the unity and drained the energy of the left-wing teachers' movement, thus reducing the union membership by about 20 percent, the cycle was now nearing completion with Nikkyōso's return to the original goals with which it had so rapidly organized the preponderant number of teachers into the fold shortly after World War II.

Miyanohara set himself the goal of reconstructing the divided union into a strong, reunified organization. The strategy, centered around struggles for increasing teachers' salaries and for regaining recognition of the right of collective bargaining with the Ministry of Education, perforce had to employ tactics other than strike action since the union was too weak to carry out nationwide unified strikes. This factor was only too clearly evidenced during the campaign against the achievement tests, when the plans of Nikkyōso's Central Executive Committee could not be carried out at the local level. Miyanohara was particularly sensitive to the hiatus between Nikkyōso's national leadership and the rank-and-file membership, which had widened as the union became increasingly militant dur-

164

ing the 1950s. He set about correcting that situation by promoting a no-strike policy, appealing for public support both nationally and internationally, and by having the many pending cases prosecuted through the courts.[2]

Chairman Miyanohara was also confronted with a new set of circumstances unprecedented in the left-wing teachers' movement. First, the number of female teachers in the elementary schools, traditionally the preserve of the male teacher in Japan, had reached nearly the 50-percent level by 1960. Since Nikkyōso's membership consisted primarily of elementary and lower secondary school teachers, the increase in the number of female teachers introduced a new constituency causing new complications for the union leadership. Second, union members who were graduates of the prewar three-year teacher training schools (*shihan gakkō*) were being superseded in dominance by those who were graduates of the new postwar university system, in which teacher training was incorporated into the four-year university education. The postwar university graduates who entered teaching reflected the new educational philosophy, introducing another element of friction into the union. Thus it became even more difficult to formulate a nationwide policy which could meet the needs and demands of an ever diversifying membership. Consequently, Miyanohara turned to the issue of teachers' salaries and rights as a way of unifying Nikkyōso members.

Simultaneously, the Japan Communist party showed a critical change of attitude through its members in Nikkyōso. Following the decline of Hiragaki's (and consequently the Communists') influence after Hiragaki lost his position of secretary general to Miyanohara, and reacting to the adverse criticism of the Communist-promoted teacher-rating struggles, the Japan Communist party notified its followers in Nikkyōso to emphasize henceforth economic struggles.[3] The Communist faction's reorientation, therefore, coincided with Miyanohara's, resulting in marked numerical gains for the Communist party where Nikkyōso membership was concerned. For example, the usually reliable National Police Agency reported that, whereas there were 5,000 Communist party members in Nikkyōso when Miyanohara assumed union leadership in 1962, there were 10,000 by 1965. The Japan Communist party had achieved this gain through pursuing a generally unprovocative policy and maintaining a cooperative attitude toward Nikkyōso. During the same three-year period, the total Nikkyōso membership declined from 582,300 to 574,420.[4]

As a result of these factors, Nikkyōso pursued a moderate policy from

1962 to 1965, relatively free from the disruptive tactics pursued with such regularity in the recent past. Miyanohara, facing the realities of an organization weakened from years of internal struggles and of a determined anti-Nikkyōso minister of education in the person of Araki Masuo, viewed the issues of teachers' salaries and teachers' rights as a single issue on the basis of a legal interpretation. Salaries of local teachers, although ostensibly determined by the local public bodies by which the teachers are employed, are based on the national salary scale for teachers in national schools, according to Article 25 of the Special Law for Educational Personnel.[5] As a result, the salaries for teachers throughout the nation are similar.

The national salary scale, which sets the standards for local scales, is recommended by the National Personnel Authority (Jinjiin), an organ appointed by the prime minister's cabinet. It collects data on salary and working conditions in private industry. In order that the government may compete effectively in the labor market, the National Personnel Authority recommends to the cabinet yearly salary increments for national civil servants, taking into account the salaries in private industries; the cabinet in turn determines the national salary scale for public employees for final Diet approval. Local bodies adjust accordingly, and teachers' salaries are thus uniformly determined throughout the nation.

The two sources of power in the entire procedure are the National Personnel Authority, which utilizes scientific statistical procedures of data analysis, and the cabinet, that is, the ruling party in the government. The government has the right either to accept the full recommendations of the NPA or to adjust them before submitting the budget to the Diet for ultimate approval. The government has traditionally adjusted the NPA's recommendations, frequently refusing to begin the new pay scales retroactively as the NPA nearly always recommends. In other words, even though teachers are locally hired and locally paid, the power that determines their wage increases lies with the national government and the ruling party.

The problem for Nikkyōso on this matter was that it was not recognized at any level, local or national, for it functioned through its federated prefectural unions of teachers, recognized only as local employees' organizations (*chihō shokuin dantai*) by the prefectural governments. Hence, Nikkyōso's new policy emphasizing economics could not be attained; that is, without recognition at the national level, Nikkyōso could not negotiate with the national government, which set teachers' salaries.

Obtaining official recognition of Nikkyōso as an organized body to fight for teachers' rights and improvement of teachers' economic plight thus became the major concern of the union between 1962 and 1965.[6]

The tactics used were unique. Confronted by the powerful ruling conservative party, intransigent on this very issue, with Minister Araki resolutely refusing to meet Nikkyōso representatives until the union dropped the Code of Ethics, Miyanohara decided to appeal for international support until the union could become strong enough to reassert itself within Japan once more. The convention in Toyama in 1962 voted to concentrate on the ratification of the International Labor Organization Convention 87. The slogan became "Restore the Fundamental Rights of Laborers" through the abolishment of the law restricting strikes and through government recognition of Nikkyōso as the negotiating body for teachers.[7] An analysis of the role played by the International Labor Organization in the disputations between Nikkyōso and the Japanese government is essential.

In November 1951 Japan joined the International Labor Organization, an independent, international organization working closely with the United Nations. The original purpose of the organization was to "inquire into the conditions of employment from the international aspect and to consider international means necessary to secure common action on matters affecting conditions of employment." As one of the ten "states of chief industrial importance," Japan has a permanent seat on the Governing Body, and a representative of the Japanese government occupies that seat. (No representative from Japanese workers has served on the Governing Body since 1957.[8])

In 1948, ILO adopted a resolution called Convention 87, Concerning Freedom of Association and Protection of the Right to Organize. Its purpose was to guarantee freedom of association against interference by public authorities. Article 2 reads as follows: "Workers and employers, without distinction whatsoever, shall have the right to establish and, subject only to the rules of the organization concerned, to join organizations of their own choosing without previous authorization." Article 3, Clause 2 reads, "The public authorities shall refrain from any interference which would restrict this right or impede the lawful exercise thereof." Finally, Article 8 provides that "the law of the land shall not be such as to impair, nor shall it be so applied as to impair, the guarantees provided for in the Convention."[9]

One important point in the wording of Article 2 is the phrase "without distinction whatsoever." The committee that drew up the document stressed in its report that, according to this provision, freedom of association was guaranteed not only to the employers and workers in private industry, but also to public employees, without distinction or discrimination of any kind as to occupation. The only exclusions were the armed forces and the police.

Then, in 1949, ILO adopted the Right to Organize and Collective Bargaining Convention 98 to supplement the resolutions stated in Convention 87. Article 4 of this document stipulates that "measures appropriate to national conditions shall be taken, where necessary, to encourage and promote the full development and utilization of machinery for voluntary negotiation between employers or employers' organizations and workers' organizations, with a view to the regulation of terms and conditions of employment by means of collective agreements."[10]

Under the general regulations of ILO, member nations have the right to accept or reject each convention. However, once a nation ratifies a convention, it is then expected to be fully subject to those provisions or risk international pressure and possibly condemnation. Japan, one of the ten members on ILO's Governing Body, ratified the Right to Organize and Collective Bargaining Convention 98 on October 20, 1953. At the time of Miyanohara's election as Nikkyōso's chairman in 1962, Convention 87 had not yet been ratified.

Nikkyōso initiated its case with ILO through a lengthy document charging that "the Japanese Government defies the important trade union rights by denying the right to strike to the present Union and interferes with its organization and administration. The root of the problem is Article 37 of the Local Public Service Law which deprives education civil servants of the right to dispute. . . . We ardently request you to make an appropriate recommendation to the Government of Japan."[11]

Minister of Education Araki immediately attacked Nikkyōso's charge, claiming the union had no right to appeal to ILO.[12] Nevertheless, Nikkyōso, in conjunction with Sōhyō, representing all public service unions, painstakingly constructed their case against the government over a period of several years. Finally, in 1964, ILO appointed a Fact-finding Commission, chaired by Erik Dreyer from Denmark, which embarked on an investigation of the complaints submitted by Nikkyōso and other public service unions. Shortly thereafter, much to the annoyance of the government and delight of the union, the long and bitter struggle between Nikkyōso and the Ministry of Education was being aired in public before an international tribunal. The proceedings were given wide publicity in Japan.

The conflicting testimony presented before the Fact-finding Commission by representatives of Nikkyōso and the Ministry of Education summed up their respective positions after nearly two decades of hostility. A summation of the testimony is warranted, juxtaposing the prosecution and the defense, in that order.

First, Nikkyōso contended that the Right to Organize and Collective Bargaining Convention 98, to which Japan was a signatory nation, had not been applied to the union on the grounds that teachers were hired and paid at the muncipal and prefectural levels. Under Article 53 of the Local Public Service Law, any organization that included more than one local public body could not be recognized by the government and was regarded merely as a voluntary organization. Because of this technicality, Nikkyōso, as a national organization, was not recognized at the bargaining table on the national level. Moreover, since local teachers' salaries, according to Article 25 of the Special Law for Education Personnel, were based on a national scale determined by the national government, prefectural school boards refused to negotiate salary matters with prefectural teachers' organizations, claiming that wages were decided on the national level and the prefecture had nothing to do with the wage problem.

Nikkyōso further contended that, when the prefectural organizations of teachers tried to negotiate matters concerning teachers' working conditions or the number of teachers at each school, the local school boards refused to negotiate on grounds that those matters were fixed by the Ministry of Education. Nikkyōso stated that, since the Ministry of Education does have the power to prepare the educational budget for Diet approval, and since the amount of money spent on education by the government has a direct bearing on the working conditions of teachers, Nikkyōso went to the Ministry of Education but that the minister refused negotiations, claiming that teachers were covered by the Local Public Service Law and the Ministry of Education had no right to negotiate with teachers. Thus, Nikkyōso's testimony concluded, under the circumstances described, there was no one with whom the union could negotiate.

The Japanese government's witness responded by claiming that standards relating to teachers' salaries in Article 25 of the Special Law for Education Personnel did not have such binding power that local school boards could not determine teachers' salaries independently. To maintain standards, though, it was necessary for the State "to assume responsibility for teachers' salaries"; so the standard number of teachers in each prefecture was decided by national law. Members of unions were "free to convey their wishes or express their views to the Minister," he continued, but they could not negotiate with the minister since he had no authority to act as employer. The witness testified that prefectural teachers' unions could negotiate with prefectural authorities but that Nikkyōso as a nation-wide organization could not. When asked whether the government sought the views of Nikkyōso when formulating the nation's policies on education and in drawing up the education budget, insofar as these matters had repercussions on the salaries and working conditions of teachers, the government representative replied that the Ministry of Education had not sought Nikkyōso's opinion.

In hearings related to "Acts of Antiunion Discrimination and Interference," Nikkyōso's witness accused the government of sponsoring rival unions, citing as an example the National Federation of Teachers, which had about twelve thousand members and which was, he alleged, organized under the sponsorship of the Ministry of Education and Jimintō. Every year, Nikkyōso charged, the Ministry of Education concentrated its efforts on a different prefecture. Nikkyōso also accused the Ministry of arbitrarily deciding supervisory classifications in an attempt to disrupt the membership by forcing administrative personnel to withdraw from the union.

The Ministry of Education's defendant countered to the Fact-finding Commission that Nikkyōso's excessive political inclinations and its attitude totally against the policy of the Ministry of Education were the fundamental reasons why fifteen to twenty thousand members withdrew from the union in each of the past several years. He added that in 1964 only 70 percent of newly employed teachers joined the union, whereas in 1958, 96.5 percent had joined.

Nikkyōso's witness charged the government with discriminatory treatment of union members in Ehime Prefecture, where the Teacher's Efficiency-rating Plan originated, citing statistics to show that prefectural union membership of 9,664 in 1957 had fallen to a mere 940 by 1964. The witness testified that the prefectural board of education had organized a rival group, the Ehime Educational Research Conference (E.E.R.C.), whose membership was open only to those teachers who had left or promised to leave Nikkyōso. The charge was made that only E.E.R.C. members were given salary increases and that no union members were promoted to administrative positions without first withdrawing from

Nikkyōso and joining the E.E.R.C. In addition, the percentage of Nikkyōso members transferred to isolated rural districts was said to have been two to three times higher than that of E.E.R.C. members. The witness cited other prefectural examples similar to Ehime.

The Ministry of Education's witness testified that because the Ehime Prefectural Teachers Union had violently opposed the Teacher's Efficiency-rating Plan, considerate teachers, being aware of their primary mission, seceded from Nikkyōso to form the E.E.R.C. as an organization devoted to educational research. He said there was absolutely no truth in the allegations of discriminatory treatment of selected teachers. He added that, in view of E.E.R.C.'s successful research meetings and research publications, the prefectural and central governmental authorities had given the organization a grant-in-aid of 2,058,000 yen in 1963. The fact that members of Nikkyōso were excluded from the E.E.R.C. had been brought to the attention of the Ministry of Education, but the minister attached no importance to this fact and extended assistance to the new teachers' association for its worthy research activities. He explained that Nikkyōso could not receive government grants because the union had its own activities.[13]

Rebuttal followed allegation, winding through the morass of hostility and vituperation, just as Nikkyōso and the Ministry had been conducting themselves in preceding years; such a hostile relationship bewildered the Fact-finding Commission of international labor experts. The commission finally decided to visit Japan in January 1965 for further hearings and direct investigations. The arguments were merely extended in Japan. The commission, which logged over a month of hearings both in Geneva and in Japan, compiling thousands of pages of written reports, published the following major findings, conclusions, and recommendations:

1. The Commission finds that the kernel of the grievance of certain of the complaining organizations is that the Japan Teachers Union cannot at present negotiate effectively on either a national or a local basis. The Commission therefore recommends the government to decide as a matter of policy whether it prefers central or local negotiations in respect to the employment of teachers. If the government prefers central negotiation, it will be necessary to take appropriate steps to make decisions resulting from such negotiations binding upon the local authorities. If the government prefers local negotiation, it will be necessary for it to give the local authorities real freedom to negotiate. It may well be that the most appropriate solution would be to distinguish from time to time

between the matters appropriate for central negotiation and those more appropriate for local negotiations.

2. The Commission notes that the right to strike continues to be the subject of a fundamental divergence of view in Japan. We believe that both the restoration of the unlimited right to strike and the maintenance of the absolute prohibition to strike are unrealistic and that a reasonable compromise is necessary.

3. The Commission has noted the complexities of the regulations concerning labor relations in Japan. We regard excessive legalism as a major obstacle to developing mutual confidence. The government as a whole should have a general labor policy, applicable to all public employees irrespective of the department or local authority by which they are employed. As a minimum this policy should provide immediately for the full application to all public employees of the provisions of the Freedom of Association and Protection of the Right to Organize Convention, 1948 (No. 87), and the Right to Organize and Collective Bargaining Convention, 1949 (No. 98).

4. The government should develop at all levels the habit of mutual consultation.

5. It has become normally accepted practice in highly industrialized countries for trade unions, including organizations of public employees, to support the programs of democratic political parties which they consider to be in the interests of their members. But Sōhyō, and the Japan Teachers Union in particular, have systematically proceeded far beyond the point justified by economic aims and, in doing so, have called upon their local unions to utilize the strike weapon—an economic weapon—in an endeavor to force the Government of Japan to undertake particular policies in political fields which are peculiarly the responsibility of the government.

6. The future now depends on two factors: whether trade unions give the government, on a non-political basis, the measure of cooperation necessary to enable it to make a reality of the new policy; and whether the government then proceeds, on the basis of such cooperation, to resolve the innumerable questions still outstanding.[14]

Several months after the Fact-finding Commission completed its investigation in Japan, the ruling party finally consented to Convention 87, which received Diet approval on June 14, 1965, effective one year later.[15] Ratification had been considered repeatedly during earlier sessions of the Diet, only to be tabled when the government could not succeed in persuading the right-wing bloc to recognize Nikkyōso. Following ratification, the Fact-finding Commission concluded as follows:

By virtue of the ratification of the Freedom of Association and Protection of the Right to Organize Convention, 1948 (No. 87), teachers are now legally entitled to designate the Japan Teachers Union to represent them in such negotiations as may take place irrespective of whether such negotiations are conducted on a regional or national level. The Commission notes with satisfaction that this was implicitly conceded in the evidence given before them in September 1964, by the representation at the Ministry of Education.[16]

As we shall see, this was not to be the case.

During the several years when Nikkyōso was appealing its case before the International Labor Organization, Chairman Miyanohara was energetically trying to ameliorate the internal divisions of the union by organizing on the local level groups of people to study wage struggles. These study groups promoted the appeal for unity so that the union could attain its economic objectives. A notable shift in tactics was evinced when Nikkyōso began to attach new importance to the National Personnel Authority by presenting its economic demands to the NPA rather than directly to the government as in the past.

The new tactics, eschewing violence, involved the submission of union demands to the NPA. Peaceful demonstrations and sit-ins were conducted around the NPA building and in front of the Diet building as the process of determining teachers' salaries proceeded through its course. Peaceful rallies were also held in schools. Once the NPA made its recommendations to the government, Nikkyōso directed its efforts to the government rather than the NPA, demanding total acceptance of the NPA's recommendations. Because salaries of all public servants were being considered simultaneously, Nikkyōso collaborated with Sōhyō and the Socialist party in the annual wage struggles. Their efforts were not particularly encouraging since ultimate decisions on salary matters were greatly influenced by the intense internal cabinet rivalry between the traditionally powerful minister of finance and his close associates, and the remaining competing cabinet ministers, including the minister of education.

Minister of Education Araki never for a day relented his attack on Nikkyōso. During his speaking tour throughout the nation, he branded Nikkyōso teachers as thieves intent on robbing Japanese children of their spiritual health by using brainwashing techniques. He attacked the union's annual research conventions (Kyōiku Kenkyū Shūkai), under the influence of left-wing scholars (Kōshidan), for attempting to destroy the mandatory curriculum and turn children into tools of a Communist revolution.[17] After serving exactly three years as minister of education, the longest period any one man has served in that position in the postwar era, Araki was succeeded on July 18, 1963, by Nadao Hirokichi, a strong bureaucrat. Nikkyōso proposed to meet with Nadao, but he saw no reason to alter Araki's position against official contacts with the union. He felt that talks might create misunderstandings.[18]

During the tenures of Araki and Nadao, Nikkyōso made one of its major educational goals the acceptance of all students from the lower secondary school to the upper secondary school, because any student wishing to enter the upper school after completing the ninth year in the compulsory lower secondary school was required to take an entrance examination. Nikkyōso devoted considerable effort, with some success, to the campaign for the accommodation of more students in the upper secondary schools. At the time the union first considered launching this campaign in 1960, 57.8 percent of the graduates of lower secondary schools entered the upper secondary school; by 1965, over 72 percent were in the upper school.[19] Nikkyōso took considerable credit for the rapid increase.

The first half of the 1960s was also important in the history of the left-wing teachers' movement because of a number of court decisions handed down during this period. The union's Legal Affairs Department had become involved in 137 court suits as a result of the struggles over the Teacher's Efficiency-rating Plan, during the years 1956 to 1959, and the achievement-test plan, between 1961 and 1962.[20] The judicial decisions were obviously of great importance not only to Nikkyōso, but also to the Ministry of Education.

The major court decisions concerning teachers punished for their actions during the Teacher's Efficiency-rating Plan struggles, based on Article 37 of the Local Public Service Law, which stipulates that "local public servants may not resort to strikes, slowdown, or other acts of dispute against their employer, or to instigate others to do so," included the following:

1. The Osaka District Court ruled on February 13, 1959, that teachers who participated in mass paid holidays during the rating struggles were not in violation of the Local Public Service Law. The Prosecutor's office appealed the verdict to the next higher court where the case lay pending for years.[21]
2. (*a*) The Fukuoka District Court on December 21, 1962, ruled that mass holidays in April and May, 1958 were, in fact, strikes in violation of the law. Four members of the Fukuoka Prefectural Teachers Union were found guilty of instigating acts of dispute against the local body under Article 37.

(*b*) The Fukuoka Higher Court on December 18, 1967, overruled the lower court's decision.[22]

3. The Saga District Court on August 27, 1962, ruled that strikes by local public service personnel do not violate Article 37 of the Local Public Service Law if the strikes do not affect the welfare of the public. Teachers who went on strike in Saga Prefecture were not violating Article 37 since their activities did not affect the welfare of the general public.[23]

4. The Tōkyō Higher Court in November, 1965, declared that leaders of Tokyōso, the huge affiliate of Nikkyōso in the capital city, were guilty of instigating teachers to strike during a protest demonstration in 1958.[24]

The court cases concerning the achievement-test struggles and arrests revolved primarily around Nikkyōso's charge that the government had no legal basis for conducting compulsory nationwide achievement examinations. The union charged the government with violating Article 10 of the Fundamental Law of Education, which stipulates that "education shall not be subject to improper control, but it shall be directly responsible to the whole people"; and Article 54, Clause 2 of the Law for the Administration of Local Education, which says that the "Minister of Education can *motomeru* (request or demand) local school boards to submit statistical and investigative reports concerning education within their jurisdiction."

The interpretation of *motomeru,* under the so-called *yōkyū* (request or demand) clause, became extremely important in these proceedings because the legal basis of the government's increasing influence over education was the authority of the Ministry of Education to ask school boards to comply with Ministry requests. The fundamental question at stake was whether school boards had the right to refuse Ministerial directives or whether the government had the power to compel local boards to comply. Nikkyōso's case was aimed at the very heart of the interminable postwar controversy over control of Japanese education. The following verdicts were handed down:

1. (*a*) The Kumamoto District Court (Kyūshū) on September 14, 1962, concluded that the achievement tests were not a matter of legality or constitutionality and that they did not violate the spirit of the Fundamental Law of Education. Three teachers were given short-term prison sentences for obstructing the performance of a public official, the school principal, in carrying out his duties in administering the tests.

(*b*) The Fukuoka Higher Court on May 13, 1964, overruled the Kumamoto District Court's decision and declared that the tests were illegal on the basis that it was not proper for the Ministry of Education to conduct national achievement tests merely for the purpose of research.

2. (*a*) The Kōchi District Court (Shikoku) on April 24, 1963, declared that the tests did not fall within the realm of legality as tests per se. They merely represented official government documents which must be executed as instructed. In effect, the tests were legal.
(*b*) The Takamatsu Higher Court on June 3, 1964, upheld the Kōchi District Court's decision.

3. (*a*) The Kokura Branch Court of the Fukuoka District Court (Kyūshū) on March 16, 1964, ruled the tests illegal not on the basis of Article 54 of the Law for the Administration of Local Education but rather on the basis of Article 10 of the Fundamental Law of Education.
(*b*) The Fukuoka Higher Court on April 28, 1967, upheld the lower court's decision, based on Article 54 of the educational administration law, not on Article 10 of the Constitution.

4. The Asahikawa District Court (Hokkaidō) on May 25, 1966, declared the tests illegal based on Article 54 of the Law for the Administration of Local Education.[25]

The inconsistencies of the various court decisions concerning the right to strike and the legality of the achievement tests were revealing because the verdicts themselves reflected the polarization taking place in the interpretations of Japanese education laws: antithetical verdicts were given based on the same clauses of the law. Obviously, a conclusive legal decision was essential. Anxious for a hearing by the highest judicial body in the land, Nikkyōso appealed to the Supreme Court.

As a test case for the Supreme Court, Nikkyōso appealed the 1965 verdict by the Tōkyō Higher Court that leaders of Tōkyōso (Tōkyō Municipal Teachers Union), including its president, Hasegawa Shōzō (one of the founding fathers of the left-wing teachers' movement after the war), were guilty of violating Article 37 of the Local Public Service Law in instigating teachers to strike in 1958 against the Teacher's Efficiency-rating Plan. The Tōkyō Higher Court had indicted only the leaders of the union for instigating the strike, but not the thousands of teachers who had participated in the strike. Nikkyōso argued in its résumé before the Supreme Court in November 1965 that Article 37 of the Local Public Service Law, restricting strikes by local civil servants, was unconstitutional in that it violated Article 28 of the Constitution, which states that "the right of workers to organize and to bargain and act collectively is guaranteed."[26]

The Supreme Court delayed its decision for four years; on April 2,

1969, it finally overruled the lower court's findings. But the final verdict did not answer the question concerning the constitutionality of Article 37 of the Local Public Service Law, for the decision was based on the argument that the prosecution had not proven beyond a doubt that union leaders had "instigated" the strike. The Supreme Court by a narrow decision wrote that the clause prohibiting individuals or groups from instigating local public servants to strike must be strictly defined.[27] Nikkyōso considered the Supreme Court's decision the greatest judicial victory for the teachers in the history of the left-wing teachers' movement. The ultimate results of this landmark decision extend far beyond the period covered in this study.

During the first three years under Miyanohara's leadership, Nikkyōso also continued an attack on what it interpreted as the government's reactionary educational policies, in addition to the implementation of the required curriculum at the elementary school level from 1961 and at the lower secondary level from 1962. The union charged that the Ministry of Education was distorting the required curriculum and the intent of authorized textbooks by injecting reactionary and nationalistic material, particularly in the history courses. The union demanded that the curriculum be set by teachers and local administrators, that textbooks be selected by the local teaching body, and that the proposed government-sponsored national aptitude examination for university entrance (Nōken Tesuto) be rejected.

There were two developments in 1965 which aroused Nikkyōso leaders to redouble their criticisms of the government's educational policies. On January 1 the Central Advisory Council on Education, an organ of the Ministry of Education, published a controversial interim report entitled *The Ideal Image of Man*, an outgrowth of an assignment made by the minister of education in 1963 in preparation for an expansion of secondary school education. He requested the council to undertake a study of the ideal product of the school system; hence, the words *ideal image* in the title of the report.

Among other controversial items, the interim report stated, "The Emperor is the symbol of Japan. We have carried the flag, sung the anthem, and loved and revered the Emperor. We must remember that loving and revering our fatherland is identical with loving and revering the Emperor."[28] Nikkyōso joined the chorus of protests from many sources over the right-wing intent of the report, and prepared materials for local teachers' discussions. Nikkyōso claimed that it was not a legitimate function of a democratic government to establish a mold into which all students should fit. They argued that the strength of Japan rests on the diversity of her people. Opposition is essential. The union vowed to oppose in the classrooms the concept expressed in the *ideal-image* document.[29]

Following this controversy, Nikkyōso plunged into the textbook dispute when, in mid-June 1965, a left-wing scholar, Ienaga Saburō, professor of Japanese history at the University of Education in Tōkyō, sued the Ministry of Education for one million yen. Ienaga had in 1963 submitted to the Ministry for approval the revised draft of his popular textbook entitled *A New History of Japan,* which had gone through four editions since 1947. Objecting to about two hundred passages, the Ministry did not approve the revised draft. After making further revisions in accordance with the Ministry's demands, Ienaga brought suit charging that the Textbook Authorization Procedure, requiring authors to obtain Ministry authorization for the use of their books as official textbooks, constituted a form of state censorship infringing on freedom of expression guaranteed by the postwar Constitution.[30]

Nikkyōso, which had disputed the textbook-authorization system throughout the postwar period, had already been claiming that the Ministry of Education had increased its surveillance over textbook content from the early 1960s by increasingly demanding revisions of material critical of early Japanese myths, which had been taught as truths prior to World War II, and of Japan's role in the war. When Professor Ienaga took his case to court citing specific examples of sections labeled unacceptable by the Ministry of Education, Nikkyōso threw its full weight behind Ienaga by organizing study groups of teachers throughout the nation. The case received wide publicity when distinguished scholars, among them former president of Tōkyō University, Nambara Shigeru, testified on behalf of Ienaga. The case developed into a long and tedious litigation.

During the years of relative quietude between 1962 and 1965 while the ILO investigations and the legal proceedings ran their course—costing the union much time, effort, and expense—Chairman Miyanohara, with subdued diplomacy, had been emphasizing wage demands at home. By 1965 he concluded that the unity of Nikkyōso's rank and file had been sufficiently restored to allow the union to use aggressive tactics to attain its economic goals. After failing to obtain for the union the right of collective bargaining with the government, Miyanohara decided to change his tactics. He planned for a nationwide strike to demand full acceptance by the government of the National Personnel Authority's recommendation of a 6.4 percent increase in teachers' salaries, retroactive to May.[31] The government had announced its acceptance of the salary increase but on the condition that it take effect only from September. Strike action was approved for October 22, 1965, by the twenty-eighth national convention in May.[32]

Miyanohara, being still wary of the gap between national union planning and local implementation, maneuvered carefully for the first unified action since he assumed the chairmanship. He decided that before strike action could be executed, Nikkyōso should conduct an unprecedented nationwide union referendum on the question whether the members would approve of a strike demanding a monthly pay increase of 7,000 yen, to be retroactive to May 1, extra payment for overtime duties, and the abolishment of daytime security duty in the school building. The purpose of the referendum was to instill into each union member a sense of responsibility for the strike action, thus linking the rank and file with the national executive in a truly unified struggle. Miyanohara felt that if all members were responsible, all would participate.[33] The plan was to strike on October 22 with five other public service employees' unions; the combined forces gave a total of over two million unionists.

Shortly before the scheduled strike, Minister of Education Nakamura Umekichi, appointed by Prime Minister Satō Eisaku (younger brother of former Prime Minister Kishi; he succeeded Ikeda Hayato who resigned from the nation's supreme office because of failing health in 1964), proposed to meet with Nikkyōso representatives. His decision was based ostensibly on the recommendations of the International Labor Organization's Fact-finding Commission that the government and unions should hold periodic consultations. The meeting represented the first such direct talks between a minister of education and Nikkyōso representatives in five and a half years, that is, since Araki Masuo became minister in 1960. The union interpreted the meeting as an indication of concern by the minister of education over the well-publicized strike plans. At the highly heralded meeting, Minister Nakamura proposed suspension of the union's strike plans; he stated that the Ministry of Education, in turn, would carefully consider Nikkyōso's wage demands. Nikkyōso refused to call off the strike unless the Ministry gave a definite promise that it would meet the union's demands.

Minister Nakamura, during the hour-and-a-half encounter, laid down three conditions of the government before further talks would be considered. The significance of this famous troika of conditions is that each succeeding minister of education referred to them as a necessary basis for talks. They were: the abolishment or fundamental revision of the union's Code of Ethics, the adoption of a policy of political neutrality, and the discontinuance of force to impede the educational measures taken by the school boards.[34] Nikkyōso rejected the minister's terms.

The referendum on the strike question was conducted by the union in mid-September. Seventy-five percent of those voting approved the strike plan. Based on the results of the referendum, Nikkyōso, on September 30, held its thirtieth Extraordinary Convention to vote on the motion to take a half-day mass leave on October 22 as part of the unified action by the Public Service Personnel Unified Struggle Committee (Kōmuin Kyōtō). The convention passed the motion to strike by a vote of 427 to 29.[35] The plans had been carefully prepared.

But by October 20 the Unified Struggle Committee began to disintegrate. Certain unions, either under the threat of government censure or reacting to minor government concessions, modified their plans by reducing the length of the strike. When one union deviated from the original unified plan, it set off a ripple that quickly turned into a wave. By late evening of October 20, Nikkyōso was standing alone. Prefectural Nikkyōso officers lost their confidence in the face of mass defections of the other public employees' unions. At the very last minute, Miyanohara altered the original plan from a half-day strike to a walkout beginning at 3 P.M., just at the end of a regular school day.

The first nationwide strike sponsored by Nikkyōso since the late 1950s thus ended in failure. The government endorsed most of the National Personnel Authority's wage recommendations but refused to make them retroactive to May. No concessions were granted. Self-reflection was the order of the day. Miyanohara, who had spent several years planning this strike, realized he had overestimated the unity and power of his union. Nikkyōso was still too weak to carry out unified struggles. Nevertheless, he vowed to mount a successful strike campaign for higher wages in 1966.

For the remainder of 1965 and part of 1966, Nikkyōso held innumerable meetings; the 1965 debacle was discussed in an attempt to discern appropriate strike tactics for wage demands in 1966. Leaders on the prefectural level also promoted similar tactics. While the union was busy drawing up preliminary plans for the 1966 strike, the government announced that principals and assistant principals would be classified as supervisors according to the National Public Service Law. As a result, they could no longer remain in a union meant for nonsupervisory personnel. It was estimated that about forty thousand reclassified members withdrew from Nikkyōso.[36]

Then UNESCO, in conjunction with ILO, added a further stimulant to Nikkyōso's campaign for recognition, when it convened a conference in Paris in October 1966 to consider the status of teachers. The union showed more than a passing interest in the meeting because the government, although having ratified the Freedom of Association and Protection of the Right to Organize Convention 87 sixteen months earlier, was still refusing to recognize Nikkyōso. Delegates from both the union and the Ministry of Education attended. The conference drew up a document entitled Recommendations Concerning the Status of Teachers. Of the many recommendations listed, the articles most critical for Nikkyōso were the following:

Article 6. Teaching should be regarded as a profession. It is a form of public service which requires of teachers expert knowledge and specialized skills, acquired and maintained through rigorous and continued study.

Article 44. Promotion of teachers should be based on an objective assessment of the teacher's qualifications for the new post, by reference to strictly professional criteria laid down in consultation with teacher's organizations.

Article 49. Teachers' organizations should be consulted when the machinery to deal with disciplinary matters is established.

Article 62. Teachers and their organizations should participate in the development of new courses, textbooks, and teaching aids.

Article 82. Both salaries and working conditions for teachers should be determined through the process of negotiation between teachers' organizations and the employers of teachers.

Article 84. Appropriate joint machinery should be set up to deal with the settlement of disputes between the teachers and their employers arising out of terms and conditions of employment. If the means and procedures established for these purposes should be exhausted, or if there should be a breakdown in negotiations between the parties, teachers' organizations should have the right to take such other steps as are normally open to other organizations in the defense of their legitimate interests.[37]

Interpreting the final clause in Article 84—that "teachers' organizations should have the right to take such steps as are normally open to other organizations" when negotiations break down—to mean the right to strike, Nikkyōso welcomed UNESCO's report.[38] Since recognized unions have that right in Japan under the Labor Relations Adjustment Law (Rōdō Kankei Chōsei Hō), the union argued that once again an international organization in which Japan holds membership had supported Nikkyōso's position against the government. The Ministry of Education, through its representative, Sagara Iichi, argued that the government did not interpret this passage as granting Nikkyōso the right to strike. On the contrary, according to the government, the "other organizations," referred to in Article 84 were those in the same category as Nikkyōso, that is, public service unions. Since other organizations in the public sector do not have the right to strike, neither did Nikkyōso.[39] Nikkyōso would not be recognized. The relationship between the union and the Ministry thus remained as before.

At Nikkyōso's national convention in September 1966, strike plans nearly identical with those made for 1965 were approved. A unified strike of government employees' unions was scheduled for October 21, 1966, with similar demands for the full implementation of the National Personnel Authority's recommendations, including retroactive wage increases. A national union referendum was held between September 25 and October 5 to obtain approval of the half-day walkout. This time 72.2 percent of the membership approved.[40] Treading cautiously, Miyanohara would approve of strike action only in those prefectures where more than 50 percent of union members voted in favor of the strike motion, since the weaker prefectural unions had been the first to capitulate in the 1965 debacle. Twenty-three of forty-six prefectures approved the plan to strike.[41]

An entirely new ingredient was added in the 1966 strike plans. Sōhyō, of which Nikkyōso is a member, decided in August to support unified strike action also on October 21. Sōhyō had two major goals: to launch a campaign protesting American involvement in the Vietnam war, and to obtain a salary hike for public employees, who represented the majority of Sōhyō's membership. The Vietnam war was being sharply escalated at this time, thrusting the war issue into the center of the Japanese left-wing movement which was aimed directly against American involvement. At a special convention in early October, Sōhyō reaffirmed that one of its major slogans in the strike on October 21 would express opposition to the war.[42]

Miyanohara, who had organized a campaign to collect ten million signatures against American bombings of North Vietnam, was willing to place his union behind an anti-American demonstration, but he had not planned to have Nikkyōso's economic campaign turned into an ideological protest movement. Admittedly, in his speech at the 1966 convention he devoted more time to international political issues than in any of his speeches since he became chairman in 1962. He demanded an end to the American involvement in Vietnam, the return of Okinawa to Japanese control, and the annulment of the United States–Japan Security Pact. Clearly, Nikkyōso was moving cautiously back into the political arena. Be that as it may, Miyanohara claimed that the 1966 strike plans were focused primarily on economic demands.[43]

In spite of Miyanohara's appeals, antiVietnam war preparations dominated the left-wing forces, overshadowing Nikkyōso's wage campaign. The Japan Communist party joined with the Socialist party and Sōhyō to announce that the anti-Vietnam war issue would take precedence over economic issues in the strike.[44] With local Nikkyōso leaders supporting the antiwar demonstrations, it became nebulous where economic demands ended and political issues began. The minister of education warned that the government would deal sternly with teachers who participated in a political strike.[45] Miyanohara's unified strike plans were once again going astray.

Nikkyōso, on October 9, declared that teachers in over half of all prefectures had voted to participate in the strike action to demand full implementation of the National Personnel Authority's recommendations for a 6-percent salary increase, retroactive to May 1966. Seventy-two percent of the 549,000 membership had voted approval.[46] As the strike deadline approached, various unions began to scale down their plans in response to a threat that the minister of labor would punish union members participating in a political strike. Nikkyōso's strike plans once again remained the boldest.

On October 21, 1966, Sōhyō's forty-eight member unions carried out a limited strike led by Nikkyōso's selected prefectural union affiliates. The strike was only partly successful, but Nikkyōso took immediate comfort in being able to conduct strike action even though only about half of all the prefectures participated; it was the union's largest unified action since 1958. Approximately 134,000 teachers walked out of their classrooms—two-thirds for half a day and the remainder for two hours.[47] Nikkyōso leadership called the strike a great success because teachers could unite with workers from other unions in unified struggles. Their euphoria was short-lived, however.

The government reacted early the next morning. Throughout the nation, the police took swift action, raiding union-affiliate headquarters in three hundred different locations for evidence related to the conduct of a politically motivated strike. Days later, nearly all the leaders of the Tōkyō Municipal Teachers Union were arrested because seventeen thousand teachers in Tōkyō had walked out of their classrooms on October 21. In all, thirty-six Nikkyōso leaders were arrested, including Chairman Miyanohara and Secretary General Makieda, who were arrested in their homes at dawn on December 21 for instigating the strike.[48] A total of twenty thousand teachers were dismissed or suspended for their part in the strike.[49] A number of cases were taken to court, including Miyanohara's and Makieda's, as the turbulent year ended.

For Nikkyōso, the year 1967, its twentieth anniversary, began in much the same manner as did the year 1947, when Nikkyōso was inaugurated amidst militant acts of opposition against the government. In action reminiscent of the abortive general strike planned for February 1, 1947, to topple the Yoshida government, the thirty-third national convention in August 1967 voted to conduct a nationwide teachers' strike on October 26 against the wage policy of the Satō government. The circumstances were nearly identical with those of the previous two years when strikes were planned for the month of October. Minister of Education Kennoki Toshihiro declared the strike illegal. He also announced that he would not meet with union representatives until they renounced their Code of Ethics, practiced political neutrality, and refrained from resorting to force to impede the educational policy of the government.[50]

The Kagoshima Prefectural Board of Education then made public the dismissal of Nikkyōso Chairman Miyanohara Sadamitsu from its local teachers' register for leading the teachers' political strike on October 26, 1966; Miyanohara by this dismissal had to forfeit his teaching license.[51] At the time of the announcement, Miyanohara was busily engaged in arranging for a nationwide union referendum in the hope of winning approval for the 1967 strike—for "ensuring individual responsibility for unified struggles."[52] Defiantly, he returned the notice of dismissal, two days prior to Nikkyōso's twentieth-anniversary celebration, a fitting gesture with which to conclude Nikkyōso's first two decades and to perpetuate the militant antigovernment traditions of the Japanese left-wing teachers' movement.

NOTES

1. Nikkyōso (Japan Teachers Union), *Nikkyōso Nijūnenshi* (Twenty-Year History of the Japan Teachers Union) (Tōkyō: Rōdō Junpōsha, 1967), p. 732.
2. Interview with Miyanohara Sadamitsu, Nikkyōso chairman, Tōkyō, January 21, 1970.
3. Interview with Mochizuki Muneaki, Nikkyōso historian, Tōkyō, January 29, 1970.
4. Japan National Police Headquarters' unpublished table entitled "Nihon Kyōshokuin Kumiai nai ni Okeru Nendobetsu Nikkyōso Seiryoku Shintō Jōkyōhyō" (Table of Japan Communist Party Members within Nikkyōso), Tōkyō, August, 1968.
5. Mombu Hōrei Kenkyūkai (Educational Law Research Association), *Shin Kyōiku Roppō* (Revised Edition of the Fundamental Education Laws) (Tōkyō: Daiichi Hōki Shuppansha, 1969), p. 866.
6. Interviews with Miyanohara Sadamitsu and Mochizuki Muneaki, Tōkyō, January 21, 1970 and January 29, 1970, respectively.
7. Mochizuki Muneaki, *Nikkyōso Nijūnen no Tatakai* (Twenty-Year Struggle of the Japan Teachers Union) (Tōkyō: Rōdō Junpōsha, 1967), pp. 228, 231.
8. Ayusawa Iwao, *A History of Labor in Modern Japan* (Honolulu: East-West Center Press, 1966), pp. 112, 315–316.
9. International Labor Office (ILO), *Report of the Fact-finding and Conciliation Commission on Freedom of Association Concerning Persons Employed in the Public Sector in Japan,* Special Supplement to the ILO Official Bulletin, vol. 49, no. 1 (Geneva: ILO, 1966), pp. 156, 169.
10. Ibid., pp. 169–170.
11. Correspondence from Nikkyōso to the ILO, Tōkyō, November 9, 1960.
12. *Japan Times,* October 25, 1960.
13. ILO, *Fact-finding Commission,* pp. 296, 305, 364–373, 427.
14. Ibid., pp. 488, 513–518.
15. Ibid., p. 514.
16. Ibid., p. 513.
17. *Japan Times,* June 7, 1963.
18. Ibid., July 23, 26, 1963.
19. Mochizuki, *Nikkyōso Nijūnen,* p. 289.
20. Nikkyōso, *Outline of the Movement of the Japan Teachers Union,* Tōkyō, May, 1967, p. 10.
21. Interview with Kiriyama Makoto, chief, Legal Affairs Section, Nikkyōso, Tōkyō, February 24, 1970.
22. Nikkyōso, *Chikōhō Jiken Hanketsu Shū* (Judicial Decisions Concerning Violations of Local Public Service Laws), Tōkyō, June, 1968, pp. 69–132.
23. Ibid., pp. 176–179.
24. Nikkyōso, *Jōkoku Shuisho* (Prospectus for the Appeal to the Supreme Court), Tōkyō, October 30, 1966, p. 1.
25. Nikkyōso, *Gaku Te Jiken Jōkyō Ichiran* (Summary of Current Movements Concerning the Achievement-Test Incidents), leaflet, Tōkyō, July 15, 1968.
26. Nikkyōso, *Jōkoku Shuisho,* p. 27.
27. *Asahi Shimbun* (Asahi Newspaper), April 12, 1969; *Japan Times,* April 3, 1969.
28. Mombushō (Japanese Ministry of Education), "Kitaisareru Ningenzō" (Image of an Ideal Man), *Mombu Kōhō* (Ministry of Education Report), leaflet, Tōkyō, January 13, 1965.

29. Interview with Mochizuki Muneaki, Tōkyō, January 29, 1970.
30. Ienaga Saburō, *Kyōkasho Kentei* (Textbook Authorization) (Tōkyō: Nihon Hyōronsha, 1965), p. 173.
31. Interview with Miyanohara Sadamitsu, Tōkyō, January 21, 1970.
32. Mochizuki, *Nikkyōso Nijūnen,* pp. 264–265.
33. Interview with Miyanohara Sadamitsu, Tōkyō, January 21, 1970.
34. *Japan Times,* August 26, 1965.
35. Mochizuki, *Nikkyōso Nijūnen,* p. 266–267.
36. *Japan Times,* July 10, 1966.
37. United Nations Educational, Scientific, and Cultural Organization (UNESCO), *Recommendations Concerning the Status of Teachers,* Paris, October 5, 1966, pp. 6, 20–30.
38. *Asahi Shimbun,* October 5, 1966.
39. Interview with Sagara Iichi, professor of educational administration, Kyōto University, Kyōto, July 29, 1968.
40. Mochizuki, *Nikkyōso Nijūnen,* p. 278.
41. Ibid., p. 276.
42. Munakata Seiya, *10–21 e no Shōgen* (October Twenty-first Strike Testimony) (Tōkyō: Rōdō Junpōsha, 1966), p. 87.
43. Interview with Miyanohara Sadamitsu, Tōkyō, January 21, 1970.
44. *Japan Times,* October 4, 1966.
45. *Asahi Shimbun,* October 1, 1966.
46. Ibid., October 9, 1966.
47. *Japan Times,* October 23, 1966.
48. *Asahi Shimbun,* December 21, 1966.
49. Mochizuki, *Nikkyōso Nijūnen,* p. 280.
50. *Japan Times,* March 19, 1967.
51. *Asahi Shimbun,* June 1, 1967.
52. Interview with Miyanohara Sadamitsu, Tōkyō, January 21, 1970.

PART III

Militancy

Militancy

An Analysis of the Causes

This review of the first twenty years of Nikkyōso's history, and of the left-wing teachers' movement of the prewar era has made it clear that militancy is one of the union's most salient characteristics. Nikkyōso has literally been an organization in perpetual opposition. It has opposed, among other things, the Japanese government, the Ministry of Education, Japanese rearmament, American foreign policy, capitalism, and post-Occupation reforms of Japanese education.

Opposition and resistance are inherent in Nikkyōso's attitudes. For example, when the Nikkyōso-supported Socialist party gained control of the government in 1947, the union actively opposed the Socialist government within a relatively short time, precipitating its collapse, which terminated the only period of Socialist control in postwar Japan. Nikkyōso's attitude of interminable opposition has developed into a militant tradition expressed in activities ranging from peaceful strikes and sit-ins to violent demonstrations and confrontations with local, prefectural, and national authorities.

Innumerable factors underlie Nikkyōso's militant policies, but rather than merely itemizing the many causes, I shall focus on one of the most fundamental factors—Nikkyōso's left-wing leadership. I shall do so by reviewing the careers of several of the union's leaders.

Iwama Masao, long-time Japan Communist party representative in the Diet, was the first notable leader of the left-wing teachers' movement to emerge after the war. Coming from a half-farmer, half-merchant family, he entered the Miyagi Normal School in northern Japan in 1921. Even during this period of Taishō Democracy, the militaristic normal school training was characterized by absolute obedience to authority. Bedtime and rising time, for example, were regulated by military bugle calls. Nevertheless, the liberal trends of the day affected a few students who began reading socialist publications that were circulating throughout the nation during the 1920s. Iwama was one of those students.

Upon graduation in 1925, Iwama became a teacher in a small agricultural community near Sendai in the northern part of Japan. As a teacher of the Japanese language, he participated informally in the Life in Education Movement (Seikatsu Tsuzurikata Undō) by helping his students develop individuality through writing. Deeply interested in poetry, particularly the *tanka* (the thirty-one syllable Japanese verse), Iwama had his pupils describe their lives in poetry. He was awakened to the evils of society through compositions of his pupils, compositions in which they described the hardships of living in destitute rural Japan.[1]

He returned to the normal school for a one-year special postgraduate course, and then, in 1930, found another teaching position, again in an agricultural area in the north. By then the disastrous effects of the Great Depression had reached northern Japan. Farmers could barely afford to eat the rice they themselves produced. Teaching conditions were abominable. Teachers' salaries were reduced and often delayed. Supplies were scarce. Children were undernourished, poorly clothed, and lacking in incentive. Tuberculosis was endemic.

Under these conditions, Iwama developed within himself a guilt complex about teaching the government-prescribed curriculum, conspicuously remote from and unrelated to the lives of his poverty-stricken students. Day by day he became more critical of the Japanese government and its policies. He began to read, in private, ideologically oriented publications including Marxist literature, and became more and more leftwing in spirit.

In 1932 Iwama moved to Tōkyō and joined the staff of the progressive Seijō Gakuen, which employed the teaching method of the Dalton Plan. A crisis developed within the school in 1933, when its progressiveness came under attack by influential conservative parents. Iwama defended the liberal headmaster, sacrificing his own position in the process. From then on until the end of World War II, he worked on a dictionary and an encyclopedia, wrote poetry, and undertook substitute teaching. Simultaneously, his interest in Socialist and Communist literature increased. However, because he was a known progressive, it ultimately became too dangerous for him to secure the illegal publications. He had, however, no formal contacts with the Japan Communist party prior to the war.

Several weeks after the war ended, Iwama attended a small discussion meeting of teachers at the Kyōdō Elementary School near his home in Setagaya Ward in Tōkyō. The discussion focused on the future course for Japanese education now that the war had ended. Iwama described his experiences during the prewar struggles at the Seijō Gakuen and in the process attracted a certain degree of recognition as a prewar activist who lost his position for a progressive cause. He met an "organizer" at the meeting who had probably been sent by the Communist party, although this fact was not made known.

Shortly thereafter, Iwama was invited to attend a preparatory meeting of the left-wing Zenkyō. Because his name was rather well known among prewar activists on account of the Seijō Gakuen incident, Iwama was made welcome and was promptly elected a member of the executive committee. Subsequently he was propelled into the chairmanship of the radical Tōkyō Municipal Teachers Union; eventually he became the leader of the entire teachers' movement in the general strike campaign of February 1, 1947. Two months later he was elected to the Upper House of the Diet as an independent representative. Finally, in 1949, he joined the Japan Communist party, beginning a long and successful career as Communist representative in the Japanese Diet.[2]

The career of Kobayashi Takeshi, who served as chairman of Nikkyōso longer than any of the other three chairmen during the twenty-year history of the union, also has its roots in the normal school education he received. Kobayashi attended the Sapporo Normal School in Hokkaidō, the northernmost island in Japan. The nationalistic education he acquired there molded Kobayashi into a man deeply imbued with reverence for the emperor and love of Japan.

Upon graduation in 1928, Kobayashi became an elementary school teacher in a small town in Hokkaidō, which was then severely affected by the Great Depression. His school had no electricity and very little oil for heating. Broken windows were replaced with cloth. When the winter darkness settled over that northern territory, schools were closed. Kobayashi felt great sympathy for his students, who were undernourished and poorly clothed. During this time he witnessed governmental suppression of some of his colleagues who participated in activist movements protesting the prevailing social and economic conditions. But Kobayashi did not join any of the prewar left-wing movements, despite the sympathy he felt toward the plight of the students.

Kobayashi attributes his complete loyalty to Japan and its leaders during the prewar and wartime periods to his strict normal school training, which implanted in him an intense love of his homeland and the deepest respect and love for the emperor. He endeavored to pass on these attitudes to his students and, after becoming an elementary school principal, to the teachers who served under him as well.

When the radio and newspapers during the American Occupation brought to light how the Japanese people had been deceived by the wartime leaders, Kobayashi experienced a new consciousness, a feeling of liberation—and mixed feelings of guilt and anger. He felt betrayed and misled. These feelings inevitably led him to seek a new direction for Japanese education. As a small-town higher elementary school principal in faraway Hokkaidō, however, he had little opportunity or courage to become active in the left-wing teachers' movement converging on Tōkyō.

Prompted, nevertheless, by the poor economic conditions endured by teachers immediately after the war, Kobayashi turned against the Japanese government and its educational policies. Feeling that too many prewar bureaucrats remained in the postwar government and that teachers were politically weak and needed the power of unity to confront the government, Kobayashi, by 1949, or two years after Nikkyōso was formed, was actively participating in the union movement as head of the Hokkaidō branch of Nikkyōso. In 1951 he became chairman of the Hokkaidō Teachers Union, an affiliate of Nikkyōso, and then, from 1953 until 1962, chairman of Nikkyōso itself. He entered the Upper House of Parliament in 1962 on the Socialist party ticket.

Kobayashi, as the newly elected Nikkyōso chairman in 1953, approved the union's ideological shift to the left in reaction to the government's shift to the right after the American Occupation ended in 1952. Observing that the ministers of education were being chosen from the ranks of party politicians, especially Minister Odachi who had been associated with the former Ministry of Home Affairs, Nikkyōso, under Kobayashi, hardened its attitude toward the Ministry of Education. Violence, bloodshed, and mass punishment eventually ensued. When the violence in 1958 between union members and the police continued unabated, Kabayashi belatedly threw his support behind the moderates led by his successor, Miyanohara Sadamitsu.[3]

The third career that will be reviewed is that of Miyanohara Sadamitsu, who has been chairman of Nikkyōso since 1962. Born in the city of Kagoshima in Kyūshū, the southernmost island in Japan, Miyanohara entered the Kagoshima Normal School in 1936, when the militarists were wielding an inordinate amount of influence over the Japanese government. Consequently, Miyanohara immediately found himself immersed in a very tightly controlled life, especially in the dormitory where strict discipline was maintained. He felt that he did not fit into that kind of oppressive atmosphere. Nevertheless, the concepts of Japanese superiority and love for the emperor were ingrained within him during this period. After graduating from the normal school in 1938, he entered the Japanese imperial navy for five months; upon release, he became an elementary school teacher in rural Kyūshū.

Miyanohara firmly believed in the militaristic education then being advanced by the military regime, as Japanese armies launched offensive movements on the Asian mainland. As a teacher in the higher elementary school dealing mainly with boys fourteen to fifteen years old, he took a particularly strong interest in developing among his students a sense of service to the Japanese empire. As mentioned in an earlier chapter, he encouraged volunteers to go to Manchuria to help develop that land under Japanese control; he did so through a special organization of Japanese youth. Miyanohara took considerable pride in being able to persuade many of his rural students to join this governmental project for overseas development of the Japanese empire.

When, at war's end, at least half of the youth corps which had gone to Manchuria did not return, Miyanohara began to question agonizingly and earnestly his blind acceptance of the Japanese government's policies— and of the war itself. He came to realize that Japanese education was concerned primarily with the concept of loyalty to the emperor. And because of this blind loyalty, people did not value life and unhesitatingly killed others in the name of the emperor. Miyanohara concluded that Japanese education was fundamentally evil.

In April 1946, Miyanohara had the opportunity to read the First United States Education Mission's report for the democratization of Japanese education. Comparing the old Japanese forms with the new plan, and reflecting upon his experiences under the old system, he concluded that the new education was the only hope for the future of Japan. He then and there decided to dedicate himself to the fulfillment of the new democratic education.

How he could best accomplish his ideals became of paramount concern. At first, in 1947, he formed a study group of several of his fellow teachers to discuss the future course of Japanese education and to reflect upon the past. Learning that teachers in Tōkyō, faced with spiraling inflation and low salaries, were already forming unions, his small circle of colleagues concluded that teachers in Kyūshū must also unite in order to promote their economic welfare and help mold the new education.

After Nikkyōso was formed in June 1947, Miyanohara combined his group of teachers with several others in Kagoshima Prefecture to form the Kagoshima Prefectural Teachers Union under his leadership. This union later sent Miyanohara to the national headquarters of Nikkyōso; he was elected national chairman in 1962. As chairman of Nikkyōso, he has insisted at every annual convention that a banner be unfurled over the convention hall bearing the slogan, "Never send our children to the battlefields again."[4]

The lives of these three Nikkyōso leaders illustrate many of the fundamental factors giving rise to Nikkyōso's militancy. All three men received normal school education and had teaching experience in rural or small-town elementary schools during the depression of the early 1930s and during the war. This experience was shared by all of the Nikkyōso leaders.

The first two Nikkyōso chairmen, Araki Shōzaburō and Oka Saburō, were also graduates of provincial normal schools. Araki graduated from the Ikeda Normal School near Osaka in 1925 and began teaching in a small elementary school in that area. Oka Saburō graduated from the Yamanashi Normal School in rural Japan in 1933 and became a teacher in a small elementary school in Yamanashi Prefecture during the depression. Oka believes that, as far as teaching technique is concerned, the training given by normal schools in prewar years, was superior to that given by postwar teacher-training institutions. However, the normal school of his day "produced narrow-minded teachers who taught automatically the prescribed curriculum."[5] Hiragaki Miyoji, leader of Nikkyōso's left-wing bloc during the period of violence around 1958, was also a graduate of the Ikeda Normal School and began his teaching career in a nearby rural elementary school in 1937.

One could examine the list of all the officers of Nikkyōso and find that nearly every leader attended a provincial normal school before the war. Upon graduation, all began their teaching careers in elementary schools, frequently in rural Japan, during the periods of the Great Depression and the militaristic regime. The significance of this common background must not be underestimated. The fact that none of the top union leaders had attended a university, the source of the prewar elite, placed them in a lower category, both academically and in prestige, than that enjoyed by university graduates. In addition, because the universities were much more liberal than normal schools, university graduates were more broadly educated and certainly much less restrained and less indoctrinated with ultranationalistic ideas than were normal school graduates, for university students were exposed to the more liberal thought prevailing on university campuses. Indeed, Tōkyō University was alive with Communist cells among the students in the early 1930s.

In contrast, normal schools were highly disciplined, closely regulated, restrictive institutions. Their students received a narrow education and were heavily indoctrinated; they were trained, as it were, to be dogmatists and to perpetuate those concepts and ideals selected by the government as essential for the youth of Japan in the name of the emperor. The leaders of Nikkyōso, almost to a man, were trained in this type of environment; these men showed the same rigidity and intolerance with respect to the development of the union, though in the name of democracy, not of the emperor.

Not only were the postwar leaders of the teachers' movement trained in second-class prewar institutions, they were elementary school teachers— the least prestigious position in the hierarchy of the teaching profession. Admittedly, rural elementary school teachers from normal schools, particularly those teaching in the upper grades, were held in high esteem in their local communities. Nevertheless, teachers in the middle and upper secondary schools held the truly prestigious teaching positions, next only to those teaching at the university level. Elementary school teachers, moreover, had virtually no freedom in their teaching, whereas secondary school teachers had a certain degree of freedom and independence in the classroom.

In other words, the men who led the postwar teachers' movement had held positions of inferior status in the prewar years in terms of both their professional training and experience. When they found themselves leading a postwar mass movement of teachers, it was perhaps inevitable that they would follow an aggressive policy, driven in part perhaps by an inferiority complex, in order to raise the status of union members who were mostly elementary school teachers.

Be that as it may, the postwar leaders of the teachers' unions not only led a popular movement among teachers, but also occupied influential positions as the intellectual leaders of the entire labor movement. Leaders of the proliferating labor unions were primarily either graduates of secondary technical schools or those who had had no further education beyond the level of compulsory education. Leaders of the teachers' unions, as graduates of normal schools, thus assumed a special status. As a result, Nikkyōso was often in the forefront of the burgeoning labor movement. At times, labor leaders found themselves moving more to the left in response to the militant demands from the rank and file, notably the railway and postal workers. At other times, Nikkyōso influenced the entire trade-union movement leftward when its leaders were convinced that the Japanese government was becoming reactionary and that the trade unions were not cognizant of the danger. Nikkyōso leaders took it upon themselves to enlighten other labor leaders about the evils of the Japanese government.

The general sentiment of teachers who had been subservient to the ultranationalistic military regime in the prewar and war years also sparked a militant reaction at war's end. Up until the end of the war, teachers had been compelled to teach certain facts and concepts which many of them knew were untrue. The myths about the sun goddess and the origin of Japan, the subhumanness of Western peoples, and the like, were not believed by a good many of the teachers. But they had to stand before their classes and teach such myths and false ideas as truths, or face the consequences. Most teachers simply complied with the regulations without compunction. Others, however, experienced mental anguish over this unhappy assignment. These latent feelings against the government were carried over into the postwar period.

Also unpleasant, especially to the sensitive teacher, was the task of preparing the finest of Japanese youth to fight and die courageously on the battlefields of Asia and the Pacific. When an appalling number of former students failed to return to their beloved homeland at the end of the war, the teachers ironically were exposed overnight as having been pawns of the wartime machine. The suppressed feelings of guilt among such teachers turned to anger and exploded through the channels of the teachers' unions proliferating throughout Japan in 1945 and 1946.

When the Americans arrived, with their idealistic democratic ideals for the reformation of Japanese education, including freedom of teachers from government control, the activist teachers concentrated their energies into a truculent campaign against the government. The purpose of the campaign was to transform the traditional subservient mentality of the average teacher, trained by the normal schools to follow government orders, to one of independence. Ironically, union activists exploited this very habit of subservience in order to induce the average teacher to transfer his allegiance from the government to the union when independent unions joined the larger unions *en bloc*.

Postwar poverty also caused teachers to feel deeply hostile toward the government. The average union teacher, a married man with a family, was forced to witness his meagre salary being eroded by inflation while his family subsisted on inadequate food rations. The only major avenue by which he might attempt to improve his circumstances existed with the unions. As the months of destitution dragged into years, teachers released their frustrations through strikes and demonstrations. But in 1948 General MacArthur banned strikes and collective bargaining for teachers on the grounds that teachers were civil servants. Thus the means of release of tensions was proscribed while the causes of tension and frustration continued unabated.

The American Occupation struck another blow against the union by conducting the Red Purge, following the ban on teachers' strikes. The teachers, who in 1946 had given their unqualified support to the United States Education Mission's recommendations for educational reform in Japan and who had found themselves in harmony with SCAP until then, suddenly found themselves betrayed by their American ally, first by being denied the rights to strike and to bargain collectively, and now by having their leftist union leaders purged. In response, the degree of teachers' hostility increased.

Nikkyōso lost its last hope of sustaining the American Occupation's educational reforms for Japan when, shortly after the end of the Occupation, the ruling conservative party of the Japanese government started to change the educational reforms that had been implemented by the Americans. Nikkyōso intensified its militant tactics accordingly. A rash of protest strikes and demonstrations followed, leading to violence in the years between 1957 and 1961. By the time the government started to react against Nikkyōso's violent actions, the union's militancy had already escalated to a point beyond the possibility of reconciliation.

The period following the end of the American Occupation of Japan, when the Japanese government, under conservative leadership, initiated Japanese revisions of the Occupation reforms to rectify what it considered excesses, produced the most violent acts of resistance in the union's history. In order to understand those actions, a series of events must be viewed in perspective. During the American Occupation, control of education was theoretically transferred from the Ministry of Education to local school boards. Teachers were granted considerable influence in determining local educational policy. When the school-board law was revised in 1956, much of the real power pertaining to educational decision-making was transferred back to the central government; Nikkyōso considered this a threat to local autonomy and resorted to acts of belligerence. The union lost its case.

The next stage evolved when school principals were forced out of the union and, from the union's point of view, on to the side of the school boards and the Ministry of Education. Nikkyōso increased its resistance in order to protect school autonomy. Again the union lost. The final stage involved the Teacher's Efficiency-rating Plan, interpreted by the union as a device to compel teachers to follow the prescribed curriculum. Nikkyōso pursued its most violent protest campaign to defend what it believed to be the teacher's last preserve—the autonomy of the classroom. In this instance, Nikkyōso won a partial victory but at an extravagantly high price in membership defection and disruptive internal dissension.

Related to this issue is the continuing nonrecognition of Nikkyōso by the Japanese government—a frustration which intensifies the union's aggressive policy toward the government. After being weaned, during the early heady days of the American Occupation, on Western labor concepts of collective bargaining and the right to strike, Nikkyōso found the conditions set by SCAP after 1948 unreasonable and unacceptable, for it was through these conditions that Nikkyōso, the largest labor union in Japan, not only lost those rights, but also witnessed its contract as the agency representing its members unilaterally nullified by the government: Nikkyōso's predicament only hardened its militant attitudes. Although the International Labor Organization, of which Japan is a member nation, essentially supported the union's position, the Japanese government proved to be a formidable enemy, able to thwart all attempts by the union to gain official recognition. Nonrecognition continues as a sword in the side of the union and a major factor underlying its militant antipathy toward the government.

At the local level, Nikkyōso's frustrations have been magnified by the dearth of institutional avenues available for expressing grievances. In lieu of the right to strike and bargain collectively, each prefecture and major city maintains a local Personnel Authority (Jinjiinkai), patterned after the National Personnel Authority, where grievances from civil servants are handled. Nikkyōso claims that this is a biased body because its three members are appointed by the local administrative head—the governor or the mayor. When the local school board, also appointed by the local administrative head, disciplines teachers or transfers activists from one school to another, complaints taken to the local Personnel Authority are usually rejected. Nikkyōso claims that the Personnel Authority is merely an extension of the school board since both are appointed by the governor or the mayor. The union claims that, because its members have no impartial body to adjudicate grievances, they take to the streets in protest.

The composition of the membership of Nikkyōso has also been a critical factor inducing belligerency. The Japanese elementary school has traditionally been the preserve of the male teacher, whereas in most countries women dominate elementary teaching. In Japan, the number of women elementary school teachers did not approach that of men teachers until after 1965. Hence, when Nikkyōso, consisting preponderantly of elementary teachers, aggressively campaigned for higher salaries in its early history, it was on behalf of male teachers supporting families on inadequate incomes.

The final factor underlying the militant policies of Nikkyōso concerns the highly volatile and controversial issue of Communist influence. The discussion of communism as an ideology has been avoided hitherto in this study because it was not an issue in the prewar normal school; nor was it related to the Great Depression or to the terrible economic conditions and inflation after the war. These conditions did not spawn Communist activity although Communists within Nikkyōso capitalized on the prevailing circumstances to exert an influence, which fluctuated considerably depending on the magnitude of the adverse external factors.

The degree of Communist influence on Nikkyōso can be measured in part by the number of Communist party members holding important administrative positions in the union. Figure 2 shows the percentage of Communist party members on Nikkyōso's Central Executive Committee from 1947 to 1967.

Table 9 shows the estimated number of Communist party members within Nikkyōso between 1953 and 1967. A comparison of the data in Figure 2 and Table 9 will reveal that there is virtually no correlation between the number of Communists on the Central Executive Committee and that among the rank and file. Indeed, there is no correlation between the degree of Communist power within Nikkyōso and the numerical strength of the union's Communist teachers. For example, when Commu-

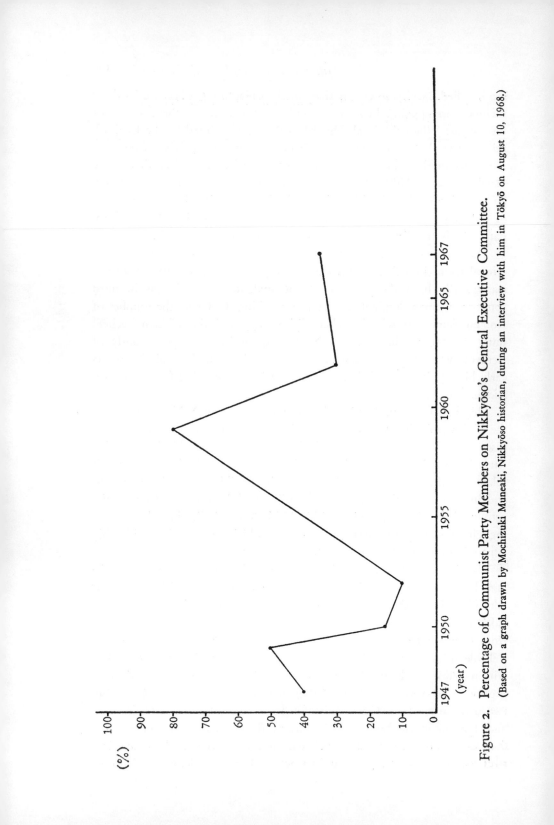

Figure 2. Percentage of Communist Party Members on Nikkyōso's Central Executive Committee.

(Based on a graph drawn by Mochizuki Muneaki, Nikkyōso historian, during an interview with him in Tōkyō on August 10, 1968.)

Table 9.   Estimated Numbers of Communist Party Members
in Nikkyōso, 1953–1967

Year	Total Nikkyōso Membership	Communist Party Members in Nikkyōso	
		Number	Percentage
1953	501,386	465	0.09
1956	549,858	989	0.18
1959	575,557	2,131	0.37
1962	582,375	5,989	1.03
1965	574,420	9,817	1.71
1967	535,816	12,729	2.38

Source: Data from Japan National Police Headquarters' unpublished table entitled "Nihon Kyōshokuin Kumiai nai ni Okeru Nendobetsu Nikkyōso Seiryoku Shintō Jōkyōhō" (Table of Japan Communist Party Members within Nikkyōso), Tōkyō, August, 1968.

nist influence on Nikkyōso was at its peak in 1958, leading the union to pursue violent tactics, less than half of 1 percent of the total union membership were members of the Japan Communist party. Obviously, Communist influence was not dependent upon numbers.

Conversely, after Miyanohara became union chairman in 1962 by purging Communists from the Central Executive Committee in order to pursue a more moderate policy stressing economics rather than ideology, total Communist membership increased among rank-and-file union members. Again, there was no positive correlation between the degree of militancy pursued by the union and the number of card-carrying Communists within the union. In fact, there is a direct relationship between the number of Communists within Nikkyōso and the degree of Nikkyōso's increasing moderation, if the years 1958 to 1967 are taken as samples.

What can be said by way of analysis is that Communist influence within Nikkyōso has been significant at selected periods during the union's twenty-year history, but not because of the appeal of communism itself. Rather, Communist influence within Nikkyōso has been dominant only when the Communist bloc on the Central Executive Committee was capable of leading the union for or against an issue about which the average union member felt strongly.

For example, the Communist members attained their zenith of power during the campaign against the Teacher's Efficiency-rating Plan between 1957 and 1959 as leaders of an implacable opposition. Teachers throughout the world have opposed teacher-rating schemes. It can also be assumed that in Japan the vast majority of teachers opposed the government's plan to evaluate teachers. The result was the rapid growth of the Communist bloc's influence within Nikkyōso as Nikkyōso's Communists maneuvered to lead a popular campaign against the rating plan. There is no evidence that Communist influence was increased because of the attraction of communism per se.

When the long and debilitating campaign against the rating plan eventually ran out of steam and lost its appeal to the average union member, Communist prestige within Nikkyōso rapidly declined in proportion. The rank and file supported the Communist bloc as long as Communist interests coincided with those of Nikkyōso's general membership. When they did not, the Communists lost their power.

In sum, communism as an ideology has not been the determining factor in the degree of influence the Communist bloc has been able to attain in the historical development of Nikkyōso; communism as an ideology has not been one of the major causes underlying the militant policies of the union. Too many other conditions and factors unrelated to communism, as discussed previously, are more directly responsible for the militancy of the union.

Support for this position can be made by a concluding syllogism. If communism had not existed and there had been no Communist bloc within Nikkyōso, it is nevertheless difficult to imagine that the union would have developed its policies much differently in reaction to the prewar and postwar conditions in Japan. However, if the prewar and postwar conditions had been diametrically different; that is, if there had been no nationalistic normal school training, no Great Depression, no postwar poverty, and no conservative reforms of the American Occupation reforms, then the militancy of a teachers' union in contemporary Japan would have been significantly moderated regardless of the presence of communism. In other words, there is sufficient cause to believe that Nikkyōso, with or without Communist influence, would have pursued a policy of militant resistance to the Japanese government and to the Ministry of Education in reaction to the peculiar set of circumstances prevailing within Japan during the prewar, the American Occupation, and the independence periods.

NOTES

1. Iwama Masao, *Hitosujini* (In One Direction) (Tōkyō: Japan Communist Party Publications Department, 1967), p. 112.
2. Adapted from Iwama Masao's *Hitosujini* and from an interview with the Honorable Iwama Masao, Japan Communist party representative, Tōkyō, August 12, 1968.
3. Interview with the Honorable Kobayashi Takeshi, Socialist party representative, Tōkyō, August 12, 1968.
4. Interviews with Miyanohara Sadamitsu, Nikkyōso chairman, Tōkyō, July 11, 21, 1968; August 15, 1969; January 21, 1970.
5. Correspondence from the Honorable Oka Saburō, Tōkyō, May 11, 1968.

Appendix

Selected Documents

General MacArthur's Letter to Prime Minister Shidehara Kijūrō
Concerning the Unionization of Labor. October 11, 1945. (Excerpts)

In the achievement of the Potsdam Declaration, the traditional social order under which the Japanese people for centuries have been subjugated will be corrected. This will unquestionably involve a liberalization of the Constitution.

The people must be freed from all forms of governmental and secret inquisition into their daily lives which holds their minds in virtual slavery and from all forms of control which seek to suppress freedom of thought, freedom of speech or freedom of religion. Regimentation of the masses under the guise or claims of efficiency, under whatever name of government it may be made, must cease.

In the implementation of these requirements and to accomplish the purposes thereby intended, I expect you to institute the following reforms in the social order of Japan as readily as they can be assimilated:

1. The emancipation of the women of Japan through their enfranchisement . . .
2. The encouragement of the unionization of Labor . . . that it may be clothed with such dignity as will permit it an initial voice in safeguarding the working man from exploitation and abuse and raising his living standard to a higher level; with the institution of such measures as may be necessary to correct the evils which now exist in child labor practices
3. The opening of the schools to more liberal education that the people may shape their future progress . . .
4. The abolition of systems which through secret inquisition and abuse have held the people in constant fear . . .
5. The democratization of Japanese economic institutions to the end that monopolistic industrial controls be revised through the development of methods which tend to insure a wide distribution of income and ownership of the means of production and trade

Source: Ayusawa Iwao, *A History of Labor in Modern Japan* (Honolulu: East-West Center Press, 1966), p. 247.

2

Administration of the Educational System of Japan.
General Headquarters, SCAP. October 22, 1945.

In order that the newly formed Cabinet of the Imperial Japanese Government shall be fully informed of the objectives and policies of the Occupation with regard to Education, it is hereby directed that:

a. The content of all instructions will be critically examined, revised, and controlled in accordance with the following policies:

(1) Dissemination of militaristic and ultranationalistic ideology will be prohibited and all military education and drill will be discontinued.

(2) Inculcation of concepts and establishment of practices in harmony with representative government, international peace, the dignity of the individual, and such fundamental human rights as the freedom of assembly, speech, and religion, will be encouraged.

b. The personnel of all educational institutions will be investigated, approved or removed, reinstated, appointed, reorientated, and supervised in accordance with the following policies:

(1) Teachers and educational officials will be examined as rapidly as possible and all career military personnel, persons who have been active exponents of militarism and ultranationalism, and those actively antagonistic to the policies of the Occupation will be removed.

(2) Teachers and educational officials who have been dismissed, suspended, or forced to resign for liberal or antimilitaristic opinions or activities, will be declared immediately eligible for and if properly qualified will be given preference in reappointment.

(3) Discrimination against any student, teacher, or educational official on grounds of race, nationality, creed, political opinion, or social position will be prohibited, and immediate steps will be taken to correct inequities which have resulted from such discrimination.

(4) Students, teachers, and educational officials will be encouraged to evaluate critically and intelligently the content of instruction and will be permitted to engage in free and unrestricted discussion of issues involving political, civil, and religious liberties.

(5) Students, teachers, educational officials, and the public will be informed of the objectives and policies of the Occupation, of the theory and practices of representative government, and of the part played by militaristic leaders, their active collaborators, and those who by passive acquiescence committed the nation to war with the inevitable result of defeat, distress, and the present deplorable state of the Japanese people.

c. The instrumentalities of educational processes will be critically examined, revised and controlled in accordance with the following policies:

(1) Existing curricula, textbooks, teaching manuals, and instructional materials, the use of which is temporarily permitted on an emergency basis, will be examined as rapidly as possible and those portions designed to promote a militaristic or ultranationalistic ideology will be eliminated.

(2) New curricula, textbooks, teaching manuals, and instructional materials designed to produce an educated, peaceful, and responsible citizenry will be prepared and will be substituted for existing materials as rapidly as possible.

(3) A normally operating educational system will be reestablished as rapidly as possible, but where limited facilities exist preference will be given to elementary education and teacher training.

d. The Japanese Ministry of Education will establish and maintain adequate liaison with the appropriate staff section of the Office of the Supreme Commander for the Allied Powers and upon request will submit reports describing in detail all action taken to comply with the provisions of this directive.

e. All officials and subordinates of the Japanese Government affected by the terms of this directive, and all teachers and school officials, both public and private, will be held personally accountable for compliance with the spirit as well as the letter of the policies enunciated in this directive.

Source: Supreme Commander for the Allied Powers, *Education in the New Japan* (Tōkyō: SCAP, 1948), 2:26–28.

3

Screening of Teachers. General Headquarters, SCAP.
October 30, 1945.

In order to eliminate from the educational system of Japan those militaristic and ultranationalistic influences which in the past have contributed to the defeat, war guilt, suffering, privation, and present deplorable state of the Japanese people; and in order to prevent the teachers and educational officials having military experience or affiliation; it is hereby directed that:

a. All persons who are known to be militaristic, ultranationalistic, or antagonistic to the objectives and policies of the Occupation and who are at this time actively employed in the educational system of Japan, will be removed immediately and will be barred from occupying any position in the educational system of Japan.

b. All other persons now actively employed in the educational system of Japan will be permitted to retain their positions at the discretion of the Ministry of Education until further notice.

c. All persons who are members of or who have been demobilized from the Japanese military forces since the termination of hostilities, and who are not at this time actively employed in the educational system of Japan, will be barred from occupying any position in the educational system of Japan until further notice.

In order to determine which of those persons who are now actively employed in or who may in the future become candidates for employment in the educational system of Japan are unacceptable and must be removed, barred, and prohibited from occupying any position in the educational system of Japan, it is hereby directed that:

a. The Japanese Ministry of Education will establish suitable administrative machinery and procedures for the effective investigation, screening, and certification of all present and prospective teachers and educational officials.

b. The Japanese Ministry of Education will submit to this Headquarters as soon as possible a comprehensive report describing all actions taken to comply with the provisions of this directive. This report will contain in addition the following specific information:

  (1) A precise statement of how acceptability of the individual is to be determined, together with lists of specific standards which will govern the retention, removal, appointment, or reappointment of the individual.

  (2) A precise statement of what administrative procedures and machinery are to be established in order to accomplish the investigation, screening, and certification of personnel, together with a statement of what provisions are to be made for review of appealed decisions and reconsideration of individuals previously refused certification.

All officials and subordinates of the Japanese Government affected by the terms of this directive, and all school officials, both public and private, will be held personally accountable for compliance with the spirit as well as the letter of the policies enunciated in this directive.

Source: Supreme Commander for the Allied Powers, *Education in the New Japan* (Tōkyō: SCAP, 1948), 2:29–30.

4

Suspension of Courses in Morals, History, and Geography.
General Headquarters, SCAP. December 31, 1945.

  1. In accordance with the basic directive AG 000.3 (15 Dec. 45) CIE proclaiming the abolition of government sponsorship and support of State Shinto and Doctrine; and inasmuch as the Japanese Government has used education to inculcate militaristic and ultranationalistic ideologies which have been inextricably interwoven in certain textbooks imposed upon students; it is hereby directed that:

    a. All courses in Morals (Shūshin), Japanese History, and Geography in all educational institutions, including government, public, and private schools, for which textbooks and teachers' manuals have been published or sanctioned by the Ministry of Education shall be suspended immediately and will not be resumed until permission has been given by this Headquarters.

b. The Ministry of Education shall suspend immediately all ordinances (hōrei), regulations, or instructions directing the manner in which the specific subjects of Morals (Shūshin), Japanese History, and Geography shall be taught.

c. The Ministry of Education shall collect all textbooks and teachers' manuals used in every course and educational institution affected by 1, a for disposal in accordance with the procedure outlined in Annex A to this memorandum.

d. The Ministry of Education shall prepare and submit to this Headquarters a plan for the introduction of substitute programs to take the place of courses affected by this memorandum in accordance with the procedure outlined in Annex B to this memorandum. These substitute programs will continue in force until such time as this Headquarters authorizes the resumption of the courses suspended herein.

e. The Ministry of Education shall prepare and submit to this Headquarters a plan for revising textbooks to be used in Morals (Shūshin), Japanese History, and Geography in accordance with the procedure outlined in Annex C to this memorandum.

2. All officials, subordinates, and employees of the Japanese Government affected by the terms of this directive, and all school officials and teachers, both public and private, will be held personally accountable for compliance with the spirit as well as the letter of the terms of this directive.

Source: Supreme Commander for the Allied Powers, *Education in the New Japan* (Tōkyō: SCAP, 1948), 2:36–37.

5

Political Activities of Teachers and Students. Vice-Minister of Education, Ministry of Education. January 17, 1946.

Students, teachers, and school officials may enter political activities, and join political organizations. Such political activities, however, must not be allowed to interfere in any way with their normal duties.

Although free discussions on politics will be allowed in schools, political canvassing or recommending of specific political parties or personnel will not be allowed in school time.

Source: Supreme Commander for the Allied Powers, *Education in the New Japan* (Tōkyō: SCAP, 1948), 2:163.

6

Concerning Teachers' Associations (To Educational Administrators).
Ministry of Education April 11, 1946.

Various questions have recently been sent in from different quarters concerning teachers' associations. Mr. Abe, Minister of Education, spoke of this matter at the recent meeting of prefectural governors as follows:

"Everyone recognizes that measures taken by the government cannot keep pace with the problems which arise from difficulties in our daily life, caused by a shortage of commodities, inflation, etc. It is, therefore, necessary that attempts be made by teachers to help themselves. It is desirable for them to organize some sort of self-aid organizations. They must be careful, however, not to be too radical, or to allow themselves to be taken advantage of by any political parties. It is hoped that these will be developed into a beneficial organization. Therefore, you are requested not to impose too many restrictions on such groups.

"Teachers are at liberty to identify themselves with any of the political parties according to their choice, but they must be very careful not to forget their fundamental mission of education and not to cause any conflict in the schools, thereby disrupting the education of the young people.

"We understand that there are many school farms and other various organizations, supported by parents, which contribute toward the living of elementary school and secondary school teachers. We consider this to be a good thing as it is a sign of appreciation of teachers on the part of parents. But it is requested that you take care not to let the relationship become too personal."

We desire that you inform all teachers under your supervision concerning the details of this notice.

Source: Supreme Commander for the Allied Powers, *Education in the New Japan* (Tōkyō: SCAP, 1948), 2:162.

7

Screening of Teachers. Imperial Ordinance No. 263.
May 6, 1946. (Excerpts)

ARTICLE I. A person now holding an educational position and designated by the competent Minister "as falling under the categories of career military personnel, notorious militarist, ultranationalist, or notorious antagonist of the objectives and policies of the occupation of Japan by the Allied Powers as specified in the Memorandum of the Supreme Commander for the Allied Powers dated 22 October 1945" shall be removed and henceforth disqualified.

If suitable replacement cannot be found, however, he may be retained for not over six months.

ARTICLE II. A person who may be employed within six months from this date is also subject to Article I above.

ARTICLE III. A person, previously removed from an educational position and now designated by the competent Minister as liberal or anti-militaristic under SCAP directives, will be preferentially reinstated up to six months hence.

ARTICLE IV. Positions included under the term "position in the educational service" shall be designated by the competent minister.

ARTICLE V. Questionnaires necessary for application of Articles I, II, and III above shall be collected by appropriate government agencies.

DISQUALIFICATION BY INQUIRY COMMITTEES

States six categories of those who are to be designated as nonacceptable persons for educational service according to the inquiry and decision of the inquiry committees, as follows:

1. Persons who by lecture, speech, book, essay, or other actions fall in any of the following groups:

    a. Persons who have advocated or actively cooperated in propagating aggressive policy or militant nationalism, and persons who by their doctrines laid an ideological basis for Great Asia Policy, the New-Order-East-Asia or other similar policies, the Manchurian Affair, the Chinese Affair, or the Recent War.

    b. Persons who have advocated dictatorship or Nazi or Fascist totalitarianism.

    c. Persons who have persecuted or expelled others on the grounds of race.

    d. Persons who have propagated Shinto ideology with a view to advocating racial superiority.

    e. Persons who have persecuted or expelled those who have liberal or anti-militaristic opinions, etc., or those who believe in any religion on grounds of their opinions or religions.

    f. Persons who, though they fall under none of the above items, have advocated militarism or ultranationalism or persons who have so ingratiated themselves with these tendencies that they lack ideological integrity as educators.

2. Persons who have been advisors, or nonofficial staff of, or who have had other special connections with the Nazi or Fascist regime or its organs and have cooperated in carrying out its policies.

3. Persons who have publicly stated opinions antagonistic to the objectives and policies of the occupation of Japan by the Allied Powers or who have led others to oppose objectives and policies.

4. Government or public officials who in discharging their duties have persecuted or oppressed religion.

5. Persons who have compiled textbooks or publications concerning education with a militaristic or ultranationalistic intention.

6. Persons who have, under the protection of the Japanese armed forces, directed or taken part in scientific expeditions or excavation works in the territory of the Allied Powers occupied by the Japanese forces since 1 January 1928.

Source: Supreme Commander for the Allied Powers, *Education in the New Japan* (Tōkyō: SCAP, 1948), 2:80–87.

8

The Collective Bargaining Contract between the Council of All–Japan Teachers' Unions (Zenkyōkyō) and the Ministry of Education. March 19, 1947. (Excerpts)

The Ministry of Education, hereinafter referred to as *A,* and Zen Nihon Kyōin Kumiai Kyōgi Kai (The Council of All-Japan Teachers' Unions), hereinafter referred to as *B,* hereby make an agreement for collective bargaining based upon the spirit of the Labor Union Law, as follows:

Chapter I. *PRINCIPLES*

ARTICLE I

A shall recognize *B* as an agent for collective bargaining. *A* shall be responsible for the security of the living and the members of *B*. *A* and *B* shall cooperate and be responsible for the enhancement of democratic education.

Chapter II. *MATTERS CONCERNING PAY*

ARTICLE III

A shall undertake to establish a pay system that will secure for the members of *B* and their families the standards of wholesome and cultured living. In deciding fundamental principles of pay, the representatives of both parties shall participate.

Chapter III. *MATTERS CONCERNING WORKING HOURS AND BUSINESS AFFAIRS*

ARTICLE V

The working hours of teachers shall be as follows:
1. There shall be 42 working hours a week.
2. The standard daily teaching time shall be 4 hours.
3. As to other working hours, *A* and *B* shall decide by mutual agreement within the limits of preceding rules.

ARTICLE VI

Twenty free study days shall be granted every year.

Chapter VI. *MATTERS CONCERNING PERSONNEL AFFAIRS*

ARTICLE XI

The fundamental standards relative to personnel affairs, including appointment, discharge, transfer, rewards and punishments, shall be considered by the Personnel Affairs Committee composed of members of *A* and *B*.

ARTICLE XII

A shall not discharge any of the union members:

1. For participation in the union movement
2. During the period necessary for medical treatment of injuries or sickness contracted while on duty, and for 90 days thereafter
3. During a resting period before and after childbirth, and 90 days thereafter

Chapter VII. *MATTERS CONCERNING THE UNION MOVEMENT*

ARTICLE XIII

A shall allow members of *B* to engage fully in union affairs while occupying their regular posts. The number of such members shall be decided at a conference of *A* and *B*.

ARTICLE XIV

A shall permit members of *B* to engage in union movement activities. A trip on union business shall be treated as an official trip after the principal has been informed, but no travelling expenses shall be granted.

ARTICLE XV

A shall allow *B* the use of buildings or facilities under its control for union activities.

ARTICLE XVI

If a dispute, or the threat of one, should arise, *A* will not take any step against the union by applying the Administrative Order.

ARTICLE XVII

A, when engaged in a dispute with *B*, will not negotiate with a union or its members who have seceded.

Chapter VIII. *MATTERS CONCERNING THE COUNCIL OF BUSINESS AFFAIRS*

ARTICLE XVIII

A and *B* shall set up a Council of Business Affairs, based on the aims of this contract. As to the constitution of the Council and the application of its rules, another agreement will be made between the two contracting parties.

ARTICLE XIX

The Council of Business Affairs, based on this contract, will concern itself with the following affairs:

1. Matters concerning pay, injury compensation, personnel, and positions
2. Matters concerning working hours, free days, and vacations
3. Matters concerning the educational budget
4. Matters concerning the handling of business affairs

5. Matters concerning welfare
6. Matters concerning education and culture
7. Other matters recognized by the Council as necessary

ARTICLE XX

Both parties shall be responsible for the bona fide enforcement of the decisions of the Council of Business Affairs. Any of the preceding items shall be included in a written agreement, if both parties deem it necessary to do so.

Chapter IX. *MATTERS CONCERNING THE STANDARDS OF PREFECTURAL COLLECTIVE BARGAINING*

ARTICLE XXI

A, considering it proper for the prefectural chapters of *B* to enter into collective bargaining agreements with the prefectural government, shall encourage the realization of the following:

1. Matters concerning vacations
2. Matters concerning the number of union officials
3. Matters concerning personnel affairs

Chapter X. *OTHER AFFAIRS*

ARTICLE XXII

A shall not interfere with the political interests of the members of *B*.

ARTICLE XXIII

A shall recognize the freedom of a member of *B* to hold another public office, insofar as it does not conflict with his regular duties. *A* shall provide facilities necessary to execute duties of office.

ARTICLE XXIV

The duration of this agreement shall be for six months. *A* and *B* may change the effective duration of this agreement before the end of the prescribed period by mutual agreement, if they find that general economic conditions or some other unavoidable situation makes it necessary. If no announcement be made by either of the parties concerned of the invalidation of this agreement one month before its expiration, it will be effective for six more months. If the intention to invalidate the agreement is announced, the agreement will remain effective until the new one comes into being.

UNDERSTANDING

1. *A* and *B* shall make efforts to realize as soon as possible the following:
   (1) The uniting of all the teachers' unions in the country into one single union, so that it will be the only agent for collective bargaining with *A*.
   (2) The including of all the teachers, in principle, as members of the union mentioned in the preceding clause.
2. If a union affiliated with *B* is the only one in a metropolis or prefecture, it will be authorized to make agreements on the basis of the above understanding.

March 3, 1947
Provisionally signed by
    Seiichiro Takahashi, Minister of Education
    Masao Iwama, Chairman of the Campaign Committee of the
    Council of All–Japan Teachers' Unions
    Yoshihei Himuro, Superintendent of the Central Labor Committee

Source: Supreme Commander for the Allied Powers, *A History of Teachers' Unions in Japan* (Tōkyō, March 25, 1948), pp. 68–72.

9

Political Activities of Teachers. Directive of the Minister of Education. March 26, 1947. (Excerpts)

A teacher is free to run as a candidate for election to either the House of Representatives or the House of Councillors, but it is stipulated by law that a teacher at a government or public school who becomes a member of either house of the Diet cannot retain the post of a teacher.

A teacher is free to run as a candidate for the Metropolitan, prefectural, municipal, ward, town, or village assembly. When returned, he is authorized by law to be a teacher concurrently. In this case, however, he cannot accept membership, if he is a government official, without approval of the officer in charge. When a local educational official, that is, an educational official at a secondary, youth, or elementary school, is elected a member of a local assembly, he may be given permission for accepting the membership as an additional post, as long as the additional duties do not interfere with his duties as a teacher.

A teacher is free to run as a candidate for a prefectural governor, mayor, or a headman of a ward, town, or village, but in case he is returned, he cannot hold concurrently any of such offices, which are stipulated by law as exclusive offices. If he is a government official, approval of the officer in charge must be obtained before accepting the office. In any case care should be taken that election campaigns do not interfere with teaching as far as possible.

In view of the importance of the coming elections, which will mark a turning-point for a new democratic Japan founded upon the new Constitution, and in view of the fact that the world is deeply interested in the democratization of Japan, it is necessary to carry out impartial and uncorrupted elections. Therefore, it shall be the last thing for a teacher to take advantage of his position in election campaigns.

A teachers' union is free to carry on an election campaign so long as it does not deviate from its essential aims and status as a labor union or restrain its members from their political liberty.

Source: Supreme Commander for the Allied Powers, *A History of Teachers' Unions in Japan* (Tōkyō, March 25, 1948), pp. 205–206.

10

The Fundamental Law of Education. March 31, 1947.

Having established the Constitution of Japan, we have shown our resolution to contribute to the peace of the world and welfare of humanity by building a democratic and cultural state. The realization of this ideal shall depend fundamentally on the power of education.

We shall esteem individual dignity and endeavor to bring up the people who love truth and peace, while education which aims at the creation of culture, general and rich in individuality, shall be spread far and wide.

We hereby enact this Law, in accordance with the spirit of the Constitution of Japan, with a view to clarifying the aim of education and establishing the foundation of education for new Japan.

ARTICLE 1. *Aim of Education*
Education shall aim at the full development of personality, striving for the rearing of the people, sound in mind and body, who shall love truth and justice, esteem individual value, respect labor and have a deep sense of responsibility, and be imbued with the independent spirit, as builders of the peaceful state and society.

ARTICLE 2. *Educational Principle*
The aim of education shall be realized on all occasions and in all places. In order to achieve the aim, we shall endeavor to contribute to the creation and development of culture by mutual esteem and cooperation, respecting academic freedom, having a regard for actual life and cultivating a spontaneous spirit.

ARTICLE 3. *Equal Opportunity in Education*
The people shall be given equal opportunities of receiving education according to their ability, and they shall not be subject to educational discrimination on account of race, creed, sex, social status, economic position, or family origin.

The state and local public bodies shall take measures to give financial assistance to those who have, in spite of their ability, difficulty in receiving education for economic reasons.

ARTICLE 4. *Compulsory Education*
The people shall be obligated to have boys and girls under their protection receive nine years' general education.

No tuition fee shall be charged for compulsory education in schools established by the state and local public bodies.

ARTICLE 5. *Coeducation*
Men and women shall esteem and cooperate with each other. Coeducation, therefore, shall be recognized in education.

ARTICLE 6. *School Education*
The schools prescribed by law shall be of public nature and, besides the

state and local public bodies, only the juridical persons prescribed by law shall be entitled to establish such schools.

Teachers of the schools prescribed by law shall be servants of the whole community. They shall be conscious of their mission and endeavor to discharge their duties. For this purpose, the status of teachers shall be respected and their fair and appropriate treatment shall be secured.

ARTICLE 7. *Social Education*

The state and local public bodies shall encourage home education and education carried out in places of work or elsewhere in society.

The state and local public bodies shall endeavor to attain the aim of education by the establishment of such institutions as libraries, museums, civic halls, by the utilization of school institutions, and by other appropriate methods.

ARTICLE 8. *Political Education*

The political knowledge necessary for intelligent citizenship shall be valued in education.

The schools prescribed by law shall refrain from political education or other political activities for or against any specific political party.

ARTICLE 9. *Religious Education*

The attitude of religious tolerance and the position of religion in social life shall be valued in education.

The schools established by the state and local public bodies shall refrain from religious education or other activities for a specific religion.

ARTICLE 10. *School Administration*

Education shall not be subject to improper control, but it shall be directly responsible to the whole people.

School administration shall, on the basis of this realization, aim at the adjustment and establishment of the various conditions required for the pursuit of the aim of education.

ARTICLE 11. *Additional Rule*

In case of necessity, appropriate laws shall be enacted to carry the foregoing stipulations into effect.

Source: Mombushō (Japan Ministry of Education), *Education in Japan* (Tōkyō: Mombushō, 1967), p. 21.

11

The Board of Education Law. July 15, 1948. (Excerpts)

ARTICLE III. Boards of Education shall be established in Tōkyō-to, Hokkaidō, prefectures, cities, towns and villages. . . . "Prefectural Boards of Education" referred to in this law shall be those established in Tōkyō-to, Hokkaidō, and the prefectures, and "local Boards of Education" shall be those established in cities, towns and villages.

ARTICLE IV. Boards of Education shall administer and execute affairs concerning education, science, and culture that have hitherto been under the control of prefectures or prefectural governors or cities, towns, or mayors of cities and towns, and headmen of villages. . . . Universities and private schools shall not be under the jurisdiction of Boards of Education. . . .

ARTICLE VII. A prefectural Board of Education shall consist of seven members, and a local Board of Education shall consist of five members. The Board members . . . shall be elected by the inhabitants of . . . public bodies consisting of citizens of Japan in accordance with the provisions of the Public Service Election Law.

ARTICLE VIII. The term of office of the Board members by popular vote shall be four years.

ARTICLE XLI. The Board of Education shall have a superintendent of education (Kyōikuchō) . . . appointed by the Board of Education. The term of office shall be four years.

ARTICLE XLVIII. Prefectural Boards of Education shall have control over all Schools and other educational institutions established by the prefectures concerned, and local Boards of Education shall have control over all schools and other educational institutions established by the local public bodies concerned.

ARTICLE XLIX. The Board of Education shall take charge of the matters . . . concerning curriculum contents and . . . the appointment, dismissal, and other personnel affairs of the staffs of the Board of Education, schools, and other educational institutions.

ARTICLE LIX. When the budget is approved by the local assembly, the chief of the local public body shall allocate the budget under control of the Board of Education to the Board concerned.

Source: Supreme Commander for the Allied Powers, *Postwar Developments in Japanese Education* (Tōkyō: SCAP, 1952), 2:231–244.

12

The Freedom of Association and Protection of the Right to Organize Convention 1948 (No. 87). International Labor Organization. (Excerpts)

ARTICLE 1

Each Member of the International Labor Organization for which this Convention is in force undertakes to give effect to the following provisions.

ARTICLE 2

Workers and employers, without distinction whatsoever, shall have the right to establish and, subject only to the rules of the organization concerned, to join organizations of their own choosing without previous authorization.

ARTICLE 3

1. Workers' and employers' organizations shall have the right to draw up their constitutions and rules, to elect their representatives in full freedom, to organize their administration and activities and to formulate their programs.

2. The public authorities shall refrain from any interference which would restrict this right or impede the lawful exercise thereof.

ARTICLE 4

Workers' and employers' organizations shall not be liable to be dissolved or suspended by administrative authority.

ARTICLE 5

Workers' and employers' organizations shall have the right to establish and join federations and confederations and any such organization, federation or confederation shall have the right to affiliate with international organizations of workers and employers.

ARTICLE 6

The provisions of Articles 2, 3 and 4 hereof apply to federations and confederations of workers' and employers' organizations.

ARTICLE 7

The acquisition of legal personality by workers' and employers' organizations, federations and confederations shall not be made subject to conditions of such a character as to restrict the application of the provisions of Articles 2, 3 and 4 hereof.

ARTICLE 8

1. In exercising the rights provided for in this Convention workers and employers and their respective organizations, like other persons of organized collectivities, shall respect the law of the land.

2. The law of the land shall not be such as to impair, nor shall it be so applied as to impair, the guarantees provided for in this Convention.

ARTICLE 10

In this Convention the term "organization" means any organization of workers or of employers for furthering and defending the interests of workers or of employers.

ARTICLE 11

Each Member of the International Labor Organization for which this Convention is in force undertakes to take all necessary and appropriate measures to ensure that workers and employers may exercise freely the right to organize.

Source: International Labor Office, *Report of the Fact-finding and Conciliation Commission on Freedom of Association Concerning Persons Employed in the Public Sector in Japan,* Special Supplement to the ILO Official Bulletin, vol. 49, no. 1 (Geneva: ILO, 1966), pp. 168–169.

13

The Right to Organize and Collective Bargaining Convention 1949
(No. 98). International Labor Organization. (Excerpts)

ARTICLE 1

1. Workers shall enjoy adequate protection against acts of antiunion discrimination in respect of their employment.
2. Such protection shall apply more particularly in respect of acts calculated to
    (a) make the employment of a worker subject to the condition that he shall not join a union or shall relinquish trade union membership;
    (b) cause the dismissal of or otherwise prejudice a worker by reason of union membership or because of participation in union activities outside working hours or, with the consent of the employer, within working hours.

ARTICLE 2

1. Workers' and employers' organizations shall enjoy adequate protection against any acts of interference by each other or each other's agents or members in their establishment, functioning or administration.
2. In particular, acts which are designed to promote the establishment of workers' organizations under the domination of employers or employers' organizations, or to support workers' organizations by financial or other means, with the object of placing such organizations under the control of employers or employers' organizations, shall be deemed to constitute acts of interference within the meaning of this Article.

ARTICLE 4

Measures appropriate to national conditions shall be taken, where necessary, to encourage and promote the full development and utilization of machinery for voluntary negotiation between employers or employers' organizations and workers' organizations, with a view to the regulation of terms and conditions of employment by means of collective agreements.

Source: International Labor Office, *Report of the Fact-finding and Conciliation Commission on Freedom of Association Concerning Persons Employed in the Public Sector in Japan,* Special Supplement to the ILO Official Bulletin, vol. 49, no. 1 (Geneva: ILO, 1966), pp. 169–170.

14

Local Public Service Law. 1950 (With revisions). (Excerpts)

ARTICLE 1 (Purpose)
1. This law realizes local autonomy by establishing standards for employment, ranking, salary, working conditions, punishment, duties and evaluation of local public servants by the local public body.

ARTICLE 8 (Personnel Committee—Jinjiinkai)
1. Qualified local bodies may establish a local Personnel Committee which studies working conditions, salaries, regulations, collects documents for employment, etc., and submits its findings to the appropriate appointing officer and administrative officer concerning local administration.
2. The Personnel Committee is composed of three members appointed for a four-year term by the head of the local body with the approval of the locally elected governing body. Two members may not belong to the same political party.

ARTICLE 36 (Political Activities)
1. Local public service personnel may not contribute to the formation of political parties or become officers in them. They also may not induce others to become members of any political party.
2. Local public service personnel may not participate in any of the following activities in support of, or opposition to, a particular political party, person, or event in a public election:
   a. engage in soliciting votes
   b. participate in a signature campaign
   c. engage in fund raising campaigns
   d. use or allow others to use public funds or public buildings

ARTICLE 37 (Dispute Tactics)
Local public servants may not resort to strikes, slowdown, or other acts of dispute against their employer, who is the local people as represented by the agencies of the local public body, or to conduct such idling tactics as will deteriorate the functional efficiency of the local public body, or to instigate others to do so.

ARTICLE 40 (Efficiency Rating)
The appointment officer of local public servants must conduct periodic efficiency ratings of all employees under his responsibility and must act appropriately according to the results.

ARTICLE 52 (Organization)
Public servants' organizations whose purpose is to promote the improvement of working conditions will be recognized. Local public servants may join such an organization.

ARTICLE 55 (Negotiations)
Local public servants' organizations may negotiate with the local public

body concerned with regard to compensation, work hours, and other working conditions of their personnel. However, such negotiations do not include the right of collective agreement with the authorities of the local public body.

ARTICLE 61

Anyone who plans, instigates, or carries out acts prohibited in Article 37 shall be liable for punishment of not more than three years imprisonment, or fined 100,000 yen.

Source: Mombu Hōrei Kenkyūkai (Educational Law Research Association), *Shin Kyōiku Roppō* (Revised Edition of the Fundamental Education Laws) (Tōkyō: Daiichi Hōki Shuppansha, 1969), pp. 871–902.

15

A Code of Ethics for Teachers. Nikkyōso. 1952.

Until the present time the teachers of Japan, under the pressures of a half-feudalistic ultranationalistic system, have been forced into a logic of subservience. Because the Japanese social system today has reached a point where reconstruction from a completely different point of view is necessary, we must cut our ties with past conventions and embrace a new ethic.

A code of ethics is not merely a set of universal and eternal rules, but rather a set of changing principles which must be grasped through a fight to accomplish the historical tasks which have been bestowed upon a people within a specific historical period. Today, however, the workings of our society are causing poverty and unemployment to become more and more universal and are forcing even the independence of the country onto dangerous ground.

The threat of a modern destructive war is distorting our recognition of these historical tasks and deflecting our will to overcome them. In such a state of affairs our earnest desire to seek a peaceful society in which human rights are respected, industrial production is increased, and the exploitation of man by man is no longer permitted cannot be attained without a high degree of autonomous growth toward maturity on the part of the laboring class. Needless to say, teachers are laborers. The more the difficulty of the situation increases, the more the teachers of Japan, along with all laborers, must increase their unity, protect the youth of the country, and face these historical tasks with courage and intelligence. Based on a recognition of the above facts, we hereby establish the following code of ethics:

ARTICLE I.   *Teachers Shall Work with the Youth of the Country in Fulfilling the Tasks of Society*

Upon our shoulders have been laid the historical tasks of protecting peace, insuring the independence of the country, and realizing a society free from exploitation, poverty and unemployment. Believing in democracy, we are unswerving in our desire to fulfill these tasks.

The youth of the country must be raised and educated to become capable workers who will give themselves, each according to his own abilities, to the accomplishment of these tasks. There is no other road by which the youth of Japan can attain freedom and happiness.

Teachers shall live and work with the youth and shall be the organizers of and counselors in a schooling designed to meet this necessity. Each teacher shall make an intensive critical examination of himself and shall study and make efforts to prepare himself for his new role in education.

ARTICLE 2. *Teachers Shall Fight for Equal Opportunity in Education*

Equal opportunity in education and respect for the dignity of the individual, as guaranteed by the Constitution, are today still dead letters. The youth of today are severely restricted in their educational opportunities because of the social and economic limitations placed upon the individual. It may be said in particular that no serious consideration has been given to educating either the multitudes of working young people or mentally and physically handicapped children. Children are not being guaranteed equality of conditions for life and growth either within or without the schools. We have reached a point where eighteenth century individualism no longer opens the way to the development of the individual. Today social procedures must be followed in order to create equal opportunities in education.

Teachers shall of themselves be keenly aware of this necessity and shall in all quarters fight for equality in education.

ARTICLE 3. *Teachers Shall Protect Peace*

Peace is the ideal of mankind; war destroys all the hopes of mankind. Without peace the historical tasks facing Japanese society cannot be accomplished. The desire of the people for peace becomes strongest when individual rights are respected and when the people are able to hold hopes for an improvement in social conditions and have strong faith in progress. Discontent and loss of hope on the part of the people may serve to impel a country down the road to war.

Teachers shall be advocators of the brotherhood of man, leaders in the reconstruction of life attitudes, and pioneers in respecting human rights, and as such they shall stand as the most courageous defenders of peace against all those who advocate war.

ARTICLE 4. *Teachers Shall Act on Behalf of Scientific Truth*

Progress takes place within a society when the members of that society, acting on behalf of scientific truth, seek a rational approach to historical tasks. Actions which ignore the fruits of science serve to suppress that in man which makes him seek progress. Teachers shall respect the progress-seeking element in man, shall carry out scientific explorations on nature and society, and shall create a rational environment conducive to the growth and development of young people.

To these ends teachers shall share their experiences and shall work closely with scholars and specialists in all fields.

ARTICLE 5. *Teachers Shall Allow No Infringements on Freedom in Education*

Our freedom of research in education as well as of action is often suppressed by improper forces. Academic freedom as well as freedom of speech, thought and assembly, although guaranteed in the Constitution, are nevertheless actually being restricted severely. Infringements on freedom in education serve to obstruct healthy learning by young people, to hinder intellectual activity, and furthermore to endanger the proper development of the nation. Teachers, being deeply aware of this, shall fight against all improper pressures in education.

ARTICLE 6. *Teachers Shall Seek after Proper Government*

Successive governments, under the pretext of making education politically neutral, have long deprived the teachers of Japan of their freedoms and have forced them to serve in whatever way the government has desired. After the war, having been given the freedom to participate in political activities, teachers banded together and fought for proper government, but now such political freedom is again being taken from them. Government is not something to serve the interests of any one group; it belongs to all the people. It is the means for us to attain our desires in a peaceful manner.

Teachers, together with all working men, shall participate in political activities and shall pool their resources in seeking proper government.

ARTICLE 7. *Teachers Shall Fight Side by Side with Parents against Corruption in Society and Shall Create a New Culture*

In our towns and villages our young people are surrounded day and night by corruption of all kinds which is exerting a degenerative influence on their wholesome minds. Unwholesome amusements are suggested in movies, plays and even in the tales told by the neighborhood children's storytellers; degenerative tendencies are to be found in newspapers, radio programs, and in books and magazines; the type of atmosphere surrounding bicycle and race tracks and urban amusement districts tends to weaken the soul of the nation. All these exert a particularly strong and poisonous influence on the youth of the country.

Teachers shall combine their efforts with parents in protecting youth from the corrupting influences of society, shall live and work with youth in a proper manner, and shall create a new culture of the working man.

ARTICLE 8. *Teachers Are Laborers*

Teachers are laborers whose workshops are the schools. Teachers, in the knowledge that labor is the foundation of everything in society, shall be proud of the fact that they themselves are laborers. At the present stage of history, the realization of a new society of mankind which respects fundamental human rights, not only in word but in deed as well, and which utilizes resources, technology, and science for the welfare of all men is possible only through the power of the working masses whose nucleus is the laboring class. Teachers shall be aware of their position as laborers, shall live forcefully believing in the historical progress of man, and shall consider all stagnation and reaction as their enemies.

ARTICLE 9. *Teachers Shall Defend Their Right to Maintain a Minimum Standard of Living*

Having been forced thus far to live in noble poverty under the proud name of educator, teachers have been ashamed to voice their demands for even the minimum material benefits necessary for their existence. To demand just recompense for their own labors would have been unthinkable to teachers of the past. Because of this situation, teachers have lost all desire and zeal for imparting to their students a proper education, and their lives have come to be ruled by exhaustion, indolence and opportunism.

Teachers shall consider it their right and duty to protect their own right to maintain a minimum standard of living and to fight for optimum conditions under which to live and labor.

ARTICLE 10. *Teachers Shall Unite*

The obligations which history has given to the teacher can only be fulfilled if teachers unite. The strength of the teacher is exhibited through organization and unity; organization and unity give constant courage and strength to the activities of the teacher. Moreover, there is no other way today in which the teacher can establish himself as an individual except through unity of action. The teachers of Japan, through the labor movement, shall unite with the teachers of the world and shall join hands with all laborers.

Unity is the highest ethic of the teacher.

Source: Center for Japanese Social and Political Studies, *Journal of Social and Political Ideas in Japan* 1, no. 3:129–131.

16

New Board of Education Law (Law for the Administration of Local Education). June 30, 1956. (Excerpts)

ARTICLE 2. A Board of Education shall be established for each prefecture, city, town and village.

ARTICLE 3. The Board will consist of five members, or three at the village level.

ARTICLE 4. Each member of the Board will be appointed by the head of the local government with the approval of the local representative body.

ARTICLE 5. The term of the Board members shall be four years. Members may be reelected.

ARTICLE 16. A Superintendent of Education (Kyōikuchō) will be appointed by the Board of Education. At the prefectural level the Ministry of Education must approve the Board's recommendation. At the city, town or village level, the Superintendent appointed by the local School Board must be approved by the Prefectural Board of Education.

ARTICLE 33. The Board of Education, within the limits of other laws and regulations, shall regulate the management and administration of the schools under its jurisdiction.

ARTICLE 35. The Board of Education shall appoint, dismiss and punish educational personnel subject to the provisions of the Local Public Service Law.

ARTICLE 46. An efficiency rating of the educational personnel will be undertaken by the appropriate administrative officer under provisions of Article 40 of the Local Public Service Law.

ARTICLE 52. The Minister of Education, if he determines that the local education body is violating the fundamental laws of education, or is deviating from the original purposes of education, has the right to "motomeru" (request or demand) that measures necessary to correct the situation be taken.

ARTICLE 54. The Minister of Education has the right to "motomeru" (request or demand) local school boards to submit necessary statistics, investigative reports, and other materials to the Ministry of Education.

Source: Mombu Hōrei Kenkyūkai (Educational Law Research Association), *Shin Kyōiku Roppō* (Revised Edition of the Fundamental Education Laws) (Tōkyō: Daiichi Hōki Shuppansha, 1969), pp. 112–142.

17

Nikkyōso's Convention Goals. 1966

1. Intensify the joint struggles of all public servants for the early attainment of a large salary increase.
2. Oppose dismissals of teachers, increase the number of teachers over and above the limit set by the government, and increase the education budget for the improvement of education and our working conditions.
3. Intensify our struggles for teachers' rights and recapture our fundamental labor rights.
4. Oppose education controlled by the central government, promote the independent research and study of education, and abolish the achievement tests and the Nōken Test. Promote the People's Movement for a New Education in order to provide secondary education for all.
5. Oppose the "invasion" of Vietnam, destroy the United States–Japan Security Treaty, prohibit the nuclear rearmament of Japan, return Okinawa from American control, and intensify the People's Movement for Peace.
6. Establish our labor union at each workshop (school), intensify the unity and solidarity of our 600,000 members, and expand our organization.

Source: Nikkyōso (Japan Teachers Union), *Dai Sanjūnikai Teiki Taikai Gian* (Proposals of the Thirty-second National Convention), Tōkyō, May, 1966, p. 1.

Index